Lecture Notes in Computer Scier

T0238067

Commenced Publication in 1973
Founding and Former Series Editors:
Gerhard Goos, Juris Hartmanis, and Jan van Leeuwen

Editorial Board

Diego Zamboni (Ed.)

Detection of Intrusions and Malware, and Vulnerability Assessment

5th International Conference, DIMVA 2008
Paris, France, July 10-11, 2008
Proceedings

 Springer

Volume Editor

Diego Zamboni
IBM Zurich Research Laboratory
Säumerstr. 4, 8803 Rüschlikon, Switzerland
E-mail: dza@zurich.ibm.com

Library of Congress Control Number: 2008930154

CR Subject Classification (1998): E.3, K.6.5, K.4, C.2, D.4.6

LNCS Sublibrary: SL 4 – Security and Cryptology

ISSN   0302-9743
ISBN-10   3-540-70541-4 Springer Berlin Heidelberg New York
ISBN-13   978-3-540-70541-3 Springer Berlin Heidelberg New York

Springer is a part of Springer Science+Business Media

springer.com

© Springer-Verlag Berlin Heidelberg 2008
Printed in Germany

Typesetting: Camera-ready by author, data conversion by Scientific Publishing Services, Chennai, India
Printed on acid-free paper   SPIN: 12326570   06/3180   5 4 3 2 1 0

Preface

On behalf of the Program Committee, it is my pleasure to present the proceedings of the 5th GI International Conference on Detection of Intrusions and Malware, and Vulnerability Assessment (DIMVA).

Every year since 2004 DIMVA has brought together leading researchers and practitioners from academia, government and industry to present and discuss novel security research. DIMVA is organized by the Security–Intrusion Detection and Response (SIDAR) special interest group of the German Informatics Society (GI).

The DIMVA 2008 Program Committee received 42 submissions from 16 different countries, and from governmental, industrial and academic organizations. All the submissions were carefully reviewed by several members of the Program Committee and evaluated on the basis of scientific novelty, importance to the field and technical quality. The final selection took place at the Program Committee meeting held on March 28, 2008 at the IBM Zürich Research Laboratory in Switzerland. Thirteen full papers and one extended abstract were selected for presentation and publication in the conference proceedings.

The conference took place during July 10-11, 2008, in the France Télécom R&D/Orange Labs premises of Issy les Moulineaux, near Paris, France, with the program grouped into five sessions. Two keynote speeches were presented by Richard Bejtlich (Director of Incident Response, General Electric) and by Tal Garfinkel (VMware Inc./Stanford University). The conference program also included a rump session organized by Sven Dietrich of the Stevens Institute of Technology, in which recent research results, works in progress, and other topics of interest to the community were presented.

A successful conference is the result of the joint effort of many people. In particular, I would like to thank all the authors who submitted papers, whether accepted or not. I also thank the Program Committee members and additional reviewers for their hard work in evaluating the submissions. In addition, I want to thank the General Chair, Hervé Debar from France Télécom R&D, for handling the conference arrangements and website, Tadeusz Pietraszek from Google for publicizing the conference, and Ludovic Mé from Supélec for finding sponsor support. Finally, I would like to express our gratitude to Google and EADS for their financial sponsorship.

July 2008   Diego Zamboni

Organization

Organizing Committee

General Chair	Hervé Debar, France Télécom R&D, France
Program Chair	Diego Zamboni, IBM Zürich Research Laboratory, Switzerland
Sponsor Chair	Ludovic Mé, Supélec, France
Publicity Chair	Tadeusz Pietraszek, Google, Switzerland

Program Committee

Kostas Anagnostakis	Institute for Infocomm Research, Singapore
Thomas Biege	SuSE, Germany
David Brumley	Carnegie Mellon University, USA
Roland Büschkes	RWE AG, Germany
Weidong Cui	Microsoft Research, USA
Marc Dacier	Institut Eurecom, France
Sven Dietrich	Stevens Institute of Technology, USA
Holger Dreger	Siemens CERT, Germany
Ulrich Flegel	SAP Research, Germany
Marc Heuse	Baseline Security Consulting, Germany
Thorsten Holz	University of Mannheim, Germany
Ming-Yuh Huang	Boeing, USA
Bernhard Hämmerli	HTA Lucerne, Switzerland
Martin Johns	University of Hamburg, Germany
Erland Jonsson	Chalmers University, Sweden
Klaus Julisch	IBM Zurich Research Laboratory, Switzerland
Christian Kreibich	International Computer Science Institute, USA
Christopher Kruegel	Technical University of Vienna, Austria
Pavel Laskov	Fraunhofer FIRST and University of Tübingen, Germany
Wenke Lee	Georgia Institute of Technology, USA
John McHugh	Dalhousie University, Canada
Michael Meier	University of Dortmund, Germany
Ludovic Mé	Supélec, France
John Mitchell	Stanford University, USA
George Mohay	Queensland University of Technology, Australia
Benjamin Morin	Supélec, France
Tadeusz Pietraszek	Google, Switzerland
Phil Porras	SRI International, USA
Stelios Sidiroglou	Columbia University, USA
Robin Sommer	ICSI/LBNL, USA
Morton Swimmer	City University of New York, USA
Peter Szor	Symantec, USA

Additional Reviewers

Christopher Alm	Wolfgang John	Carsten Willems
Vika Felmetsger	Henry Stern	Yves Younan
Felix Freiling	Elizabeth Stinson	Jacob Zimmermann

Steering Committee

Chairs	Ulrich Flegel (SAP Research)
	Michael Meier (University of Dortmund)
Members	Roland Büschkes (RWE AG)
	Marc Heuse (Baseline Security Consulting)
	Bernhard Hämmerli (HTA Lucerne)
	Klaus Julisch (IBM Zürich Research Laboratory)
	Christopher Kruegel (Technical University of Vienna)
	Pavel Laskov (Fraunhofer FIRST and University of Tübingen)
	Robin Sommer (ICSI/LBNL)

DIMVA 2008 was organized by the Special Interest Group Security — Intrusion Detection and Response (SIDAR) of the German Informatics Society (GI).

Support

Financial sponsorship for DIMVA 2008 was provided by Google (Gold Sponsor) and by EADS. We sincerely thank them for their support.

Table of Contents

Intrusion Detection and Activity Correlation

Data Space Randomization[*]

Sandeep Bhatkar[1] and R. Sekar[2]

[1] Symantec Research Laboratories, Culver City, CA 90230, USA
[2] Stony Brook University, Stony Brook, NY 11794, USA

Abstract. Over the past several years, US-CERT advisories, as well as most critical updates from software vendors, have been due to memory corruption vulnerabilities such as buffer overflows, heap overflows, etc. Several techniques have been developed to defend against the exploitation of these vulnerabilities, with the most promising defenses being based on randomization. Two randomization techniques have been explored so far: address space randomization (ASR) that randomizes the location of objects in virtual memory, and instruction set randomization (ISR) that randomizes the representation of code. We explore a third form of randomization called data space randomization (DSR) that randomizes the representation of data stored in program memory. Unlike ISR, DSR is effective against non-control data attacks as well as code injection attacks. Unlike ASR, it can protect against corruption of non-pointer data as well as pointer-valued data. Moreover, DSR provides a much higher range of randomization (typically 2^{32} for 32-bit data) as compared to ASR. Other interesting aspects of DSR include (a) it does not share a weakness common to randomization-based defenses, namely, susceptibility to information leakage attacks, and (b) it is capable of detecting some exploits that are missed by full bounds-checking techniques, e.g., some of the overflows from one field of a structure to the next field. Our implementation results show that with appropriate design choices, DSR can achieve a performance overhead in the range of 5% to 30% for a range of programs.

Keywords: memory error, buffer overflow, address space randomization.

1 Introduction

Memory errors continue to be the principal culprit behind most security vulnerabilities. Most critical security updates from software vendors in the past several years have addressed memory corruption vulnerabilities in C and C++ programs. This factor has fueled a lot of research into defenses against exploitation of these vulnerabilities. Early research targeted specific exploit types such as stack-smashing, but attackers soon discovered alternative ways to exploit memory errors. Subsequently, randomization based defenses emerged as a more

---

[*] This research is supported in part by an ONR grant N000140710928 and an NSF grant CNS-0627687. This work was part of the first author's Ph.D. work [8] completed at Stony Brook University.

D. Zamboni (Ed.): DIMVA 2008, LNCS 5137, pp. 1–22, 2008.

systematic solution against these attacks. So far, two main forms of randomization defenses have been explored: *address-space randomization (ASR)* [32,9] that randomizes the locations of data and code objects in memory, and *instruction set randomization (ISR)* [6,27] that randomizes the representation of code.

Although ASR and ISR have been quite effective in blocking most memory exploits that have been used in the past, new types of exploits continue to emerge that can evade them. As defenses such as ASR begin to get deployed, attackers seek out vulnerabilities and exploits that go beyond them. One class of attacks that can evade coarse-grained ASR is based on corrupting non-control data [13]. In particular, buffer overflows that corrupt non-pointer data are not captured by coarse-grained ASR. Moreover, ASR implementations that are deployed today suffer from the problem of low entropy. This enables brute-force attacks that succeed relatively quickly — with about 128 attempts in the case of Windows Vista, and 32K attempts in the case of PaX [32,35]. Finally, ASR techniques are vulnerable to information leakage attacks that reveal pointer values in the victim program. This can happen due to a bug that sends the contents of an uninitialized buffer to an attacker — such data may contain pointer values that may have been previously stored in the buffer. We therefore develop an alternative approach for randomization, called *data space randomization (DSR)*, that addresses these drawbacks of previous randomization-based techniques.

The basic idea behind DSR is to *randomize the representation of different data objects.* One way to modify data representation is to xor each data object in memory with a unique random mask ("encryption"), and to unmask it before its use ("decryption"). DSR can be implemented using a program transformation that modifies each assignment $x = v$ in the program into $x = m_x \oplus v$, where m_x is a mask associated with the variable x. Similarly, an expression such as $x + y$ will have to be transformed into $(x \oplus m_x) + (y \oplus m_y)$.

To understand how DSR helps defeat memory corruption attacks, consider a buffer overflow attack involving an array variable a that overwrites an adjacent variable b with a value v. As a result of DSR, all values that are written into the variable a will use a mask m_a, and hence the value stored in the memory location corresponding to b would be $v \oplus m_a$. When b is subsequently used, its value will be unmasked using m_b and hence the result will be $(v \oplus m_a) \oplus m_b$, which is different from v as long as we ensure $m_a \neq m_b$. By using different masks for different variables, we can ensure that even if the attacker manages to overwrite b, all she would have accomplished is to write a random value into it, rather than being able to write the intended value v.

Although inspired by PointGuard [17], which proposed masking of all pointer values with a random value, our DSR technique differs from it in many ways.

- First, PointGuard is focused on preventing pointer corruption attacks — otherwise known as *absolute-address-dependent attacks.* In contrast, the primary goal of DSR is to prevent *relative address attacks,* such as those caused by buffer overflows and integer overflows. Consequently, DSR is able to detect non-control data attacks that don't involve pointer corruption, such as attacks that target file names, command names, userids, authentication data, etc. Moreover, since pointer corruption attacks rely on a preceding buffer overflow, absolute-address-dependent attacks are also defeated by DSR.

– Second, DSR randomizes the representation of *all types of data*, as opposed to PointGuard which randomizes only pointer-typed data. (Indeed, as a result of optimizations, the representation of many pointer variables are left unchanged in DSR.) DSR uses different representations for different data objects in order to prevent buffer overflows on one object from corrupting a nearby object in a predictable way.

– Third, DSR corrects an important problem with PointGuard that can break legitimate C-programs in which pointer and non-pointer data are aliased. For instance, suppose that an integer-type variable is assigned a value of 0, and subsequently, the same location is accessed as a pointer-type. The zero value won't be interpreted as a null value since PointGuard would xor it with a mask m, thus yielding a pointer value m. We note that such aliasing is relatively common due to (a) unions that contain pointer and non-pointer data, (b) use of functions such as `bzero` or `bcopy`, as well as assignments involving structs, and (c) type casts. DSR considers aliasing and hence does not suffer from this drawback.

– Finally, like other previous randomization based defenses, PointGuard is susceptible to *information leakage* attacks that leak the values of encrypted pointers to a remote attacker. Since a simple xor mask is used, leakage of masked data allows the attacker to compute the mask used by PointGuard. She can then mount a successful attack where the appropriate bytes within the attack payload have been masked using this mask. In contrast, DSR is able to discover all instances where masked data is being accessed, and unmask it before use. As a result, an information leakage attack will not reveal masked values.

As compared to ASR, DSR provides a much larger range of randomization. For instance, on 32-bit architectures, we can randomize integers and pointers over a range of 2^{32} values, which is much larger than the range possible with ASR. Moreover, DSR can, in many instances, address the weakness of even the fine-grained ASR techniques [10] concerning their inability to randomize relative distances between certain data items, e.g., between the fields of a struct. Since the C-language definition fixes the distance between struct fields, even bounds-checking techniques do not provide protection from overflows across the fields of a structure. In contrast, DSR has the ability to protect from such overflows as long as there is no aliasing between these fields[1]. (However, this feature is not currently supported due to our use of field-insensitive alias analysis in our implementation.)

---

[1] Typically, aliasing of multiple fields is induced by low-level functions such as `bcopy` and `bzero`. DSR can use different masks for different fields of a struct object if the object is not involved in these operations. In some cases, it is possible to improve this further by incorporating the semantics of these block move operations into the DSR implementation.

A direct implementation of DSR concept can lead to nontrivial runtime overheads due to the need for masking/unmasking after every memory access, and due to the additional memory overheads for accessing mask data. To provide better performance, observe that the first step in memory corruption attacks involve a buffer overflow, i.e., an operation that starts with the base address of an object a in memory, but then accesses a different object b as a result of out-of-bounds subscript or invalid pointer arithmetic operation. Our implementation focuses on disrupting this step. Note that this is possible even without masking b, as long as we ensure that a uses a non-zero mask. A static analysis can be used to identify *overflow candidates*, i.e., objects such as a that can serve as a base address in an address arithmetic computation that goes out-of-bounds. In its simplest form, this analysis would identify all arrays, structures containing arrays, and any other object whose address is explicitly taken in the code. This optimization provides significant benefits since most variables accessed in C-programs are simple local variables that can be determined to be non-overflow candidates.

One of the main limitations of the DSR approach is the need to use the same mask for overflow candidate objects that may be aliased. To mitigate the impact of this limitation, our implementation attempts to allocate different objects with the same mask in different memory regions that are separated by unmapped pages. This ensures that even when two objects are assigned the same mask, overflows from one of these objects to the other would be detected since it would cause a memory fault due to the protection memory page in between the objects. However, the number of overflow candidate objects with the same mask may become very large for heap-allocated objects, and hence this approach may not be appropriate for such objects. In those cases, our implementation essentially provides probabilistic protection against overflows involving such objects.

1.1 Paper Organization

In Section 2, we describe the transformations to introduce data space randomization. In Section 3, we describe a prototype implementation of our technique. In section 4, we evaluate performance overhead, and analyze the effectiveness of our technique against different attacks. Related work is covered in Section 5, followed by concluding remarks in Section 6.

2 Transformation Overview

Our transformation approach for DSR is based on a source-to-source transformation of C programs. The basic transformation is quite simple. For each data variable v, we introduce another variable m_v which stores the mask value to be used for randomizing the data stored in v using an exclusive-or operation. The mask is a random number that can be generated at the beginning of program execution for static variables, and at the time of memory allocation for stack and heap variables. The size of m_v depends on the size of the data stored in v. Ideally, we can store a fixed size (say, word length) random number in the mask variable, and depending on the size of the associated variable, we can generate bigger or smaller masks from the random number. However, for simplicity of notation, we will use mask variables having the same size as that of the variables being masked.

The variables appearing in expressions and statements are transformed as follows. Values assigned to variables are randomized. Thus, after every statement that assigns a value to a variable v, we add the statement v = v ^ m_v to randomize the value of the variable in the memory. Also, wherever a variable is used, its value is first derandomized. This is done by replacing v with v ^ m_v.

So far the transformations seem straightforward, but we have not yet considered a case in which variable data is accessed indirectly by dereferencing pointers, as in the following C-code snippet:

```
    int x, y, z, *ptr;
    ...
    ptr = &x;
    ...
    ptr = &y;
    ...
L1: z = *ptr;
```

In the above code, the expression *ptr is an alias for either x or y. Since *ptr is used in the assignment statement at L1, we need to unmask it before using its value in the assignment. Therefore, the line should be transformed as:

    z = m_z ^ (m_starptr ^ *ptr),

where m_z and m_starptr are respectively masks of z and *ptr. Unfortunately, statically we cannot determine the mask m_starptr to be used for unmasking; it can be the mask of either variable x or y.

One way to address this problem is to dynamically track the masks to be used for *referents*[2] of all the pointers. This requires storing additional information (henceforth called metadata) about pointers. Similar information is maintained in some of the previous techniques that detect memory errors. In particular, they store metadata using different data structures such as *splay tree* [26] and *fat pointers* [4,30]. These metadata storing techniques lead to either high performance overheads or code compatibility problems. For this reason, we chose to avoid dynamic tracking of masks.

Our solution to the above problem is based on using static analysis[3]. More specifically, we use the same mask for variables that can be pointed by a common

---

[2] A *referent* of a pointer is an object that the pointer points to.

[3] A static analysis typically assumes the absence of memory errors. Yet, in our work, we expect that memory errors will occur, and expect the technique to defend against them. In this regard, note that the effect of a memory error is to create additional aliases at runtime — for instance, if p was a pointer to an array a, due to a buffer overflow, it may also end up pointing to an adjacent object b. However, since the static analysis did not report this possible aliasing, we would have assigned different masks for a and b. As a result, the buffer overflow would corrupt b with values that will appear "random," when unmasked using m_b.

pointer. Thus, when the pointer is dereferenced, we know the mask to be used for its referents statically. This scheme requires "points-to" information which can be obtained by using *pointer analysis*, further described in Section 2.1. In the above example, from the results of any conservative pointer analysis technique, we can conclude that both variables x and y can be pointed by the pointer variable ptr. Hence we can use the same mask for both x and y, and this mask can be then used for unmasking *ptr, i.e., m_x = m_y = m_starptr. Mask assignment based on the results of pointer analysis is described in Section 2.2.

The principal weakness of the DSR approach arises due to potential aliasing. In particular, if two objects *a* and *b* can be aliased, then the same mask will be used for both, which means that overflows from *a* to *b* cannot be detected. To address this problem, we allocate objects that share the same mask in different memory regions that are separated by an unmapped memory page. In this case, a typical buffer overflow from *a* to *b* will attempt to modify data in this inaccessible page, which causes a memory fault. We will revisit this solution in the discussion of optimization later in this section.

2.1   Pointer Analysis

Ideally, we would like to associate a distinct mask with each variable. Unfortunately, the use of pointers in C language potentially forces the assignment of the same mask for different variables. As a result, variables are divided into different equivalence classes. All the variables in a class are assigned the same mask, and those belonging to different classes are assigned different masks. The number of the equivalence classes depends on the precision of pointer analysis. Intuitively, greater the precision, there will be more number of the equivalence classes.

A pointer analysis is, in general, computationally undecidable [33]. As a result, existing pointer analysis algorithms use approximations that provide varying degree of precision and efficiency. The worst-case time complexities of these algorithms range from linear to exponential. We need to consider the time complexity for the analysis to be efficient and scalable. There are several factors that affect precision and efficiency of analysis. Such factors include flow-sensitivity, context-sensitivity, modeling of heap objects, modeling of aggregate objects, and representation of alias information [24]. We need to consider these factors while choosing the analysis.

Algorithms involved in existing flow-sensitive analyses [25] are very expensive in terms of time complexity (high order polynomials). Context-sensitive approaches [21,39] have exponential time complexity in the worst case. We avoid these two types of analyses as they do not scale to large programs. Among the flow-insensitive and context-insensitive algorithms, Andersen's algorithm [3] is considered to be the most precise algorithm. This algorithm has the worst case cubic time complexity, which is still high for it to be used on large programs. On the other hand, Steensgaard's algorithm [37] has linear time complexity, but it gives less precise results. Interestingly, as we shall show in the next section, it turns out that the results of Andersen's and Steensgaard's analyses give us the

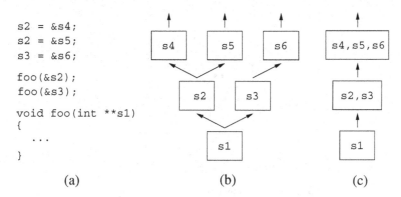

```
s2 = &s4;
s2 = &s5;
s3 = &s6;

foo(&s2);
foo(&s3);

void foo(int **s1)
{
    ...
}
```

(a)   (b)   (c)

Fig. 1. Figure (a) above shows a sample C program for which points-to graph is computed. Figures (b) and (c) show the points-to graphs computed by Andersen's algorithm and Steensgaard's algorithm respectively.

same equivalence classes of variable masks. Therefore, we implemented Steensgaard's algorithm for our purpose.

Steensgaard's algorithm performs flow-insensitive and context-insensitive inter-procedural points-to analysis that scales to large programs. It computes points-to set over named variables corresponding to local, global and heap objects. We use single logical object to represent all heap objects that are allocated at the same program point. We perform field-insensitive analysis, i.e., we do not distinguish between different fields in the same structure or union. Our implementation is similar to the one described in [37].

2.2   Mask Assignment

Consider points-to graphs computed by Steensgaard's and Andersen's algorithms as shown in Figure 1. A points-to graph captures points-to information in the form of a directed graph, where nodes represent equivalence classes of symbols and edges represent pointer relationships. Points-to information computed by Andersen's algorithm is more precise than that computed by Steensgaard's algorithm. For instance, according to Steensgaard's graph, s2 may point to s6. However, this relationship appears unlikely if we look at the program. Andersen's graph does not capture this relationship, hence it is more precise. In Steensgaard's analysis, two objects that are pointed by the same pointer are unioned into one node. This may lead to unioning of the points-to sets of formerly distinct objects. This kind of unioning makes the algorithm faster, but results in less precise output as shown in the above example.

Now let us see how we can use the points-to information to determine the equivalence classes of masks for the above example; we do this for Andersen's graph. Objects s2 and s3 can be accessed using the pointer dereference *s1. This suggests that s2 and s3 should have the same mask, and therefore they belong to the same equivalence class. Similarly, pointer dereference **s1 can be used to access any of the objects pointed by s2 or s3. This implies that the objects

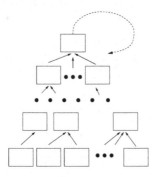

Fig. 2. A Steensgaard's point-to graph

pointed by s2 and s3 should have the same mask, and hence objects s4, s5 and s6 should be merged into the same equivalence class. This merging is similar to the unioning operation in Steensgaard's algorithm. Therefore, the equivalence classes of masks will be the same even in the case of Steensgaard's graph. For the above example, the complete set of equivalence classes of masks is {{s1}, {*s1, s2, s3}, {**s1, *s2, *s3, s4, s5, s6}}. As Steensgaard's and Andersen's graphs are equivalent from the point of view of determining masks, we use Steensgaard's algorithm for our purpose as it is more efficient than Andersen's algorithm.

Now we formally define the procedure for determining masks using a Steensgaard's points-to graph (refer Figure 2). In general, a points-to graph of a program consists of disconnected components. Hence we consider the procedure only for one component which can be similarly applied to all the graph components. For this, let us first look at the properties of a Steensgaard's points-to graph. The unioning operation in Steensgaard's algorithm enforces following properties in the points-to graph. A node in the graph has at most one outdegree and zero or more indegree. Owing to this, a connected component in the graph assumes a tree-like structure, where a node can have multiple children corresponding to the indegree edges, but at most one parent depending on the presence of an outdegree edge. However, this does not imply that the component is always a tree. There is a possibility that the root node of the tree-like structure may have an outward edge pointing to any of the nodes in the component, resulting in a cycle. Figure 2 shows such an edge as a dashed line.

We assign a distinct mask to each node of the points-to graph. Note that a node may correspond to multiple variables. The mask of the node is thus used for masking all of its variables.

The mask of an object that is accessed using a pointer dereference is determined as follows. Let ptr be the pointer variable. First, the node N corresponding to the pointer variable is located in the points-to graph. For the object *ptr, its mask is the mask associated with the parent node $parent(N)$. Similarly, the mask of **ptr is the mask associated with $parent(parent(N))$, and so on. Since each node has at most one parent, we can uniquely determine the masks of objects accessed through pointer dereferences. Note that this procedure also works for dereferences of a non-pointer variable that stores an address because the points-to graph captures the points-to relation involved. The procedure for dereferences of pointer expressions involving pointer arithmetic is similar.

Optimization

Indiscriminate introduction of masking/unmasking operations can degrade performance. For instance, many programs make use of a large number of variables that hold integer (or floating-point) values. If we can avoid masking/unmasking for such variables, significant performance gains are possible. At the same time, we want to ensure that this optimization does not have a significant impact on security. We show how this can be achieved by masking only the overflow candidate objects.

There are two types of memory corruption attacks: absolute address-dependent attacks and relative address-dependent attacks. Absolute address-dependent attacks involve corruption of a pointer value. However, mechanisms used for corrupting a pointer value, such as buffer overflows, heap overflows and integer overflows, are in fact relative address-dependent. So if we can defeat relative address-dependent attacks, we get automatic protection for absolute address-dependent attacks. Relative address-dependent attacks involve overflows from overflow candidate objects, and we make these attacks difficult as described below.

All non-overflow candidate objects are allocated in one memory region and we separate memory for this region from the overflow candidate objects with an unmapped memory page. As a result, overflows from overflow candidate objects into non-overflow candidate objects become impossible.

Overflows from an overflow candidate object into another overflow candidate object is possible. To address this problem, first we mask all the overflow candidate objects. Second, we identify objects that may be aliased, and allocate them in disjoint areas of memory that are separated by an unmapped memory page. Now, any attempt to overflow from one of these objects to the other will cause a memory exception, since such a write must also write into the intervening unmapped page[4]. The number of memory regions needed is equal to the number of different objects that use the same mask at runtime. This number can be statically estimated and is small for static data, and hence each such object can be allocated in a disjoint memory area. In typical programs, this number appears to be small for stack-allocated data, so we have been able to allocate such objects across a small number of disjoint stacks. (We call them buffer stacks.) Note that the strategy of removing overflow candidate objects from the main stack has some additional benefits: it removes the possibility of a stack-smashing attack — not only is the return address protected this way, but also other data such as

---

[4] The details of this step are somewhat complicated by our choice of implementing this technique using a source-to-source transformation, as opposed to modifying a compiler. With this choice, we cannot control how the memory for objects is allocated. We therefore borrowed a technique from [10] which uses an extra level of indirection for accessing objects. Intuitively, this technique can be viewed as a means to control the layout of objects.

saved registers and temporaries. This is important since, as a source-to-source transformation, we cannot ensure that saved registers and temporaries use a mask. Since this data cannot be corrupted by buffer overflows, we mitigate this weakness. If the number of stack objects with the same mask is large, we can move the objects into the heap. Protection of these objects will then be the same as that of heap objects.

For the heap, however, the number of distinct objects with the same mask may be large, thereby making it difficult to allocate those objects from different memory regions. As a result, our approach is to use a fixed number of memory regions, and cycle the heap allocations through these regions as successive objects with the same masks are allocated. This approach increases the likelihood of successful buffer overflows across two heap blocks, but note that traditional heap overflows, which are based on corrupting metadata stored at the beginning (or end) of heap blocks will fail: an attempt to overwrite metadata value with x will instead end up writing x^m_h, where m_h denotes the mask associated with the heap block.

The technique of separating aliased objects with a guard page prevents the common form of buffer overflows, which involve writing a contiguous (or closely spaced) set of locations beyond the end of a buffer. However, there can be buffer overflows that allow an attacker to corrupt memory that is far from the base of the buffer. Such overflows are common in conjunction with integer overflows. The guard-page technique does not protect against this attack. We therefore rely on our relative-address randomization technique [10] as a second line of defense against such attacks.

The technique described so far contains a vulnerability that occurs due to reuse of storage for non-overflow candidate objects. For instance, such a vulnerability may arise in a program that uses an uninitialized pointer variable for which we do not assign any mask. Now, if an attacker can control the previous use of the memory corresponding to this pointer, she can potentially corrupt the pointer with a chosen value. We address this vulnerability by ensuring that all objects are initialized before use, which is any way necessary to prevent information leakage attacks. An information leakage attack targets randomization techniques by exploiting a vulnerability that leaks the random values. An uninitialized non-overflow candidate variable may hold a masked value of a previously used data, and if this value is leaked, it is possible for an attacker to derive the mask. The attacker can then target other variables that share the derived mask. Note that an overflow candidate object is not vulnerable to information leakage attacks because any attempt to read this object will cause the mask associated with the object to be applied. In other words, the attacker receives the plaintext data rather than the masked data.

3   Implementation

Our transformation approach is applicable to C programs. We use CIL [29] as the front end, and Objective Caml as the implementation language. We describe our implementation approach for a 32-bit x86 architecture and Linux operating system.

```
int *p1, *p2, **pp1, **pp2, intval;
...
int main()
{
    ...
    p1 = &intval;
    pp1 = &p1;

    pp2 = pp1;
    p2 = *pp2;
    ...
    ... = &pp2;
    ...
}
```

(a) A sample C code

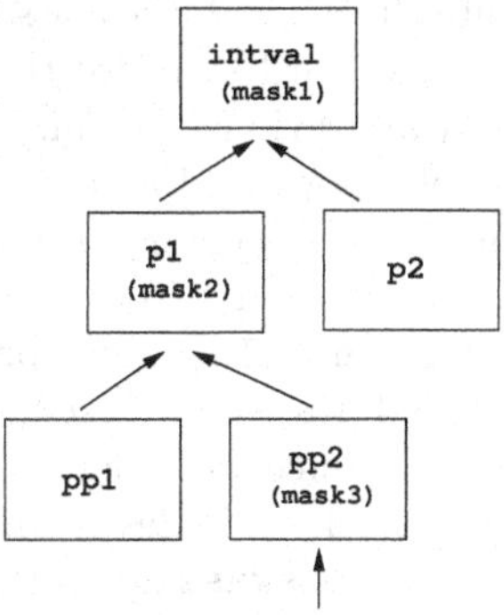

(b) Points-to graph for the code

```
static unsigned int mask1, mask2, mask3;
int **p1_ptr, *p2, **pp1, ***pp2_ptr, *intval_ptr, ...;
int main()
{   ...
    (*p1_ptr) = intval_ptr;
    (*p1_ptr) = (int *)((unsigned int)(*p1_ptr) ^ mask2);
    pp1 = p1_ptr;
    (*pp2_ptr) = pp1;
    (*pp2_ptr) = (int **)((unsigned int)(*pp2_ptr) ^ mask3);
    p2 = (int *)((unsigned int)(*((int **)
        ((unsigned int)(*pp2_ptr) ^ mask3))) ^ mask2);
    ...
}
static void (__attribute__((__constructor__)) __dsr_init)()
{   ...
    /* code to allocate memory for intval, p1 and pp2 using their
    pointers intval_ptr, p1_ptr and pp2_ptr respectively. */
    ...
    __dsr_maskassign(mask1); __dsr_maskassign(mask2);
    __dsr_maskassign(mask3);
}
```

(c) Transformed code for the code in (a)

Fig. 3. A sample example illustrating basic DSR transformations

As a first step in the transformation of a program, we first perform pointer analysis in order to determine masks associated with different data. Our current implementation supports Steensgaard's pointer analysis. One of the limitation of our current implementation is that it is based on whole program analysis and transformation. The whole program analysis approach requires a merged source file. The CIL toolkit provides an option to automatically generate such a merged file. Sometimes this kind of merging can fail due to type mismatch of variable declarations present in different files. Such cases can be handled by manual changes to the declarations. With some extra effort, our implementation can be extended to a separate file compilation-based transformation approach. Even with the current implementation approach, we have demonstrated its practicality by transforming several "real-world" programs without any manual changes.

In the second step, we generate the program's points-to graph, from which we then compute the equivalence classes needed for assigning random masks to data variables. In the third step, we transform the code as per the transformations described in the previous section.

The example shown in Figure 3 illustrates the above transformation steps. In this example, variables p2 and pp1 correspond to non-overflow candidate objects, which are not required to be masked due to our optimization. On the other hand, variables intval, p1 and pp2 correspond to overflow candidate objects because their addresses are taken. So we mask these variables, and for this we respectively introduce variables mask1, mask2, and mask3 to store their masks. Each of these mask variables is initialized with a different random value using the macro __dsr_maskassign in the constructor function __dsr_init() that is automatically invoked before the start of the execution in main(). Recall from Section 2 that we need to allocate memory for overflow candidate objects in different memory regions. For this to be possible, we access overflow candidate objects with an extra level of indirection using pointers, e.g., a variable v is accessed using (*v_ptr), where v_ptr is a pointer to v. In this example, we introduce pointers intval_ptr, p1_ptr, and pp2_ptr to access intval, p1, and pp2 respectively. The memory for these overflow candidate objects is allocated in the initialization code present in __dsr_init(). Since the overflow candidate objects in this example do not share masks, we allocate their memory in the same region, in between two unmapped memory pages. As a result, overflows from overflow candidate objects cannot corrupt non-overflow candidate objects. Moreover, overflows among overflow candidate objects are detected because all of them use different masks.

The statements are transformed as follows. If an overflow candidate variable is assigned a value, the value is first masked and then stored in the memory; if it is used in an expression, its masked value is unmasked before its use.

Now we discuss a few issues concerning the basic implementation approach.

3.1   Handling Overflows within Structures

According to C language specifications, overflows within structures are not considered as memory errors. However, attackers can potentially exploit such overflows also. For instance, an overflow from an array field inside a structure corrupting adjacent fields in the same structure may lead to an exploitable vulnerability. Thus, it is desirable to have some protection from these overflows. Unfortunately, even bounds-checking detection techniques do not provide defense against these types of overflows. ASR too fails to address this problem due to the inherent limitation of not being able to randomize relative distances between fields of a structure because of language semantics. DSR can be used to provide some level of protection in this case. The basic idea is to use field-sensitive points-to analysis so that we can assign different masks to different fields of the same structure. However, our current implementation does not support field-sensitive points-to analysis. As a part of future enhancement, we plan to implement Steensgaard's points-to analysis [36] to handle field-sensitivity. The time complexity of this analysis, as reported in [36], is likely to be close to linear in the size of the program in practice. Hence, this enhancement would not affect the scalability of our approach. Moreover, it does not increase runtime performance overhead.

Library functions such as `memcpy`, `memset` and `bzero`, which operate on entire structures, need a special transformation. For instance, we cannot allow `bzero` to zero out all the fields of a structure. Instead it should assign each field a value corresponding to its mask. This would require computing points-to set for pointer arguments of these functions in a context-sensitive way (as if the functions are inlined at their invocation point). As a result, the pointer arguments would most likely point to specific type of data including structures and arrays. So if the data pointed by an argument is a structure, we would use corresponding masks for the individual fields of the structures using summarization functions.

3.2   Handling Variable Argument Functions

Variable argument functions need special handling. In effect, we treat them as if they take an array (with some maximum size limit) as a parameter. This effectively means that the same mask is assigned to all the parameters, and if some of these parameters happen to be pointers, then all their targets get assigned the same mask, and so on. However, the imprecision in resulting pointer analysis can be addressed by analyzing such functions in a context-sensitive manner. Our implementation currently does not support this.

3.3   Transformation of Libraries

A source-code based approach such as ours requires the source code for the program as well as the libraries, as all of them need the transformation.

A few extra steps are required for handling shared libraries. Using the steps described in Section 2, we would obtain points-to graphs for all the shared libraries and the main executable. Since these graphs could be partial, we need to compute the global points-to graph. This could potentially lead to merging of some equivalence classes of masks, which in turn can make an object in a shared library an alias of another object from the executable or other shared libraries. In such situation, mask values are needed to be shared across the executable and the libraries.

A natural way to implement the above steps is to enhance the functionality of the dynamic linker. For this, each binary object (an executable or a shared library) needs to maintain dynamic symbol information about the points-to graph, which is a general yet an important piece of information that could be useful to many program analysis and transformation techniques. In addition, the binary objects need storage for mask variables and also dynamic symbol information about them. Using this information, at link-time, the dynamic linker can compute the global points-to graph, and resolve the mask variables just like it resolves other dynamic symbols. Additionally, it needs to initialize the mask variables with random values.

At times, source code may not be available for some libraries. Such libraries cannot be directly used with our DSR technique. The standard approach for dealing with this problem is to rely on summarization functions that capture the effect of such external library functions.

Given the prototype nature of our implementation, we did not transform shared libraries, and instead used the approach of summarization functions. For the test programs used in our experiments, we needed to provide summarizations for 52 `glibc` functions. In addition, we do not mask external variables, (i.e., shared library variables) and any internal variable that gets aliased with an external variable, so as to make our technique work with untransformed libraries.

4   Evaluation

4.1   Functionality

We have implemented DSR technique as described in the previous section. The implementation is robust enough to handle several "real-world" programs shown in Figure 4. We verified that these programs worked correctly after the transformation. We also manually inspected the source code to ensure that the masking and unmasking operations were performed on data accesses, and that variables were grouped into regions guarded by unmapped pages as described earlier.

4.2   Runtime Overheads

Figure 4 shows the runtime overheads, when the original and the transformed programs were compiled using `gcc-3.2.2` with optimization flag `-O2`, and run on a desktop running RedHat Linux 9.0 with 1.7 GHz Pentium IV processor and 512 MB RAM. Execution times were averaged over 10 runs.

Program	Workload	% Overhead
`patch-1.06`	Apply a 2 MB patch-file on a 9 MB file	4
`tar-1.13.25`	Create a tar file of a directory of size 141 MB	5
`grep-2.5.1`	Search a pattern in files of combined size 108 MB	7
`ctags-5.6`	Generate a tag file for a 17511-line C source code	11
`gzip-1.1.3`	Compress a 12 MB file	24
`bc-1.06`	Find factorial of 600	27
`bison-1.35`	Parse C++ grammar file	28
	Average	15

Fig. 4. Runtime performance overhead introduced by transformations for DSR

For DSR transformations, the runtime overhead depends mainly on memory accesses that result in masking and unmasking operations. In I/O-intensive programs, such as `tar` and `patch`, most of the execution time is spent in I/O operations, and hence we see low overheads for such programs. On the other hand,

CPU-intensive programs are likely to spend substantial part of the execution time in performing memory accesses. That is why we observe higher overheads for CPU-intensive programs. The average overhead is around 15%, which is a bit higher than the overheads for ASR techniques. Nonetheless, DSR technique is still practical and provides a stronger level of protection.

4.3 Analysis of Effectiveness Against Different Attacks

Effectiveness can be evaluated experimentally or analytically. Experimental evaluation involves running a set of well-known exploits against vulnerable programs, and showing that our transformation stops these exploits. Instead, we have relied on an analytical evaluation for the following reasons. First, exploits are usually very fragile, and any small modification to the code, even if it they are not designed for attack protection, will cause the exploit to fail. Clearly, with our implementation, which moves objects around, the attacks would fail even if we used a zero-valued mask in all cases. Modifying the exploit so that it works in this base case is quite time-consuming, so we did not attempt this. Instead, we rely on an analytical evaluation that argues why certain classes of existing exploitation techniques will fail against DSR; and estimate the success probability of other attacks.

Stack buffer overflows. Memory for all the overflow candidate local variables is allocated in a buffer stack or the heap. Typical buffer overflow attacks on the stack target the data on the main stack, such as the return address and the saved base pointer. These attacks will fail deterministically, since the buffer and the target are in different memory regions, with guard pages in between. Similarly, all attacks that attempt to corrupt non-aggregate local data, such as integer or floating-point valued local variables, saved registers, and temporaries will also fail.

Attacks that corrupt data stored in an overflow candidate variable by overflowing another overflow candidate variable is possible if they are both in the same memory region. However, such attacks have low probability of success (2^{-32}) because we ensure that objects with the same mask are allocated in different memory region. As mentioned before, in our implementation, we could do this without having to maintain a large number of buffer stacks. If this assumption did not hold for some programs, then we could resort to moving those overflow candidate variables to the heap, and falling back on the technique (and analysis of effectiveness) as overflows in the heap.

Static buffer overflows. Static overflow candidate objects are separated from static non-overflow candidate objects with inaccessible pages. So overflows in static memory cannot be used for corrupting non-overflow candidate static data.

Overflows from a static overflow candidate object into another overflow candidate object (not necessarily a static object) that is allocated in a different memory region are impossible due to the use of guard pages in between regions. However, overflows within the same static data region are possible. For such overflows, since our implementation ensures that the masks for different variables within each region will be different, the probability of a successful data corruption attack is reduced to 2^{-32}. In our experiments, we needed less than 150 distinct memory regions in the static area.

Heap overflows. Heap overflows involve overwriting heap control data consisting of two pointer-values appearing at the end of the target heap block (or at the beginning of a subsequent block). This sort of overwrite is possible, but since our technique would be using a mask for the contents of the heap block (which, as pointed out earlier, is an overflow candidate data), whereas the heap-control related pointer values would be in cleartext. As a result, the corruption has only 2^{-32} probability of succeeding.

Overflows from one heap block to the next are possible. If the two heap blocks are masked with different masks, then the attack success probability is 2^{-32}. However, heap objects tend be large in numbers, and moreover, possible aliasing may force us to assign the same mask to a large number of them. An important point to be noted in this case is that the number of different memory regions required for heap objects is a property of input to the program, rather than the program itself. Hence we use a probabilistic approach, and distribute heap objects randomly over a bounded number of different memory regions. Moreover, it should be noted that inter-heap-block overflows corrupt the heap control data in between, so the program may crash (due to the use of this corrupted data) before the corrupted data is used by the program. Nevertheless, it is clear that the success probability can be larger than 2^{-32}. In practice, this is hard because (a) heap allocations tend to be unpredictable as they are function of previous computations performed and inputs processed, (b) the control data will also be corrupted, and so it will likely be detected.

Format string attacks. Traditional format-string attacks make use the %n directive to write the number of bytes printed so far, and require the attacker to be able to specify the location for this write. Note that the attacker has control only over the format string, which being an overflow candidate object does not reside on the main stack. The location for the write is going to be a parameter, which will reside on the main stack. Thus the attacker cannot control the target into which the write will be performed, thus defeating traditional format-string attacks.

Other ways of exploiting format string attacks may be possible. The attacker may use %n to refer to a pointer value or an attacker-controlled integer value that is already on the stack. Also, the attacker can use other format specifiers such as %x and %d to print out the contents of the stack.

We point out that this weakness is shared with most existing defenses against memory error exploits. Nonetheless, the best way to deal with format-string attacks is to combine DSR with an efficient technique such as FormatGuard[16].

Relative address attacks based on integer overflows. Note that the base address used in any relative address attack must correspond to an overflow candidate variable. There is a small probability that the target location overwritten by the attack will have been assigned the same mask as the one corresponding to the base address. It is hard to predict this probability independent of the program, as it is the same as the probability of possible aliasing between the base address and the target address of the attack. In any case, relative-address randomization of overflow candidate objects in DSR provides probabilistic protection against these attacks.

Attacks Targeting DSR. We discuss possible attacks targeted at DSR.

- **Information leakage attack.** Randomization based defenses are usually vulnerable to information leakage attacks that leak the random values. For instance, ASR is vulnerable to attack that leaks the values of pointers that are stored on the stack or the heap. Interestingly, DSR is not susceptible to this attack. This is because any attempt to read a pointer value will automatically cause the mask associated with the pointer to be applied, i.e., the result of the read will be in plaintext rather than being in encrypted form. Thus, information regarding the masks is not leaked.
- **Brute force and guessing attacks.** The probability calculations in the previous sections indicate the difficulty of these attacks.
- **Partial pointer overwrites.** These attacks involve corruption of the lower byte(s) of a pointer. Partial pointer overflows can decrease the attacker's work because there are only 256 possibilities for the LS byte. But these vulnerabilities are difficult to find and exploit. Even when exploitable, the target usually must be on the stack. In our implementation, since the main stack does not contain overflow candidate variables, it becomes impossible to use buffer overflows to effect partial overflow attack on stack-resident data.

5   Related Work

Runtime Guarding. These techniques transform a program to prevent corruption of specific targets such as return addresses, function pointers, or other control data. Techniques such as StackGuard [18], RAD [15], StackShield [5], Libverify [5] and Libsafe [5], in one way or another, prevent undetected corruption of the return address on the stack. ProPolice [22] additionally guards against corruption of non-aggregate local data. FormatGuard [16] transforms source code to provide protection from format-string attacks.

As above techniques provide only an attack-specific protection, attackers find it very easy to discover other attack mechanisms for bypassing the protection.

Runtime Enforcement of Static Analysis Results. Static analysis based intrusion detection techniques such as [38] were based on using a static analysis to compute program control-flow, and enforcing this at runtime. However, since enforcement was performed only on system call invocations, control-flow hijack attacks were still possible. Control-flow integrity (CFI) [1] addressed this weakness by monitoring all control-flow transfers, and ensuring that they were to locations predicted by a static analysis. As a result, control-flow hijack attacks are detected, but the technique does not detect data corruption attacks.

Data-flow integrity [12] addresses this weakness by enforcing statically analyzed *def-use* relationships at runtime. However, it incurs much higher performance overheads than CFI as well as DSR.

Write-integrity testing (WIT) [2] proposes a faster way to perform runtime checking of validity of memory updates. Specifically, they use a static analysis to identify all memory locations that can be written by an instruction, and assign the same "color" to all these locations. This color is encoded into the program text as a constant. At runtime, a global array is used to record the color associated with each memory location. Before a memory write, WIT ensures that the color associated with the write instruction matches the color of the location that is written. Although developed independent of our work [8], the techniques behind WIT share some similarities with DSR. In particular, their color assignment algorithm is also based on alias analysis.

WIT reports lower overheads than DSR, but this is achieved by checking only the write operations. In contrast, DSR addresses reads as well as writes, and hence can address memory corruption attacks that may be based on out-of-bounds reads. In terms of strength of protection, DSR and WIT are comparable in the context of buffer overflows where the source and target objects are *not* aliased. If they are aliased, then WIT can still offer deterministic protection against typical buffer overflows that involve writing a contiguous (or closely spaced) set of locations beyond the end of a buffer. DSR can also provide deterministic protection in such cases, but its implementation technique for achieving this, namely, the use of unwritable memory pages, does not scale well for heap objects. However, WIT fails to provide any protection in the case of buffer overflows where the source and target objects are aliased and are far apart — this happens often in the case of integer overflows. In contrast, DSR offers probabilistic protection in this case due to its use of relative address randomization as a second line of defense.

Runtime Bounds and Pointer Checking. Several techniques have been developed that maintain, at runtime, metadata related to memory allocations and pointers [4,26,30,34,41,20]. Pointer dereferences are then checked for validity against this metadata. While the techniques differ in terms of the range of memory errors that they are able to detect, they all cover a broad enough range to protect against most memory error exploits. As compared to the techniques described in previous paragraph, these techniques tend to be more precise since they rely on runtime techniques (rather than static analysis) for metadata-tracking. However, this also translates to significant additional overheads.

Randomization Techniques. Our DSR technique is an instance of the broader idea of introducing diversity in nonfunctional aspects of software, an idea first suggested by Forrest et al. [23]. The basic idea is that the diversified programs maintain the same functionality, but differ in their processing of erroneous inputs. As a result, different variants exhibit different behaviors when exposed to the same exploit. In the context of memory error vulnerabilities, several recent works have demonstrated the usefulness of introducing automated diversity in the low level implementation details, such as memory layout [32,40,23,28], system calls [14], and instruction sets [27,6]. System call and instruction set randomization techniques only protect against injected code attacks, but not from return-to-libc (aka existing code) or data corruption attacks. On the other hand, the techniques which randomize memory layout, popularly known as address space randomization (ASR) techniques, provide protection against injected code as well as data corruption attacks. ASR techniques that only perform absolute address randomization [32,9] (AAR) don't directly address buffer overflows, but are still able to defeat most attacks as they rely on pointer corruption. ASR techniques that augment AAR with relative address randomization (RAR) [10] are effective against all buffer overflows, including those not involving pointer corruption. DieHard [7] and DieFast [31] approaches provide randomization-based defense against memory corruption attacks involving heap objects.

Randomization techniques with relatively small range of randomization, e.g., PaX with its 16-bits of randomness in some memory regions, can be defeated relatively quickly using guessing attacks [35]. As mentioned earlier, they are also susceptible to information leakage attacks. Cox et al. [19] and Bruschi et al. [11] have shown how process replication can be used to address these deficiencies, and hence provide deterministic (rather than probabilistic) defense against certain classes of memory exploits. However, they come with a significant overhead due to the need to run two copies of the protected process. In contrast, DSR incurs only modest overheads to mitigate guessing attacks (using a much larger range of randomization) as well as information leakage attacks.

6   Conclusion

In this paper, we introduced a new randomization-based defense against memory error exploits. Unlike previous defenses such as instruction set randomization that was effective only against injected code attacks, our DSR technique can defend against emerging attacks that target security-critical data. Unlike address space randomization, which is primarily effective against pointer corruption attacks, DSR provides a high degree of protection from attacks that corrupt non-pointer data. Moreover, it is not vulnerable to information leakage attacks. Finally, it provides much higher entropy than existing ASR implementations, thus providing an effective defense from brute-force attacks.

We described the design and implementation of DSR in this paper. Our results show that the technique has relatively low overheads. In addition to reducing the likelihood of successful attacks to 2^{-32} in most cases, the technique also provides deterministic protection against attacks such as stack-smashing, and traditional format-string attacks. In future work, we expect to address some of the limitations of current prototype, such as the inability to address intra-field overflows.

References

1. Abadi, M., Budiu, M., Erlingsson, U., Ligatti, J.: Control-flow integrity - principles, implementations, and applications. In: ACM conference on Computer and Communications Security (CCS), Alexandria, VA (November 2005)

2. Akritidis, P., Cadar, C., Raiciu, C., Costa, M., Castro, M.: Preventing memory error exploits with wit. In: IEEE Symposium on Security and Privacy (May 2008)
3. Andersen, L.O.: Program analysis and specialization for the C programming language. PhD Thesis, DIKU, University of Copenhagen (May 1994), ftp.diku.dk/pub/diku/semantics/papers/D-203.dvi.Z
4. Austin, T.M., Breach, S.E., Sohi, G.S.: Efficient detection of all pointer and array access errors. In: ACM SIGPLAN Conference on Programming Language Design and Implementation, Orlando, Florida, pp. 290–301 (June 1994)
5. Baratloo, A., Singh, N., Tsai, T.: Transparent run-time defense against stack smashing attacks. In: USENIX Annual Technical Conference, Berkeley, CA, pp. 251–262 (June 2000)
6. Barrantes, E.G., Ackley, D.H., Forrest, S., Palmer, T.S., Stefanović, D., Zovi, D.D.: Randomized instruction set emulation to disrupt binary code injection attacks. In: ACM conference on Computer and Communications Security (CCS), Washington, DC (October 2003)
7. Berger, E.D., Zorn, B.G.: DieHard: Probabilistic memory safety for unsafe languages. In: ACM SIGPLAN Conference on Programming Language Design and Implementation, Ottawa, Canada, pp. 158–168 (June 2006)
8. Bhatkar, S.: Defeating memory error exploits using automated software diversity. Ph.D. Thesis, Stony Brook University (September 2007), http://seclab.cs.sunysb.edu/seclab/pubs/thesis/sandeep.pdf
9. Bhatkar, S., DuVarney, D.C., Sekar, R.: Address obfuscation: An efficient approach to combat a broad range of memory error exploits. In: USENIX Security Symposium (August 2003)
10. Bhatkar, S., Sekar, R., DuVarney, D.C.: Efficient techniques for comprehensive protection from memory error exploits. In: USENIX Security Symposium, Baltimore, MD (August 2005)
11. Bruschi, D., Cavallaro, L., Lanzi, A.: Diversified process replicae for defeating memory error exploits. In: International Workshop on Information Assurance (WIA) (April 2007)
12. Castro, M., Costa, M., Harris, T.: Securing software by enforcing data-flow integrity. In: USENIX Symposium on Operating Systems Design and Implementation (OSDI), Seattle, WA (November 2006)
13. Chen, S., Xu, J., Sezer, E.C.: Non-control-hijacking attacks are realistic threats. In: USENIX Security Symposium (2005)
14. Chew, M., Song, D.: Mitigating buffer overflows by operating system randomization. Technical Report CMU-CS-02-197, Carnegie Mellon University (December 2002)
15. Chiueh, T., Hsu, F.: RAD: A compile-time solution to buffer overflow attacks. In: IEEE International Conference on Distributed Computing Systems, Phoenix, Arizona (April 2001)
16. Cowan, C., Barringer, M., Beattie, S., Kroah-Hartman, G.: FormatGuard: Automatic protection from printf format string vulnerabilities. In: USENIX Security Symposium (2001)
17. Cowan, C., Beattie, S., Johansen, J., Wagle, P.: PointGuard: Protecting pointers from buffer overflow vulnerabilities. In: USENIX Security Symposium, Washington, DC (August 2003)
18. Cowan, C., Pu, C., Maier, D., Walpole, J., Bakke, P., Beattie, S., Grier, A., Wagle, P., Zhang, Q., Hinton, H.: StackGuard: Automatic adaptive detection and prevention of buffer-overflow attacks. In: USENIX Security Symposium, San Antonio, Texas, pp. 63–78 (January 1998)

19. Cox, B., Evans, D., Filipi, A., Rowanhill, J., Hu, W., Davidson, J., Knight, J., Nguyen-Tuong, A., Hiser, J.: N-variant systems: A secretless framework for security through diversity. In: USENIX Security Symposium (August 2006)
20. Dhurjati, D., Adve, V.: Backwards-compatible array bounds checking for c with very low overhead. In: International Conference on Software Engineering (2006)
21. Emami, M., Ghiya, R., Hendren, L.J.: Context-sensitive interprocedural points-to analysis in the presence of function pointers. In: ACM SIGPLAN Conference on Programming Language Design and Implementation, pp. 242–256 (June 1994)
22. Etoh, H., Yoda, K.: Protecting from stack-smashing attacks (June 2000), http://www.trl.ibm.com/projects/security/ssp/main.html
23. Forrest, S., Somayaji, A., Ackley, D.H.: Building diverse computer systems. In: Workshop on Hot Topics in Operating Systems, pp. 67–72. IEEE Computer Society Press, Los Alamitos (1997)
24. Hind, M.: Pointer analysis: Haven't we solved this problem yet? In: ACM SIGPLAN-SIGSOFT Workshop on Program Analysis for Software Tools and Engineering (2001)
25. Hind, M., Burke, M., Carini, P., Choi, J.-D.: Interprocedural pointer alias analysis. In: ACM Transactions on Programming Languages and Systems (TOPLAS) (July 1999)
26. Jones, R.W.M., Kelly, P.H.J.: Backwards-compatible bounds checking for arrays and pointers in C programs. In: International Workshop on Automated and Algorithmic Debugging, pp. 13–26 (1997)
27. Kc, G.S., Keromytis, A.D., Prevelakis, V.: Countering code-injection attacks with instruction-set randomization. In: ACM conference on Computer and Communications Security (CCS), Washington, DC, pp. 272–280 (October 2003)
28. Li, L., Just, J., Sekar, R.: Address-space randomization for windows systems. In: Annual Computer Security Applications Conference (ACSAC) (December 2006)
29. McPeak, S., Necula, G.C., Rahul, S.P., Weimer, W.: CIL: Intermediate language and tools for C program analysis and transformation. In: Conference on Compiler Construction (2002)
30. Necula, G.C., McPeak, S., Weimer, W.: CCured: type-safe retrofitting of legacy code. In: ACM Symposium on Principles of Programming Languages (POPL) (January 2002)
31. Novark, G., Berger, E.D., Zorn, B.G.: Exterminator: Automatically correcting memory errors with high probability. In: ACM SIGPLAN Conference on Programming Language Design and Implementation, San Diego, CA, pp. 1–11 (June 2007)
32. PaX (2001), http://pax.grsecurity.net
33. Ramalingam, G.: The undecidability of aliasing. ACM Transactions on Programming Languages and Systems (TOPLAS) 16(5), 1467–1471 (1994)
34. Ruwase, O., Lam, M.S.: A practical dynamic buffer overflow detector. In: Network and Distributed System Security Symposium, San Diego, CA, pp. 159–169 (February 2004)
35. Shacham, H., Page, M., Pfaff, B., Goh, E., Modadugu, N., Boneh, D.: On the effectiveness of address-space randomization. In: ACM conference on Computer and Communications Security (CCS), Washington, DC, pp. 298–307 (October 2004)
36. Steensgaard, B.: Points-to analysis by type inference of programs with structures and unions. In: Gyimóthy, T. (ed.) CC 1996. LNCS, vol. 1060, pp. 136–150. Springer, Heidelberg (1996)
37. Steensgaard, B.: Points-to analysis in almost linear time. In: ACM Symposium on Principles of Programming Languages (POPL), pp. 32–41 (January 1996)

38. Wagner, D., Dean, D.: Intrusion detection via static analysis. In: IEEE Symposium on Security and Privacy (May 2001)
39. Wilson, R.P., Lam, M.S.: Efficient context-sensitive pointer analysis for C programs. In: ACM SIGPLAN Conference on Programming Language Design and Implementation (1995)
40. Xu, J., Kalbarczyk, Z., Iyer, R.K.: Transparent runtime randomization for security. In: Symposium on Reliable and Distributed Systems (SRDS), Florence, Italy (October 2003)
41. Xu, W., DuVarney, D.C., Sekar, R.: An efficient and backwards-compatible transformation to ensure memory safety of C programs. In: ACM SIGSOFT International Symposium on the Foundations of Software Engineering, Newport Beach, CA (November 2004)

XSS-GUARD: Precise Dynamic Prevention of Cross-Site Scripting Attacks

Prithvi Bisht and V.N. Venkatakrishnan

Systems and Internet Security Lab, Department of Computer Science,
University of Illinois, Chicago
{pbisht,venkat}@cs.uic.edu

Abstract. This paper focuses on defense mechanisms for cross-site scripting attacks, the top threat on web applications today. It is believed that input validation (or filtering) can effectively prevent XSS attacks on the server side. In this paper, we discuss several recent real-world XSS attacks and analyze the reasons for the failure of filtering mechanisms in defending these attacks. We conclude that while filtering is useful as a first level of defense against XSS attacks, it is ineffective in preventing several instances of attack, especially when user input includes content-rich HTML. We then propose XSS-GUARD, a new framework that is designed to be a prevention mechanism against XSS attacks on the server side. XSS-GUARD works by dynamically learning the set of scripts that a web application intends to create for any HTML request. Our approach also includes a robust mechanism for identifying scripts at the server side and removes any script in the output that is not intended by the web application. We discuss extensive experimental results that demonstrate the resilience of XSS-GUARD in preventing a number of real-world XSS exploits.

Keywords: Cross-site scripting (XSS), Attack Prevention, Filtering, Security.

1 Introduction

The growth of JavaScript based client-side programming has given rise to several serious security problems related to web applications. The most notorious problem is *cross site scripting* (XSS), cited as the topmost threat, accounting for nearly 30% of the reported vulnerabilities in web applications today [6]. Web application worms such as Samy [21] spread through these attacks, affecting millions of users worldwide. More recently, XSS attacks have become vectors for a much broader class of attacks, and researchers suggest that they can be used to create a distributed botnet without the need for user involvement [5].

The problem of cross-site scripting results from JavaScript code that can be injected into a document through untrusted input. A typical scenario is the following code in a Java web application, that prints the supplied username on its output:

```
out.println("<P> Hello "+uname+"! Welcome</P>");
```

Unfortunately, this code is vulnerable to XSS attacks, as the input can contain scripting commands: e.g., `<script>...stealCookie()...</script>`. When such injected code is executed in the client browser, it can result in stealing cookies, defacing

D. Zamboni (Ed.): DIMVA 2008, LNCS 5137, pp. 23–43, 2008.

the document or unauthorized submission of forms. We refer to such JavaScript code as *unauthorized* code, to distinguish it from code that was *authorized*, i.e., inserted into the HTTP response by the web application without being influenced by untrusted input.

Input validation is the most commonly employed defense against XSS attacks. In the code of the web application, untrusted input is processed by a filtering module that looks for scripting commands or meta-characters in untrusted input, and filters any such content before these inputs get processed by the web application. Filtering can be used to place constraints on input before they are processed by a web application (such as "zip codes contain exactly five characters from the set [0-9]"). From a practical standpoint, employing filters provides a first layer of defense against XSS attacks. However, there are many scenarios where filtering is difficult to get right, especially when dealing with arbitrary user input that could include content-rich HTML. In this case, every character in the HTML character set is legal, which implies that the filter cannot reject any individual character that may result in script content. Therefore, the filter has to identify sequences of characters that may result in script content. Furthermore, the filter has to "guess" how particular character sequences may appear to a browser. For instance, some browsers typically ignore the "/" character and read the string <script/> as a script tag, whereas this view may not be shared by a validation routine seeking to remove script tags.

Other approaches that defend applications against attacks on the server side, such as dynamic tainting, track the use of untrusted information by the application. They further ensure that this untrusted information passes through a filter routine before it is output by the web application. While they correctly track whether a filter routine is called before untrusted information is output, they do not reason about the correctness of employed filters, assuming the filtering is "done right". (Some progress has been made in reasoning about the correctness of filters in recent works [13,11], but these works still do not address all the problems discussed in Section 2.)

In this paper, we present the results of a study that involved a large number of recent real-world XSS attacks, and discuss the reasons for the failure of filtering mechanisms used in the applications that were subject to these attacks. We present this study using a generic example of a web application in Section 2.

We then propose a new framework called XSS-GUARD for detecting XSS attacks on the server side. XSS-Guard works by discovering intentions of the web application, and uses this in order to stave attacks. It rests mainly on two simple observations:

(a) web applications are written implicitly assuming benign inputs, and encode programmer intentions to achieve a certain HTML response on these inputs, and
(b) maliciously crafted inputs subvert the program into straying away from these intentions, leading to a HTML response that leads to XSS-attacks.

Since intentions are implicit, we propose to dynamically elicit these intentions from the web application during every run. In our approach, the main idea for discovering intentions is to generate a *shadow* response for every (real) HTTP response generated by the web application. The purpose behind generating the shadow response is to elicit the intended set of *authorized scripts* that correspond to the HTTP response. Whenever an HTTP response is generated by a web application, XSS-GUARD identifies the set of scripts present in the (real) response. The process of identifying scripts in the real response involves robust identification techniques involving real world browser code. XSS-GUARD then checks whether there is any script in this set that is not authorized (i.e., not intended) by the web application. This is accomplished by using the shadow response, which only contains scripts intended by the application. An unauthorized script is an instance of XSS attack, and XSS-GUARD removes it from the response and then sends the response to the client.

The key benefits of the XSS-GUARD approach are:

- *Deployment friendly.* Our approach does not require any significant level of human involvement in terms of code changes to be applied for XSS defense. It is based on a fully automated program transformation technique that removes the injected scripts.
- *Strong resilience.* Our approach is highly resilient to some very subtle scenarios that occur in XSS inputs, as illustrated by our comprehensive evaluation.
- *Acceptable overheads.* Our approach does not impose an undue burden on web application performance.

This paper is organized as follows: In Section 2, we discuss several real-world examples that challenge conventional filtering, especially in the context of legacy applications. Section 3 starts with the overall design of XSS-GUARD followed by the technical details behind our approach. Section 4 discusses a comprehensive evaluation of XSS-GUARD on several metrics including attack detection, resilience and performance. Section 5 analyzes contemporary XSS defenses and compares them with our approach. In Section 6 we conclude after a general discussion about future directions.

2   Challenges in Preventing XSS Attacks

We use an abstract example of a web application to discuss the challenges in preventing XSS attacks. (This example has been modeled based on several real-world attack scenarios.) Fig. 1 depicts an arbitrary run of this application. The application accepts a set of inputs $(I_1, I_2, \ldots, I_n)$. Each node in the graph of the application denotes a program location P_i where the web application generates HTML. Each output statement contributes to the HTTP response in sequence, which taken together, forms the web page that constitutes the HTTP response. For the sake of brevity, the figure does not depict other nodes in the web application that involve computation (these are abstracted along the edges).

Two views of the generated HTML response from each output location P_i are shown: one at the server side, based on the program locations where it was output from (on the left), and the view at the browser (on the client). The scripts identified by the browser are shown as S_1 through S_4.

Filtering. The web application in the Fig. 1 also includes filtering routines; the routine F shown after the application reads inputs is an *input validation* function. In addition, the routines $f_1, f_2, \ldots, f_m$ shown in the figure are *output sanitization* functions; these look for script commands in outputs being generated by each output statement, and possibly sanitize them. In the rest of this section, using several examples, we argue that these routines are not adequate in preventing several well-known types of XSS attacks.

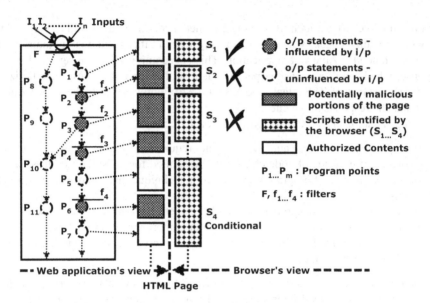

Fig. 1. Web application's HTML response and a browser's view of response

Browser view. As noted in the figure, the browser identifies the scripts and executes them. It is important to note that the scripts S_1 through S_4 identified at the browser are precisely those that will be executed when the page is viewed in the browser. The browser cannot distinguish between scripts that were crafted by malicious input or were intended by the web application in the response. Therefore, it simply executes all scripts, and this can result in XSS attacks. The web-application could communicate the set of intended scripts to a specially-equipped browser as suggested in BEEP [17], but this approach has problems of scalability from the web application's point of view; every client user needs to have a copy of this specialized browser that can understand this non-standard communication.

Output sanitization. Note that each of the filter functions f_i can HTML-encode all the output characters, so that the corresponding characters can be rendered by the browser. This can prevent all XSS attacks since all the characters will be escaped and interpreted literally by the browser. For instance, the string `<script>` will be encoded to `&lt;script&gt;`. However, this will disallow any HTML to be input by the user, and will break web applications such as wikis and blogs as they render user-supplied HTML.

2.1 Some XSS Attack Scenarios

Let us now consider in detail several scenarios outlined in the Fig. 1. We consider the HTTP response both from the web application's and browser's points of view.

1. *Authorized Scripts.* The web application may output content that did not depend on user input in any fashion, and a browser identifies the script content in this

output. This is the scenario depicted as script S_1 in Fig. 1. Since this behavior (script execution) was intended by the application, the browser can be allowed to execute S_1.

2. *Unauthorized scripts.* The web application may write user input (or content derived from it) in its output. This is depicted by script S_2 identified by the browser. This script may appear in the output either because there was no filter function, or it failed to identify the injected script in the input. Note that there is a large set of vectors for XSS; there are several possible HTML entities that can be used to embed script content (1) tags and URI schemes (such as `<script>` and `javascript:`) (2) tag attributes such as `src`, `background`, etc., and (3) event handlers such as `onload`, `onclick etc.` (at least 94 event handlers reported [4]).

3. *Scripts resulting from multiple output locations.* A script may result from multiple output locations in a web application, such as the script S_3 identified by the browser. In this case, a single filter function (say f_2 or f_3) may not be sufficient if it looks for scripting commands, as injected input may be split across these output statements. For instance, a simple splitting of a prohibited keyword into `innerH` and `TML...` in two output locations may appear as an `innerHTML` keyword in the final output on the browser.

4. *Content in existing execution environment.* Most XSS attack prevention techniques target identifying execution environments such as `<script>` tags. However, script content S_4 (which may be an attack) in our example is constructed by making use of an existing execution environment. This is an example of a *XSS-locator* based attack [4], where user input is sandwiched between existing (authorized) script code. A simple concrete example that illustrates this is the following code: `<SCRIPT>var a=$ENV_STRING;</SCRIPT>` which embeds an environment variable in an existing (authorized) `<script>` environment. In this case, a filter such as f_4 that relies on locating scripting content does not help. A successful injection in this context can make use of *any* JavaScript construct that allows execution of arbitrary commands. For instance, the Samy MySpace Worm [21] introduced keywords prohibited by the filters (`innerHTML`) through JavaScript code that resulted the output at the client end (`eval('inner' + 'HTML')`). It is hard to isolate and filter input that builds such constructs, without understanding the syntactical context in which they are used.

The above examples illustrates why filtering is hard to get right, especially in the presence of HTML input. Furthermore, an existing exploit can be obfuscated to avoid detection through filtering. Such obfuscation can be achieved by encoding it in various ways - `UTF-8`, `HEX`, foreign languages etc. Such encoding can even be provided *on-the-fly* and filters have to cope up with such dynamic scenarios.[1] When such encodings can be set dynamically in the presence of other factors listed above, it is difficult for filtering techniques to identify script content. Static analysis techniques to detect sanitization violations will fail to detect script content that is injected through these encodings.

---

[1] A typical instance is web applications that provide response to natural language query requests. Typically these allow the end user to make use of a dynamic parameter to specify the expected character set for the response. For instance, Google search queries take `ie` and `oe` parameters that specify the input encoding and output encodings respectively.

(i) Web Application

```
String uName =
  request.getParameter("uName");
out.println("<html><body>");
out.println("<script>f()</script>");
out.println("Hi " + uName + "!");
if(uName == "admin")
  out.print("<script>Admin-script()");
else
  out.print("<script>Non-Admin-script()");
out.println("</script>");
out.println("</body></html>");
```

(ii) Benign Access, uName = Alan

```
1. <html><body>
2. <script>f()</script>
3. Hi Alan!
4. <script>Non-Admin-script()</script>
5. </body></html>
```

(iii) Real Page : uName exploited

```
1. <html><body>
2. <script>f()</script>
3. Hi <script>evil();</script>!
4. <script>Non-Admin-script()</script>
5. </body></html>
```

Fig. 2. Example server side application and generated HTML pages

Summarizing, the salient points from this section are:

1. Filtering is difficult to get right in the presence of user input that includes HTML.
2. The output of a web application must be analyzed in its entirety to identify script content.
3. A robust mechanism to identify script content is needed, as there are a myriad of ways to encode the unauthorized script content that may escape filters but may appear on the client browser.

Furthermore, from a usability and deployment point of view, any proposed solution must allow users to specify harmless (without scripts) HTML and must be easy to deploy. The solution discussed in the next section satisfies all the above requirements.

3   Our Approach

Objective. The objective of our approach is to prevent unauthorized script content from being output on the response from the server side. We want to detect any malicious scriptable content that may go undetected through any input filtering mechanism present in the web application code.

The central theme of the XSS injection attacks is to introduce script code that would perform malicious operations, instead of the operations that were *intended by the web application*. A web application is written by a programmer implicitly assuming benign inputs, and encode programmer intentions to output a particular web page on these inputs. The presence of an unauthorized script in the output, which will be executed by the browser is an example of a deviation from the web application's intentions.

The key idea in our approach is to learn the *intention* of the web application while creating the HTTP response page. This is done through *shadow* pages, which are generated every time a HTTP response page is generated. These pages are similar to the real HTTP responses returned by the web application with mainly one crucial difference: they *only* retain the (authorized) scripts that were intended by the web application to be included, and do not contain any injected scripts.

Given the real and shadow pages, one can compare the script contents present in the real page with web-application intended contents, present in the shadow page. Any

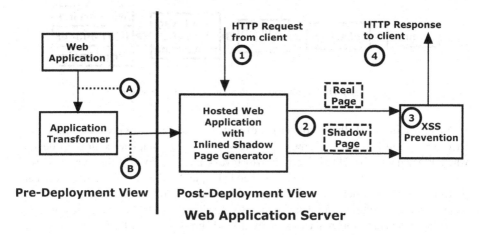

Fig. 3. The XSS-GUARD server side defense approach

"difference" detected here indicates a deviation from the web application's intentions, and therefore signals an attack.

As a running example, consider the code snippet of a simple web application given in Fig. 2 (i). This code embeds the user specified name and generates `Admin-script` / `Non-Admin-script` based on whether the user is `admin`. Notice that the parameter `"uName"` is vulnerable to injection and can be exploited by specifying malicious values. Fig. 2 (ii) and (iii) show responses generated for a benign user `uName=Alan`, and for a malicious user name `uName=<script>evil();</script>`, respectively.

Conceptually, Fig. 2 (ii) is a shadow page (contains only the intended scripts for a non-admin user - `f(), Non-Admin-script()`) for the response shown in part (iii). The injected attack at line 3 in part (iii), has no equivalent script at line 3 of the shadow page part(ii), and presents an intuitive example of attack detection in our approach.

Fig. 3 depicts the block level architecture of our approach. In the pre-deployment view, a web application is retrofitted (step A) through an automated transformation to facilitate generation of shadow pages and then deployed (step B) in place of the original application. In the post deployment view for any HTTP request received (step 1) by the web application, the instrumented application generates (step 2) a shadow page corresponding to the actual HTTP response (real page). The real and shadow pages are compared (step 3) for equivalence of script contents and any attacks found in the real page are eliminated. The modified HTTP response page is sent (step 4) to the client.

In the following sections, we elaborate the mechanisms used by XSS-GUARD for robust script identification and comparison.

3.1 A Generic Mechanism for Identifying Script Content

We want to identify the set of scripts present in the real page in order to check if they are intended by the web application. In order to do this, we need to first identify the set of all scripts in the real page.

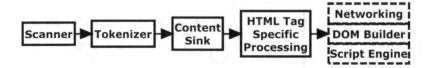

Fig. 4. High level content flow in the Firefox browser

As shown in Fig. 1, the set of scripts executed at the client are precisely those that have been identified by the browser. A browser has the complete context to decide whether a sequence of HTML entities will invoke a script. Even if the input is based on a specific encoding, browser sees all encoded input "in-the-clear" and therefore can perform sound identification of all script content in a HTML page. In other words, a real browser is a natural candidate for identifying all the scripts present in a web page.

Our approach therefore makes use of a real-world browser's code base for precise identification of scripts in a web page. The portion of the browser code base that is of interest to us is the one responsible for tokenizing HTML content and parsing it, and ultimately invoking the JavaScript interpreter on script content. To this end, we analyzed the script content identification schemes employed by one of the popular web browsers - Firefox, and describe our customizations of Firefox components that identify script content.

Firefox mechanisms to identify script content
Fig. 4 depicts a high level diagram of the content flow in Firefox with regards to script identification. We ignore any browser component that is not relevant to script identification, and describe the behavior at an abstract level, thus making the discussion applicable to other browsers in general.

The component scanner identifies character boundaries, and the tokenizer aggregates them into lexical tokens. The results of this lexical analysis is given to a *content sink*, a component responsible for HTML-tag specific browser action. For instance, when the content sink encounters a tag that has a `src` attribute, it calls the networking component that downloads additional data that is pointed to by the `src` attribute. Similarly, when a `<script>` tag is encountered, the content sink calls the JavaScript interpreter.

We then further studied the browser code base to identify when the JavaScript interpreter is called from a content sink. The browser invokes the JavaScript interpreter in three distinctive situations:

Entities causing external resource downloads. These are the tags / attributes designated by the HTML specification to embed external resources in HTML pages. Such entities can be used to directly or indirectly introduce script content in the embedding HTML pages. An example is `<script src=...>`, which directly introduces script contents, whereas `<embed src=xss.swf>` can indirectly introduce script contents.

Inlined script content and event handlers. These tags / attributes are designated by the HTML specification to introduce inlined scripts and event handlers. Examples are `<script>` which introduces script code, or `<body onload=...>` where the script code corresponding to `onload` is executed when this entity is loaded in the browser.

URI Schemes that can have scripts. The above two techniques are based on the HTML specification and thus provide exact knowledge of the tags / attributes utilizing these techniques. However, script content based on *URI schemes* present other subtle ways of embedding script content in non-obvious contexts. These schemes are the mechanisms by which an HTML entity can direct the browser to perform special processing. Browsers implement protocol handlers to cater to these special processing requests. An example is an image tag `<img src="javascript:script">` that makes use of javascript URI scheme and directs the browser to execute the specified script.

Using a custom content sink to identify script content

An important inference from our study of the Firefox identification mechanisms is that the content sink phase possesses sufficient information to enable identification of all script content. Also, for above purpose, the rest of the components in a typical browser stack are not required. Hence, a code stack from the Firefox browser comprising of the scanner, tokenizer and content sink would result in a much smaller script identifier that is sufficient for our purposes. The XSS-GUARD framework makes use of this lightweight code stack from the Firefox code base to perform precise identification.

We extended the content sink implementation in Firefox to record the identified script content. Our implementation handles all the three kinds of script content discussed above. Overall, our identification of the script content at the content sink component is quite robust. Also, re-using components such as the tokenizer and scanner from an existing browsers' stack provides this scheme immunity against various encoding schemes and browser quirks. Moreover, being a part of actual browser stack, the tokenizer obviates the need for identifying tokens / keywords through error prone algorithms.

Incorporating behaviors of other browsers. Utilizing a single browser's identification mechanisms would not be sufficient to identify script constructs specific to other browsers. This can be remedied by selectively incorporating other browser specific mechanisms. For this purpose, we built a custom content sink based on Firefox browser stack and then extended its identification to encompass behaviors specific to other browsers. For instance, Firefox only checks for 38 event names, but our custom content sink supports an extended list comprising of 94 event names from [4] that are supported by other browsers. More details of our specific extensions are provided in the Section 4.

3.2 Shadow Pages: Computing Web Application Intent

A web application is written implicitly assuming benign inputs (with filtering to remove malicious input). It encodes programmer intentions to output a particular web page on these inputs. The XSS-GUARD approach is to capture these intentions using shadow pages.

Naturally, the shadow page will differ according to the input provided to the web application; a shadow page is therefore defined for a particular run of the web application. Formally, a shadow page of a web application P on any input u is the output response of the web application on some benign input v, on which P traverses the same path as it traverses on u.

(i) Transformed Web Application : real shadow page

```
String uName =
  request.getParameter("uName");
String uName_c = beginCandidate(uName);
StringBuffer re = ""; // real response
StringBuffer sh = ""; // shadow response
re.append("<html><body>");
sh.append("<html><body>");
re.append("<script>f()</script>");
sh.append("<script>f()</script>");
re.append("Hi " + uName + "!\n");
sh.append("Hi " + uName_c + "!\n");
if(uName == "admin"){
  re.append("<script>Admin-script()");
  sh.append("<script>Admin-script()");
}
else{
  re.append("<script>Non-Admin-script()");
  sh.append("<script>Non-Admin-script()");
}
re.append("</script>\n");
sh.append("</script>\n");
re.append("</body></html>");
sh.append("</body></html>");
re = XSS-PREVENT(re, sh);
out.print(re);
```

(ii) Real page for benign Access, uName = Alan

```
1. <html><body>
2. <script>f()</script>
3. Hi Alan!
4. <script>Non-Admin-script()</script>
5. </body></html>
```

(iii) Shadow page for benign Access, uName = Alan

```
1. <html><body>
2. <script>f()</script>
3. Hi aaaa!
4. <script>Non-Admin-script()</script>
5. </body></html>
```

(iv) Real page : uName exploited

```
1. <html><body>f
2. <script>f()</script>
3. Hi <script>evil();</script>!
4. <script>Non-Admin-script()</script>
5. </body></html>
```

(v) Shadow page : uName exploited

```
1. <html><body>
2. <script>f()</script>
3. Hi aaaaaaaaaaaaaaaaaaaaaaaaaa!
4. <script>Non-Admin-script()</script>
5. </body></html>
```

Fig. 5. Transformed running example and generated HTML pages (real and shadow)

Finding such benign inputs v, in general, is undecidable. We avoid this problem by using some manifestly benign inputs (such as a string of a's), and force the web application to act on these benign inputs along the same control path dictated by these real inputs. This technique has been used to successfully defend SQL injection attacks in our previous work [8].

More specifically, in order to construct the shadow page, we use explicitly benign user inputs; those that do not contain any meta characters of the scripting language. As these inputs are manifestly benign and do not contain any script content, the corresponding web application output will be free of injected script content, while retaining content authorized by the web application. Hence, an HTTP request with explicitly benign inputs will result in an exploit free HTML response from the web application.

We automatically transform the original web application to generate the shadow response pages apart from the real response pages. We refer the readers to our previous work [8] for a comprehensive treatment of this program transformation, and provide the key ideas here to make the discussion self-contained.

– For every string variable v in the program, we add a variable v_c that denotes its shadow. When v is initialized from the user input, v_c is initialized with an explicitly benign value of the same length as v. If v is initialized by the program, v_c is also initialized with the same value.
– For every program instruction on v, our transformed program performs the same operation on the shadow variable v_c. Departure from these mirrored operations

comes in handling conditionals, where the shadow computation needs to be forced along the path dictated by the real inputs. Therefore, the logic for path-selection in the program is not transformed and acts on the real inputs.

– Each output generating statement (writing output to the client), is replaced by appending the arguments to a buffer. This is done both for the real and the shadow values.
– After the last write operation, transformation adds invocation to a method responsible for detecting and disabling the XSS attacks.

The transformed web application for the running example is shown in the Fig. 5. It also shows real and shadow pages generated by this transformed application. The real and the shadow pages are stored in variables re and sh respectively and follow the transformation outlined previously. On line 23 in the transformed application real and shadow pages are passed on to a routine XSS-PREVENT that identifies and removes all the injected attacks and returns a retrofitted page, which is then returned to the client.

The generated shadow pages possess the following properties:

– The set of scripts in the shadow page is precisely that intended for the control path dictated by the real inputs. This is by virtue of a transformation that "mirrors" the computation on manifestly benign values on the same control path dictated by the real inputs. More specifically, when the user input is admin, the shadow page will contain the scripts f and Admin-script (and only those), and for a non-admin user, the shadow page will only contain the scripts f and Non-Admin-script.
– The transformation maintains the length of the shadow page to be the same as the real page. This is true as long as the functions defined in the web application are length preserving [8], a criterion satisfied by all the functions in the Java Standard library string manipulation suite. As a result the shadow and real pages are of the same length. Moreover, the offsets of the script content in the real and shadow pages are the same e.g., Non-Admin-script start and end offsets are same in both the real and the shadow pages.

3.3   Distinguishing XSS Attack Instances from Authorized Scripts

Equipped with the knowledge of script content in the real page and corresponding intended script content in the shadow page, our approach asks the following two questions about each script content identified in the real page:

1. *Web application intent mining.* For each identified script content, did the web application intend to create it?
2. *Script checking.* If so, are the actual script content "equivalent" to the application intended script content?

To see consider our example Fig. 5 (iv) (attack), on reaching line 3, the script identifier described in the previous section will reach a state that will identify the content as script. Whereas, in corresponding shadow page Fig. 5 (v) line 3, the parser will not identify any script content.

	Benign case	XSS attack
User Input	uName = John	uName = ";evil();c="
Real Script Content	var name = "John";	var name = ""; evil(); c = "";
Shadow Script Content	var name = "aaaa";	var name = "aaaaaaaaaaaaaaaa";

Fig. 6. Syntactically different content are generated with benign and hostile user inputs

If the identified script content and the web application intended content are not "equivalent", it is an XSS attack instance. We elaborate on the notion of equivalence below.

All identified script content (including attacks) originate from one of the following three categories of web application action:

1. *Created without untrusted inputs* - script content that are created without any influence of the untrusted inputs, and hence are benign. The script created on line 2 of Fig. 5 (ii), provides an example of such content creation. Interestingly, corresponding shadow page also contains the exact same script at the same offsets as the real page, and a direct content comparison suffices to establish their equivalence.
2. *Created by embedding untrusted inputs* - script content that embed untrusted inputs, and depending on the user inputs may be benign or hostile. The code snippet presented in Fig. 6 uses the untrusted data to initialize a variable in the script. Looking at the corresponding shadow script confirms that unlike the previous case, directly comparing the content does not work here.
3. *Not intended by the web application* - script content not intended by the web application, and hence are the attack instances. The script found on line 3 of Fig. 5 (iv), is such an instance. Here as well, a direct comparison with shadow content does not work.

Although we cannot check equivalence of last two cases mentioned above by directly comparing the content, both these cases share a well researched insight about injection attacks - a successful injection attack changes the syntactical structure of the exploited entity [18]. In case 3 above, an adversary injects script content in a context where it is not expected. Whereas, in case 2, the main goal of an attacker is to perform semantically different operations through the use of malicious input. Hence the syntactical structure of the real script generated with hostile user inputs, would be different, when compared to corresponding shadow script.

Based on the above discussion, we compare the (JavaScript) syntax structure of script elements, in absence of an exact match in the content.

JavaScript parse tree comparison details. To establish syntactical structure equivalence, we compare the JavaScript parse tree structures of the real and shadow scripts. However, a straightforward comparison of parse trees would cause false negatives e.g., parse trees for a = b; and c = d; are same. We compare the parse trees such that their structures are same along with an exact match of lexical entities - including the JavaScript comments, variable names and operators, and function names. String literals are not compared literally; in this case, we check if they have same lexical token value.

An exception to this rule for string literals arises when strings are used as arguments to functions such as document.write, when we demand exact equality, as demands a match in lexical token values will allow an attack to succeed.

Filtering out hostile script content. Any identified script content that fails the equivalence check (exact content match or parse tree comparison), is marked as an XSS attack instance. As we precisely know the offsets of the script content in the real page, such non-conforming content is replaced with explicitly benign values. The script content evil(); found in the real page of Fig. 5 (iv) fails to match due to the parse tree comparison. As a result, evil(); is identified as an XSS attack and is replaced with the shadow counterpart aaaaaaa.

Conditional Copying Procedures. There are a few instances where our approach fails and requires user involvement. Consider the following code from a routine that simply copies a character x to y using the following code:

```
if x='a' then y='a'
else if x='b' then y='b'
else if ...
```

We can extend the above routine to copy a string x to a string y, iterating through each character in the input by matching the correct conditional. Let us call this a *conditional-copy* function. If the web application has such a function, then our candidate evaluation technique will copy a user-input string <script> to the shadow page, while completely ignoring its candidate value (of a string of a's). This is one example of a case our approach fails to protect filtering, and is in fact an example where every known server-side technique against XSS defense will fail, including dynamic tainting.

The above example is simple but contrived, however there are practical examples of such "table-lookup" code. One instance we encountered is charset-decoding, where every character in a particular character set is decoded using a similar table lookup. Here too, our approach and dynamic tainting will fail. In case of our approach and tainting, the information about untrusted input is lost due to the conditional-copy of one character to another. Our solution for handling these functions is to include (user supplied) summarization functions, that summarize the effect of these functions and preserve the shadow values. For instance, the copy function given above has a summarization function that will simply return the candidate string instead of the real string as its return value.

Implementation. Our web application transformation is for Java / JSP applications. The program transformation to enable the shadow page generation, is implemented in Java SOOT optimization framework [2]. For the script content identification module, we implemented a custom content sink phase that used scanner and tokenizer from the Firefox browser. The HTML tokenizer / scanner modules are modified to generate the offsets for identified content. For the equivalence check, we leveraged the Firefox SpiderMonkey engine's parse tree creation for JavaScripts. We added support to create a flat string representation of these parse trees for comparison purposes.

4   Experimental Evaluation

Experimental Setup. Our experimental setup for evaluating attacks consisted of a server (1GB RAM, 1.66 GHz dual core processor) and a client (2GB RAM, 2.0 GHz dual core processor) both running Ubuntu OS and connected over the same Ethernet network. We deployed the original and XSS-GUARD protected applications under separate but identically configured Apache Tomcat servers.

CVE	Program	Version	XSS Attack Description	Detection
CVE-2007-5120	JSPWiki	2.4.103	via group name etc.	Success
CVE-2007-5121	JSPWiki	2.4.103	via redirect parameter	Success
CVE-2007-2450	Tomcat Html Manager	6.0.13	via name to html/upload option	Success
CVE-2007-3386	Tomcat Host Manager	6.0.13	via aliases to html/add option	Success
CVE-2007-3383	Tomcat SendMail App	4.1.31	via from field	Success
CVE-2007-3384	Tomcat Cookie App	3.3.2	via name/value fields	Success
CVE-2007-2449	Tomcat Snoop App	6.0.4	via HTTP method argument	Success
CVE-2006-7196	Tomcat Calendar App	4.1.31	via time parameter	Success

Fig. 7. The real XSS exploits used in effectiveness evaluation

4.1   Effectiveness Evaluation

One of our objectives was to evaluate the effectiveness of the XSS-GUARD approach against the real-world attacks. Since our framework is targeted towards Java applications, we analyzed the CVE repository [20] and chose the JSP / Java based applications that had reported vulnerabilities in 2007. In all, we chose seven such applications: JSPWiki, Tomcat HTML Manager, Tomcat Host Manager and Tomcat example web applications (Cookie, SendMail, Calendar and Snoop). These applications were diverse in sizes and complexity - ranging from a large and complex Wiki engine to small and simple example web applications. Below, we discuss the nature of these exploits and our experience in evaluating the XSS-GUARD approach against them.

JSPWiki (CVE-2007-5120, CVE-2007-5121). The JSPWiki engine facilitates a collective privilege management by creating groups of users. Unfortunately, the group creation process is vulnerable to XSS attacks. On presenting malformed group names, such as those containing characters that are forbidden by the filter in JSPWiki e.g., <, >, JSPWiki responds with an error message which embeds the malformed group name verbatim, thus making way for XSS exploits.

Tomcat HTML Manager (CVE-2007-2450, CVE-2007-3386). For deploying new web applications, Tomcat has a built-in application called Manager that accepts a WAR (Web Archive) file name from the user. In this vulnerability, an error message is shown with the user specified WAR file name if it does not end with a .war extension. The following code snippet provides a sample exploit code -

```
<form action="http://server/manager/html/upload" method="post">
<input TYPE="hidden" NAME='deployWar";
    filename="<script>alert(&#39&#120&#115&#115&#39)</script>"
exploit code based on: http://www.securityfocus.com
```

This exploit circumvents an input restriction (quotes disallowed), by partially encoding the exploit - `alert('xss')` as `alert(&#39&#120&#115&#115&#39)`. Our approach is resilient to alternate encodings as the HTML parser used for content identification receives all data after being decoded.

Tomcat Web Applications (CVE-2007-(3383, 3384, 2449, 7196)). In all the previous cases, vulnerable applications display user inputs in their HTTP responses. The Send-Mail web application is different. It accepts the message subject, recipient and email body from the user and sends an email to the recipient. This application does not display the user data in any HTTP response. However, when *from* field contains a malicious email address, an external class `javax.mail.internet.AddressException` raises an exception, which generates a stack trace. The SendMail subsequently displays this stack trace, which contains the malicious *from* field. Such exceptional cases are typically not checked by the input filters, and illustrates the need for dynamic protection mechanisms such as ours.

Attack evaluation summary. Our solution successfully defended all 8 exploits mentioned above. This demonstrates that the XSS-GUARD can be used successfully to safeguard the real world applications against XSS exploits.

4.2 A Comprehensive Evaluation of Resilience

To evaluate the resilience of XSS-GUARD we selected RSnake CheatSheet [4], a collection of 92 unique exploits based on different attack vectors to evade the server side filters. Many of these exploits are quite subtle, and explore a significant portion of the attack surface. In our evaluation, we focused on 36 out of the 92 RSnake cheat sheet exploits that are applicable to the Firefox. Out of 92, four exploits were not applicable - SSI, PHP, one does not introduce scripts and one exploit could not be reproduced. We evaluated the remainder of 32 exploits in our experiments. These exploits are classified into various categories, for brevity we only mention a few interesting cases here below.

XSS exploits based on Firefox quirks. Exploits based on this vector rely on the "ad-hoc(quirk)" behavior of the Firefox HTML parser e.g., only the Firefox executes - `<SCRIPT/XSS SRC="http://evil/e.js"></SCRIPT>`. Note that the filters oblivious to this quirk will miss out such attacks. As our approach uses the Firefox HTML parser, we were able to identify these tags without any special handling.

XSS Vector embedded in the Flash object. This vector embeds the exploit in the ActionScript of a Flash object, which invokes client side JavaScript interpreter when rendered. When this exploit requires exploit code to embed the flash object, our approach disallows it. However, if the exploit is embedded in a Flash object included by the web application, our technique cannot prevent it.

XSS exploit vector based on a pre-existing execution environment. This vector is useful in situations where user input is added to a existing execution environment e.g., between `<script>` and `</script>` tags. This poses additional difficulties for filters. In our case such attempts prevented by script parse tree comparison as such vectors cause the JavaScript parse tree structures to vary.

XSS exploit vector based on self generating scripts. In this interesting vector the prohibited keywords or constructs may not even appear in the exploits at the server side, but dynamically generated at the client. Variations of this scheme were used in the MySpace Samy worm which constructed the prohibited keyword `innerHTML` on the client side by using `"eval('inne' + 'rHTML')"`. However, such attacks require script code and are disallowed by XSS-GUARD.

Summary. We used vulnerable JSPWiki application from CVE to recreate all the 32 applicable exploits of the cheat sheet. We then tested these exploits on the XSS-GUARD protected JSPWiki application, which was able to defend all. The successful defense of several subtle attacks demonstrates that the XSS-GUARD approach is highly resilient.

4.3 Performance

We conducted another set of experiments to evaluate acceptability of our solution in terms of performance overheads. We measured the browser end response times using benchmarking tool JMeter [7] for the original and the XSS-GUARD protected applications.

The performance overheads ranged from 5% to 24%. The least overhead resulted for the SendMail application (response page 266B, 2 scriptable attributes). The Tomcat HTML Manager application incurred the highest overhead in terms of the response time (response page 12.75KB, 67 scriptable entities).

To assess the scalability of our approach to safeguard widely accessed websites, we analyzed one level GET page responses (without downloading embedded resources) of the ten most accessed websites in the United States [1]. The largest page response was 75KB (www.youtube.com), four were in the range of 32-50KB and rest all were less than 12KB. Based on this data we created a web application that generated response pages of different sizes (1KB to 75KB). We then transformed this web application with XSS-GUARD and measured the response times for original and guarded application for varying response sizes. Overheads incurred were reasonably moderate (2.8% - 13.64%).

To evaluate the impact of JavaScript parse tree comparisons on the performance, we enabled above application to also generate varying number of scripts with embedded user inputs. For 1-5 scripts in a 20KB response page, overheads varied in the range of 37%-42%. As mentioned earlier, the JavaScript parse tree comparison is needed only rarely (in presence of attacks or scripts that embed user inputs). We did not encounter any such case while measuring the performance of the applications from the CVE.

This extensive performance analysis demonstrates that this approach has acceptable overheads in real world situations. These numbers are indicative of the worst case performance of our approach. In our experiments client and server were connected over the same Ethernet and hence the impact of network latency, that dominates response time, is negligible. We believe that the overheads in a real world deployment of our solution would be significantly less than the reported numbers here.

4.4   Verifying Safe-Passage of Benign HTML Tags in Untrusted Contents

Web applications such as Wikis and Blogs allow end user to input HTML. This is highly desirable as it allows users to format their input data using HTML tags. We also wanted to study the possibility of our solution working smoothly with applications that allow selective HTML input.

To understand the degree of freedom granted to the users in specifying HTML, we analyzed several Wiki / blog applications (Pebble, Drupal, Plone, Geeklog, JSPWiki, JChatBox)[2] that allow a limited set of HTML entities to pass through. We also analyzed the HTML specification 4.01 and identified following entities to be allowable - text, lists, tables, links, alignment, font styles, and horizontal rules. We compiled these into a comprehensive test suite consisting of benign tags and attributes.

Equipped with above test suite, we decided to assess any loss of functionality of the XSS-GUARD protected applications in the presence and absence of the selective HTML filters.

XSS-GUARD *in the presence of HTML filters.* For co-existence evaluation we chose the selective HTML filtering mechanisms employed by the following two applications:

– *Pebble:* filters allow limited / no HTML, and strip the `<script>` tags.
– *JChatBox:* filters forbid all HTML, and encode the URLs with `<a>` tags.

We modified the Tomcat Calendar application to process the user inputs with above filters and then transformed it using XSS-GUARD. For JChatBox filter, XSS-GUARD allowed the filter created `<a>` tags and all the escaped HTML to pass through and echoed the same behavior for Pebble filters. However, the script filter allowed the XSS attacks to pass through e.g., `<script>nada</script><script src=URL>` resulted in `<script src=URL>`. This attack, however, was caught by the XSS-GUARD and removed from the response page.

In absence of filters, we used the XSS-GUARD protected Tomcat calendar application and verified that all the entities listed in our testbed were allowed in user inputs. These experiments demonstrate usefulness of layering XSS-GUARD protection on top of the existing filtering mechanisms. The XSS-GUARD protected applications do not forbid benign HTML allowed by selective filtering mechanisms, but are able to prevent any attacks missed by the filters. We also note that XSS-GUARD allows a rich set of benign HTML thus allowing users to input content rich HTML input.

4.5   Discussion

As the script identification in the current implementation of the XSS-GUARD is based on components from the Firefox browser family, it does not identify all script contents

---

[2] http://pebble.sourceforge.net, http://drupal.org, http://plone.org, http://www.geeklog.net, http://www.javazoom.net/jzservlets/jchatbox/jchatbox.html

based on 'quirks' specific to other browsers (say Internet Explorer). We tested our current implementation against 56 exploits from XSS cheatsheet that were based on quirks specific to non-Firefox browsers; XSS-GUARD defended 35 out of these 56 exploits. However, to uniformly identify scripts across the browser families a "universal" parser is required.

- To build a browser independent URI scheme identification, the custom content sink could unify identification of schemes implemented in different browsers.
- The custom content sink could be modified to identify and parse URI schemes specific to other browsers e.g., `<img src="vbscript:xss">`.
- If the quirk is based on the tokenization process specific to a browser family, universal parser could handle it by incorporating necessary changes in it's tokenization process.

Attacks specific to other browsers. XSS-GUARD may produce a different output page when an attack specific to a browser is attempted. For instance, `<img src=javascript:xss>` is an XSS vector for Internet Explorer (IE), but is not a valid attack vector for Firefox, which simply ignores the javascript `src` attribute for image URLs. Disabling this exploit code does not impact Firefox user agents, as XSS-GUARD results in an output page with a broken image link, when viewed in Firefox. However, if the client user agent is IE, then XSS-GUARD protects the browser from any attacks through XSS vector.

False Negatives. We also found XSS-GUARD to produce false negatives in cases when attacks utilized non-Firefox quirks that were not identified by the custom content sink. One typical missed attack instance was based on IE conditional comments. However, as mentioned before, such attacks can be prevented by appropriately modifying the content sink.

5   Related Work

Research on cross-site scripting can be broadly classified into approaches that (a) detect vulnerabilities (b) prevent attacks against applications. Our contribution in this paper falls into the second category.

5.1   Vulnerability Analysis Based Approaches

There are several approaches that rely on static analysis techniques [19,22,14] to detect programs vulnerable to XSS injection attacks. As mentioned in the introduction, these tools are typically intended to be used by a developer during the code development process. These techniques are limited to identifying sources (points of input) and sinks (query issuing locations), and checking whether every flow from a source to the sink is subject to input validation ([19] is flow-insensitive while [22] is flow-sensitive, and [14] adds more support for aliasing). However, these tools do not themselves check the correctness of input validation functions.

Recently, [13] and [11] proposed solutions to the important question of checking filter functions. In [13] the code of a filter function is abstracted into a context-free grammar, and the XSS exploits are modeled as a regular expression and detection is done by checking whether the intersection of these two languages is non-empty. Since their modeling is based on static string analysis, it does not work for arbitrary custom filtering code based on dynamic string operations. Balzarotti et al. [11] check sanitization code between input locations (sources) and output locations (sinks) through static analysis, and construct exploits through dynamic analysis. Both these approaches use some form of "blacklist" for checking whether scripting commands contained in this blacklist appear in the output of sanitization functions. Based on our discussion in Section 2, putting together this blacklist will require identifying every possible string sequence that would result in a scripting command in a browser, while excluding all valid HTML. This is certainly a challenging task. We avoid the need for a blacklist, by using a real-world browser and the actual output of an application, thus achieving precise script detection and XSS prevention.

All the previous static approaches do not track vulnerabilities across web application modules, and typically lose precision. [10] refers to these vulnerabilities as multi-module vulnerabilities and develop an approach called MiMosa. It models an application's extended state to identify vulnerabilities that traverse modules. Extended state based attacks pose no problem for our approach. Data carried through session variables have their candidate (shadow) counterparts which denote corresponding benign input, and can be used to prevent attacks.

5.2   Attack Prevention Approaches

Server side detection approaches [9,16,18,23] track the user specified inputs through mechanisms like taint tracking. In particular, [16] and [18] briefly suggest in their discussion that placing syntactical restrictions on tainted data may lead to precise XSS attack detection. Restricting the tainted data to specific syntactical contexts is a powerful idea. Our approach makes use of dynamic candidate evaluation, a real world HTML parser and a JavaScript engine to obtain the contextual information and place such syntactic restrictions on output of a web application. Thus our approach demonstrates a realization of this idea in a practical setting for detecting XSS attacks.

Commercial solutions. These are many web applications (KaVaDo InterDo, NetContinuum NC-1000 Web Security Gateway, Sanctum AppShield, and others that can be referenced from [3]) that perform filtering at a proxy level to detect injection attacks. Since these apply a set of (application independent) filters, these are subject to the same limitations that were discussed in Section 2.

Client side protection. Client side approaches [12,15] try to protect sensitive information leakage by preventing attempts to send the sensitive data to third party servers. These schemes treat symptoms of an XSS attack (such as a cookie stealing script). Therefore, these schemes do not prevent XSS attacks that violate the same-origin policy e.g., attacker injected scripts can update user information on the trusted server, or perform malicious transactions within the same domain. However, such schemes have the advantage of empowering end users by being readily deployable on the clients without relying on the server side to provide the protection.

Browser-Web application collaboration. [17] propose a solution that requires web applications and browsers to collaborate. Web application provides policies (a while list of all benign scripts), which when enforced by the browsers (only white-listed scripts execute), ensures protection against injection attacks. This is a very sound idea. However current framework requires web applications and browsers to collaborate - which may be a big challenge in adoption of such solutions. Further, in [17], white-list construction is mostly done by hand, and does not automatically include dynamically generated scripts. Our scheme can be complimentary to the solution provided by [17] to determine the set of scripts in the whitelist.

6   Conclusion

In this paper, we presented a novel and precise defense against XSS attacks. As a standalone mechanism or with widely used schemes like filtering, our approach can provide a robust defense against XSS attacks. We provided extensive experimental results that corroborate effectiveness, scalability and applicability of our solution to real world applications and subtle attacks. We also highlighted limitations in our current implementation (some non-Firefox quirks), and presented our thoughts on developing a technique for browser independent script identification.

Overall, we believe that the approach presented in this paper has underscored the promising idea of building solutions based on web application's output and actual script identification behaviors of the browsers to counter the serious threats raised by cross-site scripting attacks.

Acknowledgments. This research is supported in part by NSF grants CNS-0716584 and CNS-0551660. Thanks are due to Mike Ter Louw and Kalpana Gondi for their suggestions on improving the draft. Finally, we thank the anonymous referees for their feedback.

References

1. Alexa top sites United States, http://www.alexa.com
2. Soot: A Java Optimization Framework, http://www.sable.mcgill.ca/soot/
3. The Web Application Security Consortium,
   http://www.webappsec.org/projects/wafec
4. XSS (Cross Site Scripting) Cheat Sheet. Esp: for filter evasion,
   http://ha.ckers.org/xss.html
5. Hackers broaden reach of cross-site scripting attacks. ComputerWeekly.com (March 2007)
6. Symantec Internet Security Threat Report. Technical report, Symantec Corporation (March 2007)
7. Apache. The JMeter Project, http://jakarta.apache.org/jmeter
8. Bandhakavi, S., Bisht, P., Madhusudan, P., Venkatakrishnan, V.N.: CANDID: Preventing SQL Injection Attacks using Dynamic Candidate Evaluations. In: Proceedings of the 14th ACM Conference on Computer and Communications Security, pp. 12–24 (2007)

9. Nguyen-Tuong, A., et al.: Automatically Hardening Web Applications using Precise Tainting. In: 20th International Information Security Conference (2005)
10. Balzarotti, D., et al.: Multi-Module Vulnerability Analysis of Web-based Applications. In: 14th ACM Conference on Computer and Communications Security, pp. 25–35 (2007)
11. Balzarotti, D., et al.: Saner: Composing Static and Dynamic Analysis to Validate Sanitization in Web Applications. In: IEEE Symposium on Security and Privacy (2008)
12. Kirda, E., et al.: Noxes: A Client-Side Solution for Mitigating Cross-Site Scripting Attacks. In: Proceedings of the 2006 ACM Symposium on Applied Computing (2006)
13. Wassermann, G., et al.: Static Detection of Cross-Site Scripting Vulnerabilities. In: Proceedings of the 30th International Conference on Software Engineering (May 2008)
14. Jovanovic, N., et al.: Pixy: A Static Analysis Tool for Detecting Web Application Vulnerabilities. In: IEEE Symposium on Security and Privacy (May 2006)
15. Vogt, P., et al.: Cross-Site Scripting Prevention with Dynamic Data Tainting and Static Analysis. In: NDSS, San Diego (2007)
16. Pietraszek, T., et al.: Defending Against Injection Attacks through Context-Sensitive String Evaluation. In: Recent Advances in Intrusion Detection (2005)
17. Jim, T., et al.: BEEP: Browser-Enforced Embedded Policies. In: International WWW Conference (2007)
18. Su, Z., et al.: The Essence of Command Injection Attacks in Web Applications. In: ACM Symposium on Principles of Programming Languages (POPL) (2006)
19. Livshits, V.B., Lam, M.S.: Finding Security Vulnerabilities in Java Applications with Static Analysis (2005)
20. MITRE. Common Vulnerabilities and Exposures List, http://cve.mitre.org
21. Samy. I'm popular (2005), http://namb.la/popular
22. Xie, Y., Aiken, A.: Static Detection of Security Vulnerabilities in Scripting Languages. In: USENIX Security Symposium (2006)
23. Xu, W., Bhatkar, S., Sekar, R.: Taint-Enhanced Policy Enforcement: A Practical Approach to Defeat a Wide Range of Attacks. In: USENIX Security Symposium (2006)

VeriKey: A Dynamic Certificate Verification System for Public Key Exchanges

Brett Stone-Gross, David Sigal, Rob Cohn,
John Morse, Kevin Almeroth, and Christopher Kruegel

Department of Computer Science,
University of California, Santa Barbara
{bstone,dsigal,rcohn,morse,almeroth,chris}@cs.ucsb.edu

Abstract. This paper presents a novel framework to substantiate self-signed certificates in the absence of a trusted certificate authority. In particular, we aim to address the problem of web-based SSL man-in-the-middle attacks. This problem originates from the fact that public keys are distributed through insecure channels prior to encryption. Therefore, a man-in-the-middle attacker may substitute an arbitrary public key during the exchange process and compromise communication between a client and server. Typically, web clients (browsers) recognize this potential security breach and display warning prompts, but often to no avail as users simply accept the certificate since they lack the understanding of Public Key Infrastructures (PKIs) and the meaning of these warnings. In order to enhance the security of public key exchanges, we have devised an automated system to leverage one or more vantage points of a certificate from hosts that have distinct pathways to a remote server. That is, we have a set of distributed servers simultaneously retrieve the server's public key. By comparing the keys received by peers, we can identify any deviations and verify that an attacker has not compromised the link between a client and server. This is attributable to the fact that an attacker would have to compromise all paths between these vantage points and the server. Therefore, our technique greatly reduces the likelihood of a successful attack, and removes the necessity for human interaction.

1   Introduction

As e-commerce and subsequent online transactions emerged on the Internet, there became a need to protect sensitive communication. This requirement was partially fulfilled by introducing public key cryptography to secure key exchanges. Public key cryptography utilizes certificates to bind an entity to a specific public key with a digital signature. This digital signature may belong to a well-known Certificate Authority (CA) or the creator of the certificate. The former is generally regarded as more secure, but has been exploited previously due to improper implementations [3]. The latter poses a greater security risk, because there is no way (other than manually verifying the certificate's fingerprint) to confirm the identity of the owner. As a result, a malicious host can exploit this

D. Zamboni (Ed.): DIMVA 2008, LNCS 5137, pp. 44–63, 2008.

uncertainty through the use of a man-in-the-middle attack by intercepting and altering a certificate to impersonate the same party with another key known to the attacker. When the public key on the certificate is replaced with the key of an attacker, the integrity of the encrypted session is compromised if the forged certificate is accepted.

The most popular public key encryption protocol for the World Wide Web has been the Secure Sockets Layer (SSL) and its successor, the Transport Layer Security (TLS) protocol. While these protocols have proven to be relatively effective, they are also vulnerable to man-in-the-middle attacks in situations where the user or the client implementation is not able to detect the fraudulent certificate. These attacks are normally a consequence of other insecure protocols that allow a malicious host to easily become a man-in-the-middle. Some of these exploitable protocols include the Address Resolution Protocol (ARP), Domain Name System (DNS), and Dynamic Host Configuration Protocol (DHCP). Wireless networks are also particularly vulnerable since attackers can easily deploy rogue access points, modify unencrypted link layer frames, and are susceptible to most switched Local Area Network (LAN) attacks. Only in large networks with sophisticated Intrusion Detection Systems (IDS) are these attacks routinely detected and prevented.

In order to prevent SSL man-in-the-middle attacks on the Internet, several companies operate as certificate authorities to digitally sign X.509 certificates. Certificates from these CAs are assumed to be secure, since their public keys are well-known and are included with standard web browser distributions. Therefore, a web browser only needs to confirm that the digital signature on a certificate matches one of these trusted CAs. For the majority of cases, the certificates signed by these CAs function well. However, the service that these CAs provide comes at a fairly high cost, which deters some web server administrators from purchasing certificates from them. Current rates for a single domain certificate cost approximately $100-$200 USD per year, and a wildcard domain certificate costs about $500-$1,000 USD per year[1]. To avoid this expensive surcharge, smaller web sites often create their own self-signed certificates, or purchase a certificate for only a single domain.

When a certificate is self-signed or if the common name and fully qualified domain name do not correspond, nearly all web browsers will display a prompt that requests user input on whether to accept the certificate. These warning dialogs occur even when visiting popular sites like https://amazon.com and https://bankofamerica.com because the common name on their certificates are registered only to https://www.amazon.com and https://www.bankofamerica.com, respectively. The problem derives from the fact that many web users do not understand the meaning of these "cryptic" messages, and will accept almost any certificate [21]. Therefore we believe that it is important to develop a system that does not require user attention for normal users, while offering supplemental knowledge for expert computer users to

---

[1] http://www.digicert.com/

determine the legitimacy of a certificate, without having prior knowledge of the remote web server's public key.

In this paper, we propose a novel solution to augment the security of SSL certificate exchanges. The primary objective of our system is to remove certificate prompts from the web browser, and instead rely on what peers elsewhere on the Internet observe. We term these outside peers *verification servers* and refer to them as such throughout the paper. By combining multiple views from verification servers, our system greatly reduces the likelihood that an attacker can intercept and inject their own certificate during the SSL handshake without being detected. This follows from our method to select verifications servers such that they have *different* pathways to a remote web server. As a result, our approach considerably minimizes the potential man-in-the-middle attack vectors because an attacker would have to compromise all these paths to launch a successful man-in-the-middle attack. To select servers that have different paths, our system leverages Autonomous System (AS) level topological mappings. Another benefit our of design is that it is based on existing protocols. Therefore, our system can be readily deployed, since it requires no modifications to web servers, and can be implemented in current web browsers through an extension or plug-in. In order to evaluate our system's relative effectiveness and performance, we deployed our prototype on PlanetLab [15]. Further applications of our design also extend to other non-web-based public key protocols including Secure Shell (SSH), Internet Message Access Protocol (IMAPS), and Secure Copy (SCP).

The remainder of this paper is organized as follows. In Section 2, we introduce relevant work that has been previously performed. Section 3 explains how and why SSL man-in-the-middle attacks work and the potential attack vectors. Section 4 presents our design considerations, system architecture, and certificate verification process. We then provide an evaluation of our system and potential extensions in Section 5. Finally, Section 6 concludes with a summary of our contributions.

2   Related Work

There are various protocols from the link layer to the application layer that have been exploited using man-in-the-middle attacks. As a result, there have been numerous studies to detect and prevent the root causes of each vulnerability. One of the most prominent man-in-the-middle attacks on a LAN is ARP poisoning [20]. This link layer protocol is insecure since it neither provides any form of message authentication nor maintains any state information. In order to mend these vulnerabilities, several solutions have been proposed that authenticate hosts and record the bindings of link layer MAC addresses to network layer IP addresses [2][10][12]. The problem with these solutions is that they are difficult to deploy due to added infrastructure, operating system modifications for all connected hosts, and complexities in key distribution for authentication.

Another common local man-in-the-middle attack exploits the DHCP protocol, which is used to automate network configurations. Since DHCP lacks message authentication, an attacker can impersonate and forge DHCP replies to other hosts, thus manipulating the victim's IP address, gateway address, and DNS server information. To mitigate this vulnerability, several authentication and access control systems have been proposed [1][6][11]. These approaches share the same limitations as the ARP prevention systems in that all hosts require operating system modifications to access the network. Moreover, they require the configuration and setup of authentication servers.

Potentially the most dangerous man-in-the-middle vulnerability stems from the weaknesses of DNS. Due to the hierarchical structure of DNS, an attacker may spoof DNS responses that may affect not only a local network, but also remote networks. To address these shortcomings, the Domain Name System Security Extensions (DNSSEC) protocol was proposed [8]. DNSSEC is designed to prevent manipulation of DNS queries and replies via authentication and data integrity. Current deployment of this protocol has been impeded by a lack of backward-compatibility with existing DNS servers and hosts. ConfiDNS is another system that monitors DNS replies from multiple vantage points, with the goal of identifying inconsistencies [16]. However, ConfiDNS is only effective against attacks on local DNS servers, and has difficulty with discrepancies produced by DNS load balancing.

An alternative approach to improve current PKIs was introduced by Zhou *et al.* through a distributed online certificate authority with a fault-tolerant algorithm that uses Byzantine quorums, called COCA [22]. While this solution is elaborate, there are numerous complexities in the distributed infrastructure that make it impractical to deploy, configure, and maintain.

Unfortunately, all of the preceding solutions require extensive modifications to hosts, lack support for non-compliant hosts, or both. Instead of developing multiple protocols to address all possible man-in-the-middle attack vectors, we take a different approach and provide a method to avert these attacks at the application level. This solution permits users of our system to install a web browser plug-in, which will run silently in the background. This technique makes our system backward-compatible with all existing protocols. When we combine this method with lightweight verification servers, we are able to attain a considerably more deployable solution.

3   SSL Man-in-the-Middle Attack Overview

A man-in-the-middle attack occurs when a malicious host deceives others into forwarding their traffic to them by impersonating the intended receiver. The potential for these attacks exist in virtually all networks that use unauthenticated communication (*e.g.*, no encryption and/or message integrity checks). Consequently, these packet manipulations facilitate man-in-the-middle attacks on encrypted protocols that exchange public keys through certificates. This weakness is due to the fact that most implementations of cryptographic algorithms allow user interaction to accept self-signed certificates and their associated public keys. Tools that automate these exploits include `webmitm`[7] and `ettercap`[9].

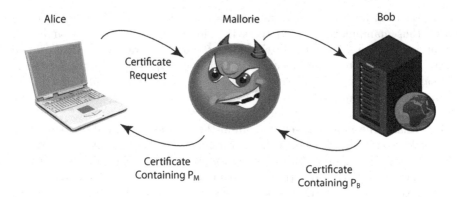

Fig. 1. Example of an SSL Man-in-the-Middle Attack

An attacker using these tools is able to redirect all of a victim's traffic to himself instead of the original destination. Figure 1 demonstrates a classic SSL man-in-the-middle attack. In this example, Alice and Bob want to communicate with each other using SSL. The first step in the SSL handshake requires Alice to contact Bob and request his certificate containing his public key, P_B. However, without Alice's knowledge, Mallorie, who is on the same physical network as Alice, has previously poisoned her ARP cache, causing Alice to address all of her packets to Mallorie. When Mallorie observes Alice's SSL request, she is able to intercept her request and make her own SSL connection to Bob. Mallorie then replies to Alice's request with her own public key, P_M. Alice is prompted by her web browser that the certificate that she received was valid, but not signed by a trusted CA. Unfortunately, Alice does not know the meaning of the warning and accepts the forged certificate. Alice now begins encrypting her traffic to Bob using the public key of Mallorie, P_M. Consequently, Mallorie is able to decrypt, monitor, and modify all communications before relaying messages between Alice and Bob.

As illustrated in the preceding example, most current web browsers display warning prompts when certificates cannot be validated. These dialogs commonly appear in the following cases:

- A certificate has expired.
- A certificate is signed by a trusted CA and belongs to a domain (without wildcards), but is not associated with any subdomain
  (*e.g.*, https://bankofamerica.com *vs.* https://www.bankofamerica.com).
- The common name on the certificate does not match the domain name of the host.
- A certificate is not signed by a trusted certificate authority (*e.g.*, a self-signed certificate or a certificate signed by a non-trusted CA).

Figure 2 shows an example of a typical certificate mismatch dialog displayed by web browsers.

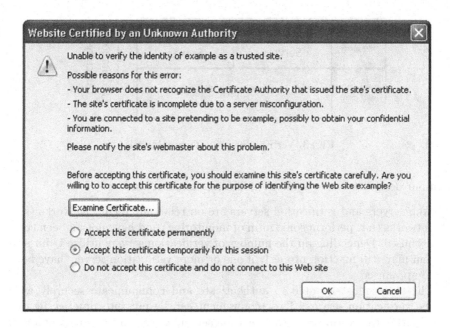

Fig. 2. Mozilla Firefox warning that a certificate is not signed by a trusted CA

4   System Architecture

In this section, we first present the considerations that went into our design, as well as the assumptions that were made. Next, we introduce our system's architecture and explain each component in detail. We then discuss our certificate verification process. Finally, we describe how clients determine which verification servers to contact.

4.1   Design Considerations

Before we examine the details of our design, we first present our security threat model and our assumptions.

The basis for our design is derived from our security threat model shown, in Figure 3. We believe that because most users of web applications are not experts in public key cryptography, they are the weakest link in the process when given the power to make a decision to accept a certificate. In contrast, verification and web servers are generally deployed by security-conscious network administrators (*i.e.*, experts), who are knowledgeable about certificates, PKIs, and common network vulnerabilities. Since attackers are more likely to exploit the easiest target, which is frequently the user's inexperience with certificates, it is critical to assist the client in making the correct decision to reduce this vulnerability. Therefore, our system focuses particularly on protecting the client from these man-in-the-middle attacks during public key exchanges.

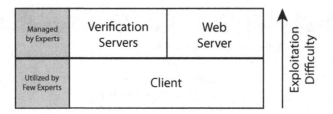

Fig. 3. VeriKey Security Threat Model

In our design, we have made the following assumptions.

1. Web servers and verification servers are on relatively secure networks (*i.e.*, networks that perform some form of monitoring) and have not all been compromised. Depending on the number of verification servers utilized, our system may still function properly if one or more verification servers have been compromised.
2. The client must be able to authenticate and communicate securely with the verification servers. This requirement can be put into practice by distributing the certificates of verification servers to the client as part of a web browser extension. This serves as a pre-shared key mechanism so that the client can authenticate the verification server as well as communicate over a secure, encrypted connection. Alternatively, verification servers may obtain certificates from well-known CAs and eliminate the need to acquire each verification server's public key from the browser plug-in.
3. There exists at least one non-compromised pathway to a web server. Our system depends on this notion to identify inconsistencies reported by different verification servers. Therefore, if a man-in-the-middle is located on or near the web server's network, or if only one pathway to the web server exists, our system would not be able to detect an attack. We are confident, however, that in most cases this assumption holds because an attacker will normally exploit vulnerable client networks (*e.g.*, an insecure wireless hotspot). We discuss the impacts of this assumption later in Section 5.4.

4.2   Certificate Verification Components

In this section, we present the components that make our system effective in subverting man-in-the-middle attacks based on the preceding set of assumptions. As previously mentioned, the general idea of our system is to add an extra layer of security to public key exchanges by coalescing diverse views from trusted peers, and verifying that they are the same. We achieve this verification with an automated process, which is critical in removing user interaction that may otherwise compromise security. The fundamental principles that we incorporated in our design are based on the inherent lack of user understanding about the operation of public key cryptography. Therefore, the client-side of the verification system must be extremely easy to use. On the server-side, simplicity and compatibility

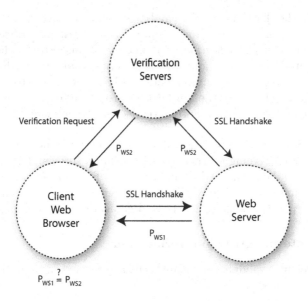

Fig. 4. Components of the VeriKey System Architecture

with existing web servers is essential. Hence, a web server should be able to interface with our system with no modifications. For certificate validation, we have developed a lightweight verification server that provides the client with its own perception of a remote certificate.

As shown in Figure 4, there are three main components of our system that implement our objectives: the client, verification servers, and web server. The client that we refer to includes standard web browsers with extension support (*e.g.*, a Mozilla Firefox/Opera plug-in or Internet Explorer add-on). The second component can be almost any existing web server with SSL support such as Apache, IIS, or Tomcat. These web servers will function with our system with no alterations or additional modules. The verification servers operate as the intermediary between the client and web server and handle certificate exchanges, caching, and verification.

4.3   System Deployment

Deploying our system is straightforward. The only requirement for a client is to install a web browser plug-in. We also provide the option for advanced users to deploy their own verification servers (although not necessary). The deployment process to interface with VeriKey is described below.

Client. The client must perform a one-time installation of our web browser extension. This extension contains a pairwise set of IP addresses and certificates containing the public keys for the default verification servers $\{\{IP_1, P_{V_1}\}, \{IP_2, P_{V_2}\}, \{IP_n, P_{V_n}\}\}$. As mentioned previously, verification servers may also attain a digitally signed certificate from a well-known CA such as VeriSign. In that case, only the distribution of their IP addresses is necessary. In addition, pre-computed AS topology maps are bundled that assist in verification server selection (discussed later in Section 4.5). The extension also has the ability to automatically update, revoke, and add new verification servers. Expert users may configure extra security requirements and have the option to integrate the information obtained during the verification process into the default security warning rather than allowing an automatic decision to be made on their behalf.

Verification Server. As previously discussed, more advanced users have the ability to deploy and configure their own verification servers. The web browser extension can then be configured to update its verification server set to point to these new custom servers. These verification servers may be deployed at research institutions, corporations, and other large organizations.

4.4 Certificate Integrity and Verification

In order to efficiently validate certificates, we have devised the following methodology as demonstrated in Figure 5.

Case 0: The initial step involves retrieving the web server's certificate. This exchange ensues during the SSL handshake, and the client must then confirm whether a trusted CA has signed the certificate.

Case 1: If the certificate has been signed by a trusted CA, the common name on the certificate is compared with the domain name of the web server.

– If the common name matches the domain name of the web server, the certificate should be trusted and the SSL connection can proceed normally. We ignore any mismatch between a domain and its possible subdomains, which commonly occurs when web sites do not purchase wildcard certificates and thus trigger warning messages. We justify this rationale based on the fact that it would be extremely difficult for an attacker to acquire a legitimate certificate for a subdomain that belonged to another entity.
– If the common name does not match the domain of the web server, the certificate (although valid), should not be trusted and the SSL connection between the client and web server should be blocked. This would occur when a man-in-the-middle has obtained a legitimate signed certificate from a trusted CA but for a different domain. Thus the man-in-the-middle could inject his own certificate (*e.g.*, www.hacker.com) during communications with another web server (*e.g.*, www.bank.com).

Case 2: If the certificate has not been signed by a trusted CA (*e.g.*, is self-signed), then the VeriKey certificate verification process will commence accordingly. Each of the following steps are illustrated in Figure 6.

1. **Client communication with verification servers.** The client connects to a number of verification servers. How these servers are selected will be

discussed in the following section. After completing the handshake, the client verifies that the SSL handshake results in the reception of the correct public key of the verification server, P_v. If the certificate does not match, there is a man-in-the-middle between the client and verification server. Otherwise, the client sends the full domain name and IP address of the web server to the verification server. The purpose of sending the pair (domain, IP) is to enable the verification server to determine if its own DNS resolution matches that of the client. In addition, these pairs are required when a single domain name may resolve to multiple IP addresses.

2. **Certificate Request.** The verification server checks its internal cache to see if it has previously retrieved the certificate. If the public key is not found in the cache, it connects to the web server to retrieve the server's certificate. Otherwise, the verification server forwards the cached public key of the web server to the client and Step 3 is omitted.

3. **Certificate Exchange.** The verification server (a) connects to the web server to retrieve its public key and (b) forwards it to the client.

4. **Public Key Verification.** At this stage, the client can now compare the certificate and public key of the server. If the public keys match, the client can communicate with the web server. Otherwise, there is a problem with the connection (*e.g.*, a man-in-the-middle) and the client will be notified that a potential security risk has been identified and the web server connection will be terminated. If the client's browser plug-in has been configured with higher security requirements, multiple verification servers will be utilized to verify the public key of the web server. When this option is chosen, a variable-based threshold τ is used in determining the number of public key matches μ that are required from the verification servers such that $\mu > \tau$. When the plug-in is configured in expert mode, the observed results are presented to the user, enabling them to make a manual decision instead of aborting the connection. In Section 5.5, we propose a mechanism to use the verification server as an SSL proxy, which may offer an alternative secure communication channel to the web server when a man-in-the-middle has been detected.

5. **(Optional) Verification Status Report.** This last step is optional, but allows a client to provide feedback to verification servers on the results of the certificate verification. This step enables the verification servers to determine if a certificate on the remote web server has changed and needs to be updated as well as to construct records of man-in-the-middle attacks.

4.5   Verification Server Selection

The architecture of our system provides support for utilizing multiple verification servers. A client may elect to query several verification servers for their view of a particular web server's certificate, which in the general case, will enhance a client's perspective. However, this technique may neither be the most effective nor efficient method to validate certificates. There is the possibility that one or more verification servers will share the same pathway to the web server. This scenario would occur if an attacker was positioned on one of these shared pathways

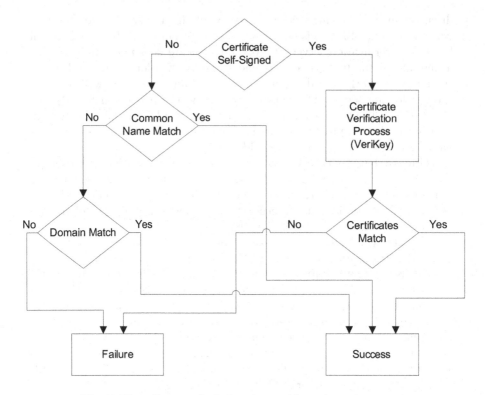

Fig. 5. Flow diagram depicting the certificate integrity process

between the client and server. Thus, the security of the verification process does not always increase with the number of responses from additional verification servers. In order to determine the number and locations of verification servers to query, we have developed our own selection algorithm.

Before presenting our verification server selection technique, we first introduce other potential selection options and the relevant effects. In order to assist our analysis, we define the distance between two hosts as the number of Autonomous System (AS) links on the shortest path between them and denote this as $\mathbf{d}$(source, destination). The selection procedure may optimize for latency, limited resources, and/or security. The easiest way to reduce the latency of the verification process is to minimize the sum of the distances between client, verification server, and web server (*i.e.,* min $\{\mathbf{d}(C, V_{Si}) + \mathbf{d}(V_{Si}, W_S)\}, \forall : V_{Si}$). However, this method is naïve, because when the combined distance is minimal there is a higher probability that more than one of these hosts have paths that overlap.

If limiting the amount of resources (*e.g.,* CPU time and bandwidth) is an important consideration, a client can randomly select a single verification server. This approach has several limitations including an increased response time, particularly if the verification server is located far from the client and web server.

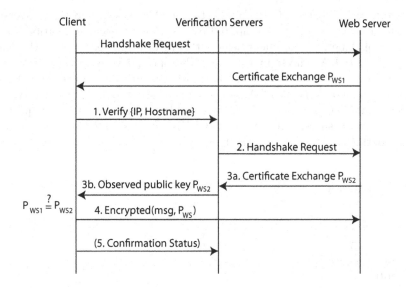

Fig. 6. The VeriKey certificate verification process

Our approach, however, enhances security while reducing latency and resources when selecting a verification server. We achieve this functionality by computing the shortest AS pathways in advance and then utilize the information to compare the overlap among a set of verification servers. This data can be collected from publicly available Internet topology maps that analyze BGP routing dynamics to discover AS adjacencies. The data sources and the details of our implementation are discussed later in this section.

We denote the path between client and web server as $C \Rightarrow W_S$ and the path between verification server and web server as $V_S \Rightarrow W_S$, where C, V_S, and W_S represent the client, verification server(s), and web server respectively. We first calculate the shortest path between the AS of the source and the AS of the destination (given our topology information). After this computation, we select the verification server that has the *least amount of link overlap* between the two paths (*i.e.*, $min\{C \Rightarrow W_S \cap V_{Si} \Rightarrow W_S\}$, $\forall : V_{Si}$). If more than one shortest pathway exists between hosts, we calculate the average overlap between paths according to the equation $\frac{1}{n} \sum_{i=1}^{n} \lambda_i$ where λ is the number of links that overlap. This rationale follows from the fact that an attacker cannot influence or predict the exact path between any two hosts, and packets are more probable to follow shorter pathways. If there are multiple paths that have equivalent overlap, one path will be selected randomly from the potential paths with a uniform probability.

An example of our verification selection algorithm is shown in Figure 7. In this instance, the client is located within the UCSB AS, and is connecting to a Bank of America web server. The client has three verification server options to choose from that include UC Berkeley, Stanford University, and the University of Washington. Using the pre-computed routes between each verification server and Bank of America, the client selects the verification server with the least number of shared AS links. In this case, the optimal verification server is at Stanford University since it shares no path overlap with the connection between the UCSB client and Bank of America. Conversely, the verification server at Berkeley would be considered the least suitable of the three, since its path to Bank of America shares two AS links (CENIC and Level 3 Communications) with the path from the client to the bank.

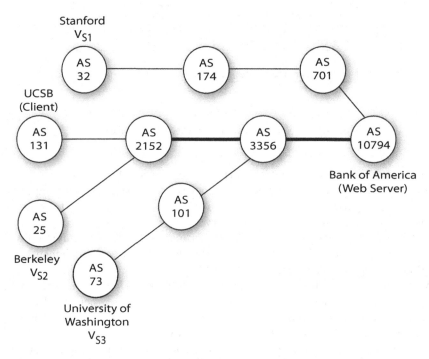

Fig. 7. Verification server selection example for a client at UCSB to the web server at Bank of America. Path overlaps are highlighted in bold.

Our path selection algorithm provides an important advantage, since the IP to AS mappings enable us to determine *a priori* the relative security of the verification process. Thus, we can ensure that the client, verification server, and web server are not on the same networks by analyzing each host's AS number (AS{C}, AS{VS}, AS{WS}). If any two have the same AS number, there is a higher risk of a man-in-the-middle since one or more links will likely be in common. In addition, the path selection algorithm that we utilize also enables us to determine the relative effectiveness of a chosen verification server. In the worst case, $(C \Rightarrow W_S \subseteq V_S \Rightarrow W_S)$, which signifies that the client and verification server share the same path to the web server and the verification process will not be effective. Furthermore, our topological maps allow us to select verification servers efficiently even when a client machine is physically relocated (*e.g.*, a laptop that may frequently change locations).

We implemented our selection process by computing the shortest paths and locations of verification servers in relation to various netblocks using AS topological mapping engines such as CAIDA's `skitter`[2], Route Views [13], and the Routing Information Service (RIS) [18]. We then correlated these maps with publicly available AS to IP address netblock mappings [14], and from the Routing Assets Database (RADb) [17]. After obtaining this data, we corroborated these paths using multiple trace routes on PlanetLab using `Scriptroute` [19]. These measurements confirmed that these paths were approximately 80% accurate with errors occurring in resolving IP addresses to AS numbers, and due to alternative AS paths. When the IP address of a host could not be resolved to an AS, we chose verification servers at random.

5 Evaluation

In this section, we analyze the performance impact of VeriKey and discuss the security of the system against man-in-the-middle attacks. We then follow with a discussion about our system's limitations and how it can be extended for enhanced performance and added security.

5.1 Experimental Setup

After implementing our system, we deployed 47 verification servers across five continents using PlanetLab. We then recorded measurements of the certificate verification process from a range of locations for the client, verification servers, and web server. The purpose of our experiments was to determine approximate bounds on the time necessary for the certificate verification process to complete. We estimated these bounds by taking geographically diverse measurements from regional, national, and multi-national locations. More specifically, the regional test involved machines across California, the national test involved machines traversing the entire United States, and the multi-national experiments entailed global pathways. Each experiment consisted of a single client, verification server, and web server.

5.2 Verification Process Overhead

Before we examine the experimental measurements, we first present the overhead for a single session. Table 1 demonstrates the bandwidth overhead involved for the certificate verification process from a single verification server, which is independent of the location of the verification server. Assuming symmetric connectivity between the client, web, and verification servers (*i.e.*, the verification

---

[2] http://www.caida.org/tools/measurement/skitter/

Table 1. Approximate VeriKey overhead for non-cached certificates

	Standard SSL Handshake		Certification Verification	
	Bytes Transferred	RTTs	Bytes Transferred	RTTs
C ↔ S	2,411	5x	2,411	5x
C ↔ V	-	-	2,857	7x
V ↔ S	-	-	2,411	5x
Total	2,411	5x	7,679	17x

server is roughly half the distance between the client and web server), the round-trip-time is approximately 3.5 times a standard SSL handshake without caching. The overhead in bytes is slightly over three times the standard SSL handshake. The absolute amount of time and overhead, however, are relatively small as only about five extra kilobytes are required, and the latency for certificate verification is typically on the order of one second (more precise numbers based on the locations of the verification servers are shown in Table 2). More importantly, this process is only a one-time cost, and after the initial verification process, the SSL session resumes with no additional overhead. The round-trip-time can be further reduced by more than 50% when temporary certificate caching is enabled on the verification servers. This diminishes the need for the SSL handshake between the verification server and web server, reducing the overhead to only double that of a standard SSL handshake.

Table 2 displays the results of the verification delay for servers from various geographical locations averaged over ten consecutive trial runs. We executed two types of verification tests for each web server. In the initial test, the verification server had not previously cached the certificate of the web server. In the following test, the verification server had already cached the web server's certificate and directly returned it to the client, thereby reducing response time and subsequent connections to the web server. Each set of tests was performed ten times and the measurements were recorded. When the client, verification server, and web server were physically closer, the overall performance gain of caching (measured in latency) decreased by about 16%. This reduction in performance was due to the limit on the latency between the client and verification server.

In the approximate worst case, the verification process could take almost three seconds. While this delay would be evident to a user, we could potentially leverage this delay to query closer verification servers. Depending on the number and density of the deployed verification servers, the average case would most likely appear similar to the regional and national examples with verification times of less than one second.

5.3   Man-in-the-Middle Attack Prevention

In this section, we examine the protective measures of VeriKey against man-in-the-middle attacks. The potential for a man-in-the-middle attack can exist

Table 2. Verification process delay perceived by clients

Test	Client	V_S	W_S	Verification Time	
				Non-cached	Cached
Multi-National 1	ucsb.edu (USA)	uestc1.edu.cn (China)	univie.ac.at (Austria)	2.876s	1.830s
Multi-National 2	canterbury.ac.nz (New Zealand)	u-tokyo.ac.jp (Japan)	berkeley.edu (USA)	2.303s	1.891s
Multi-National 3	mit.edu (USA)	utoronto.ca (Canada)	zib.de (Germany)	1.040s	0.691s
National	harvard.edu (USA)	colorado.edu (USA)	uci.edu (USA)	0.885s	0.674s
Regional	uci.edu (USA)	berkeley.edu (USA)	ucsb.edu (USA)	0.236s	0.204s

on the same network as the client establishing the egress SSL connection, the ingress web server's network, or anywhere in between. Our system successfully prevents most of the possible attack vectors, and prevents all attacks that we consider likely under our set of assumptions.

The most likely location for man-in-the-middle attacks are on client networks since they are not routinely monitored and most operating systems do not implement proper safeguards. However, we can establish secure communication between the client and verification server. As previously discussed, this is a result of requiring clients to install a web browser plug-in that stores the IP addresses and public keys of the verification servers. This prevents the primary classes of attacks including a rogue DHCP server, an attacker who has poisoned the ARP caches of nearby hosts, and DNS spoofing that would redirect users to a malicious server. Because all messages are encrypted with the verification servers' public keys, only the trusted verification servers are able to decrypt the packets. If a client receives any certificate other than that of the verification server, it becomes trivial to detect malicious behavior, and block further SSL communications.

The verification servers' networks could contain a man-in-the-middle attacker. However, on the client-side, the attacker would be trivial to detect during the SSL handshake since the certificate would not match that in the client's trusted CA root. In addition, our verification server path selection algorithm will choose a verification server with the least amount of overlap between the path from the web server to the client, and the path from the web server to the verification server. Hence, a successful attack would essentially require a coordinated attack on multiple autonomous systems. A VeriKey client can also detect a compromised verification server by maintaining a history, and comparing the results from other verification servers. If a particular verification server consistently responds with invalid keys over a prolonged period of time, the client may remove the verification server from its trusted list.

In our system, we eliminate user dialog messages for the average user because we believe the messages do more harm than good. Hence, we systematically verify or reject the certificate without the need for human interaction. For advanced users, VeriKey offers additional information about the potential threat and the number of inconsistencies among the verification servers. Thus, our system provides versatility and security for both average and expert users.

5.4 System Limitations

In this section, we address the limitations of our system, which include man-in-the-middle attacks that occur on the web server's network, and the potential for a denial of service.

A man-in-the-middle can exist on the web server's network, which is the hardest attack to detect from the viewpoint of the client and verification server. However, we believe that it is also the least likely place for an attack to occur since most web servers are on networks that employ firewalls, actively monitor for malicious behavior, and employ IDS systems. The only possible way to detect an attack near the web server is to require prior registration (*e.g.*, obtaining a signed certificate from a CA).

Another potential weakness of the system is that a man-in-the-middle could potentially detect and block all traffic to or from verification servers. By creating a denial of service (DoS) attack against verification servers, the attacker would prevent a client from being able to verify any certificates. However, since it would be rather trivial to detect this type of abuse, the system would still be constructive in preventing SSL man-in-the-middle attacks (even though the client would no longer be able to communicate with the server).

VeriKey's distributed architecture also protects against DoS attacks against individual verification servers by removing any single point of failure. Therefore we maintain constant availability with a large distributed set of servers, and in the event that a verification server is attacked, it will not affect the entire system.

5.5 Security and Performance Optimizations

In this section, we analyze possible extensions to our system to provide better security and performance. As mentioned previously, a man-in-the-middle attack detected by our system may cause a denial of service for the client because the client's connection to the web server would be blocked for the duration of the attack. On the other hand, if a man-in-the-middle has not compromised the connection between the client and verification server, we may be able to use the proxy connection to the web server. Thus, the verification server could operate as an SSL proxy server, allowing the client to securely browse the remote web server as shown in Figure 8. In order to prevent a man-in-the-middle between the verification server and web server, the verification proxy server would function as a client web browser. That is, the verification server would follow the same process described in Section 4.4 and connect to other verification servers to ensure that it has not become compromised by a man-in-the-middle attack itself.

The major downside of this design is that it puts substantial trust into the verification proxy server and assumes that the verification server itself has not

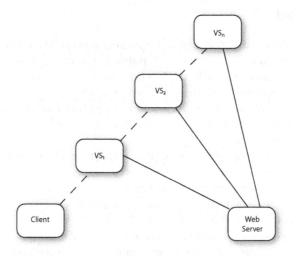

Fig. 8. Verification servers operating as SSL proxies

been compromised. In terms of overhead, this approach would also place a larger resource burden particularly on verification proxy servers. The client would also notice an increase in latency for the entire duration of the session rather than just the initial connection setup.

Another optimization to improve our framework's response time is to cache public keys from previous verification requests. This optimization works well, provided that the remote certificate has not recently changed. In order to determine when the verification server needs to update a certificate, we propose a method to maintain a history of client feedback during prior verification sessions. That is, when clients report a certificate mismatch, the verification servers will contact the web server to update the certificate. This would employ the knowledge gained from the optional confirmation status at the end of the VeriKey process as described earlier in Section 4.4. We introduce the concept of a reputation [4] to prevent a malicious host from deceiving verification servers into launching denial of service attacks by directing them to persistently contact a web server. This procedure would provide the ability for verification servers to identify compromised networks and construct a reputation-based scheme per IP Class C netblock, in addition to determining whether any of its own cached public keys may be outdated. Verification servers would refresh public keys from a web server only when a client with a positive reputation reported a key that did not correspond to the one stored in its own internal cache. This method serves two primary purposes: to establish that there is no man-in-the-middle between verification server and web server, and to update the verification server's public key cache when a web server's certificate changes. The downside of utilizing the reputation scheme is that it may not always be trustworthy and would require additional storage resources on the verification servers.

6   Conclusion

In this paper, we presented the design, implementation, and evaluation of an architecture to augment the security of SSL public key exchanges. In particular, we have introduced a means to verify the integrity of self-signed certificates. For average clients, we have substituted user interaction with an automated technique to utilize the views of remote peers, while empowering expert users with supplemental information about public key exchanges to make better assessments when accepting certificates.

We have shown the benefits, performance impacts, and the limitations of our system. Although our system is not free of weaknesses, we believe that the advantages that it provides far outweigh the potential drawbacks. Through our analysis, we are confident that our approach significantly increases the level of difficulty for a miscreant to launch a successful attack. As more insecure wireless networks are deployed, the number of attacks will likely increase because these networks provide a more susceptible environment in comparison to traditional wired LANs. Therefore, we see the need for a cost-effective and lightweight solution, such as the one that we have proposed, to protect and prevent users from becoming victims of these attacks.

References

1. Bahl, P., Balachandran, A., Venkatachary, S.: Secure Wireless Internet Access in Public Places. In: Proc. of the International Communications Conference (ICC), Helsinki, Finland (June 2001)
2. Bruschi, D., Ornaghi, A., Rosti, E.: S-ARP: A Secure Address Resolution Protocol. In: Proc. of the Annual Computer Security Applications Conference (ACSAC), Las Vegas, NV (December 2003)
3. Burkholder, P.: SSL Man-in-the-Middle Attacks. The SANS Institute (February 2002)
4. Cahill, V., Shand, B., Gray, E.: Using Trust for Secure Collaboration in Uncertain Environments. Pervasive Computing 2(3), 52–61 (2003)
5. Chomsiri, T.: HTTPS Hacking Protection. In: Proc. of Advanced Information Networking and Applications Workshops (AINAW), Mahasarakham, Thailand (May 2007)
6. Demerjian, J., Serrhrouchni, A., Achemlal, M.: Certificate-based Access Control and Authentication for DHCP. In: Proc. of the International Conference on E-Business and Telecommunication Networks (ICETE), Setubal, Portugal (August 2004)
7. DSniff, http://monkey.org/~dugsong/dsniff/
8. Eastlake, D.: Domain Name System Security Extensions. RFC 2535 (March 1999)
9. Ettercap, http://ettercap.sourceforge.net/
10. Gouda, M., Huang, C.: A Secure Address Resolution Protocol. The Computer Networks Journal 41(1), 57–71 (2003)
11. Komori, T., Saito, T.: The Secure DHCP System with User Authentication. In: Proc. of Local Computer Networks (LCN), Washington DC (November 2002)
12. Lootah, W., Enck, W., McDaniel, P.: TARP: ticket-based address resolution protocol. In: Proc. of the Annual Computer Security Applications Conference (ACSAC), Tucson, AZ (December 2005)

13. Meyer, D.: University of Oregon Route Views Project,
    http://www.antc.uoregon.edu/route-views/
14. Morley Mao, Z., Rexford, J., Wang, J., Katz, R.: Towards an Accurate AS-Level
    Traceroute Tool. In: Proc. of the Special Interest Group on Data Communication
    (SIGCOMM), Karlsruhe, Germany (August 2003)
15. PlanetLab: An Open Platform for Developing, Deploying, and Accessing Planetary-
    Scale Services,http://www.planet-lab.org/
16. Poole, L., Pai, V.S.: ConfiDNS: Leveraging scale and history to improve DNS secu-
    rity. In: Proc. of Third Workshop on Real, Large Distributed Systems (WORLDS),
    Seattle, WA (November 2006)
17. Routing Assets Database (RADb), http://www.radb.net/
18. Routing Information Service (RIS), http://www.ripe.net/ris/ris-index.html
19. Spring, N., Wetherall, D., Anderson, T.: Scriptroute: A Public Internet Measure-
    ment Facility. In: Proc. of the Internet Technologies and Systems (ITS), Seattle,
    WA (March 2003)
20. Wagner, R.: Address Resolution Protocol Spoofing and Man-in-the-Middle Attacks.
    The SANS Institute (August 2001)
21. Xia, H., Brustoloni, J.C.: Hardening Web Browsers Against Man-in-the-Middle
    and Eavesdropping Attacks. In: Proc. of the 14th International World Wide Web
    (WWW) Conference, Chiba, Japan (May 2005)
22. Zhou, L., Schneider, F., van Renesse, R.: COCA: A Secure Distributed On-line
    Certification Authority. ACM Transactions on Computer Systems 20(4), 329–368
    (2002)

Dynamic Binary Instrumentation-Based Framework for Malware Defense

Najwa Aaraj[1], Anand Raghunathan[2], and Niraj K. Jha[1]

[1] Department of Electrical Engineering, Princeton University
Princeton, NJ 08544, USA
[2] NEC Laboratories America, Princeton, NJ 08540
{naaraj,jha}@princeton.edu, anand@nec-labs.com

Abstract. Malware is at the root of a large number of information security breaches. Despite widespread effort devoted to combating malware, current techniques have proven to be insufficient in stemming the incessant growth in malware attacks. In this paper, we describe a tool that exploits a combination of virtualized (isolated) execution environments and dynamic binary instrumentation (DBI) to detect malicious software and prevent its execution. We define two isolated environments: (i) a *Testing* environment, wherein an untrusted program is traced during execution using DBI and subjected to rigorous checks against extensive security policies that express behavioral patterns of malicious software, and (ii) a *Real* environment, wherein a program is subjected to run-time monitoring using a behavioral model (in place of the security policies), along with a continuous learning process, in order to prevent non-permissible behavior.

We have evaluated the proposed methodology on both Linux and Windows XP operating systems, using several virus benchmarks as well as obfuscated versions thereof. Experiments demonstrate that our approach achieves almost complete coverage for original and obfuscated viruses. Average execution times go up to 28.57X and 1.23X in the *Testing* and *Real* environments, respectively. The high overhead imposed in the *Testing* environment does not create a severe impediment since it occurs only once and is transparent to the user. Users are only affected by the overhead imposed in the *Real* environment. We believe that our approach has the potential to improve on the state-of-the-art in malware detection, offering improved accuracy with low performance penalty.

Keywords: Malware, control-data flow, execution context, dynamic binary instrumentation, virtualization.

1   Introduction

Defending computer systems against malicious software is one of the primary concerns in information security. Recent years have witnessed a steady increase in the prevalence and diversity of malware, resulting in escalating financial, time, and productivity losses, as testified to by disclosures from various organizations (*e.g.*, Computer Security Institute (CSI) [1], Virus Bulletin [2], Symantec [3],

D. Zamboni (Ed.): DIMVA 2008, LNCS 5137, pp. 64–87, 2008.
© Springer-Verlag Berlin Heidelberg 2008

etc.). This trend has occured in spite of widespread awareness and increasing efforts towards the deployment of anti-malware tools. Therefore, the development of new approaches to address malicious software is an important research front in information security.

Malware takes myriad shapes and forms, including viruses, worms, Trojan horses [4], *etc.*, and varies in severity, propagation media, and frequency of occurrence. In this work, we propose a new approach to malware detection and explore it in the context of viruses. However, our work can be adapted to defend against other forms of malware.

Computer virus research is described in [5] as a "rich, complex, and multifaceted subject. It is about reverse engineering, developing detection, disinfection, and defense systems with optimized algorithms". The constant rise in the sophistication of viruses has been continuously scrutinized by malicious code experts in order to deploy efficient and well-tuned anti-virus techniques. Signature-based techniques have been the mainstay of virus detection, and form the basis for most current commercial products. More advanced products rely on heuristic analysis and sandboxing techniques [3,6]. Testing and evaluation procedures for anti-virus tools have been developed by various academic and commercial entities [7,8]. A fundamental limitation of signature-based techniques is the need to keep the signature database up-to-date in order to provide protection against the latest threats. While significant progress has been made in this regard through automatic update tools, the emergence of zero-day and even zero-hour attacks has clearly stretched the capabilities of current approaches to virus defense.

From a research point of view, various techniques have been proposed that extend or build upon the capabilities of signature-based techniques. The work by Zhou [9] builds a flexible virus detection and vulnerability remediation system using distributed network devices and network traffic analyzers. Centralized and distributed virus detection schemes based on automatic program signature generation are presented by Shin-Jia et al. [10]. Detection based on established heuristics, pattern recognition and machine learning techniques, such as data mining, Bayesian networks, *etc.*, have also been proposed [11,12]. Panorama, by Yin el al. [13], uses taint propagation information at the hardware and operating system (OS) levels in order to detect privacy-threatening malware. Other techniques use reverse engineering [14] in order to analyze viruses. Semantics-aware techniques for discovering obfuscations of viruses or worms are presented by Christodorescu et al. [15,16]. A known program code with malicious intent is formalized using a template, embedding within its blocks instruction variables and constants. A template-based matching is then proposed to detect obfuscations of the code in question. Moser et al. [17] propose a solution to improve test coverage in malware analysis systems. The solution relies on tracking the input dependency of the program control flow, generating input values to force execution along a specific path, and then exploring the actions that the program performs under those input values. A widely used preventive technique for addressing viral and non-viral malware proliferation on computer systems consists of executing untrusted code in containment or protection domains, wherein specific access privileges are assigned to each domain. For example, the security risks of helper applications are alleviated by restricting their access to the underlying OS by defining several dispatch tables [18]. Similar other approaches have also been presented [19,20]. Since the web browser is a common source of malware attacks, tools such as VMWare's secure browser appliance [21] run the browser in a separate virtual machine to confine the negative impact of browser exploits on the system.

We conjecture that minor enhancements to current structural approaches to virus detection are unlikely to succeed in the face of ever-increasing sophistication in the techniques (such as obfuscation, payload encryption, *etc.*) used by virus writers. In the extreme case, the only way to detect a virus may be to realize, after it has executed, that it has had malicious effects. Fortunately, a solution to this conundrum is made possible by the emergence of technologies such as virtualization and dynamic binary instrumentation (DBI), which allow us the luxury of executing untrusted code without compromising the system.

In this paper, we propose a novel approach for the detection and prevention of computer malware, in particular, computer viruses. We have designed and implemented a tool to automatically analyze and identify malicious software based on a compiled list of fundamental and evolving malicious behavioral traits. We exploit isolated software execution capabilities provided by virtualization and DBI. Virtualization is a useful technology for addressing security concerns and has several applications to information security. It allows for the creation of isolated execution environments, *e.g.*, for implementation of honeypots [22] and execution of security-critical functions such as anti-virus tools, *etc.* [23]. We especially exploit this provided isolation, which enables us to safely test untrusted code without the danger of corrupting a "live" execution environment. In order to preserve a system's integrity, an isolated compartment, duplicating a system's configuration and state, can be built and used for defending against malicious software.

Our specific approach to virus detection is based on observing the execution of unknown programs (whose source code is not available), modeling safe/unsafe behavior with respect to specified security policies, and ensuring that the program does not deviate from safe behavior. We utilize the concept of isolated execution by defining two virtual execution environments, namely a *Testing* environment and a *Real* environment. Our tool performs the following steps:

1. While executing an untrusted program in the *Testing* environment, we use DBI to collect specific information in the form of execution traces.
2. We analyze the execution traces to construct a hybrid model that represents the program's dynamic control and data flow in terms of regular expressions and data invariants. The regular expression R_U has an input alphabet Σ = $\{BB_1, ..., BB_n\}$, where BB_i is a basic block of the execution trace. For each basic block, several data properties are captured that are relevant to detecting malicious software execution.

3. We design security policies that represent fundamental traits of a malicious program behavior. We express the policies using the same hybrid model as the program execution traces (we use R_P to denote this model).
4. Through an enhanced regular expression intersection of hybrid models R_U and R_P, we detect malicious behaviors in the unknown program.
5. By combining the previous intersection result, program properties, and data invariants, we extract appropriate checkpoints and derive a behavioral model M, which can be used as an efficient proxy for the security policies.
6. After extensive testing of the unknown program, it is moved into the *Real* environment, where we monitor its execution and ensure that it conforms with model M. Checks are performed at the granularity of extracted checkpoints. If a new execution path is encountered, restrictive security policies are enforced at run-time, thus, preventing any malicious execution, and M is updated with information regarding the newly executed path.

We implemented the proposed framework using the Pin DBI tool from Intel, and evaluated its utility and performance using multiple in-the-**wild** viruses, *i.e.,* those that are currently infecting computer systems, and in-the-**zoo** viruses, *i.e.,* those that are not being currently spread or are only available online. We applied our tool to both Linux and Windows OSs. The tested viruses cover a wide range of malicious traits and behaviors. Results show that our tool enables an almost complete detection and prevention of all the considered attacks.

Our work is differentiated from previous work in that it bases its detection on the fundamental traits of malware behavior, enabling it to achieve high coverage of both new malware and new variants or obfuscations of known malware. Most previous approaches, including heuristic- and behavior-based approaches, cannot discern subtle differences between benign and malicious execution, and are thus forced to incur high false alarm rates. The proposed framework can allow a program to execute past the point where a malicious behavior is triggered, due to the "safety net" provided by virtualization, and execution trace analysis occurs after a program has finished or aborted execution. This is very attractive when the execution of malware closely resembles that of a benign program. Moreover, we believe that our hybrid model, based on regular expressions and data invariants, offers a general framework to combine control- and data-based analysis. Together, these factors lead to an improvement in detection accuracy, as underscored by our experimental results. We note that our approach is not limited to defending against the aforementioned malicious software; it promises coverage of a wider range of software vulnerabilities and malicious software behavior, provided that appropriate security policies are designed. Our work in [24] applies this approach to various software vulnerabilities with promising results.

The rest of the paper is organized as follows. The next section provides a high-level overview of our approach. Section 3 discusses the details of the proposed framework in the *Testing* and *Real* environments. Section 4 presents the experimental methodology and results, and Section 5 concludes the paper.

2   Overview

Figures 1(a) and (b) present the architecture of the proposed tool in both execution environments. Figure 1(a) depicts the different components in the *Testing* environment (Section 3.1): (1) the execution trace generator, (2) the regular expression generator, (3) the security policy generator, (4) the detection module, and (5) the behavioral model generator. The execution trace generator executes the untrusted program under a series of automatically-generated input sequences (in addition to any user-provided inputs). While building the program execution traces, DBI, based on the Pin [25] framework, is used to intercept execution and generate information that is necessary for analyzing the execution of malicious behavior. The regular expression generator combines each sequence of instructions that terminates in a control flow transfer instruction into a basic block (*BB*). Consequently, the execution trace is expressed as a regular expression R defined over alphabet $\Sigma = \{BB_1, ..., BB_n\}$, which represents the set of all basic blocks in the program. The union of all generated regular expressions (each representing a separate program execution) is performed to combine the program execution paths into a single regular expression R_U. Meanwhile, regular expressions are passed through a data invariance detector, which formulates invariants obeyed by the data associated with each basic block. When no new input sequence is able to activate new execution paths, R_U is analyzed to determine

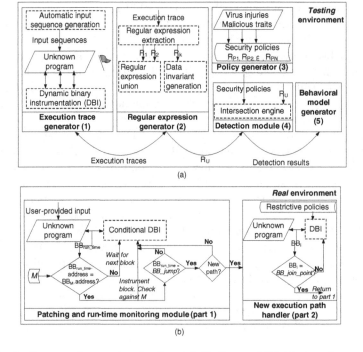

(a)

(b)

Fig. 1. Framework overview for the: (a) *Testing* and (b) *Real* environments

whether the corresponding program has manifested any malicious behavior. To this end, R_U is subjected (through a regular expression intersection operation) to rigorous security policy checks. Security policies are expressed using the same hybrid model along which R_U is designed and they encapsulate within their model fundamental malicious behaviors. The intersection procedure also allows identification of "checkpoints" – trace segments whose monitoring is critical for preventing any security exploits. Checkpoints and invariants are consequently used by a behavioral model generator, which filters out basic blocks that are significant for the tool's purposes and defines a fixed set of blocks, which capture properties indicative of permissible or non-permissible program behavior. The behavioral model, M, also maintains a record of the application's control transfer points in order to keep track of the executed paths. M is then migrated to the *Real* environment.

Figure 1(b) depicts the *Real* environment. After an application is moved to the *Real* environment, it is subjected to instrumentation at the basic block granularity and to run-time monitoring, wherein only checkpointed basic blocks are monitored [part 1 in Figure 1(b)]. Run-time monitoring also involves the application of restrictive security policies in the case where new execution paths are encountered [part 2 in Figure 1(b)], as described in Section 3.2.

3   Details of the Proposed Approach

This section describes the operation of our system in the *Testing* and *Real* environments in Sections 3.1 and 3.2, respectively.

3.1   Design and Implementation of the *Testing* Environment

This section describes the implementation of the *Testing* environment and its various components.

Execution Trace Generator. Our tool is built on top of Pin [25], which transparently performs DBI at run-time, by inserting extra code into an application for behavioral observation and information (data and control) logging. Using the Pin API, we developed our tool to execute each instruction intercepted by Pin and generate data and control information, which reflects actions of the code under test that need to be checked against the security policies. The program state information that is observed for the malware instances tackled in this work (*i.e.,* viruses) is the following:

1. Calls to and arguments of "exec" function and its variants.
2. System or library calls involving modifications of any file or directory.
3. Calls to functions that create symbolic and hard links.
4. Instructions performing memory reads and writes.

When an unknown application is executed, DBI monitors its control flow and that of dynamically-linked libraries (*e.g.,* the GNU C library) mapped into its

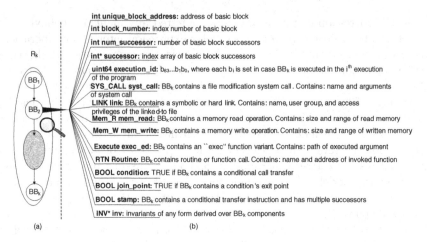

int unique_block_address: address of basic block

int block_number: index number of basic block

int num_successor: number of basic block successors

int* successor: index array of basic block successors

uint64 execution_id: $b_{83}...b_1b_0$, where each b_i is set in case BB_k is executed in the ith execution of the program

SYS_CALL syst_call: BB_k contains a file modification system call. Contains: name and arguments of system call

LINK link: BB_k contains a symbolic or hard link. Contains: name, user group, and access privileges of the linked-to file

Mem_R mem_read: BB_k contains a memory read operation. Contains: size and range of read memory

Mem_W mem_write: BB_k contains a memory write operation. Contains: size and range of written memory

Execute exec_ed: BB_k contains an ``exec'' function variant. Contains: path of executed argument

RTN Routine: BB_k contains routine or function call. Contains: name and address of invoked function

BOOL condition: TRUE if BB_k contains a conditional call transfer

BOOL join_point: TRUE if BB_k contains a condition's exit point

BOOL stamp: BB_k contains a conditional transfer instruction and has multiple successors

INV* inv: invariants of any form derived over BB_k components

(a)   (b)

Fig. 2. Overview of (a) regular expression R_k, and (b) basic block BB_i structure

address space. Dynamically-linked libraries are considered potentially unsafe and subjected to the same analysis as the application.

While most computer viruses operate independently of user inputs, those in infected files may only be triggered when a particular path, which may be input-dependent, is executed. Therefore, we design an automatic input generation technique, described later, in order to exercise as many paths as possible, thus, triggering a virus along an input-dependent path execution.

Regular Expression Generator. We describe below the key steps performed by the regular expression generator, namely regular expression extraction, regular expression union, and data invariant generation.

Regular Expression Extraction

In addition to generating an execution trace corresponding to each run of the untrusted binary, we transform each execution trace into a regular expression. Each constructed regular expression presents a codified method that allows parsing and isolation of specific properties within the body of the execution trace. It is defined over alphabet $\Sigma = \{BB_1, ..., BB_n\}$. At the highest level of granularity, each literal, BB, is a basic block derived as a sequence of instructions terminating at a control flow transfer instruction. Upon building a basic block, we map the information observed within its scope to various properties, which can indicate malicious effects when they assume specific values or when they occur in a specific sequence. Each property captured in a basic block is coded into a concise representation. Figures 2(a) and (b) present, respectively, a regular expression example and the various properties that are encoded within a basic block. Note that each BB is uniquely identified by its standardized address *unique_block_address* and its *block_number*. If BB's entry point corresponds to a static executable address A, then *unique_block_address* $= A$. On the other hand, if this entry point corresponds to a dynamically-linked entry, we calculate address offset O in an execution trace with respect to a pre-defined value A' that we specify. Given that the value of the first dynamically-linked address that follows an application's entry point virtual address is equal to D_A, $O = D_A - A'$. Thereafter, the address of each such BB is adjusted by this offset in order to allow for efficient and correct comparison by the regular expression union module, thus yielding the value of *unique_block_address*. Constituents of each BB_i in regular expression R_k are extracted from the kth execution trace and R_k is generated accordingly.

Regular Expression Union and Data Invariant Generation

After all regular expressions are generated, we need to find the union expression R_U, and subject it to defined security policies in order to determine whether the tested program manifests any malicious behavior. The union module operates on the control flow of the application and is complemented by a data invariance module, which operates on the data properties of the application.

Regular expression union: Regular expression union is presented in Figure 3.
It recursively combines single-trace regular expressions, R_k, into R_U, *i.e.*, when R_k is generated, the following operation is performed: $R_U = R_U \bigcup R_k$. As a starting point, $R_U = \lambda$ (empty regular expression). Upon combining R_U and R_k, if a path (by path, here, we mean a sequence of basic blocks executed successively) in R_k already exists in R_U, the *execution_id* of the BBs in the corresponding path are updated (step 1 in Figure 3). When a control transfer basic block (denoted by BB_jump) is encountered, if a new execution path is simulated, the latter is handled by adding it as a new successor block of BB_jump (step 2). If no new path is executed, *Union* is recursively called on

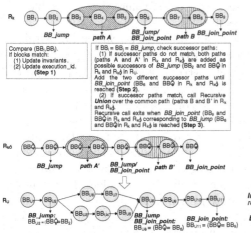

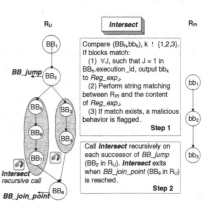

Fig. 3. Generating union regular expression R_U

Fig. 4. Malicious behavior detection: Intersecting regular expression R_U with policy R_{Pi}

the repeated execution path (step 3). **Union**'s recursive call exits when a join-point (denoted by BB_join_point) is encountered. A BB_join_point is defined as the point where different execution paths converge, *i.e.*, the exit point of the corresponding BB_jump.

Data invariance module: This module formulates invariants obeyed by data at specific blocks of R_U. It gives insight into the properties of the program data that might be useful in identifying malicious exploits. Although data invariants have been proposed before to identify program bugs [26] or understand a program's behavior [27], our system tracks data modification across multiple executions of a program and applies data invariants to the problem of detecting viruses. The on-line data invariance module maintains multiple data invariant types at various blocks of R_U, which correspond to stored basic block properties.

A) Fields over which data invariants are defined: For the type of computer viruses addressed in this paper, the data invariance module operates on the following data elements of a regular expression basic block:

- Arguments of system and function calls that involve modification of a system file or directory.
- Arguments of the "exec" function or any variants thereof.
- Arguments of functions creating symbolic and hard links.
- Size and address range of memory region access.
- Routine/thread/function names, addresses, and arguments.

B) Types of data invariants: The invariant types used are:

- Acceptable or unacceptable constant values – a value that a variable should or should not assume, respectively.
- Acceptable or unacceptable range limits – the minimum and maximum values that a variable can assume or should not assume, respectively.
- Acceptable or unacceptable value sets – the set of values that a variable can assume or should not assume, respectively.
- Acceptable or unacceptable functional invariants – a relationship within a number of variables that should or should not be satisfied, respectively.

C) Updating data invariants: For each instrumented block, the data invariance module extracts invariants, if any, that are obeyed by the basic block fields. The module maintains single or multiple types of invariants for each field, starting with the strictest invariant form (acceptable or unacceptable constant value) and progressively relaxing the stored invariants to any of the forms listed above, when combining R_k and R_U and when new run-time values of the corresponding fields are observed. When a data value from R_k does not satisfy a data invariant stored in R_U, this invariant is removed from within the basic block. For example, let us observe a memory read size, $Size_{memR}$, which assumes a constant value, $Size_R$, until execution run i. If at execution run $i + 1$, the value of the memory read size is $Size_{R'}$, we eliminate the constant invariant type for the corresponding memory size value and update the invariant to the following acceptable invariant set type: $Size_{memR} \in \{Size_R, Size_{R'}\}$. Deduced data invariants are used by the detection and behavioral model generation modules described later.

Security Policy Generator. This section describes the security policy generation process. We first describe various manifestations of virus behavior considered in this work. Second, we explain the advantages of the proposed approach. Finally, we detail the security policies that we constructed based on the behavioral traits of viruses.

Injuries and Infections of Malicious Code

While our approach can be applied to any form of malware and viruses, in this paper, we focus our attention on defending against program/file viruses, which target program and file objects and run independent of the file system in use or the format of the file under attack, and exhibit various behaviors, injuries, and infections. We next provide an overview of a compiled list of various effects, injuries, and infections resulting from virus execution. This compilation is based on the results of multiple research surveys, virus reverse engineering efforts, and digital immune system findings [5,28]. We assume that a virus can inflict damage in two ways: (i) direct injuries and (ii) injuries through the exploit of system vulnerabilities. Although direct injuries can be alleviated by always running untrusted programs as a user whose privileges to security-critical resources are minimal, a virus can overcome such security measures, *e.g.*, by modifying kernel source files, provided it has write access on these files at a certain point. We do not tackle the problem of how the virus gained access to the system (*e.g.*, by exploiting vulnerabilities). We are interested in detecting this virus through run-time instrumentation and monitoring of its execution, after it has gained access to the system.

A) Link attacks (L.A.): Link attacks are a common form of virus injuries. They are possible through exploitation of a window of vulnerability between two system calls executed by a program, which, if executed with root privileges, allows the virus code to gain privilege to sensitive information. Common malicious injuries and infections executed after a link attack include:

- I_1: Monopolizing executables, companion files, device drivers and loadable kernel modules, kernel source files, *etc.* This includes overwriting, appending, pre-pending, code injection, entry point obscuring, compression, *etc.*
- I_2: Installing random benign or malicious applications.
- I_3: Creating virus copies in a system directory under the existing OS (*e.g.*, /sbin directory), and modifying configuration files to prompt virus execution.

B) Direct injuries and infections: These include I_1, I_2, and I_3, mentioned above, denoted here by DI_1, DI_2, and DI_3, and other direct infections, *e.g.*, creating new executable files, such as decrypted virus files in the case of obfuscated viruses (DI_4). Such injuries are possible if the virus is running with high system privileges or with the same privileges associated with different components of the file system.

C) Synchronized thread execution: A common property of many viruses is that they work through multiple threads (multi-threaded or multi-fiber viruses) working by mutual exclusion. Threads can assume a multitude of roles, including:

- Execute virus code on the underlying system.
- Listen to a network port accepting remote attacks.
- Modify system files needed by the virus in order to accomplish its intent.
- Send abnormal network traffic over a network, thus, depleting its resources.
- Exploit a local vulnerability and install a backdoor.
- Kill the virus process and delete its traces from the system.

Pin is able to instrument all threads present in a process. On the other hand, since we do not address viruses from a network point of view, the *Testing* environment is not configured for network access. If an internal infinite loop is caused by lack of Internet connectivity, we trick the running process by changing the value of the internal register holding the Internet connection status to **one** [14].

D) Scheduled execution and environmental constraints: Some viruses have the property of executing upon satisfaction of a specific condition, such as time or date, system start-up, *etc.* If those constraints are satisfied in the *Testing* environment, the corresponding code is executed and subjected to the *Testing* environment security policies. If constraints are satisfied only when execution is moved to the *Real* environment, the associated code is treated as new and subjected to the approach discussed in Section 3.2.

E) Depletion of memory and storage space (mem. depletion): Another virus injury is utilizing system resources, such as memory, disk spaces, CPU cycles, and exhausting them through chunks of code embedded within their software, *e.g.*, infinite and scanning loops, infinite attempts to write to read-only memory, *etc.*

Advantages of Our Approach

Relying on virus symptoms in order to detect a virus (as performed by the majority of heuristic-based defense mechanisms) is not always accurate since these same symptoms can result from hardware or software failures. Moreover, deriving a signature for each virus variant is not a scalable approach, especially, if we consider the various ways of performing virus obfuscations. Therefore, we believe that our approach, wherein detection is based on the fundamental functional behavior of virus execution and its interactions with system components, is a more powerful defense against known and unknown viruses. Our method, which monitors a virus in both *Testing* and *Real* environments, applies the concept of sandboxing. Sandboxing can take two different forms: (1) isolation of an untrusted binary and restricting access privileges of the isolated environment [18,19,20], and (2) confinement of untrusted code into an isolated environment, wherein extensive analysis of the code behavior is performed (only few commercial products claim to perform this form of sandboxing [6]). We are not aware of any previous work that performs malware defense based on fundamental behavioral analysis, using the second form of sandboxing.

Generated Security Policies

We design the security policies to specify the fundamental traits of each malicious behavior listed above. Each policy is translated into a regular expression R_P defined over alphabet $\sigma = \{bb_1, bb_2, ..., bb_m\}$, where bb_i is a basic block of the

Table 1. Security policies in both high-level and regular expression-based specifications

High-level language specification $\Rightarrow$ Regular expression-based specification [*Malicious behavior*]
Direct security policies
$H_1 = \begin{cases} A\ symbolic\ or\ hard\ link\ of\ file\ X \\ to\ file\ Y\ with\ root\ read/write/ \\ execute\ privilege\ \Rightarrow\ apply\ R_{P2} \end{cases}$ $\Rightarrow R_{P1} = [bb_1.(bb_k, k \neq 2)^*]^*.bb_2 \Rightarrow$ apply P_2 [*L.A.*]
bb_1: system calls **link** and **symlink** with arguments Y and X,   *: Kleene closure, $(bb_k, k \neq 2,...,n)$: any block not equal to subsequent security-critical bb, bb_2: X.inode $= Y$.inode or X.links $= Y$
$H2 = \begin{cases} Modifications\ of\ file\ X\ by \\ instructions\ within\ another \\ vulnerable\ program\ B\ and\ no \\ link\ operation\ is\ contained \\ within\ B \Rightarrow\ Security\ violation \end{cases}$ $\Rightarrow R_{P2} = [(bb_k, k \neq 1)^*]^*.bb_2 \Rightarrow$ Security violation $[I_1]$
bb_1: symbolic or hard link of file X to Y in B, bb_2: modification of linked file X within file B **Programs B are detected by a thread running**   **in parallel to Pin, each B is instrumented thereafter**
$H3 = \begin{cases} Malicious\ executable\ modification \\ (Table\ 2)\ \Rightarrow\ Security\ violation \end{cases}$ $\Rightarrow R_{P3} = bb_1 \Rightarrow$ Security violation $[I_1, DI_1]$
bb_1: file-related system call/function call   (malicious executable modification)
$H4 = \begin{cases} Modification\ of\ non\text{-}executables\ pointing \\ at\ instrumented\ untrusted\ code\ or\ code \\ generated\ by\ untrusted\ programs \\ \Rightarrow\ Security\ violation \end{cases}$ $\Rightarrow R_{P4} = bb_1 \Rightarrow$ Security violation $[I_1, DI_1]$
bb_1: malicious modifications of a non-executable file
$H5 = \begin{cases} Infinite\ or\ quasi\text{-}infinite \\ loops\ requiring\ extensive \\ access\ to\ resource\ R \\ \Rightarrow\ Security\ violation \end{cases}$ $\Rightarrow R_{P5} = [bb_1.bb_2...bb_j]_N \Rightarrow$ Violation [*mem. depletion*]
$[bb_1.bb_2...bb_j]$: sequence of basic blocks requiring   intensive access to resource R, $N \gg 1$
Recursive security policies
$H6 = \begin{cases} Non\text{-}malicious\ executable\ (E)\ modification \\ \Rightarrow\ Instrument\ modified\ executable \\ when\ executed \end{cases}$ $\Rightarrow R_{P6} = bb_1 \Rightarrow$ DBI of E $[I_1, DI_1]$
bb_1: file-related system call (modification of E)
$H7 = \begin{cases} "exec"\ function\ variant\ calls \\ \Rightarrow\ Instrument\ "exec"\ argument\ (arg_1) \end{cases}$ $\Rightarrow R_{P7} = bb_1 \Rightarrow$ DBI of arg_1 $[I_2, DI_2]$
bb_1: call to "exec" function variants
$H8 = \begin{cases} Newly\ installed\ programs\ (P) \\ \Rightarrow\ Instrument\ new\ programs \end{cases}$ $\Rightarrow R_{P8} = bb_1 \Rightarrow$ DBI of P $[I_2, DI_2, I_3, DI_3, DI_4]$
bb_1: newly installed program or newly created binary

security policy and embeds an action as specified in the high-level specification. Equation (1) shows a high-level language specification template of a policy and its regular expression structure. Policies given in Table 1 take the form of direct and recursive policies. Recursive policies are applied a jth time when we cannot determine whether the unknown program has manifested malicious behavior after applying the policies $j - 1$ times. The rule of thumb we have applied is to flag a malicious behavior when more than 10 recursive policy calls have occurred. Table 2 presents the specific case of malicious executable modifications we have taken into consideration (corresponding to security policy R_{P3}).

$$H = \begin{cases} \textbf{if } Action_1 \textbf{ then} \\ ... \textbf{ then } Action_m \Rightarrow (R_P = [bb_1.(bb_k, k \neq 2, ..., m)^*]^*.[...]^*.bb_m \Rightarrow A) \quad (1) \\ \Rightarrow \textbf{ Action A} \end{cases}$$

Detection Module. In order to check the application's R_U against security policy R_{Pi}, we design a regular expression intersection engine, which operates as depicted in Figure 4. Intersection enables program analysis and automatic malicious behavior detection. It works as follows: R_U is scanned block by block in a top-down manner (Step 1 in Figure 4), comparing the properties of its successive basic blocks against the properties of R_{Pi}'s basic blocks. When a control transfer block (BB_jump) is encountered and BB_jump has multiple successors, **Intersect** is called recursively over each successor path (Step 2). In case basic block BB_h in R_U matches basic block bb_k in R_{Pi}, **Intersect** outputs bb_k into file Reg_exp_J for each bit $J = 1$ in $BB_h.execution\_id$. At each match between BB_h and bb_k, the string of bb_i's in each Reg_exp_J is matched, using a standard string matching functionality, against the string representation of R_{Pi}'s regular expression. If a match occurs, a malicious behavior is captured in untrusted program execution.

Checkpointing and Behavioral Model Generation. This module extracts basic blocks of R_U to constitute a behavioral model M. M embeds, through its reduced basic block set, permissible (or non-permissible) real-time behavior of the unknown tested program. It is a model against which the execution of the program should be monitored in the *Real* environment. Basic blocks in R_U that are checkpointed and added to model M can be one of the following: (1) conditional control transfer basic blocks in order to keep track of executed program paths, (2) basic blocks in R_U, whose components reveal a security violation when checked with the help of the policies in Table 1 (invariants stored in such blocks are formulated as unacceptable), and (3) basic blocks in R_U, whose components confirm a permissible behavior (acceptable invariants are stored in such blocks). By deriving model M, we reduce the number of invariants and the required

Table 2. Malicious modifications of executable files

Malicious modifications of executable files
File appending, pre-pending, overwriting with virus content or content derivatives
Overwriting executable cavity blocks (*e.g.*, CC-00-99 blocks)
Code regeneration and integration of virus code within executable
Executable modifications to incorrect header sizes
Executable modifications to multiple headers
Executable modifications to headers incompatible with their respective sections
Modifications of control transfer instructions to point to malicious code
Modifications of function entry points to point to malicious code (API and function hooking)
Executable entry point obfuscations
Modifications of Thread Local Storage (TLS) table
Modifications to /proc/pid/exe

Table 3. Flags and invariants embedded within behavioral model M

Flag	Content of relevant BB in R_U	Run-time response	Stored invariants
1. File_Store	Symbolic or hard link from file X to file Y	Store $X.Path$	None
2. Indirect_Verify	Modification of X at stored $X.Path$ by process B	Verify $B.path$ against invariants. Abort execution if B satisfies invariants	a. Inv_1: $B.path = P$ (P: acceptable invariant of constant type) b. Inv_2: $B.path \in set_1$ (set_1: acceptable invariant set) c. Inv_3: $B.path \in_R f(\mathbf{X})$ ($f(\mathbf{X})$: acceptable functional invariant, $\mathbf{X}$: environmental value upon which $B.path$ depends)
3. Mod_Verify	Allowed modification of file F	Verify $F.name$ against data invariants. Abort execution if invariants are not satisfied	a. Inv_1: $F.name = C$ (C: acceptable invariant of constant type) b. Inv_2: $F.name \in set_2$ (set_2: acceptable invariant set) c. Inv_3: $F.name = \in_R f(\mathbf{X})$ ($f(\mathbf{X})$: acceptable functional invariant)
4. No_Mod_Verify	Not allowed modification of file F	Verify $F.name$ against data invariants. Abort execution if invariants are satisfied	a. Inv_1: $F.name = C'$ (C': unacceptable invariant of constant type) b. Inv_2: $F.name \in set'_3$ (set'_3: unacceptable invariant set) c. Inv_3: $F.name = \in_R f'(\mathbf{X})$ ($f'(\mathbf{X})$: unacceptable functional invariant)
5. Loop_Verify	Loop requiring extensive memory usage/access	Limit a loop execution to τ iterations	a. Inv_1: $loop.n$ [n = # of times a loop has been executed] $< \tau$ (τ: a constant value derived empirically)
6. Exec_Verify	Call to an "exec" function variant	Verify $exec.arg_1.path$ against data invariants. Abort execution if invariants are not satisfied. Else, check the execution of $exec.arg_1.path$ against its derived model M	a. Inv_1: $exec.arg_1.path = P$ (P: acceptable invariant of constant type) b. Inv_2: $exec.arg_1.\mathbf{path} \in set_4$ (set_4: acceptable invariant set)
7. Prog_Verify	Installation of a new program or binary	Verify $Pr.name$ against data invariants. Abort execution if invariants are not satisfied. Else, check the execution of Pr against its model M	a. Inv_1: $Pr.name = C$ (C: acceptable invariant of constant type) b. Inv_2: $Pr.name \in set_5$ (set_5: acceptable invariant set)

storage space (as compared to the number of invariants and storage required by R_U) by an average of 75.46% and 64.81%, respectively, for the different virus benchmarks used.

In each basic block BB_M of M, in addition to stored data invariants, a flag is added in order to instruct the run-time monitor what kind of action needs to be taken when BB_M is reached. In Table 3, Column 1 lists the flags that can be associated with any BB_M, Column 2 the actions performed in the corresponding R_U's basic block, Column 3 the run-time actions to take when a flagged BB_M is reached, and Column 4 the various invariants stored at BB_M.

Automatic Input Sequence Generation Technique. The effectiveness of our tool considerably depends on code coverage, *i.e.*, the number of paths executed in the *Testing* environment and the number of triggered malicious executions.

In this section, we review a system (originally presented in [24]) that allows automatically generated input sequences to exercise a high percentage of a program's paths and is based on static binary analysis and symbolic propagation. While we realize the conservative nature of static analysis, we adopt this technique since it is able to leverage complete knowledge of a program's structure and to resolve first-level dependencies between a program input and its control flow. Moreover, pure dynamic analysis on unknown programs, used with a random initial input, would be unable to explore all path possibilities. Future work involves input generation based on a more efficient hybrid approach combining static analysis refined by dynamic analysis performed in the *Testing* environment.

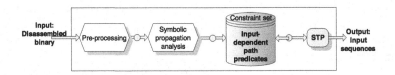

Fig. 5. Automatic input sequence generation technique

Figure 5 depicts the flow of the input generation technique. Our system operates on a disassembled binary. It proceeds by using symbolic propagation analysis to identify different input-dependent paths. It is basically a three-part system: (i) pre-processing, (ii) generating path predicates, and (iii) solving path predicates.

A) Pre-processing: Prior to static analysis, disassembled binaries are pre-process- ed in order to resolve loop unrolling and function calls. (1) *Loop analysis* is used to avoid infinite iterations. We limit the number of loop iterations to τ, where τ iterations are sufficient for approximating a loop behavior and the dependency of the loop condition on the input ($\tau = 5$ worked well in our experiments). (2) *Function call analysis* is necessary to allow a more accurate propagation of symbolic inputs. Unless functions are linked dynamically, they are replaced by their corresponding code in the disassembled binary.

B) Generating path predicates: Our system operates by generating the following formulas:
- Symbolic formulas representing input constraints at input-dependent instructions, which depend (or operate) on the symbolically propagated user-input values.
- Two symbolic formulas representing input constraints at input-dependent control transfer instructions.
- Concrete input-independent formulas at input-independent instructions.

Given each instruction, our system checks whether it depends on the symbolic input, in which case, we translate the instruction to a Simple Theorem Prover (STP) [29] conditional formula. STP is an efficient decision procedure for the validity of a set of formulas. The translation is based on techniques presented in [30] and [31].

1. For instructions that perform binary, unary, and assignment operations, we generate an **STP LET** expression, which binds a generated variable name to the expression computed by the assembly instruction. For each operation, we use the corresponding bitwise and arithmetic STP functions.
2. For conditional control transfers, we generate two formulas, thus resulting in two sets of path predicates, one path where the current path continues with the *True* branch and another path where the current path continues with the *False* branch. Each control transfer instruction is translated into two symbolic formulas using the corresponding STP predicates.
3. For assembly instructions that do not depend on the input, the operands are set or abstracted to concrete values using the **ASSERT** STP function.

C) Solving path predicates: The solver that we use is **STP**, which has its own built-in language with specific functions and predicates. For all generated path conditions, the solver checks if the conditions are satisfiable. In case conditions are satisfiable, it generates an input sequence triggering a new path execution.

We have implemented the approach above and tested it on various benchmarks infected with known in-the-**wild** viruses. Results show that it is automatically and efficiently able to generate (offline) inputs used in the *Testing* environment. In the case where input sequences do not achieve a high coverage of an application's possible execution paths, they can be augmented with user-provided inputs. Note that since **STP** is provided as a Linux library, Windows executables in the Portable Executable (PE) format are first disassembled using the *PEdump* Windows utility, the output of which is processed on a Linux system, following the flow of Figure 5. *Objdump* is used to disassemble Linux executables in the Executable and Linkable Format (ELF).

3.2   Design and Implementation of the *Real* Environment

This section describes the architecture of the *Real* environment, which performs run-time monitoring and on-line prevention of malicious code execution. The run-time monitoring mechanism is composed of two parts: the first part prevents malicious execution in program paths already analyzed in the *Testing* environment by checking the basic blocks in the instrumented path against those of the extracted behavioral model M; the second part applies the conservative security policies shown in Table 4 on newly executed paths. Both components, embedded in the run-time monitor, prevent malicious attacks in the *Real* environment.

Table 4. Restrictive policies used in the *Real* environment

Restricted actions	Restrictive policies
"exec" function variants	Not allowed if model M was not generated for the executed argument
New installed programs	Not allowed if model M was not generated for the programs
Non-executable modification	Not allowed if files have root privileges
Loop execution	Any loop is allowed to execute τ times only. τ is derived empirically
Executable modification	Not allowed

Figure 1(b) depicts a detailed architecture of the exploit prevention system in the *Real* environment. The system consists of (1) the patching and run-time monitoring module, and (2) the new execution path handler.

Patching and Run-time Monitoring Module: This module first loads the extracted model M and then runs the application (using a user-provided input sequence, in case the application is input-dependent) under DBI. The module identifies the first instruction executed within a basic block and delineates its boundaries. When a new basic block BB is identified, its run-time loaded address is transformed into its standardized address format, which is checked against the address of basic block BB_M in M scanned so far. In case the two addresses do not match, the instrumentation of instructions in BB is suspended until a new basic block is identified. Otherwise, the instructions in BB need to be instrumented, and appropriate components listed in Figure 2(b) are extracted and checked against properties and components of BB_M (Table 3, Column 3). If check results do not reveal any security breach, BB's instructions are allowed to execute and commit. Otherwise, execution is aborted. If the instrumented BB is a conditional control transfer basic block (*i.e.*, $BB = BB\_jump$), the run-time monitor identifies whether the first basic block executed after BB_jump corresponds to a path previously tested in the *Testing* environment.

New Execution Path Handler: If no new path is executed, the run-time monitor compares the series of basic blocks in the given path against their corresponding blocks in model M. If a new path is executed, the set of restrictive policies (Table 4) is enforced at run-time before any instruction completes execution in order to prevent any malicious attack. The new path instrumentation proceeds until BB_join_point corresponding to BB_jump is encountered. While the restrictive policies would eventually result in some false positives, they keep the overhead in the *Real* environment low and prevent the execution of malicious code.

Basic blocks in newly executed paths, which did not cause execution to be aborted due to violation of the restrictive security policies, are added to M. In case a newly executed path violates a restrictive security policy, the execution of an application is aborted.

4   Evaluation

This section presents the experimental evaluation of our approach in the *Testing* and *Real* environments on both Windows and Linux OSs. Our results consist of two parts. First, we investigate the accuracy of our tool in terms of detection and prevention metrics, and false positives (FP) and negatives (FN) (Section 4.1). We then present how execution time is affected by our tool (Section 4.2).

4.1   Virus Detection Results

In order to explore the feasibility of our approach, we have designed and implemented a prototype on both Linux and Windows OSs. On both OSs, our system is implemented as an on-access detection mechanism, in the sense that all programs are first run in the *Testing* environment. Thus, any malicious code will be intercepted and analyzed prior to execution in its *Real* environment.

For the Linux OS, the system used is a 3.2GHz Intel Pentium IV PC running XenLinux 2.6. Xen [32] is an open-source virtual machine monitor that supports the execution of multiple OSs. We use Xen to build two virtual domains, executed in isolation, in order to set up the *Testing* and *Real* execution environments. Xen's domain 0, which is a privileged management domain, is used in order to create both domains, and securely migrate information (behavioral model M), through Xen's S-Hype security hooks, between them. For the Windows OS, we have implemented each of the environments as a custom-installed VMWare [33] virtual Windows XP OS image on a 3.2GHz Intel Pentium IV PC running Windows XP. M is migrated manually between the two environments.

On both OSs, we developed our tool based on Pin [25], which provides a rich API for building a variety of instrumentation tools. Under Linux, detection of file modifications occurs at the *system call-interception* level. Under Windows, detection of file modifications occurs at the *Windows API (WinAPI) function call/CRC-based WinAPI function call/system call-interception* levels. (CRC corresponds to Cyclic Redundancy Check, CRC-based WinAPI function calls basically mean that WinAPI function names are not visible in the virus code image. Instead, function calls occur through matching of the checksum of the function names or addresses to CRC values calculated within the virus code.)

Our virus collection consisted of 72 real-world Linux viruses and 45 Windows viruses [34,35]. The virus collection contained both in-the-**wild** [*e.g.,* the Binom, Bliss, and Neox viruses on Linux and the Zombie (Zmist virus version for Windows XP), Cleevix, Looked-BG, and Shrug viruses on Windows] and in-the-**zoo** viruses. Furthermore, we obfuscated the available Linux and Windows viruses using ELFCrypt [36] and UPX [37], and Obfuscator [38], respectively. We also ran our tool on multiple benign programs that exhibit behaviors that closely resemble those manifested by computer viruses, such as gcc, javac, gawk, and nasm for Linux, and tasm, tlink, and lcc for Windows (45 programs for Linux and 28 programs for Windows). We also tested our approach on infected versions of those programs.

Next, we present the code and path coverage of the tested applications, the virus detection result in the *Testing* environment, and finally the effectiveness of the prevention mechanism in the *Real* environment.

Code and Path Coverage. The efficiency of our approach is bounded by the number of paths covered in the *Testing* environment. Following the input generation method described earlier, we cover 93.68% of the paths in input-dependent programs on an average. Generated input sequences can be augmented with user-provided input in the case where they do not achieve a high coverage of an application's possible execution paths. Another issue to address while defending against computer viruses is time and environmental constraints that restrain virus execution. The approaches in [17,31] detect such constraints, as specified in a pre-compiled constraint list, and force them to become true in order to analyze a malware instance. Such a framework can be integrated within our system; however, for the time being, we assume that any non-executed path in the *Testing* environment is compensated for in the *Real* environment.

Virus Detection Rate in the *Testing* Environment. We have evaluated the effectiveness of our tool in the *Testing* environment by running it on the aforementioned viruses and benchmarks. Table 5 summarizes the results of our experiments, and Table 6 details the specific malicious executable modifications (as listed in Table 2) that were observed amongst tested viruses. Note that a single virus can have multiple malicious effects and can inflict multiple malicious modifications. We can see that our system has correctly classified almost all viruses and benign programs. It falsely declared one Linux virus and two Windows viruses [rows 6 and 19 (last rows corresponding to the virus category under the Linux and Windows XP OSs, respectively) in Table 5] to be benign. By manually checking the control data flow graph related to the three non-identified viruses and their resulting effects on our system, we observed that their execution did not inflict any of the malicious effects specified in our security policies. Table 7 compares the performance of our system, in detecting original [Det. rate (Orig.V.)] and obfuscated [Det. rate (Obf.V.)] viruses, with that of widely used anti-virus (AV) products. We can see that our approach largely outperforms all tested AV tools, and even the combination of all tools (union of the sets of viruses detected by each of the tools), as shown in the **Union AV** row in Table 7. However, one limitation of our approach, as can be seen for the case of non-detected virus instances, is its dependency on the accuracy of the security policies, and the completeness of the set of malicious behaviors these policies cover.

Virus Defense in the *Real* Environment. Behavioral models extracted in the *Testing* environment, in addition to the restrictive security policies of Table 4, successfully halted the execution of any malicious code in the *Real* environment. For input-dependent binaries, we have tested our approach in the *Real* environment using a set of inputs that was used in the *Testing* environment and another that was not used. Experiments in the *Real* environment resulted in new execution paths only 6.8% of the time. No false positives were encountered. However, due to the nature of the restrictive policies imposed on the new execution paths, we expect a small percentage of false positives to occur if spawned by adequate user-inputs.

4.2   Execution Time Overheads

This section describes how execution time is affected by our tool in both the *Testing* and *Real* environments.

Testing Environment: The key components in this environment that contribute to execution time are: (i) t_1: time required by binary instrumentation, (ii) t_2: time required by the regular expression module, (iii) t_3: time required by the detection module, and (iv) t_4: time required by the checkpointing and behavioral model generation module. Table 8 reports execution times for the different sets of viruses and benign and infected open-source benchmarks on both

Table 5. Detection and false alarm results in the *Testing* environment

Category	#viruses	Suspicious effects triggering recursive policy calls	Malicious effects	FN	FP
		Linux OS			
Viruses	60	0	malicious ELF modifications	0	0
Viruses	5	"exec" function variant	malicious exec.arg$_1$	0	0
Viruses	3	newly created binaries	malicious binary	0	0
Viruses	2	0	extensive memory access	0	0
Viruses	1	non-malicious ELF modifications	malicious ELF execution	0	0
Viruses	1	0	ELF modification not specified in Table 2	1	0
Obfuscated viruses	153	0	malicious ELF modifications	0	0
Obfuscated viruses	15	"exec" function variant	malicious exec.arg$_1$	0	0
Obfuscated viruses	12	newly created binaries	malicious binary	0	0
Obfuscated viruses	6	0	extensive memory access	0	0
Obfuscated viruses	3	non-malicious ELF modifications	malicious ELF execution	0	0
Benign programs	36	0	0	0	0
Benign programs	3	"exec" function variant	0	0	0
Benign programs	1	non-executable modifications	0	0	0
Benign programs	5	newly created binaries	0	0	0
Infected programs	45	0	malicious ELF modifications	0	0
		Windows XP OS			
Viruses	42	0	malicious PE modifications	0	0
Viruses	1	0	extensive memory access	0	0
Viruses	2	0	ELF modification not specified in Table 2	2	0
Obfuscated viruses	21	0	malicious PE modifications	0	0
Benign programs	1	non-malicious PE modifications	0	0	0
Benign programs	2	non-executable modifications	0	0	0
Benign programs	2	newly created binaries	0	0	0
Benign programs	23	0	0	0	0
Infected programs	20	0	malicious PE modifications	0	0

Table 6. Observed malicious ELF/PE modifications

#viruses	Malicious executable modification type
	Linux OS - ELF modifications
53	Entry point obfuscation [entry point virtual address (e_entry), replace **nop** with **jmp** instructions, jump addresses]
10	Virus appending [end of ELF file, end of .debug section, end of .text section]
4	Overwriting with virus code [.text section]
2	proc/pid/exe modification
7	Cavity block overwriting [.text section, insertion of jmp instructions]
	Windows XP OS - PE modifications
34	Entry point obfuscation [relative virtual address entry (AddressofEntryPoint), .reloc entries, jump addresses]
7	API hooking [Kernel32.dll, .idata section]
4	Cavity block overwriting [.reloc section, PE header]
6	Virus appending [end of PE file, end of .reloc section]
1	TLS table modification
2	Overwriting with virus code [.reloc section]
1	Header incompatible with .reloc section
1	Virus integration within PE file

Table 7. Comparison of detection results against anti-virus products

AV product	Detection type	Det. rate (Orig.V.) (%)	Det. rate (Obf.V.) (%)
		Linux OS	
Clam	Signature-based	80.55	38.89
F-prot	Signature/heuristics	44.44	1.39
Avira	Signature/heuristics	97.22	50.00
AVG	Signature-based	97.22	34.72
Sophos	Signature/heuristics/emulation	76.39	0.00
Union AV		97.22	51.39
Our system		100.00	100.00
		Windows XP OS	
Avira	Signature/heuristics	85.71	47.61
Kaspersky	Signature/heuristics	28.57	9.52
Panda	Signature/heuristics	33.33	4.76
F-prot	Signature/heuristics	95.23	57.14
Eset	Signature/heuristics/emulation	90.48	57.14
Union AV		95.23	57.14
Our system		100.00	100.00

Table 8. Execution times in the *Testing* and *Real* environments

Benchmarks	*Testing* environment						*Real* environment					
	$\#BB$	t_1 (sec.)	t_2 (sec.)	t_3 (sec.)	t_4 (sec.)	T.I. (X)	$\#BB_M$	t'_1 (sec.)	t'_2 (msec.)	t'_3 (msec.)	t.i. (X)	T.R. (X)
						Linux OS						
Viruses	2102	0.82	8.66	0.34	0.11	20.82	951	0.44	56.92	14.61	1.07	19.41
Obfuscated viruses	3686	1.01	8.92	0.42	0.13	21.59	1482	0.47	62.70	14.62	1.12	19.11
Benign programs	10601	16.11	209.47	2.12	0.32	32.07	5925	8.82	372.22	68.00	1.30	24.62
Infected programs	11972	19.99	230.28	2.58	0.37	32.74	6299	9.75	381.12	n/a	1.31	24.99
						Windows XP OS						
Viruses	2740	1.10	9.82	0.47	0.13	22.47	1247	0.54	60.41	n/a	1.17	19.21
Obfuscated viruses	3977	1.46	10.48	0.48	0.16	22.81	1629	0.61	70.04	n/a	1.23	18.49
Benign programs	15395	17.57	273.91	2.48	0.41	37.18	8562	9.93	482.93	n/a	1.31	28.28
Infected programs	17937	20.47	286.19	2.60	0.43	38.92	9001	10.23	490.41	n/a	1.35	28.89

Linux and Windows OSs. Column 1 corresponds to the executed benchmark set, Column 2 lists the number of basic blocks in R_U ($\#BB$) extracted as an average for all benchmarks in a given set. Columns 3-6 report the average total time required by each of the above-mentioned components. Reported times are based on an average of 40 executions per benchmark. User input-dependent benign and infected open-source programs were tested using automatically generated inputs, augmented with user-provided inputs when necessary. Column 7 reports the average total increase in execution time (T.I.) induced by all modules (as compared to running the benchmarks without any security checks).

The execution time induced in the *Testing* environment (Table 8) is quite significant (the execution time goes up to an average of 26.81X on Linux and 30.35X on Windows). However, we can argue that this incurred time is acceptable and does not impose a severe limitation, since our tool performs off-line detection in the *Testing* environment, transparently to the user, while subjecting the application to rigorous checks.

Real Environment: Performance in this environment is evaluated while the run-time monitor is running in parallel with the program, and performing checks against behavioral model M and the list of restrictive security policies (Table 4). The key components that contribute to execution time in the *Real* environment are: (i) t'_1: time required by binary instrumentation, (ii) t'_2: time required for checking against behavioral model M, and (iii) t'_3: time required for testing a new execution path and rebuilding M. Table 8 reports an average (over 32 executions) of the different time components for different benchmark sets in Columns 9-11. Column 8 lists the average number of basic blocks checked at run-time [*i.e.,* number of blocks in M ($\#BB_M$)]. Column 12 reports the average total execution time increase (t.i.) in the *Real* environment as compared to running a standalone benchmark set without any security prevention measurements applied to it. Column 13 reports the average execution time reduction (T.R.) between the *Testing* and *Real* environments. The execution time goes up to an average of 1.20X (1.26X) on the Linux (Windows) OS in the *Real* environment [maximum of 1.31X (1.35X) and minimum of 1.07X (1.17X)]. This increase in execution time is quite minimal and compensates for the high slowdowns imposed in the *Testing* environment [to an average of 22.03X (23.72X)].

5   Conclusion

Current techniques fall short of meeting the challenges posed by the dramatic increase of malware threats, leading to escalating financial, time, productivity, and information losses. This suggests the need for a new approach for designing defense mechanisms against malware. We believe that the system we introduced in this paper is a highly efficient, practical, and scalable way to prevent a wide range of computer malware, in particular computer viruses, which are tackled here, from inflicting damage. We applied our tool to successfully detect a number of real-world computer viruses. The use of an abstracted behavioral model for system monitoring in the *Real* execution environment results in an acceptable performance penalty incurred by the user at run-time.

Limitations of our approach include its dependency on the accuracy of the security policies used and the number of observed paths, in particular, observed malicious paths, in the *Testing* environment. In our future work, we plan to explore ways to augment our static input generation technique with dynamic analysis, as the software is executed in the *Testing* environment. Also, we plan to investigate the efficiency of our approach in defending against polymorphic, self-modifying, and code integration-based viruses.

Acknowledgments

We thank the anonymous reviewers for their comments and suggestions. This work is supported by the National Science Foundation under Grant No. CNS-0720110.

References

1. Computer Security Institute, CSI Survey 2007 (2007), http://www.gocsi.com
2. Virus Bulletin (2007), http://www.virusbtn.com/news/2007
3. Symantec Security Response (2007), http://www.symantec.com
4. The difference between a virus, worm and trojan horse (2004),
   http://www.webopedia.com/DidYouKnow/Internet/2004/virus.asp
5. Szor, P.: The Art of Computer Virus Research and Defense. Addison-Wesley Professional, Reading (2005)
6. Norman SandBox Pro-active virus protection (2004),
   http://lan-aces.com/Norman_Sandbox.pdf
7. Gordon, S., Howard, F.: Antivirus software testing for the new millenium. In: Proc. National Information Systems Security Conf., pp. 125–139 (October 2000)
8. Westcoast labs: Checkmark certification (2007),
   http://www.westcoastlabs.com/checkmark
9. Zhou, Q.: A service-oriented solution framework for distributed virus detection and vulnerability remediation (VDVR) system. In: Proc. Int. Cryptology Conf. Services Computing, pp. 569–573 (July 2007)
10. Shin-Jia, H., Kuang-Hsi, C.: A proxy automatic signature scheme using a compiler in distributed systems for unknown virus detection. In: Proc. Int. Conf. Advanced Information Networking and Applications, pp. 649–654 (March 2005)
11. Yoo, I., Ultes-Nitsche, U.: Adaptive detection of worms/viruses in firewalls. In: Proc. Int. Conf. Security Technology (October 2004)
12. Henchiri, O., Japkowicz, N.: A feature selection and evaluation scheme for computer virus detection. In: Proc. Int. Conf. Data Mining, pp. 891–895 (December 2006)
13. Yin, H., Song, D., Egele, M., Kruegel, C., Kirda, E.: Panorama: Capturing system-wide information flow for malware detection and analysis. In: Proc. ACM Conf. Computer and Communication Security, pp. 116–127 (October 2007)
14. Rozinov, K.: Reverse code engineering: An in-depth analysis of the Bagle virus. In: Proc. Wkshp. Information Assurance and Security, pp. 380–387 (June 2005)
15. Christodorescu, M., Jha, S., Seshia, S.A., Song, D., Bryant, R.E.: Semantics-aware malware detection. In: Proc. IEEE Symp. Security and Privacy, pp. 32–46 (May 2005)
16. Preda, M.D., Christodorescu, M., Jha, S., Debray, S.: A semantics-based approach to malware detection. In: Proc. Conf. Principles of Programming Languages, pp. 377–388 (January 2007)
17. Moser, A., Kruegel, C., Kirda, E.: Exploring multiple execution paths for malware analysis. In: Proc. IEEE Symp. Security and Privacy, pp. 231–245 (May 2007)
18. Goldberg, I., Wagner, D., Thomas, R., Brewer, E.A.: A secure environment for untrusted helper applications confining the wily hacker. In: Proc. Conf. USENIX Security Symp., pp. 1–13 (July 1996)
19. Peterson, D.S., Bishop, M., Pandey, R.: A flexible containment mechanism for executing untrusted code. In: Proc. Conf. USENIX Security Symp., pp. 207–225 (August 2002)
20. Lam, L.-C., Yu, Y., Chiueh, T.-C.: Secure mobile code execution service. In: Proc. Conf. Large Installation System Administration, pp. 53–62 (December 2006)
21. VMWare Inc., Palo Alto, VMWare browser appliance (2006),
    http://www.vmware.com/appliances/directory/browserapp.html
22. Provos, N., Holz, T.: Virtual Honeypots: From Botnet Tracking to Intrusion Detection. Addison-Wesley, Reading (2007)

23. Intel vPro Processor Technology (2007), http://www.intel.com/business/vpro
24. Aaraj, N., Raghunathan, A., Jha, N.K.: Virtualization-assisted framework for prevention of software vulnerability based security attacks. Tech. Rep. CE-J07-001, Dept. of Electrical Engineering, Princeton University (December 2007)
25. Luk, C.-K., Cohn, R., Muth, R., Patil, H., Klauser, A., Lowney, G., Wallace, S., Reddi, V.J., Hazelwood, K.: Pin: Building customized program analysis tools with dynamic instrumentation. In: Proc. Programming Language Design and Implementation Forum, pp. 190–200 (June 2005)
26. Hangal, S., Lam, M.S.: Tracking down software bugs using automatic anomaly detection. In: Proc. Int. Conf. Software Engineering, pp. 291–301 (May 2002)
27. Ernst, M.D., Cockrell, J., Griswold, W.G., Notkin, D.: Dynamically discovering likely program invariants to support program evolution. In: Proc. Int. Conf. Software Engineering, pp. 213–224 (May 1999)
28. Symantec corporation, Cupertino, The digital immune system (2007), http://www.symantec.com/avcenter/reference/dis.tech.brief.pdf
29. STP: A decision procedure for bitvectors and arrays (2007), http://theory.stanford.edu/~vganesh/stp.html
30. Cadar, C., Ganesh, V., Pawlowski, P.M., Dill, D.L., Engler, D.R.: EXE: Automatically generating inputs of death. In: Proc. ACM Conf. Computer and Communications Security, pp. 322–335 (November 2006)
31. Brumley, D., Hartwig, C., Liang, Z., Newsome, J., Song, D., Yin, H.: Automatically identifying trigger-based behavior in malware (2007), http://bitblaze.cs.berkeley.edu/papers/botnet_book-2007.pdf
32. XenSource: Delivering the Power of Xen (2007), http://www.xensource.com
33. VMWare Inc., Palo Alto, Virtual Appliance Marketplace (2007), http://www.vmware.com/appliances
34. VX Heavens (2007), http://vx.netlux.org
35. Computer Virus Codes (2007), http://virus-codes.blogspot.com
36. ELFCrypt (2005), http://www.infogreg.com/source-code/public-domain/elfcrypt-v1.0.html
37. UPX: the Ultimate Packer for eXecutables (2007), http://upx.sourceforge.net
38. Obfuscator download (2006), http://www.soft32.com/download_186322.html

Embedded Malware Detection Using Markov n-Grams

M. Zubair Shafiq[1], Syed Ali Khayam[2], and Muddassar Farooq[1]

[1]Next Generation Intelligent Networks Research Center (nexGINRC)
National University of Computer & Emerging Sciences (NUCES)
Islamabad, Pakistan
{zubair.shafiq,muddassar.farooq}@nexginrc.org
[2]School of Electrical Engineering & Computer Science (SEECS)
National University of Sciences & Technology (NUST)
Rawalpindi, Pakistan
khayam@niit.edu.pk

Abstract. Embedded malware is a recently discovered security threat that allows malcode to be hidden inside a benign file. It has been shown that embedded malware is not detected by commercial antivirus software even when the malware signature is present in the antivirus database. In this paper, we present a novel anomaly detection scheme to detect embedded malware. We first analyze byte sequences in benign files to show that benign files' data generally exhibit a 1-st order dependence structure. Consequently, conditional n-grams provide a more meaningful representation of a file's statistical properties than traditional n-grams. To capture and leverage this correlation structure for embedded malware detection, we model the conditional distributions as *Markov n-grams*. For embedded malware detection, we use an information-theoretic measure, called entropy rate, to quantify changes in Markov n-gram distributions observed in a file. We show that the entropy rate of Markov n-grams gets significantly perturbed at malcode embedding locations, and therefore can act as a robust feature for embedded malware detection. We evaluate the proposed Markov n-gram detector on a comprehensive malware dataset consisting of more than $37,000$ malware samples and $1,800$ benign samples of six well-known filetypes. We show that the Markov n-gram detector provides better detection and false positive rates than the only existing embedded malware detection scheme.

1 Introduction

Malware sophistication has evolved considerably during the last decade. In particular, due to emerging financial motivations for attackers, malware trends are now shifting towards stealthy attacks. The challenge faced by stealthy malcode is to reach vulnerable hosts undetected and then to stay undetected on the hosts. 'The longer a threat remains undiscovered in the wild, the more opportunity it has to compromise computers before measures can be taken to protect against it. Furthermore, its ability to steal information increases the longer it remains

D. Zamboni (Ed.): DIMVA 2008, LNCS 5137, pp. 88–107, 2008.

undetected on a compromised computer' [1]. Code obfuscation, (self-)encryption and polymorphism are commonly-used code transformations that are used by stealthy malware to avoid detection.

In their seminal work, Stolfo et al. discovered a new type of stealthy threat called *embedded malware* [2]. Under this threat, the attacker embeds the malicious code or file inside a benign file on the target host. It was shown that embedded malware cannot be detected by signature-based antivirus detectors even if a malware's exact signature is present in the detector's database [2], [3]. In fact, intelligently infected files can even be opened by their respective application software without providing any observable hint of the infection. Intelligent embedding can be further enhanced to allow automatic execution of embedded malcode when the benign file is opened [3]. Embedded malware is potentially a serious security threat and accurate anomaly detection techniques must be developed to mitigate it.

In this paper, we propose a novel statistical anomaly detection scheme for embedded malware detection. Using correlation analysis, we first show that benign files exhibit a clear 1-st order dependence structure which can be modeled using Markov chains. We therefore propose to characterize the statistical properties of a benign file using conditional n-gram distributions, referred to as *Markov n-grams*, instead of the traditional n-grams. For embedded malware detection, we compute running Markov n-grams over non-overlapping windows in a file. We then use an information-theoretic measure, called *entropy rate*, to quantify perturbations in the Markov n-grams due to embedded malware. The results of our experiments show that the entropy rate of Markov n-grams gets significantly perturbed at malware embedding locations. For automated detection, we observe that the aggregate entropy rate distribution of benign files approaches Gaussianity for large training samples[1]. Therefore, a statistical range of benign entropy rates can be defined using the parameters of the baseline Gaussian distribution. Entropy rate values outside this range can then be classified as malicious.

We compare the proposed Markov n-gram detector with the only known embedded malware detector [2] using two comprehensive and diverse infected datasets. The first dataset is created by randomly embedding malware into benign files. The second dataset is created by randomly embedding naively encrypted malware into benign files. Both datasets are generated from $1,800$ benign samples (including DOC, EXE, JPG, MP3, PDF and ZIP files) and $37,420$ malware samples (containing viruses, worms trojans, spyware, and exploit codes). We show that the Markov n-gram detector consistently outperforms the only existing embedded malware detector [2] in terms of both detection and false positive rates. In comparison to commercial-of-the-shelf (COTS) antivirus (AV) software, our detector provides a significantly higher detection rate at the cost of higher false positive rates. Therefore, we argue that, due to their complementary strengths, very high accuracy can be achieved when the Markov n-gram detector is deployed in conjunction with COTS AV software.

---

[1] This is a direct consequence of the central limit theorem.

Organization of the Paper. The rest of the paper is organized as follows. We present realistic attack scenarios for embedded malware in Section 2. In Section 3, we provide an overview of related research in the field of embedded malware detection. We then discuss in detail the infected datasets created for our research work in Section 4. Section 5 summarizes the results of our pilot experimental studies. In Section 6, we propose our Markov n-gram detector and in Section 7 we compare the detection accuracy of our proposed detector with other relevant techniques and state-of-the-art antivirus products using the infected datasets. In Section 8, we discuss the limitations of the proposed Markov n-gram detector. Finally, we conclude the paper with an outlook to our future work.

2   Attack Scenarios

In this section, we discuss potential real world attack scenarios that can be realized using embedded malware:

- As demonstrated in [3] and independently verified by us, 'intelligently' embedded malware inside benign (document, media or application) files does not affect their integrity as these infected files continue to open by their respective application software. In fact, our experimental studies have shown that even in the case of naive (i.e., completely random) malware embedding, 10% DOC files, 13% EXE files, 90% JPG files, 100% MP3 files, 92% PDF and 95% ZIP continue to open with or without an error message. Moreover, most of the infected files are undetected by COTS AV software. Thus an attacker can embed malware inside common benign files –for instance, a PDF help file or a common executable file like WINWORD.EXE– and the infected file will go unnoticed through the COTS AV software deployed inside the network or on the host. Such infected files can be transported to different hosts using well-known peer-to-peer file sharing software or by making the file freely available for download. Later on, a user can be tricked into starting a trigger program (in the form of a plug-in or a macro) to launch the malicious code. Examples of similar attacks have recently been reported in [3]–[6].
- Disabling macros and plug-ins is not a viable option because there are many useful benign programs (e.g., MathType, Adobe PDF printer, flash player, etc.) that are launched as macros or plug-ins. Also, in [3] the authors show that the 'object oriented dynamic composability of modern document' formats such as DOC, PPT and PDF allows the user to include embedded objects such as video clips, wave sounds or bitmap images inside a document. The embedded objects can be invoked by simply clicking on the object. An attacker can create a fake embedded object which, in addition to some benign looking activity, executes the malcode [3].
- In our pilot studies, we have observed that MP3 song files can serve as very potent carriers of embedded malware; 100% infected MP3 files (with embedded malware) play from start to finish without any error or degradation in

quality[2]. Since most Internet song sharing portals use the MP3 file format, an attacker can use random embedding to infect a benign MP3 file by a malware and then can distribute the infected file via Internet song sharing portals or peer-to-peer file sharing software.

3   Related Work

A significant amount of research effort has recently been focused towards malware detection. To maintain focus, in this section, we describe only those approaches that target embedded malware.

– Stolfo et al. extended their previous work on identification of filetypes using n-gram analysis in [2]. In their earlier analysis, called fileprint analysis, they calculated 1-gram byte distribution of a file and compared it to various models of different file types for eventual identification of the filetype. In the context of malware detection, their work focused on embedded malware detection only in PDF and DOC files. They used 3 different models for representing the benign distributions namely single centroid, multi-centroids and exemplar files as centroids. Mahanalobis distance was calculated between the distributions obtained from these models and the n-gram distribution of a given file. To avoid repetition, details of these techniques will be provided in subsequent sections.

   The authors experimented with 1-gram (byte level) and 2-gram (word level) distributions. They tested their proposed scheme on a dataset comprising 31 benign application executables, 331 benign executables in the System32 folder and 571 viruses. The results of their experiments demonstrated that their scheme was able to detect a considerable proportion of the malicious files. However their approach was not capable of identifying the exact location of the embedded malware in a benign file. Therefore, it is impossible to devise an effective healing strategy for the infected files using their approach.

– In [3], the authors proposed two approaches for embedded malware detection in Microsoft Word documents. The first approach is based on static analysis and the second approach is based on run time dynamic analysis. In the static analysis approach, they used an open source application to decompose Word files into their constituent structures. They used a 5-gram model for benign and malicious documents because it provided reasonable memory and detection accuracy. Based on the 5-gram model for benign and malicious word documents, a "similarity" score was generated for both models for eventual classification. In dynamic analysis approach, they have employed sandbox-based tests to check OS crashes, unexpected changes to the underlying environment, and nonfatal application errors. However, it is acknowledged by the authors that the dynamic analysis approach is not practical to be used as an independent detection scheme.

---

[2] This is due to the frame-based structure of MP3 files. Each frame in the MP3 file format is preceded by a re-sync marker. Corrupt frames (without re-sync markers) are simply bypassed by the media players during playback.

Table 1. Statistics of Benign Files used in this Study

File type	Quantity	Average Size (kilo-bytes)	Minimum Size (kilo-bytes)	Maximum Size (kilo-bytes)
DOC	300	1,015.2	44	7,706
EXE	300	4,095.0	48	15,005
JPG	300	1,097.8	3	1,629
MP3	300	3,384.4	654	6,210
PDF	300	1,513.1	25	20,188
ZIP	300	1,489.6	8	9,860

4   Data

In this section, we first describe the benign and malware datasets used in this paper. We then introduce our tool NERGAL that embeds any given infection at any random location within a benign file. Using this tool, we produce a large embedded malware dataset[3].

4.1   Benign Dataset

The benign dataset for our experiments consists of six different filetypes: DOC, EXE, JPG, MP3, PDF and ZIP. These filetypes encompass a broad spectrum of commonly used files ranging from compressed to redundant and from executables to document files. Each set of benign files contained 300 typical samples of the corresponding filetype, which provide us a total of 1,800 benign files. We ensured the generality of the benign dataset by randomizing the sample sources. More specifically, we queried well known search engines with random keywords to collect these files. In addition, we also collected typical samples on the local network of our virology lab.

Some pertinent statistics of the benign dataset used in this study are tabulated in Table 1. It can be observed from Table 1 that the benign files have diverse sizes varying from 3 KB to 20 MB, with an average file size of approximately 2 MB. We show later in the paper that this diversity in file sizes provides valuable insights into an important aspect of embedded malware detection, that is, whether or not a detector is able to detect the embedded malware in large files where the statistical contents of the malicious code are simply averaged out.

The executable files collected for this study include both compiled and compressed (installation) executables. The ZIP, JPG, and MP3 file formats are inherently compressed so the n-grams on the data portion of these files should provide distributions that are fairly uniform. Evaluation and detection of embedded malware in these uniform distributions is an important issue which was originally raised in [2].

4.2   Malware Dataset

Malware samples, especially recent ones, are not easily available on the Internet. Computer security corporations do have an extensive malware collection, but

---

[3] The complete dataset and the tool, NERGAL, are publicly available at http://www.nexginrc.org

Table 2. Statistics of Malware used in this Study

Major Category	Minor Category	Quantity	Average Size (kilo-bytes)	Minimum Size (bytes)	Maximum Size (kilo-bytes)
Backdoor	Win32	3,444	285.6	56	9,502
Constructor	DOS	178	104.2	62	7,241
Constructor	Win32	172	398.5	371	5,971
Email Flooder	-	148	343.5	1,430	4,262
Email Worm	Win32	935	73.5	148	762
Exploit	-	242	101.1	370	1,912
Flooder	-	154	168.1	486	981
IRC Worm	-	485	34.4	56	1,072
Nuker	-	140	188.1	4,000	680
Trojan	BAT	649	20.2	12	708
Trojan	DOS	971	27.0	4	1,818
Trojan	Win32	983	125.4	12	2,998
Virus	Boot	1,514	32.5	108	1,490
Virus	DOS	16,236	18.7	5	1,860
Virus	MS Office	2,596	53.5	118	4,980
Virus	Win32	991	44.3	175	1,018
Worm	Win32	153	110.5	97	2,733

unfortunately they do not share their malware databases on the Internet. We could only locate 'VX Heavens Virus Collection' [11] database which is available for free download in the public domain. This is a comprehensive database that contains a total of 37,420 malware samples. The sample consists of backdoors, constructors, flooders, nukers, sniffers, droppers, spyware, viruses, worms and trojans etc.

A detailed description of the malware used in our study is provided in Table 2. The average malware size in this dataset is 64.2 KB. Note that this size is significantly larger than the average size (2 MB) of the benign files. Moreover, the sizes of malware samples used in our study vary from 4 bytes to more than 14 MB. Clearly, small sized malware are harder to detect than larger ones.

4.3   Infected Dataset

We developed an inhouse software tool, called NERGAL, that could insert an infection into benign files at any given location in the benign file. NERGAL ensure that the infections are inserted after the header of the benign files to avoid file corruption. The tool also generates a detailed infection report, which provides details about the sample malware that was used to infect each benign sample and its offset in each sample.

We have created two infected datasets for this study. The first infected dataset is created by simple embedding malware inside benign files. The second infected dataset is created by encrypting the malware before embedding. We use the ROT-13 Caesar cipher for malware encryption. While more sophisticated encryption techniques are certainly possible, we use a simple substitution cipher because it does not alter the inherent statistical properties of the malcode. Therefore, while COTS AV software will not be able to detect this naively encrypted malcode, we can intuitively argue that the accuracy of anomaly detection techniques should remain unaffected under this simple encryption. (We show later that this is not the case.)

The complete virus dataset is used for every filetype mentioned in the benign dataset. Therefore, the embedded malware dataset for each filetype consists of $37,420$ files and the total number of files in both infected datasets are $449,040$. The average file size in both datasets is $2,267.5$ KB.

5 Pilot Experimental Studies

In this section, we repeat and extend the pilot experiments of [2] on our infected dataset. Moreover, we evaluate the accuracy of the Mahanalobis distance based detector which was proposed in [2].

In [2], the authors proposed to use n-gram analysis for embedded malware detection. An n-gram of a sequence is a normalized frequency histogram (or the distribution) of n bit symbols in the sequence. Stolfo et al. [2] used 1-Centroid, Multi-Centroids and Exemplar files as centroids for modeling benign and malware files. 1-gram and 2-gram distributions were used for this purpose. Mahanalobis distances of a given (unknown) file from the benign and the malware model were used for classification. We also wanted to compare our proposed scheme with the static detection approach proposed of [3]. However, it was not possible because their approach is specific to Microsoft Word and similar document formats.

Before evaluating the previous work, we highlight that two desirable accuracy objectives of an embedded malware detector are: 1) to detect infected files and 2) to identify the likely location of the embedded infection. We refer to these two objectives as *detection* and *location identification*, respectively. The technique of [3] reported a reasonable detection accuracy when the infection appeared at the start or the end of a file. However, their proposed scheme could not provide location identification.

5.1 Whole File n-Grams for Embedded Malware Detection

One major assumption of the prior study was that the infection appears only at the start or the end of the benign file [2]. Therefore, n-gram analysis was applied only on the truncated files [2]. We argue that this assumption is unrealistic because it is not capable of detecting embedded malware in the middle of the file. In fact, in our experiments we observed that malware embedded at the start of benign files is detected more frequently by COTS AV software than malware embedded in the middle. Therefore, a pragmatic embedded malware detector should look at the statistical contents of an entire file rather than focussing on a specific location[4]. We hence revoke the assumption of file truncation and compute n-grams on whole files.

---

[4] Here we acknowledge the complexity incurred by n-gram analysis of whole files. Nevertheless, we tradeoff complexity for accuracy throughout this paper. In other words, we expect that the proposed detector will be complemented by signature-based detector.

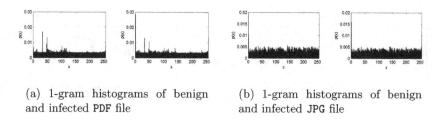

(a) 1-gram histograms of benign and infected PDF file

(b) 1-gram histograms of benign and infected JPG file

Fig. 1. Comparison of 1-gram histograms of benign and infected files

Figures 1(a) and 1(b) show the comparison of whole file 1-grams of sample benign and infected PDF and JPG files, respectively[5]. It can be clearly seen that no discernable change in the 1-grams is evident in Figures 1(a) and 1(b). It can be intuitively argued that whole file 1-grams of infected files do not change when the size of the benign file is significantly larger than the malware size because the statistical contents of the embedded malware are averaged out by large amounts of benign data. (Recall that the average sizes of the benign and malware files in Tables 1 and 2 were 2 MB and 64.2 KB, respectively.) This situation is quite common because malware are generally designed to have small sizes to make them fit inside buffer overflows/file pads/email attachments or to avoid network-based detection during an initial downloading stage.

5.2   Block-Wise n-Grams for Embedded Malware's Location Identification

The authors in [2] carried out n-gram analysis of a file in a block-wise manner in order to detect the exact location of the embedded malware. Experiments were repeated using block sizes of 500 bytes and 1000 bytes. The significance of the block size is that it sets an approximate bound on the minimum size of malware that can be possibly detected. We repeated these block-wise n-gram experiments on our datasets as well. Figure 2 shows some representative results of the Mahanalobis distance between the block-wise 1-gram distribution and the benign file model. We use a block size of 1000 bytes and plot the Mahanalobis distance between every block and the benign file model; qualitatively similar results were obtained for other block sizes. One can see in Figure 2 that the block-wise 1-gram Mahanalobis distance does not provide significant perturbations that could help in detecting the embedded malware. Figure 2(a) shows the best results with a considerable drop in the Mahanalobis distance. However, one can also observe similar or even larger drops in the benign file regions as well.

Another trend to be observed from Figures 2(a) and 2(b) is that the distance value stays more or less constant in the embedded malware blocks. Interestingly, however, even these trends could not be considered as a common feature across

---

[5] Byte value 0 has the highest frequency because of zero padding that is used for block alignment.

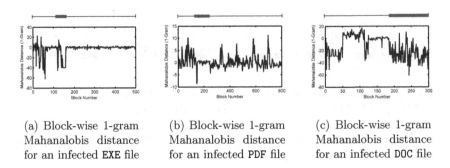

(a) Block-wise 1-gram Mahanalobis distance for an infected **EXE** file

(b) Block-wise 1-gram Mahanalobis distance for an infected **PDF** file

(c) Block-wise 1-gram Mahanalobis distance for an infected **DOC** file

Fig. 2. Block-wise 1-gram Mahanalobis distance is unable to show significant perturbations in the infected regions. The horizontal thick bars show the location of the embedded malware.

all our experiments as depicted in Figure 2(c). Thus, the Mahanalobis distance of 1-gram distribution of the infected files does not provide us with any concrete measure to robustly detect the embedded malware.

As a logical improvement of 1-gram analysis, we repeated our experiments to analyze the behavior of block-wise Mahanalobis distances of 2-gram distributions; block size is 1000 bytes. Figure 3 shows some representative results for the 2-gram block-wise Mahanalobis distance. These experiments reveal that, despite the increased computational complexity, the performance of the Mahanalobis distance based detector does not improve significantly. Figure 3(a) is an exception where the 2-gram clearly shows discernable decrease in the Mahanalobis distance. Here, we can intuitively argue that the block size of 1000 bytes does not provide enough data to compute an effective statistical distribution. Specifically, in case of 2-gram distribution we only have 1000 data values to fill $65,536$ bins. The ratio (data values to distribution bins) of about $1 : 65$ for 2-gram is in stark contrast to the ratio of about $4 : 1$ for 1-gram using the block size of 1000 bytes. A simple solution to this problem is to increase the block size. However, as stated previously, the block size roughly defines the lower bound on the minimum size of malware that can be detected. Therefore, there is an inherent tradeoff between the block size and the minimum malware size that can be detected: increasing the block size means higher false negative rates thereby degrading the accuracy of the detector. This reason stopped us from increasing the value of n and we did not extend our study beyond 2-grams.

5.3 Discussion

The pilot studies of this section indicate that the block-wise Mahanalobis distance of 1- and 2-gram distributions cannot accurately detect embedded malware. At this point, we conjecture that either n-gram analysis is not a good method for embedded malware detection or Mahanalobis distance is not a good enough quantification measure for differentiating between benign and malicious

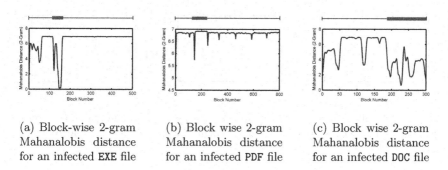

(a) Block-wise 2-gram Mahanalobis distance for an infected **EXE** file

(b) Block wise 2-gram Mahanalobis distance for an infected **PDF** file

(c) Block wise 2-gram Mahanalobis distance for an infected **DOC** file

Fig. 3. Block-wise 2-gram Mahanalobis distance is also unable to show significant perturbations in the infected regions. The horizontal thick bars show the location of the embedded malware.

n-grams. Let us first analyze the latter conjecture which will inadvertently lead us to a substantiation of the former. To quantify changes in the n-gram distributions, we use the *entropy* measure which has been quite effective in quantifying changes in traffic feature distributions [9].

Entropy measures the degree of dispersal or concentration of a distribution [10]. In information-theoretic terms, entropy of a probability distribution defines the minimum average number of bits that a source requires to transmit symbols according to that distribution. Let X be a discrete random variable such that $X = \{x_i, i \in \Delta_n\}$, where Δ_n is the image of the random variable. Then entropy of X is defined as:

$$H(X) = - \sum_{i \in \Delta_n} p(x_i) \log_2 p(x_i). \tag{1}$$

For the present embedded malware detection problem, if the statistical contents of the malware are different from the benign file, then entropy of the block-wise distribution on the infected file should change at the embedding location. We, however, observed that entropy calculation on 2-grams provide qualitatively similar results to the Mahanalobis distance.

The failure of both Mahanalobis distance and entropy measures further strengthens our conjecture that a simple n-gram distribution does not provide sufficient information to detect embedded malware. Consequently, a detector based on simple n-grams meets neither the detection nor the location identification objectives that we set at the beginning of this section. To rectify this shortcoming in the n-gram distributions, in the following we provide a different method of computing n-grams in the following sections.

6   Modeling and Quantification of n-Gram Information

We first note that the 2-gram distribution is in fact the joint distribution of two 1-gram symbols. This joint distribution may contain some redundant information

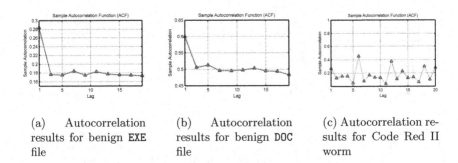

(a)   Autocorrelation results for benign EXE file

(b)   Autocorrelation results for benign DOC file

(c) Autocorrelation results for Code Red II worm

Fig. 4. Autocorrelation function of byte distributions of benign files shows 1-st order dependence. Autocorrelation function of the byte distribution for Code Red II worm shows that the structure of the 1-st order spatial dependence is disturbed.

which is not pertinent to the present embedded malware detection problem. For accurate detection, it is important that this redundancy is removed. To this end, we analyzed a number of statistical properties of the benign files' n-grams. One relevant property that provided us interesting insights into statistical properties of file data was the analysis of byte level autocorrelation of benign files.

6.1   Correlation in File Data

Autocorrelation describes the correlation between the random variables in a stochastic process at different points in time. For a given lag k, the autocorrelation function of a stochastic process, X_i (where i is the time index) is defined as:

$$\rho[k] = \frac{E\{X_0 X_k\} - E\{X_0\}E\{X_k\}}{\sigma_{X_0}\sigma_{X_k}}, \tag{2}$$

where $E\{.\}$ represents the expectation operation and σ_{X_i} is the standard deviation of the random variable at time lag i. The value of the autocorrelation function lies in the range $[-1, 1]$, where $\rho[k] = 1$ means perfect correlation at lag k (which is obviously true for $k = 0$) and $\rho[k] = 0$ means no correlation at all at lag k.

To observe the level of spatial dependence in the byte sequences of benign files, we computed their sample autocorrelation functions. Figures 4(a) and 4(b) show the autocorrelation function plotted versus the lag for EXE and DOC files, respectively. These autocorrelation results clearly show that the byte sequences in benign files have 1-st order dependence because the autocorrelation value takes a fairly significant dip at $k = 2$ and remains constant for higher values of lag. In other words, once a byte S_i appears, it is more likely that it will be followed by S_i at the next byte location. Clearly, if we are in a zero padded region of a benign file, a zero valued symbol is highly likely to be followed by another zero valued symbol.

This 1-st order spatial dependence of benign files has direct implications on the present embedded malware detection problem mainly because this structure is not observed in malware files, see Figure 4(c). In fact, instead of the 1-st order dependence, we can instead observe high correlation at $k = 6, 12$, and 18. This lack of 1-st order spatial dependence of a malware can be easily observed by examining the signature of the Code Red II Worm given below [8]:

```
GET /default.ida?XXXXXXXXXXXXXXXXXXXXXXXXXXXXXXXXXXX
XXXXXXXXXXXXXXXXXXXXXXXXXXXXXXXXXXXXXXXXXXXXXXXXXXXX
XXXXXXXXXXXXXXXXXXXXXXXXXXXXXXXXXXXXXXXXXXXXXXXXXXXX
XXXXXXXXXXXXXXXXXXXXXXXXXXXXXXXXXXXXXXXXXXXXXXXXXXXX
XXXXXXXXXXXXXXXXXXXXXXXXXXXXXXXX%u9090%u6858%ucbd3
%u7801%u9090%u6858%ucbd3%u7801%u9090%u6858%ucbd3%u7801
%u9090%u9090%u8190%u00c3%u0003%u8b00%u531b%u53ff
%u0078%u0000%u00=a HTTP/1.0
```

We can see in the signature of Code Red II that it consists of sub-blocks of 6 bytes, as a result, the high correlation values are observed at $k = 6$ or its integral multiples.

Discussion. In addition to the CodeRed example shown in Figure 4(c), we also conducted correlation experiments on other malware and benign filetypes. These correlation results were consistent with the already presented results. We hence deduce that the 1-st order dependence structure due to zero pads in benign files is not present in malcode. This result is also intuitive because a main objective of effective malcode development is to limit the size of the malcode. (Small sized malware can fit into buffer overflows and can avoid arousing suspicion during transmission over the network.) This objective is clearly defeated if an attacker allows a large zero pads inside the malcode file.

We note that the difference in 1-st order correlation structure of benign and malicious files is actually a distinguishing feature that can be used to detect embedded malware. Therefore, in the following section we model and quantify this distinguishing feature.

6.2 A Statistical Model of Benign Byte Sequences

We now focus on developing a model for the correlation structure observed in benign files. Since the correlation shows 1-st order dependence, the underlying random process (i.e., the byte sequence of benign files in the present context) can be modeled using an order-1, discrete time Markov chain [10]. Here we note that a Markov chain characterizes a process in terms of conditional distribution of its states. For a byte level distribution, a Markov representation simply implies $2^8 = 256$ conditional probability distributions, each corresponding to a different byte value. These conditional distributions reduce the size of the underlying sample space which in the present problem corresponds to removing redundant information from the joint distribution.

The Markov Chain used to model the conditional byte distribution is an order-1 (256 state) Markov chain. The transition probabilities are computed by counting the number of times byte i is followed by byte j. These probabilities can also be expressed as a transition probability matrix. If the probability of moving from state i to j is $p_{i,j}$, then the transition matrix for the present problem is given by:

$$
\mathbf{P} =
\begin{bmatrix}
p_{0,0} & p_{0,1} & \cdots & p_{0,255} \\
p_{1,0} & p_{1,1} & \cdots & p_{1,255} \\
\vdots & \vdots & \ddots & \ddots \\
p_{255,0} & p_{255,1} & \cdots & p_{255,255}
\end{bmatrix}
$$

Each row of this transition probability matrix provides the conditional distribution for a distinct byte value. Thus the total number of variables that characterize this random process ($65, 536$ floating point values) is the same as the 2-gram distribution. However, these Markov chains provide an alternative, non redundant and conditional representation of the jointly distributed 2-gram values. Henceforth, we refer to this representation as *Markov n-grams*.

We now need an accurate measure that can quantify changes in the Markov transition probabilities. This measure is presented in the following section.

6.3   Quantification of Perturbations in Markov n-Grams

We need a mathematical measure to quantify changes or perturbations in the Markov n-gram's transition probability matrix. To this end, we use an information theoretic measure, called *entropy rate*, which quantifies the time density of the average information in a stochastic process [10]. Entropy rate for a sequence of discrete finite random variables $X_1, X_2,..., X_n$ is defined as:

$$
R = \lim_{N \to \infty} \frac{H(X_1, X_2, ..., X_n)}{N}, \tag{3}
$$

where $H(X_1, X_2, \ldots, X_n)$ is the joint entropy of random variables $X_1, X_2, \ldots, X_n$. R does not exist in general. However, for the present n-gram Markov chain with 256 states, the entropy rate can be computed using (1) as:

$$
R = \sum_{i=0}^{255} \pi_i H(X_i), \tag{4}
$$

where π_i represents the equilibrium probability of being in state i and $H(X_i)$ is the entropy of the conditional distribution of state i (i.e., the entropy of row i of the transition probability matrix).

Asymptotic properties of the entropy rate measure are applicable only in case of stationary Markov chains [10]. We acknowledge that in general stationarity will not hold for the present problem. However, the entropy rate expression does provide us with the *expected entropy* of a discrete time Markov chain. Since we rely on the premise that the statistical properties of the embedded malware will be different from the statistical properties of the benign file in which it is embedded, *expected entropy* of the consequent Markov chain (derived from the infected file) should be perturbed at the embedding locations.

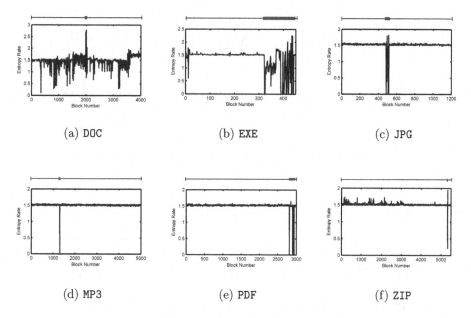

(a) DOC   (b) EXE   (c) JPG

(d) MP3   (e) PDF   (f) ZIP

Fig. 5. Entropy Rate of infected files. The horizontal thick bars show the location of the embedded malware.

Figure 5 shows the entropy rate of infected files of every filetype used in our study. It is clear from Figure 5 that the perturbation is more profound as compared to those obtained using 1-gram Mahanalobis distance or 2-gram Mahanalobis distance. This clearly verifies our earlier hypothesis that the conditional distribution discards the redundant information contained in the joint n gram distribution, thus providing us a compact representation of the file data.

The results of Figure 5 show that the entropy rate of Markov n-grams can quantify and highlight perturbations at the locations of the embedded malware. Thus this measure satisfies the detection and location identification objectives that we have set for an effective embedded malware detector. However, for automated detection, we must threshold entropy rate values above and below which an infection would be detected. The following section provides a flexible yet accurate method of defining this threshold.

6.4 Classification Using Entropy Rate Thresholding

For classification purposes, we need to set an appropriate threshold value on the block-wise entropy rate values. For this purpose, we develop a generic model of block-wise entropy rate values in the benign files. During our pilot studies, we observed that the block-wise values of entropy rates varied in the range of $[0, 3]$. Therefore, we generated an entropy rate histogram using 300 equal sized bins. We normalized this histogram to obtain the *sampled entropy rate distribution*. Figure 6 shows that the sum of sampled entropy rate distributions

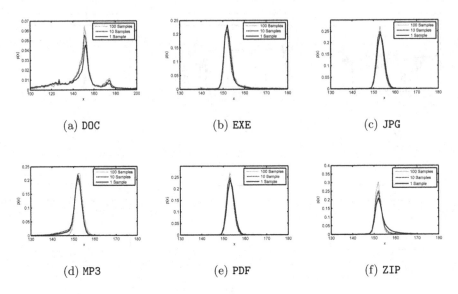

(a) DOC   (b) EXE   (c) JPG

(d) MP3   (e) PDF   (f) ZIP

Fig. 6. Sampled entropy rate distributions for different filetypes

approaches Gaussianity as the number of samples (i.e., the benign files used for training) approaches infinity. This is a consequence of the central limit theorem which asserts that, for independent finite variance entropy rate distributions, an aggregated distribution should be normally distributed.

Normal distribution is completely specified by its first and second central moments: mean (μ) and variance (σ^2). Since 99.99% of the times a normal distribution does not deviate from its mean by more than 5 standard deviations, we can set the upper and lower detection thresholds as: $\eta_{low} = \mu - 5\sigma$ and $\eta_{high} = \mu + 5\sigma$, respectively. Moreover, we integrate the sampled entropy rate distribution of a test file outside these points to obtain area at the fringes of the distribution and set a classification threshold k on this area. If the area outside the $[\eta_{low}, \eta_{high}]$ range is greater than k then the test file is classified as malicious. Conversely, if the area inside the $[\eta_{low}, \eta_{high}]$ range is less than or equal to $(1-k)$ only then an alarm is raised. The value of this threshold was tuned for the best performance in the ROC space using a randomly sampled training dataset which was 5% of the total testing dataset [16]. Suitable values of this threshold were different for different filetypes. The highest value of k was observed for the DOC filetype. An intuitive feel for the high value of k for DOC files can be developed with the help of Figure 6. DOC filetype shows worst convergence to Gaussianity, i.e., significant amount of area is present at the fringes (see Figure 6(a)). This logically leads us to set a relatively higher value of the threshold (k) for DOC files.

Discussion. Based on the results of this section, we conclude that entropy rate of Markov n-grams can achieve both accuracy objectives (i.e., detection and location identification) that we expect from an embedded malware detector. To the best of the authors' knowledge, the location identification objective cannot be achieved by any existing embedded malware detector. Moreover, and again in contrast to existing techniques [2], [3], malware data is *not* required to train our proposed detector. This makes the Markov n-gram detector a true anomaly detector that detects maliciousness by flagging deviations from a robust model of normal behavior. In addition to these desirable properties, the following section shows that the proposed detector provides better accuracy than existing schemes.

7 Classification Results

As mentioned in Section 4, we perform classification on two infected datasets, each consisting of $224,520$ infected files created by infecting benign files of six common types: DOC, EXE, JPG, MP3, PDF, ZIP. For the training of our proposed scheme, we use 5% of the benign dataset.

Table 3 provides the detection rates of 3 fully updated[6] commercial antivirus products: McAfee Antivirus [12], AVG Antivirus [14] and Kaspersky Antivirus [13], and our Markov n-gram detector. The results tabulated in Table 3 reaffirm that: *commercial antivirus products are not effective in detecting embedded malware*. Moreover, and as expectd, the detection rate for all COTS AV software degrade to 0% for the encrypted dataset. The false positive rates for these AV products are also 0% because they mostly use signature-based scanning techniques. Mahanalobis n-gram detector performs much better than COTS AV software. However, its performance also degrades for the encrypted dataset. In comparison, our proposed Markov n-gram detector achieves the best average detection rate with a reasonable average false positive rate. Furthermore, the accuracy of the Markov n-gram detector persists for the encrypted dataset. This is because entropy of a random variable is not dependent on the values or image of the underlying random variable. Therefore, a shift in the histogram does not change the entropy rate values.

The reason for less than 100% detection rate of Markov n-gram detector can be traced back to our earlier comment in Section 5.2: the lower bound on size of detectable embedded malware is roughly set by the block's size. Now recall that we have used a block size of 1000 bytes, while the size of 23.6% files in the VX Heavens malware dataset ([11]) is less than 1000 bytes. Nevertheless, even under this block's size limitation, the smallest malware that the proposed Markov n-gram detector is able to detect is Worm.Win32.Netsp, which is only 343 bytes. We also note that 8.2% of files in the VX Heavens malware dataset are smaller than 343 bytes. These file comprise malware that the proposed detector is unable to detect.

We argue that it is not entirely fair to compare the accuracy of the Markov n-gram detector with the scheme proposed in [2] because their scheme focuses on *detection* while ignoring *location identification*, whereas the detector proposed in this paper caters for both of these objectives. Despite this fact, the accuracy of the Markov n-gram detector is significantly higher than the Mahanalobis

---

[6] By January 2008.

Table 3. Detection (TP) rate and False Positive (FP) rate of Antivirus and Anomaly Detectors

	McAfee Antivirus [12]	AVG Antivirus [14]	Kaspersky Antivirus [13]	Mahanalobis n-gram Detector	Markov n-gram Detector	Percentage Improvement
			unencrypted DOC			
TP rate	0.1%	0.0%	0.0%	65.6%	66.3%	**0.7%**
FP rate	0.0%	0.0%	0.0%	48.8%	29.2%	**19.6%**
			encrypted DOC			
TP rate	0.0%	0.0%	0.0%	57.6%	67.7%	**10.1%**
FP rate	0.0%	0.0%	0.0%	46.2%	31.4%	**14.8%**
			unencrypted EXE			
TP rate	2.7%	1.3%	0.1%	54.1%	84.9%	**30.8%**
FP rate	0.0%	0.0%	0.0%	47.3%	16.7%	**10.6%**
			encrypted EXE			
TP rate	0.0%	0.0%	0.0%	56.1%	84.5%	**28.4%**
FP rate	0.0%	0.0%	0.0%	54.3%	17.2%	**37.1%**
			unencrypted JPG			
TP rate	0.0%	0.0%	0.0%	76.3%	95.4%	**19.1%**
FP rate	0.0%	0.0%	0.0%	35.7%	2.7%	**33.0%**
			encrypted JPG			
TP rate	0.0%	0.0%	0.0%	68.9%	94.6%	**25.7%**
FP rate	0.0%	0.0%	0.0%	46.7%	3.5%	**43.2%**
			unencrypted MP3			
TP rate	0.0%	0.0%	0.0%	63.8%	95.0%	**31.2%**
FP rate	0.0%	0.0%	0.0%	32.3%	0.2%	**32.1%**
			encrypted MP3			
TP rate	0.0%	0.0%	0.0%	58.6%	96.1%	**37.5%**
FP rate	0.0%	0.0%	0.0%	48.3%	0.2%	**48.1%**
			unencrypted PDF			
TP rate	5.2%	2.5%	3.6%	75.4 %	84.5%	**9.1%**
FP rate	0.0%	0.0%	0.0%	46.8%	31.8%	**15.0%**
			encrypted PDF			
TP rate	0.0%	0.0%	0.0%	63.2%	84.8%	**21.6%**
FP rate	0.0%	0.0%	0.0%	45.5%	31.9%	**13.6%**
			unencrypted ZIP			
TP rate	0.0%	0.0%	0.0%	60.0%	90.4%	**30.4%**
FP rate	0.0%	0.0%	0.0%	29.9%	8.3%	**21.6%**
			encrypted ZIP			
TP rate	0.0%	0.0%	0.0%	55.5%	90.6%	**35.1%**
FP rate	0.0%	0.0%	0.0%	28.0%	8.9%	**19.1%**

detector. The bold right column in Table 3 gives the percentage improvement in the TP rate and the FP rate for the Markov n-gram detector as compared to the Mahanalobis n-gram detector. It can be observed that the TP rate of the Markov n-gram detector is on the average 20.2% and 26.4% greater than the TP rate of the Mahanalobis detector for non-encrypted and encrypted datasets, respectively. Similarly, the FP rate of the Markov n-gram detector is on the average 21.9% and 29.3% smaller than the FP rate of Mahanalobis detector for non-encrypted and encrypted datasets, respectively. The clearly indicates the superior detection accuracy and robustness of our proposed detector as compared to the detector proposed by the authors in [2].

We, however, do admit that the FP rates for DOC and PDF files are still significantly high albeit much smaller as compared to the Mahanalobis detector. Our investigation revealed that *embedded objects* are allowed both in PDF and DOC files. The entropy rate at the location of these objects, at times, also shows a significant perturbation. As a result, our detector is mislead to classify these objects as malware. We will shortly introduce our hybrid strategy that will solve this problem of high FP rate.

Another important conclusion of the research by the authors in [2] is: if the size of the benign file in which the infection is inserted is between 10 KB and 10 MB then on the average the false positive rate of their scheme surges to 50%. In comparison, our scheme has two desirable features: 1) capability to identify block/blocks of benign file in which the infection was inserted; 2) a significantly smaller false positive rate relative to the Mahanalobis n-gram detector. Here, we must note that sizes of more than 90% of the benign files in our dataset also lie in the 10 KB to 10 MB range (average size = 2 MB). This encouraging performance clearly substantiates the potential of the Markov n-gram detector for embedded malware detection.

8   Limitations of the Markov n-Gram Detector

In this section, we present the limitations of the Markov n-gram detector proposed in this paper.

- The first, and perhaps the biggest, shortcoming of the proposed Markov n-gram detector is its high false positive rate for certain types of files. We, however, believe that these false positives can be significantly reduced if we use the proposed detector as a preprocessor to the COTS AV detection software. During this preprocessing stage, the Markov n-gram detector can be utilized to detect the presence and the location of embedded malware inside a benign file, albeit with false positives. We can then extract a small portion of the file around the infected location into a separate standalone file. The COTS AV software can then scan the new (extracted) file for the presence of a known malcode signature. Clearly, this hybrid detection strategy will significantly lower the false positives, while still maintaining the high detection rate of our detector. This hybrid detection strategy is only realizable because our detector can identify the location of the embedded malware.
- One form of the embedded malware discussed in this paper is dormant (see Section 2 for more details), which does not pose any direct threat to the victim machine. The dormant form of embedded malware requires another program (such as a trojan) to extract and activate it. As a results, this problem is similar to detecting watermarks or steganographic content. It is unlikely that our scheme will detect a malware embedded using the advanced steganographic embedding schemes. However, the use of advanced steganographic schemes have two major drawbacks when considered in the context of embedded malware: 1) the steganographic embedding and extraction algorithms have high memory and computational overheads; 2) they are media specific, i.e. they are specific for images, audio or video content, so they cannot be generalized to all filetypes. The first drawback implies that the steganographic extraction algorithm should be present on the victim machine. Transfer of extraction program to the victim machine is an additional and undesirable overhead. Also, the computational overhead, at

the victim machine, imposed due to the extraction algorithm allows for host based anomaly detection. The second drawback limits the scope of the threat posed by embedded malware.

– Since the underlying principle of our proposed detector is based on statistical analysis, a crafty attacker may launch a mimicry attack [17] by modifying the malcode to have a benign looking statistical distribution [3]. Polymorphic attack engines can be used to modify the statistical distribution of a code segment to avoid detection by our proposed detector. This unfortunate limitation is not specific to the Markov n-gram detector and is applicable to any anomaly detector, including the Mahanalobis n-gram detector and COTS AV software [17].

9 Conclusions

In this paper, we proposed a novel embedded malware detection scheme based on the principles of statistical anomaly detection. This scheme, to the best of our knowledge, is the first anomaly based malware detection approach that has the capability to locate the position of the infection in an infected file. Our proposed Markov n-gram detector has significantly better detection rate than exiting detectors. Moreover, due to its ability to identify the location of an embedded malware, the proposed detector can provide very low false positive rates when used in conjunction with existing COTS AV software.

Acknowledgments. We acknowledge the help of Syeda Momina Tabish and Ch. Junaid Anwar in result collection and data set generation.

This work is supported by the National ICT R&D Fund, Ministry of Information Technology, Government of Pakistan. The information, data, comments, and views detailed herein may not necessarily reflect the endorsements of views of the National ICT R&D Fund.

References

1. Symantec Internet Security Threat Report XI: Trends for July – December 2007 (September 2007)
2. Stolfo, S.J., Wang, K., Li, W.J.: Towards Stealthy Malware Detection. Advances in Information Security, vol. 27, pp. 231–249. Springer, Heidelberg (2007)
3. Li, W.J., Stolfo, S.J., Stavrou, A., Androulaki, E., Keromytis, A.D.: A Study of Malcode-Bearing Documents. In: Hämmerli, B.M., Sommer, R. (eds.) DIMVA 2007. LNCS, vol. 4579. Springer, Heidelberg (2007)
4. Leyden, J.: Trojan exploits unpatchedWord vulnerability. The Register (May 2006)
5. Evers, J.: Zero-day attacks continue to hit Microsoft. News.com (September 2006)
6. Kierznowski, D.: Backdooring PDF Files (September 2006)
7. Damashek, M.: Gauging Similarity with n-Grams: Language-Independent Categorization of Text. Science 267, 842–848 (1995)
8. Friedl, S.: Steve Friedl's Unixwiz.net Tech Tips: Analysis of the new 'Code Red II' Variant, http://www.unixwiz.net/techtips/CodeRedII.html

9. Lakhina, A., Crovella, M., Diot, C.: Mining anomalies using traffic feature distributions. ACM SIGCOMM (September 2005)
10. Cover, T.M., Thomas, J.A.: Elements of Information Theory. Wiley-Interscience, Chichester (1991)
11. VX Heavens Virus Collection, VX Heavens, http://vx.netlux.org/vl.php
12. McAfee Anti-virus and Internet security, McAfee, CA
13. Kaspersky Antivirus, Kaspersky Lab HQ, Moscow, Russia
14. AVG Anti-Virus and Internet Security, GRISOFT Inc., FL, USA
15. Huang, Y.: Vulnerabilities in Portable Executable (PE) File Format For Win32 Architecture, TR, Exurity Inc., Canada (2006)
16. Fawcett, T.: ROC Graphs: Notes and Practical Considerations for Researchers, TR, HP Labs, CA, USA (2003-2004)
17. Wagner, D., Soto, P.: Mimicry Attacks on Host-Based Intrusion Detection Systems. ACM CCS (November 2002)

Learning and Classification of Malware Behavior

Konrad Rieck[1], Thorsten Holz[2], Carsten Willems[2],
Patrick Düssel[1], and Pavel Laskov[1,3]

[1] Fraunhofer Institute FIRST
Intelligent Data Analysis Department, Berlin, Germany
[2] University of Mannheim
Laboratory for Dependable Distributed Systems, Mannheim, Germany
[3] University of Tübingen
Wilhelm-Schickard-Institute for Computer Science, Tübingen, Germany

Abstract. Malicious software in form of Internet worms, computer viruses, and Trojan horses poses a major threat to the security of networked systems. The diversity and amount of its variants severely undermine the effectiveness of classical signature-based detection. Yet variants of malware families share typical *behavioral patterns* reflecting its origin and purpose. We aim to exploit these shared patterns for classification of malware and propose a method for learning and discrimination of malware behavior. Our method proceeds in three stages: (a) behavior of collected malware is monitored in a sandbox environment, (b) based on a corpus of malware labeled by an anti-virus scanner a *malware behavior classifier* is trained using learning techniques and (c) discriminative features of the behavior models are ranked for explanation of classification decisions. Experiments with different heterogeneous test data collected over several months using honeypots demonstrate the effectiveness of our method, especially in detecting *novel* instances of malware families previously not recognized by commercial anti-virus software.

1 Introduction

Proliferation of malware poses a major threat to modern information technology. According to a recent report by Microsoft [1], every third scan for malware results in a positive detection. Security of modern computer systems thus critically depends on the ability to keep anti-malware products up-to-date and abreast of current malware developments. This has proved to be a daunting task. Malware has evolved into a powerful instrument for illegal commercial activity, and a significant effort is made by its authors to thwart detection by anti-malware products. As a result, new malware variants are discovered at an alarmingly high rate, some malware families featuring tens of thousands of currently known variants.

In order to stay alive in the arms race against malware writers, developers of anti-malware software heavily rely on automatic malware analysis tools. Unfortunately, malware analysis is obstructed by hiding techniques such as polymorphism and obfuscation. These techniques are especially effective against byte-level content analysis [18, 20] and static malware analysis methods [8, 10, 12]. In contrast to static techniques, dynamic analysis of binaries during run-time enables monitoring of malware behavior,

D. Zamboni (Ed.): DIMVA 2008, LNCS 5137, pp. 108–125, 2008.
© Springer-Verlag Berlin Heidelberg 2008

which is more difficult to conceal. Hence, a substantial amount of recent work has focused on development of tools for collecting, monitoring and run-time analysis of malware [3, 5, 6, 15, 23, 24, 26, 28, 37, 39].

Yet the means for collection and run-time analysis of malware by itself is not sufficient to alleviate a threat posed by novel malware. What is needed is the ability to *automatically* infer characteristics from observed malware behavior that are essential for detection and categorization of malware. Such characteristics can be used for signature updates or as an input for adjustment of heuristic rules deployed in malware detection tools. The method for automatic classification of malware behavior proposed in this contribution develops such a characterization of previously unknown malware instances by providing answers to the following questions:

1. *Does an unknown malware instance belong to a known malware family or does it constitute a novel malware strain?*
2. *What behavioral features are discriminative for distinguishing instances of one malware family from those of other families?*

We address these questions by proposing a methodology for *learning* the behavior of malware from labeled samples and constructing models capable of classifying unknown variants of known malware families while rejecting behavior of benign binaries and malware families not considered during learning. The key elements of this approach are the following:

(a) Malware binaries are collected via honeypots and spam-traps, and malware family labels are generated by running an anti-virus tool on each binary. To assess *behavioral patterns* shared by instances of the same malware family, the behavior of each binary is monitored in a sandbox environment and behavior-based analysis reports summarizing operations, such as opening an outgoing IRC connection or stopping a network service, are generated. Technical details on the collection of our malware corpus and the monitoring of malware behavior are provided in Sections 3.1–3.2.

(b) The learning algorithm in our methodology embeds the generated analysis reports in a high-dimensional vector space and learns a *discriminative model* for each malware family, i.e., a function that, being applied to behavioral patterns of an unknown malware instance, predicts whether this instance belongs to a known family or not. Combining decisions of individual discriminative models provides an answer to the first question stated above. The embedding and learning procedures are presented in Sections 3.3– 3.4.

(c) To understand the importance of specific features for classification of malware behavior, we exploit the fact that our learning model is defined by weights of behavioral patterns encountered during the learning phase. By sorting these weights and considering the most prominent patterns, we obtain characteristic features for each malware family. Details of this feature ranking are provided in Section 3.5.

We have evaluated our method on a large corpus of recent malware obtained from honeypots and spam-traps. Our results show that 70% of malware instances not identified by an anti-virus software can be correctly classified by our approach. Although such accuracy may not seem impressive, in practice it means that the proposed method would provide correct detections in two thirds of hard cases *when anti-malware products fail.* We have also performed, as a sanity check, classification of benign executables against known malware families, and observed 100% detection accuracy. This confirms that the features learned from the training corpus are indeed characteristic for malware and not obtained by chance. The manual analysis of most prominent features produced by our discriminative models has produced insights into the relationships between known malware families. Details of experimental evaluation of our method are provided in Section 4.

2   Related Work

Extensive literature exists on static analysis of malicious binaries, e.g. [8, 10, 19, 21]. While static analysis offers a significant improvement in malware detection accuracy compared to traditional pattern matching, its main weakness lies in the difficulty to handle obfuscated and self-modifying code [34]. Moreover, recent work of Moser et al. presents obfuscation techniques that are provably NP-hard for static analysis [25].

Dynamic malware analysis techniques have previously focused on obtaining reliable and accurate information on execution of malicious programs [5, 6, 11, 24, 39, 40]. As it was mentioned in the introduction, the main focus of our work lies in *automatic processing* of information collected from dynamic malware analysis. Two techniques for behavior-based malware analysis using clustering of behavior reports have been recently proposed [4, 22]. Both methods transform reports of observed behavior into sequences and use sequential distances (the normalized compression distance and the edit distance, respectively) to group them into clusters which are believed to correspond to malware families. The main difficulty of clustering methods stems from their unsupervised nature, i.e., the lack of any external information provided to guide analysis of data. Let us illustrate some practical problems of clustering-based approaches.

A major issue for any clustering method is to decide how many clusters are present in the data. As it is pointed out by Bailey et al. [4], there is a trade-off between cluster size and the number of clusters controlled by a parameter called *consistency* which measures a ratio between intra-cluster and inter-cluster variation. A good clustering should exhibit high consistency, i.e., uniform behavior should be observed within clusters and heterogeneous behavior between different clusters. Yet in the case of malware behavior – which is heterogeneous by its nature – this seemingly trivial observation implies that a *large* number of *small* classes is observed if consistency is to be kept high. The results in [4] yield a compelling evidence to this phenomenon: given 100% consistency, a clustering algorithm generated from a total of 3,698 malware samples 403 clusters, of which 206 (51%) contain just one single executable. What a practitioner is looking for, however, is exactly the opposite: a *small* number of *large* clusters in which variants belong to the same family. The only way to attain this effect using consistency is to play with different consistency levels, which (a) defeats the purpose of automatic classification and (b) may still be difficult to attain at a single consistency level.

Another recent approach to dynamic malware analysis is based on mining of malicious behavior reports [9]. Its main idea is to identify differences between malware samples and benign executables, which can be used as specification of malicious behavior (*malspecs*). In contrast to this work, the aim of our approach is discrimination between families of malware instead of discrimination between specific malware instances and benign executables.

3 Methodology

Current malware is characterized by rich and versatile behavior, although large families of malware, such as all variants of the Allaple worm, share common behavioral patterns, e.g., acquiring and locking of particular mutexes on infected systems. We aim to exploit these shared patterns using *machine learning techniques* and propose a method capable of automatically classifying malware families based on their behavior. An outline of our learning approach is given by the following basic steps:

1. *Data acquisition.* A corpus of malware binaries currently spreading in the wild is collected using a variety of techniques, such as honeypots and spam-traps. An antivirus engine is applied to identify known malware instances and to enable learning and subsequent classification of family-specific behavior.
2. *Behavior Monitoring.* Malware binaries are executed and monitored in a sandbox environment. Based on state changes in the environment – in terms of API function calls – a behavior-based analysis report is generated.
3. *Feature Extraction.* Features reflecting behavioral patterns, such as opening a file, locking a mutex, or setting a registry key, are extracted from the analysis reports and used to embed the malware behavior into a high-dimensional vector space.
4. *Learning and Classification.* Machine learning techniques are applied for identifying the shared behavior of each malware family. Finally, a combined classifier for all families is constructed and applied to different testing data.
5. *Explanation.* The discriminative model for each malware family is analyzed using the weight vector expressing the contribution of behavioral patterns. The most prominent patterns yield insights into the classification model and reveal relations between malware families.

In the following sections we discuss these individual steps and corresponding technical background in more detail – providing examples of analysis reports, describing the vectorial representation, and explaining the applied learning algorithms.

3.1 Malware Corpus for Learning

Our malware collection used for learning and subsequent classification of malware behavior comprises more than 10,000 unique samples obtained using different collection techniques. The majority of these samples was gathered via *nepenthes*, a honeypot solution optimized for malware collection [3]. The basic principle of nepenthes is to emulate only the *vulnerable* parts of an exploitable network service: a piece of self-replicating malware spreading in the wild will be tricked into exploiting the emulated vulnerability. By automatically analyzing the received payload, we can then obtain a binary copy

Table 1. Malware families assigned by Avira AntiVir in malware corpus of 10,072 samples. The numbers in brackets indicate occurrences of each malware family in the corpus.

1: Backdoor.VanBot	(91)		8: Worm.Korgo	(244)
2: Trojan.Bancos	(279)		9: Worm.Parite	(1215)
3: Trojan.Banker	(834)		10: Worm.PoeBot	(140)
4: Worm.Allaple	(1500)		11: Worm.RBot	(1399)
5: Worm.Doomber	(426)		12: Worm.Sality	(661)
6: Worm.Gobot	(777)		13: Worm.SdBot	(777)
7: Worm.IRCBot	(229)		14: Worm.Virut	(1500)

of the malware itself. This leads to an effective solution for collecting self-propagating malware such as a wide variety of worms and bots. Additionally, our data corpus contains malware samples collected via *spam-traps*. We closely monitor several mailboxes and catch malware propagating via malicious e-mails, e.g., via links embedded in message bodies or attachments of e-mails. With the help of spam-traps, we are able to obtain malware such as Trojan horses and network backdoors.

The capturing procedure based on honeypots and spam-traps ensures that all samples in the corpus are *malicious*, as they were either collected while exploiting a vulnerability in a network service or contained in malicious e-mail content. Moreover, the resulting learning corpus is *current*, as all malware binaries were collected within 5 months (starting from May 2007) and reflect malware families actively spreading in the wild. In the current prototype, we focus on samples collected via honeypots and spam-traps. However, our general methodology on malware classification can be easily extended to include further malware classes, such as rootkits and other forms of non-self-propagating malware, by supplying the corpus with additional collection sources.

After collecting malware samples, we applied the anti-virus (AV) engine *Avira AntiVir* [2] to partition the corpus into common families of malware, such as variants of RBot, SDBot and Gobot. We chose Avira AntiVir as it had one of the best detection rates of 29 products in a recent AV-Test and detected 99.29% of 874,822 unique malware samples [36]. We selected the 14 malware families obtained from the most common labels assigned by Avira AntiVir on our malware corpus. These families listed in Table 1 represent a broad range of malware classes such as Trojan horses, Internet worms and bots. Note that binaries not identified by Avira AntiVir are excluded from the malware corpus. Furthermore, the contribution of each family is restricted to a maximum of 1,500 samples resulting in 10,072 unique binaries of 14 families.

Using an AV engine for labeling malware families introduces a problem: AV labels are generated by human analysts and are prone to errors. However, the learning method employed in our approach (Section 3.4) is well-known for its generalization ability in presence of classification noise [35]. Moreover, our methodology is not bound to a particular AV engine and our setup can easily be adapted to other AV engines and labels or a combination thereof.

3.2 Monitoring Malware Behavior

The behavior of malware samples in our corpus is monitored using *CWSandbox* – an analysis software generating reports of observed program operations [39]. The samples are executed for a limited time in a native Windows environment and their behavior is logged during run-time. CWSandbox implements this monitoring by using a technique called *API hooking* [14]. Based on the run-time observations, a detailed report is generated comprising, among others, the following information for each analyzed binary:

- Changes to the file system, e.g., creation, modification or deletion of files.
- Changes to the Windows registry, e.g., creation or modification of registry keys.
- Infection of running processes, e.g., to insert malicious code into other processes.
- Creation and acquiring of mutexes, e.g. for exclusive access to system resources.
- Network activity and transfer, e.g., outbound IRC connections or ping scans.
- Starting and stopping of Windows services, e.g., to stop common AV software.

Figure 1 provides examples of observed operations contained in analysis reports, e.g., copying of a file to another location or setting a registry key to a particular value. Note, that the tool provides a high-level summary of the observed events and often more than one related API call is aggregated into a single operation.

```
copy_file (filetype="File" srcfile="c:\1ae8b19ecea1b65705595b245f2971ee.exe",
   dstfile="C:\WINDOWS\system32\urdvxc.exe", flags="SECURITY_ANONYMOUS")

set_value (key="HKEY_CLASSES_ROOT\CLSID\{3534943...2312F5C0&}",
   data="lsslwhxtettntbkr")

create_process (commandline="C:\WINDOWS\system32\urdvxc.exe /start",
   targetpid="1396", showwindow="SW_HIDE", apifunction="CreateProcessA")

create_mutex (name="GhostBOT0.58b", owned="1")

connection (transportprotocol="TCP", remoteaddr="XXX.XXX.XXX.XXX",
   remoteport="27555", protocol="IRC", connectionestablished="1", socket="1780")

irc_data (username="XP-2398", hostname="XP-2398", servername="0",
   realname="ADMINISTRATOR", password="r0flc0mz", nick="[P33-DEU-51371]")
```

Fig. 1. Examples of operations as reported by CWSandbox during run-time analysis of different malware binaries. The IP address in the fifth example is sanitized.

3.3   Feature Extraction and Embedding

The analysis reports provide detailed information about malware behavior, yet raw reports are not suitable for application of learning techniques as these usually operate on vectorial data. To address this issue we derive a generic technique for mapping analysis reports to a high-dimensional feature space.

Our approach builds on the *vector space model* and *bag-of-words model*; two similar techniques previously used in the domains of information retrieval [30] and text processing [16, 17]. A document – in our case an analysis report – is characterized by frequencies of contained strings. We refer to the set of considered strings as feature set $\mathcal{F}$ and denote the set of all possible reports by $\mathcal{X}$. Given a string $s \in \mathcal{F}$ and a report $x \in \mathcal{X}$, we determine the number of occurrences of s in x and obtain the frequency $f(x, s)$. The frequency of a string s acts as a measure of its importance in x, e.g., $f(x, s) = 0$ corresponds to no importance of s, while $f(x, s) > 0.5$ indicates dominance of s in x.

We derive an embedding function ϕ which maps analysis reports to an $|\mathcal{F}|$-dimensional vector space by considering the frequencies of all strings in $\mathcal{F}$:

$$\phi : \mathcal{X} \rightarrow \mathbb{R}^{|\mathcal{F}|}, \quad \phi(x) \mapsto (f(x, s))_{s \in \mathcal{F}}$$

For example, if $\mathcal{F}$ contains the strings `copy_file` and `create_mutex`, two dimensions in the resulting vector space correspond to the frequencies of these strings in analysis reports. Computation of these high-dimensional vectors seems infeasible at a first glance, as $\mathcal{F}$ may contain arbitrary many strings, yet there exist efficient algorithms that exploit the sparsity of this vector representation to achieve linear run-time complexity in the number of input bytes [29, 32].

In contrast to textual documents we can not define a feature set $\mathcal{F}$ a priori, simply because not all important strings present in reports are known in advance. Instead, we define $\mathcal{F}$ *implicitly* by deriving string features from the observed malware operations. Each monitored operation can be represented by a string containing its name and a list of key-value pairs, e.g., a simplified string s for copying a file is given by

"`copy_file (srcfile=A, dstfile=B)`"

Such representation yields a very specific feature set $\mathcal{F}$, so that slightly deviating behavior is reflected in different strings and vector space dimensions. Behavioral patterns of malware, however, often express variability induced by obfuscation techniques, e.g., the destination for copying a file might be a random file name. To address this problem, we represent each operation by *multiple strings* of different specificity. For each operation we obtain these strings by defining subsets of key-value pairs ranging from the full to a coarse representation. E.g. the previous example for copying a file is associated with three strings in the feature set $\mathcal{F}$

$$\text{``copy\_file } \dots\text{''} \quad \longrightarrow \quad \begin{cases} \text{``copy\_file\_1 (srcfile=A, dstfile=B)''} \\ \text{``copy\_file\_2 (srcfile=A)''} \\ \text{``copy\_file\_3 ()''} \end{cases}$$

The resulting implicit feature set $\mathcal{F}$ and the vector space induced by ϕ correspond to various strings of possible operations, values and attributes, thus covering a wide range of potential malware behavior. Note, that the embedding of analysis reports using a feature set $\mathcal{F}$ and function ϕ is generic, so that it can be easily adapted to different report formats of malware analysis software.

3.4 Learning and Classification

The embedding function ϕ introduced in the previous section maps analysis reports into a vector space in which various learning algorithms can be applied. We use the well-established method of *Support Vector Machines* (SVM), which provides strong generalization even in presence of noise in features and labels. Given data of two classes an SVM determines an *optimal hyperplane* that separates points from both classes with maximal margin [e.g. 7, 31, 35].

The optimal hyperplane is represented by a vector w and a scalar b such that the inner product of w with vectors $\phi(x_i)$ of the two classes are separated by an interval between -1 and $+1$ subject to b:

$$\langle w, \phi(x_i) \rangle + b \geq +1, \text{ for } x_i \text{ in class 1},$$
$$\langle w, \phi(x_i) \rangle + b \leq -1, \text{ for } x_i \text{ in class 2}.$$

The optimization problem to be solved for finding w and b can be solely formulated in terms of inner products $\langle \phi(x_i), \phi(x_j) \rangle$ between data points. In practice these inner products are computed by so called *kernel functions*, which lead to non-linear classification surfaces. For example, the kernel function k for polynomials of degree d used in our experiments is given by

$$k(x_i, x_j) = (\langle \phi(x_i), \phi(x_j) \rangle + 1)^d.$$

Once trained, an SVM classifies a new report x by computing its distance $h(x)$ from the separating hyperplane as

$$h(x) = \langle w, \phi(x) \rangle + b = \sum_{i=1}^{n} \alpha_i y_i k(x_i, x) + b,$$

where α_i are parameters obtained during training and y_i labels ($+1$ or -1) of training data points. The distance $h(x)$ can then be used for multi-class classification among malware families in one of the following ways:

1. *Maximum distance.* A label is assigned to a new behavior report by choosing the classifier with the highest positive score, reflecting the distance to the most discriminative hyperplane.
2. *Maximum probability estimate.* Additional calibration of the outputs of SVM classifiers allows to interpret them as probability estimates. Under some mild probabilistic assumptions, the conditional posterior probability of the class $+1$ can be expressed as:

$$P(y = +1 \mid h(x)) = \frac{1}{1 + \exp(Ah(x) + B)},$$

where the parameters A and B are estimated by a logistic regression fit on an independent training data set [27]. Using these probability estimates, we choose the malware family with the highest estimate as our classification result.

In the following experiments we will use the maximum distance approach for combining the output of individual SVM classifiers. The probabilistic approach is applicable to prediction as well as detection of novel malware behavior and will be considered in Section 4.3.

3.5 Explanation of Classification

A security practitioner is not only interested in how accurate a learning system performs, but also needs to understand how such performance is achieved – a requirement not satisfied by many "black-box" applications of machine learning. In this section we supplement our proposed methodology and provide a procedure for explaining classification results obtained using our method.

The discriminative model for classification of a malware family is the hyperplane w in the vector space $\mathbb{R}^{|\mathcal{F}|}$ learned by an SVM. As the underlying feature set $\mathcal{F}$ corresponds to strings $s_i \in \mathcal{F}$ reflecting observed malware operations, each dimension w_i of w expresses the contribution of an operation to the decision function h. Dimensions w_i with high values indicate strong discriminative influence, while dimensions with low values express few impact on the decision function. By sorting the components w_i of w one obtains a *feature ranking*, such that $w_i > w_j$ implies higher relevance of s_i over s_j. The most prominent strings associated with the highest components of w can be used to gain insights into the trained decision function and represent typical behavioral patterns of the corresponding malware family.

Please note that an explicit representation of w is required for computing a feature ranking, so that in the following we provide explanations of learned models only for polynomial kernel functions of degree 1.

4   Experiments

We now proceed to evaluate the performance and effectiveness of our methodology in different setups. For all experiments we pursue the following experimental procedure: The malware corpus of 10,072 samples introduced in Section 3.1 is randomly split into three partitions, a *training*, *validation* and *testing* partition. For each partition behavior-based reports are generated and transformed into a vectorial representation as discussed in Section 3. The training partition is used to learn individual SVM classifiers for each of the 14 malware families using different parameters for regularization and kernel functions. The best classifier for each malware family is then selected using the classification accuracy obtained on the validation partition. Finally, the overall performance is measured using the combined classifier on the testing partition.

This procedure, including randomly partitioning the malware corpus, is repeated over five experimental runs and corresponding results are averaged. For experiments involving data not contained in the malware corpus (Section 4.2 and 4.3), the testing partition is replaced with malware binaries from a different source. The machine learning toolbox *Shogun* [33] has been chosen as an implementation of the SVM. The toolbox has been designed for large-scale experiments and enables learning and classification of 1,700 samples per minute and malware family.

4.1   Classification of Malware Behavior

In the first experiment we examine the general classification performance of our malware behavior classifier. Testing data is taken from the malware corpus introduced in Section 3.1. In Figure 2 the per-family accuracy and a confusion matrix for this experiment is shown. The plot in Figure 2 (a) depicts the percentage of correctly assigned labels for each of the 14 selected malware families. Error bars indicate the variance measured during the experimental runs. The matrix in Figure 2 (b) illustrates confusions

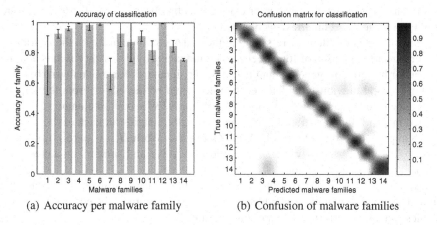

(a) Accuracy per malware family   (b) Confusion of malware families

Fig. 2. Performance of malware behavior classifier using operation features on testing partition of malware corpus. Results are averaged over five experimental runs.

made by the malware behavior classifier. The density of each cell gives the percentage of a true malware family assigned to a predicted family by the classifier. The matrix diagonal corresponds to correct classification assignments.

On average 88% of the provided testing binaries are correctly assigned to malware families. In particular, the malware families Worm.Allaple (4), Worm.Doomber (5), Worm.Gobot (6) and Worm.Sality (12) are identified almost perfectly. The precise classification of Worm.Allaple demonstrates the potential of our methodology, as this type of malware is hard to detect using static methods: Allaple is polymorphically encrypted, i.e., every copy of the worm is different from each other. This means that static analysis can only rely on small parts of the malware samples, e.g., try to detect the decryptor. However, when the binary is started, it goes through the polymorphic decryptor, unpacks itself, and then proceeds to the static part of the code, which we observe with our methodology. All samples express a set of shared behavioral patterns sufficient for classification using our behavior-based learning approach.

The accuracy for Backdoor.VanBot (1) and Worm.IRCBot (7) reaches around 60% and expresses larger variance – an indication for a generic AV label characterizing multiple malware strains. In fact, the samples of Worm.IRCBot (7) in our corpus comprise over 80 different mutex names, such as `SyMMeC`, `itcrew` or `h1dd3n`, giving evidence of the heterogeneous labeling.

4.2   Prediction of Malware Families

In order to evaluate how good we can even *predict* malware families which are not detected by anti-virus products, we extended our first experiment. As outlined in Section 3.1, our malware corpus is generated by collecting malware samples with the help of honeypots and spam-traps. The anti-virus engine Avira AntiVir, used to assign labels to the 10,072 binaries in our malware corpus, failed to identify additional 8,082 collected malware binaries. At this point, however, we can not immediately assess the performance of our malware behavior classifier as the *ground truth*, the true malware families of these 8,082 binaries, is unknown.

We resolve this problem by re-scanning the undetected binaries with the Avira An-tiVir engine after a period of four weeks. The rationale behind this approach is that the AV vendor had time to generate and add missing signatures for the malware binaries and thus several previously undetected samples could be identified. From the total of 8,082 undetected binaries, we now obtain labels for 3,139 samples belonging to the 14 selected malware families. Table 2 lists the number of binaries for each of the 14 fam-ilies. Samples for Worm.Doomber, Worm.Gobot and Worm.Sality were not present, probably because these malware families did not evolve and current signatures were sufficient for accurate detection.

Based on the experimental procedure used in the first experiment, we replace the original testing data with the embedded behavior-based reports of the new 3,139 labeled samples and again perform five experimental runs.

Figure 3 provides the per-family accuracy and the confusion matrix achieved on the 3,139 malware samples. The overall result of this experiment is twofold. On aver-age, 69% of the malware behavior is classified correctly. Some malware, most notably Worm.Allaple (4), is detected with high accuracy, while on the other hand malware

Table 2. Undetected malware families of 3,139 samples, labeled by Avira AntiVir four weeks after learning phase. Numbers in brackets indicate occurrences of each Malware family.

1: Backdoor.VanBot (169)	8: Worm.Korgo (4)
2: Trojan.Bancos (208)	9: Worm.Parite (19)
3: Trojan.Banker (185)	10: Worm.PoeBot (188)
4: Worm.Allaple (614)	11: Worm.RBot (904)
5: Worm.Doomber (0)	12: Worm.Sality (0)
6: Worm.Gobot (0)	13: Worm.SdBot (597)
7: Worm.IRCBot (107)	14: Worm.Virut (144)

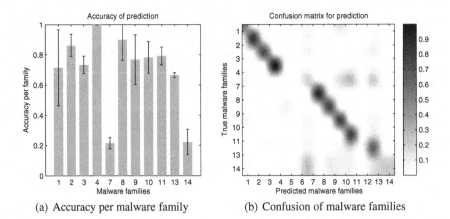

(a) Accuracy per malware family   (b) Confusion of malware families

Fig. 3. Performance of malware behavior classifier on undetected data using operation features. Malware families 5, 6 and 12 are not present in the testing data.

families such as Worm.IRCBot (7) and Worm.Virut (14) are poorly recognized. Still, the performance of our malware behavior classifier is promising, provided that during the learning phase *none* of these malware samples was detected by the Avira AntiVir engine. Moreover, the fact that AV signatures present during learning did not suffice for detecting these binaries might also indicate truly novel behavior of malware, which is impossible to predict using behavioral patterns contained in our malware corpus.

4.3   Identification of Unknown Behavior

In the previous experiments we considered the performance of our malware behavior classifier on 14 fixed malware families. In a general setting, however, a classifier might also be exposed to malware binaries that do *not* belong to one of these 14 families. Even if the majority of current malware families would be included in a large learning system, future malware families could express activity not matching any patterns of previously monitored behavior. Moreover, a malware behavior classifier might also be exposed to benign binaries either by accident or in terms of a denial-of-service attack. Hence, it is crucial for such a classifier to not only identify particular malware families with high accuracy, but also to verify the confidence of its decision and report unknown behavior.

We extend our behavior classifier to identify and reject *unknown behavior* by changing the way individual SVM classifiers are combined. Instead of using the maximum distance to determine the current family, we consider probability estimates for each family as discussed in Section 3.4. Given a malware sample, we now require *exactly one* SVM classifier to yield a probability estimate larger 50% and *reject* all other cases as unknown behavior.

For evaluation of this extended behavior classifier we consider additional malware families not part of our malware corpus and benign binaries randomly chosen from several desktop workstations running Windows XP SP2. Table 3 provides an overview of the additional malware families. We perform three experiments: first, we repeat the experiment of Section 4.1 with the extended classifier capable of rejecting unknown behavior, second we consider 530 samples of the unknown malware families given in Table 3 and third we provide 498 benign binaries to the extended classifier.

Figure 4 shows results of the first two experiments averaged over five individual runs. The confusion matrices in both sub-figures are extended by a column labeled u which contains the percentage of predicted unknown behavior. Figure 4 (a) depicts the confusion matrix for the extended behavior classifier on testing data used in Section 4.1. In comparison to Section 4.1 the overall accuracy decreases from 88% to 76%,

Table 3. Malware families of 530 samples not contained in malware learning corpus. The numbers in brackets indicate occurrences of each malware family.

a: Worm.Spybot	(63)	f: Trojan.Proxy.Cimuz	(73)
b: Worm.Sasser	(23)	g: Backdoor.Zapchast	(25)
c: Worm.Padobot	(62)	h: Backdoor.Prorat	(77)
d: Worm.Bagle	(20)	i: Backdoor.Hupigon	(96)
e: Trojan.Proxy.Horst	(29)		

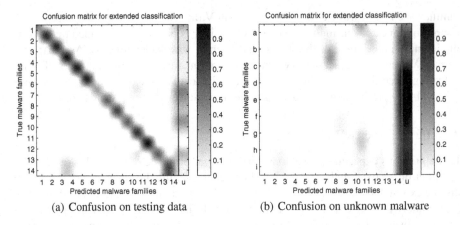

(a) Confusion on testing data   (b) Confusion on unknown malware

Fig. 4. Performance of extended behavior classifier on (a) original testing data and (b) malware families not contained in learning corpus. The column labeled "u" corresponds to malware binaries classified as *unknown behavior*.

as some malware behavior is classified as unknown, e.g., for the generic AV labels of Worm.IRCBot (7). Yet this increase in false-positives coincides with decreasing confusions among malware families, so that the confusion matrix in Figure 4 (a) yields fewer off-diagonal elements in comparison to Figure 2 (b). Hence, the result of using a probabilistic combination of SVM classifiers is twofold: on the one hand behavior of some malware samples is indicated as unknown, while on the other hand the amount of confusions is reduced leading to classification results supported by strong confidence.

Figure 4 (b) now provides the confusion matrix for the unknown malware families given in Table 3. For several of these families no confusion occurs at all, e.g., for Worm.Bagle (d), Trojan.Proxy.Horst (e) and Trojan.Proxy.Cimuz (f). The malware behavior classifier precisely recognizes that these binaries do not belong to one of the 14 malware families used in our previous experiments. The other tested unknown malware families show little confusion with one of the learned families, yet the majority of these confusions can be explained and emphasizes the capability of our methodology to not discriminate AV labels of malware but its behavior.

- Worm.Spybot (a) is similar to other IRC-bots in that it uses IRC as command infrastructure. Moreover, it exploits vulnerabilities in network services and creates auto-start keys to enable automatic start-up after system reboot. This behavior leads to confusion with Worm.IRCBot (7) and Worm.RBot (11), which behave in exactly the same way.
- Worm.Padobot (c) is a synonym for Worm.Korgo (8): several AV engines name this malware family Worm.Padobot, whereas others denote it by Worm.Korgo. The corresponding confusion in Figure 4 (b) thus results from the ability of our learning method to generalize beyond the restricted set of provided labels.
- Backdoor.Zapchast (g) is a network backdoor controlled via IRC. Some binaries contained in variants of this malware are infected with Worm.Parite (9). This coupling of two different malware families, whether intentional by the malware author or accidental, is precisely reflected in a small amount of confusion shown in Figure 4 (b).

```
0.0142: create_file_2 (srcpath="C:\windows\...")
0.0073: create_file_1 (srcpath="C:\windows\...", srcfile="vcmgcd32.dl_")
0.0068: delete_file_2 (srcpath="C:\windows\...")
0.0051: create_mutex_1 (name="kuku_joker_v3.09")
0.0035: enum_processes_1 (apifunction="Process32First")
```

Fig. 5. Discriminative operation features extracted from the SVM classifier of the the malware family *Sality*. The numbers to the left are the sorted components of the hyperplane vector w.

In the third experiment focusing on benign binaries, all reports of benign behavior are correctly assigned to the unknown class and rejected by the extended classifier. This result shows that the proposed learning method captures typical behavioral patterns of malware, which leads to few confusions with other malware families but enables accurate discrimination of normal program behavior if provided as input to a classifier.

4.4 Explaining Malware Behavior Classification

The experiments in the previous sections demonstrate the ability of machine learning techniques to effectively discriminate malware behavior. In this section we examine the discriminative models learned by the SVM classifiers and show that relations of malware beyond the provided AV labels can be deduced from the learned classifiers. For each of the 14 considered malware families we learn an SVM classifier, such that there exist 14 hyperplanes separating the behavior of one malware family from all others. We present the learned decision functions for the Sality and Doomber classifiers as outlined in Section 3.5 by considering the most prominent patterns in their weight vectors.

Sality Classifier. Figure 5 depicts the top five discriminating operation features for the family Worm.Sality learned by our classifier. Based on this example, we see that operation features can be used by a human analyst to understand the actual behavior of the malware family, e.g., the first two features show that Sality creates a file within the Windows system directory. Since both variants created during the preprocessing step (see Section 3.3 for details) are included, this indicates that Sality commonly uses the source filename vcmgcd32.dl_. Moreover, this malware family also deletes at least one file within the Windows system directory. Furthermore, this family creates a mutex containing the string kuku_joker (e.g., kuku_joker_v3.09 as shown in Figure 5 and kuku_joker_v3.04 as sixth most significant feature) such that only one instance of the binary is executed at a time. Last, Sality commonly enumerates the running processes.

Based on these operation features, we get an overview of what specific behavior is characteristic for a given malware family; we can *understand* what the behavioral patterns for one family are and how a learned classifier operates.

Doomber Classifier. In Figure 6, we depict the top five discriminating operation features for Worm.Doomber. Different features are significant for Doomber compared to Sality: the three most significant components for this family are similar mutex names, indicating different versions contained in our malware corpus. Furthermore, we can see that Doomber enumerates the running processes and queries certain registry keys.

```
0.0084: create_mutex_1 (name="GhostBOT0.58c")
0.0073: create_mutex_1 (name="GhostBOT0.58b")
0.0052: create_mutex_1 (name="GhostBOT0.58a")
0.0014: enum_processes_1 (apifunction="Process32First")
0.0011: query_value_2 (key="HKEY_LOCAL...\run", subkey_or_value="GUARD")
```

Fig. 6. Discriminative operation features extracted from the SVM classifier of the the malware family *Doomber*. The numbers to the left are the sorted components of the hyperplane vector w.

In addition, we make another interesting observation: our learning-based system identified the mutex names GhostBOT-0.57a, GhostBOT-0.57 and GhostBOT to be among the top five operation features for Worm.Gobot. The increased version number reveals that Gobot and Doomber are closely related. Furthermore, our system identified several characteristic, additional features contained in reports from both malware families, e.g., registry keys accessed and modified by both of them. We manually verified that both families are closely related and that Doomber is indeed an enhanced version of Gobot. This illustrates that our system may also help to identify *relations* between different malware families based on observed run-time behavior.

5 Limitations

In this section, we examine the limitations of our learning and classification methodology. In particular, we discuss the drawbacks of our analysis setup and examine evasion techniques that could be used by an attacker.

One drawback of our current approach is that we rely on one single program execution of a malware binary: we start the binary within the sandbox environment and observe one execution path of the sample, which is stopped either if a timeout is reached or if the malware exits from the run by itself. We thus do not get a full overview of what the binary intends to do, e.g., we could miss certain actions that are only executed on a particular date. However, this deficit can be addressed using a technique called *multi-path execution*, recently introduced by Moser et al. [24], which essentially tracks input to a running binary and selects a feasible subset of possible execution paths. Moreover, our results indicate that a single program execution often contains enough information for accurate classification of malware behavior, as malware commonly tries to aggressively propagate further or quickly contacts a Command & Control servers.

Another drawback of our methodology is potential evasion by a malware, either by detecting the existence of a sandbox environment or via mimicry of different behavior. However, detecting of the analysis environment is no general limitation of our approach: to mitigate this risk, we can easily substitute our analysis platform with a more resilient platform or even use several different analysis platforms to generate the behavior-based report. Second, a malware binary might try to mimic the behavior of a different malware family or even benign binaries, e.g. using methods proposed in [13, 38]. The considered analysis reports, however, differ from sequential representations such as system call traces in that multiple occurrences of identical activities are discarded. Thus, mimicry attacks can not arbitrarily blend the frequencies or order of operation features, so that only very little activity may be covered in a single mimicry attack.

A further weakness of the proposed supervised classification approach is its inability to find structure in new malware families not present in a training corpus. The presence of unknown malware families can be detected by the rejection mechanism used in our classifiers, yet no further distinction among rejected instances is possible. Whether this is a serious disadvantage in comparison to clustering methods is to be seen in practice.

6   Conclusions

The main contribution of this paper is a learning-based approach to automatic classification of malware behavior. The key ideas of our approach are: (a) the incorporation of labels assigned by anti-virus software to define classes for building discriminative models; (b) the use of string features describing specific behavioral patterns of malware; (c) automatic construction of discriminative models using learning algorithms and (d) identification of explanatory features of learned models by ranking behavioral patterns according to their weights. To apply our method in practice, it suffices to collect a large number of malware samples, analyze its behavior using a sandbox environment, identify typical malware families to be classified by running a standard anti-virus software and construct a malware behavior classifier by learning single-family models using a machine learning toolbox.

As a proof of concept, we have evaluated our method by analyzing a training corpus collected from honeypots and spam-traps. The set of known families consisted of 14 common malware families; 9 additional families were used to test the ability of our method to identify behavior of unknown families. In an experiment with over 3,000 previously *undetected* malware binaries, our system correctly predicted almost 70% of labels assigned by an anti-virus scanner *four weeks later*. Our method also detects unknown behavior, so that malware families not present in the learning corpus are correctly identified as unknown. The analysis of prominent features inferred by our discriminative models has shown interesting similarities between malware families; in particular, we have discovered that Doomber and Gobot worms derive from the same origin, with Doomber being an extension of Gobot.

Despite certain limitations of our current method, such as single-path execution in a sandbox and the use of imperfect labels from an anti-virus software, the proposed learning-based approach offers the possibility for accurate automatic analysis of malware behavior, which should help developers of anti-malware software to keep apace with the rapid evolution of malware.

References

[1] Microsoft Security Intelligence Report (October 2007),
    http://www.microsoft.com/downloads/details.aspx?FamilyID=4EDE2572
    -1D39-46EA-94C6-4851750A2CB0
[2] Avira. AntiVir PersonalEdition Classic (2007),
    http://www.avira.de/en/products/personal.html
[3] Baecher, P., Koetter, M., Holz, T., Dornseif, M., Freiling, F.C.: The Nepenthes Platform: An Efficient Approach to Collect Malware. In: Zamboni, D., Krügel, C. (eds.) RAID 2006. LNCS, vol. 4219, pp. 165–184. Springer, Heidelberg (2006)

[4] Bailey, M., Oberheide, J., Andersen, J., Mao, Z.M., Jahanian, F., Nazario, J.: Automated Classification and Analysis of Internet Malware. In: Kruegel, C., Lippmann, R., Clark, A. (eds.) RAID 2007. LNCS, vol. 4637, pp. 178–197. Springer, Heidelberg (2007)

[5] Bayer, U., Kruegel, C., Kirda, E.: TTAnalyze: A tool for analyzing malware. In: Proceedings of EICAR 2006 (April 2006)

[6] Bayer, U., Moser, A., Kruegel, C., Kirda, E.: Dynamic analysis of malicious code. Journal in Computer Virology 2, 67–77 (2006)

[7] Burges, C.: A tutorial on support vector machines for pattern recognition. Knowledge Discovery and Data Mining 2(2), 121–167 (1998)

[8] Christodorescu, M., Jha, S.: Static analysis of executables to detect malicious patterns. In: Proceedings of the 12th USENIX Security Symposium, p. 12(2003)

[9] Christodorescu, M., Jha, S., Kruegel, C.: Mining specifications of malicious behavior. In: Proceedings of the 6th Joint Meeting of the European Software Engineering Conference and the ACM SIGSOFT Symposium on the Foundations of Software Engineering (ESEC/FSE) (2007)

[10] Christodorescu, M., Jha, S., Seshia, S.A., Song, D.X., Bryant, R.E.: Semantics-aware malware detection. In: IEEE Symposium on Security and Privacy, pp. 32–46 (2005)

[11] Egele, M., Kruegel, C., Kirda, E., Yin, H., Song, D.: Dynamic spyware analysis. In: Proceedings of USENIX Annual Technical Conference (June 2007)

[12] Flake, H.: Structural comparison of executable objects. In: Proceedings of Detection of Intrusions and Malware & Vulnerability Assessment (DIMVA 2004) (2004)

[13] Fogla, P., Sharif, M., Perdisci, R., Kolesnikov, O., Lee, W.: Polymorphic blending attacks. In: Proceedings of the 15th USENIX Security Symposium, pp. 241–256 (2006)

[14] Hunt, G.C., Brubacker, D.: Detours: Binary interception of Win32 functions. In: Proceedings of the 3rd USENIX Windows NT Symposium, pp. 135–143 (1999)

[15] Jiang, X., Xu, D.: Collapsar: A VM-based architecture for network attack detention center. In: Proceedings of the 13th USENIX Security Symposium (2004)

[16] Joachims, T.: Text categorization with support vector machines: Learning with many relevant features. In: Proceedings of the European Conference on Machine Learning, pp. 137–142. Springer, Heidelberg (1998)

[17] Joachims, T.: Learning to Classify Text using Support Vector Machines. Kluwer Academic Publishers, Dordrecht (2002)

[18] Karim, M., Walenstein, A., Lakhotia, A., Laxmi, P.: Malware phylogeny generation using permutations of code. Journal in Computer Virology 1(1–2), 13–23 (2005)

[19] Kirda, E., Kruegel, C., Banks, G., Vigna, G., Kemmerer, R.A.: Behavior-based spyware detection. In: Proceedings of the 15th USENIX Security Symposium, p. 19 (2006)

[20] Kolter, J., Maloof, M.: Learning to detect and classify malicious executables in the wild. Journal of Machine Learning Research 7, 2721–2744 (2006)

[21] Kruegel, C., Robertson, W., Vigna, G.: Detecting kernel-level rootkits through binary analysis. In: Proceedings of the 20th Annual Computer Security Applications Conference (ACSAC) (2004)

[22] Lee, T., Mody, J.J.: Behavioral classification. In: Proceedings of EICAR 2006 (April 2006)

[23] Leita, C., Dacier, M., Massicotte, F.: Automatic Handling of Protocol Dependencies and Reaction to 0-Day Attacks with ScriptGen Based Honeypots. In: Zamboni, D., Krügel, C. (eds.) RAID 2006. LNCS, vol. 4219. Springer, Heidelberg (2006)

[24] Moser, A., Kruegel, C., Kirda, E.: Exploring multiple execution paths for malware analysis. In: Proceedings of 2007 IEEE Symposium on Security and Privacy (2007)

[25] Moser, A., Kruegel, C., Kirda, E.: Limits of static analysis for malware detection. In: Proceedings of the 23rd Annual Computer Security Applications Conference (ACSAC) (to appear, 2007)

[26] Norman. Norman sandbox information center (accessed, 2007),
     http://sandbox.norman.no/
[27] Platt, J.: Probabilistic outputs for Support Vector Machines and comparison to regularized likelihood methods. In: Smola, A., Bartlett, P., Schölkopf, B., Schuurmans, D. (eds.) Advances in Large Margin Classifiers. MIT Press, Cambridge (2001)
[28] Pouget, F., Dacier, M., Pham, V.H.: Leurre.com: on the advantages of deploying a large scale distributed honeypot platform. In: ECCE 2005, E-Crime and Computer Conference, March 29-30, Monaco (March 2005)
[29] Rieck, K., Laskov, P.: Linear-time computation of similarity measures for sequential data. Journal of Machine Learning Research 9, 23–48 (2008)
[30] Salton, G., Wong, A., Yang, C.: A vector space model for automatic indexing. Communications of the ACM 18(11), 613–620 (1975)
[31] Schölkopf, B., Smola, A.: Learning with Kernels. MIT Press, Cambridge (2002)
[32] Shawe-Taylor, J., Cristianini, N.: Kernel Methods for Pattern Analysis. Cambridge University Press, Cambridge (2004)
[33] Sonnenburg, S., Rätsch, G., Schäfer, C., Schölkopf, B.: Large scale multiple kernel learning. Journal of Maching Learning Research 7, 1531–1565 (2006)
[34] Szor, P.: The Art of Computer Virus Research and Defense. Addison-Wesley, Reading (2005)
[35] Vapnik, V.: Statistical Learning Theory. John Wiley & Sons, Chichester (1998)
[36] Virus Bulletin. AVK tops latest AV-Test charts (August 2007),
     http://www.virusbtn.com/news/2007/08 22a.xml
[37] Vrable, M., Ma, J., Chen, J., Moore, D., Vandekieft, E., Snoeren, A.C., Voelker, G.M., Savage, S.: Scalability, fidelity, and containment in the potemkin virtual honeyfarm. SIGOPS Oper. Syst. Rev. 39(5), 148–162 (2005)
[38] Wagner, D., Soto, P.: Mimicry attacks on host based intrusion detection systems. In: Proceedings of the 9th ACM Conference on Computer and Communications Security (CCS 2002), pp. 255–264 (2002)
[39] Willems, C., Holz, T., Freiling, F.: CWSandbox: Towards automated dynamic binary analysis. IEEE Security and Privacy 5(2) (2007)
[40] Yin, H., Song, D., Egele, M., Kruegel, C., Kirda, E.: Panorama: Capturing system-wide information flow for malware detection and analysis. In: Proceedings of ACM Conference on Computer and Communication Security (October 2007)

On Race Vulnerabilities in Web Applications

Roberto Paleari, Davide Marrone, Danilo Bruschi, and Mattia Monga

Dipartimento di Informatica e Comunicazione,
Università degli Studi di Milano,
Milano, Italy
{roberto,davide,bruschi,monga}@security.dico.unimi.it

Abstract. A web programmer often conceives its application as a sequential entity, thus neglecting the parallel nature of the underlying execution environment. In this environment, multiple instances of the same sequential code can be concurrently executed. From such unexpected parallel execution of intended sequential code, some unforeseen interactions could arise that may alter the original semantic of the application as it was intended by the programmer. Such interactions are usually known as *race conditions*.

In this paper, we discuss the impact of race condition vulnerabilities on web-based applications. In particular, we focus on those race conditions that could arise because of the interaction between a web application and an underlying relational database. We introduce a dynamic detection method that, during our experiments, led to the identification of several race condition vulnerabilities even in mature open-source projects.

1 Introduction

The overwhelming majority of new computer applications are now developed adopting the web paradigm. Communications relies on the HTTP protocol, and the computation is performed via a client-server model, where client and server are respectively represented by a web browser and a web server, appropriately augmented by extension modules which enable the execution of server-side code. The applications which satisfy these requirements are generally called *"web applications"*.

Originally, these applications were implemented using simple mechanisms to create dynamic web pages. One of these technologies is the Common Gateway Interface (CGI) [1], intended to provide web-based access to legacy applications by acting like a gateway between the web server and the underlying legacy application. Today, however, the most popular approach is based on extended web servers, that provide modules that implement frameworks more suitable for the development of web-based applications. Basically, the web server is able to instantiate the virtual machine needed to interpret web application programs, that are typically written in a dynamic-typed scripting language, such as PHP, Perl, Python or Ruby. Typically, web applications rely on a three-tiers architecture (web browser/web server/database manager). A very popular platform is the

D. Zamboni (Ed.): DIMVA 2008, LNCS 5137, pp. 126–142, 2008.

so called LAMP solution stack [2]: a **Linux** machine runs an **A**pache web server which is able to control a **MySQL** database management system through a **PHP** script.

Web applications have been reported to be subject to different kinds of attacks, many of which are specific of the web environment [3]. Such vulnerabilities could lead to the compromise or disclosure of sensitive information. According to a recent analysis [4], more than 60% of the software vulnerabilities annually reported are specific to web applications. This is mostly due to the fact that it is often quite easy to create simple web applications, thus many of them are written by developers with low programming or security skills. Nevertheless, web applications are valuable targets for attackers, because they often interface with a back-end server that handles sensitive information as credit card numbers, e-mail addresses, financial records, etc.

The most recurrent flaws in web-based programs arise from the interaction between the application and the underlying relational database used as a long-term storage medium [5], while others depend on the incorrect handling of trust relations between clients and servers [6]. All these types of vulnerabilities can be ascribed to the lack of proper input validation: some parameters that are under the direct control of a client are not properly validated.

In this paper we will introduce and discuss a new form of vulnerability which affects web applications. Such a vulnerability emerged by observing the behavior of some web applications when forced to be executed concurrently, and it turned out that they suffer the typical race conditions symptoms. Although race conditions are a well understood problem, in this work we will show that the impact of such an issue on web applications is still largely unexplored. More precisely, most of the web applications are made of many different scripts, each performing simple and well-defined tasks, easily described by sequential code. However, it is often neglected that any time a user requires the execution of a server side script, such a script becomes the body of a new thread that is executed in a multi-threaded environment. This could lead to more application scripts instances being concurrently executed. If scripts are conceived as sequential code and if they use some shared resources (e.g., a database), the parallel execution of these multiple instances could provoke races. For example, by exploiting such concurrency problems, in our experiments we have been able to bypass brute forcing protections, exploit SMS gateways, circumvent anti-flooding mechanisms and we managed to submit multiple votes on polls where each user was constrained to vote just one time.

We further deep our analysis in order to identify detection strategies for race conditions in web applications. In particular, we are interested in the detection of those race conditions that could arise because of the interaction between a web-based application and an underlying relational database. The problem of detecting and mitigating race conditions has been extensively discussed in literature, but the literature is entirely focused on applications expressly written as concurrent. The problem we face in this paper is very different as it is related to detecting synchronization problems in sequential code which can be executed concurrently. In other words, the problem is not, as usual, to analyze the correctness of a programmed synchronization policy, but to detect whether the implicit interprocess communication contained in a piece of sequential code could lead to security failures, when multiple instances of the code are executed concurrently.

We can summarize the key contributions of this paper as follows:

- we shed light on the impact of race conditions on web-based applications. Race conditions are a well-known problem, but the effects of those on web-based programs have not been underlined, so far.
- We propose a novel technique for the detection of race conditions that arise from the interactions between a web application and an underlying database. Our proposed method has been implemented in a prototype that led to the detection of several previously unknown vulnerabilities in mature open-source applications.
- We discuss possible countermeasures to hamper exploitation attempts.

This paper is structured as follows. In Section 2 we discuss the implications of race conditions on web-based programs and the impact of this kind of synchronization issues on real-world applications. Section 3 introduces our detection method together with some implementation details and experimental results. Possible countermeasures are analyzed during Section 4, while in Section 5 we discuss related work. Finally, Section 6 briefly concludes our paper.

2   Race Conditions in Web Applications

A *race condition* occurs when different parallel processes access shared data without proper synchronization [7]. Races are difficult to spot because the human mind is not good at extensively analyze the exceedingly high number of interleavings allowed by the operating system scheduler. Thus, concurrency is a typical source of vulnerabilities [8,9,10], and one of the oldest security problems [11]. Here we will show that the same phenomenon occurs in web applications.

Often web applications are conceived as a set of scripts that query and update an underlying database. In these situations, a programmer does not usually care about concurrency issues, and considers his scripts as executed by the web server in a strictly sequential order. So, he typically ignores the intrinsic architecture of the underlying web server, which enables multithreaded executions of code. Moreover, it is often neglected that the underlying DBMS represents a shared resource that can be concurrently accessed by multiple script instances. As we will show, by exploiting these facts, a malicious user could induce an application to behave differently from what the programmer meant.

As an example, consider the PHP script fragment depicted in Figure 1. In this example, the programmer wanted to implement an e-banking money transfer procedure: the user tries to withdraw an **amount** of money; the system checks if the user has that amount on his account (lines 1–4) and, if so, it authorizes the execution of the requested operation (line 5). Finally, the system updates the user's account by withdrawing the aforementioned amount (lines 6–7). Now

```
1   $res = mysql_query("SELECT credit FROM Users WHERE id=$id");
2
3   $row = mysql_fetch_assoc($res);
4   if($row['credit'] >= $_POST['amount']) {
5     ⟨execute the requested operation⟩
6     $new_credit = $row['credit'] − $_POST['amount'];
7     $res = mysql_query("UPDATE Users SET credit=$new_credit WHERE id=$id");
8   }
```

Fig. 1. An example of a vulnerable PHP script fragment

suppose that a script instance P executes the statement at line 3, thus retrieving from the database a tuple t of the Users relation. The procedure in Figure 1 would be prone to races if another script instance could obtain read or write access to t before P fully executes the query at line 7. In fact, it can be easily verified that the parallel execution of multiple instances of this script fragment on the same server could result in a violation of the precondition of line 4.

Some solutions to this classical *test & set* problem may be available, however here the main issue is that *a typical programmer does not conceive his web application as a multi-threaded or multi-process entity.*

In this paper we will focus on the detection of race condition vulnerabilities in PHP applications. However, our results are not language-dependent, and can easily be extended to other platforms, such as Perl, Python, and so on. Moreover, we also limit our analysis to the race conditions that could arise from the interactions between a web application and an underlying DBMS. It is worth noting that race conditions could derive from unmanaged access to any shared resource: a database is only an example of such a resource, even if probably the most common one.

Although not every race condition has necessarily security-relevant consequences, in our experiments we have been able to found a significant number of concurrency issues, so the overall probability of the security relevance of at least *one* of these defects is still significantly high.

We would also stress that the solution to these kind of problems cannot be delegated entirely to the DBMS implementors. Usually, even simple DBMSs do provide proper synchronization features that allow programmers to handle concurrency problems (e.g., locking statements, ACID transactions, ...) and they actually guarantee the atomic execution of each submitted query (or each submitted transaction). However, DBMSs cannot automatically recognize when a sequence of queries should be executed atomically, because this heavily depends on the application's logic. Thus, is up to programmers to properly use database-level synchronization primitives in order to avoid concurrency problems in their applications.

2.1   Case Studies

In order to verify the impact of race condition vulnerabilities on real-world web-based applications, we tried to exploit two remote closed-source commercial systems, having only access to their external interfaces. The first application is managed by an Internet service provider, while the second one belongs to a telecommunication provider. For obvious reasons, the names of the corporates involved will not be disclosed. Both applications are designed to permit users to send SMS messages through a web interface, allowing only a limited number of SMS per user, per day. For both applications, our conjecture was that, when an authenticated user tries to send a message, the application checks his account information from the database. We imagined that the program first sent the message and finally updated the user's account. This behavior is very similar to the bank example reported in Figure 1. Then, we tried to exploit the remote applications. In the first case, we sent 11 parallel SMS requests. The remote service was supposed to accept only 10 requests, but we received 11 SMS messages on our mobile phone. In the second case, we sent 10 parallel requests. The application was supposed to discard all but one request, so we were quite surprised when we received all the 10 SMS messages.

This simple experiment leads us to believe that a consistent number of commercial (and maybe critical) real-world applications are vulnerable to similar attacks.

We have also tested mature open-source applications (e.g., phpBB3 [12] and Joomla! [13]): not even a *single* application from those we analyzed was found to be free from concurrency problems. Even if many of these defects cannot lead to compromise the application's logic, some of them can actually allow a malicious user to violate the security properties of the web-based application. Nevertheless, exploiting race condition-based vulnerabilities requires some knowledge about the application's logic and thus their exploitation is surely more difficult with respect to other categories of web vulnerabilities, such as cross site scripting [6] or SQL injection [5]. Despite these issues, we have been able to alter the original semantics of *every* real-world application we have analyzed during our experiments.

3   Detecting Race Conditions in LAMP-Like Web Applications

In this section, we propose a method based on dynamic analysis for the detection of race conditions in LAMP-like web applications. The idea is to build a system which supports a programmer during the development of a web application, and which is able to automatically locate suspicious query sequences. Such an approach has been implemented in an experimental prototype.

We focused on those race conditions that arise from the interactions between an application and the underlying SQL-enabled relational database. Moreover, we are interested in the detection of those issues that could result from the execution of multiple instances of the *same* web application script. We leave the detection of inter-module race conditions for future work.

Our detection strategy is formed by the following components:

1. a *SQL-query logger*, which monitors a concrete execution of the web application to be analyzed and logs each query that the application submits to the DBMS;
2. an *off-line analyzer*, which examines the log files that have been produced by the SQL-query logger and detects the potential dangerous queries. Such a component is realized by two modules: the first one searches the log files for query interdependencies that could be considered as a symptom of the presence of a race condition; the second module refines the results obtained so far, by removing query pairs that are guaranteed to be race-free.

3.1 SQL-Query Logger

There are many different methods that can be employed in order to log database queries: we could for example intercept them at the DBMS level, or we could modify the module used by the application interpreter to interact with the underlying database; alternatively, we could intercept SQL queries at the application level, by hooking database-related functions. As we discuss in more detail in a following section, our current prototype implements the latter approach. Thus, at runtime, each time the application invokes a database-related function to submit a SQL statement to the DBMS, our logger module intercepts the query string. Then, each query that has been intercepted is recorded into a text file for the subsequent off-line analysis.

3.2 Off-Line Analyzer: Basic Approach

Once database queries have been collected, the resulting log files are examined by our query analyzer. The idea behind our method is to exploit query interdependencies so that likely race conditions can be detected. More precisely, let $q = \{s_1, s_2, \ldots, s_n\}$ be a query, where s_i denotes the schema objects (attributes or relations) referred to by q. We consider a schema object to be *used* by a query when its value is read. An attribute is *defined* by a query when it is altered by the execution of such a statement. Instead, we consider a relation to be *defined* by a query if it modifies the total number of tuples in that relation. As an example, a **DELETE** statement *defines* the relation that appears in its **FROM** clause, while it *uses* every schema object that appears in its **WHERE** clause.

Given a query q, we define *use(q)* and *def(q)* as the sets of schema objects that are respectively used and defined by q. Thus, we can formalize the notion of *interdependence* with the following definition:

Definition 1. *Let (p, q) be a pair of SQL queries. Then, (p, q) are said to be interdependent if $use(p) \cap def(q) \neq \emptyset$.*

Our observation is that interdependent queries could give rise to race conditions. Thus, our detection strategy consists in determining a set containing every pair of interdependent queries.

Input: $Q = \{q_i, i = 1, 2, \ldots, n\}$, a list of SQL queries.
Output: $R = \{(p, q), p \in Q \wedge q \in Q\}$, a list of paired SQL queries that suggest
         possible race conditions.

$R = \emptyset$
for $i = 1, 2, \ldots, n$ **do**
    | $q = Q[i]$
    | $D = def(q)$
    | **for** $j = i - 1, i - 2, \ldots, 1$ **do**
    | | $p = Q[j]$
    | | $U = use(p)$
    | | **if** $D \cap U \neq \emptyset$ **then**
    | | $\lfloor$ $R = R \cup \{(p, q)\}$

Fig. 2. Pseudo-code for a simplified version of the detection algorithm

        SELECT user_id
        FROM Sessions
        WHERE expiry_time $>= 1195745465;$

        DELETE FROM Sessions
        WHERE expiry_time $< 1195745465;$

Fig. 3. An example of two conflicting SQL queries with disjoint **WHERE** clauses

Definition 2. *Let* $Q = \{q_1, q_2, \ldots, q_n\}$ *be a set of SQL queries. We define a total ordering relation* $<$ *on its elements, such that* $\forall q_i, q_j \in Q, q_i < q_j$ *if and only if* $i < j$, *i.e.,* q_i *appears before* q_j *in the query log.*

Definition 3. *The set R of* interdependent query pairs *is defined as:*

$$R = \{(q_i, q_j) \in Q \times Q \mid (q_i < q_j) \wedge (use(q_i) \cap def(q_j) \neq \emptyset)\}.$$

The algorithm reported in Figure 2 formalizes these notions. The algorithm receives as input a list of SQL statements, gathered dynamically by the query logger and outputs a set of interdependent SQL query pairs (p, q). From each of these SQL query pairs, a race condition could arise.

3.3 Off-Line Analyzer: Further Heuristics

Some of the query pairs collected with the approach sketched above may represent false positives. Thus, we developed a further module to remove those pairs that are guaranteed to be race-free. Such a module is based on the following heuristics.

WHERE clauses. A significant source of false positives are interdependent queries whose relative **WHERE** clauses always identify disjoint sets of rows. As an example, consider the SQL queries reported in Figure 3: here the application extracts from the Sessions relation the user IDs not yet expired; afterwards, the application removes stale sessions from the database. Apparently, a race is possible between the two queries, because the first one uses the Sessions relation (as well as the user_id attribute) while the second statement defines it. This is however a false positive, because the intersection of the sets of rows selected by the two statements always corresponds to the empty set. To address this problem we need a method that allow us to assert when two **WHERE** clauses identify disjoint sets of rows. In such a situation, no race condition could occur between the two queries, even if they are interdependent. In the following discussion, we assume that two queries q_1, q_2 share the same **FROM** clause f but have (possibly) different **WHERE** clauses w_1, w_2.

A viable approach is to exploit the possibility of dynamically querying the DBMS. Every time we need to assert the disjunction between the sets of rows identified by w_1 and w_2 we can build the statement:

$$\textbf{SELECT} * \textbf{FROM } f \textbf{WHERE } w_1 \textbf{AND } w_2$$

If the set of rows returned by such a statement is not empty, then we can assert that there can be a race between queries q_1 and q_2. It is worth noting that if an empty set is returned, then we can only state that no race can occur in the *current* database instance (i.e. tuples currently contained in each database relation), but we cannot be sure that no race could *ever* happen.

An alternative approach consists of employing a decision procedure to assert if the sets of rows identified by w_1 and w_2 are actually disjoint. Such a method has the obvious advantage to be able to reason about *any* possible database instance, and not only about the current one, thus overcoming the major drawback of the previous approach. However, such a method would also introduce a significant overhead due to the use of an external constraint solver. Moreover, it is important to note that the constraint solver would probably not be able to handle some particular SQL constructs, such as **LIKE** expressions or nested queries. In these situations, the constraint solver would have to behave conservatively, thus reporting that the analyzed queries are not guaranteed to be independent. Nevertheless, in many practical situations this method is still effective.

Note that the constraint solver-based approach and the dynamic query approach are complementary rather than alternative: these two methods can be employed together in order to combine the efficiency of direct DBMS queries with the conservativism of the constraint solver. Every time a race condition is detected, the DBMS can be dynamically queried in order to verify if, in the current database instance, the sets of rows selected by the two **WHERE** clauses are not disjoint. If these sets of rows turn out to be disjoint in the current database instance, then we can fall back to the less efficient constraint solver-based method, in order to obtain a sound answer.

Attribute-relation bindings. Another significant source of false positives is due to the fact that we cannot always accurately deduce the relation an attribute belongs to, by only observing a single SQL query statement. Consider the query **SELECT** a_1, a_2**FROM** T_1, T_2. The a_1 attribute could belong either to the T_1

```
#! TAG get_all_ids
SELECT user_id
FROM Users;

#! SAFE get_all_ids
DELETE FROM Users
WHERE user_id = 10;
```

Fig. 4. An example of SQL queries annotated for suppressing race reports

relation or to the T_2 relation. The only thing we can do is to conservatively assume that each attribute could belong to any relation used by the analyzed query. Clearly, this could introduce a number of false positives during race detection. To overcome this limitation, in these cases we allow our race detector to actively query the application database to determine to which relation attributes belong. In the above **SELECT** statement, our race detector would actively query the underlying DBMS to determine the attributes of the T_1 and T_2 relations, in order to discover which one contains a_1 or a_2.

Annotations. Finally, it is worth pointing out that the algorithm presented above does not take into account any explicit synchronization attempt. We discuss this particular design choice during Section 3.5. The main consequence of such a limitation is that our detector will report a race condition even when a solution has been coded around it. Of course, such a behavior would seriously limit the employment of our proposed detection method in the development cycle of real-world applications. The accurate detection of every possible synchronization attempt, without relying on the knowledge of the particular set of synchronization primitives being used, is a complex task. In particular, in our situation this task becomes completely not feasible because we are only observing the interactions between the application and the database, without taking into account any information that could be extracted from the web application's code. For these reasons, we allow the programmer to explicitly specify that the race condition between a pair of SQL queries has already been fixed and should not be reported anymore by including appropriate annotations into those queries. Every annotation starts with the "#!" prefix. The '#' character indicates that the current line contains a comment[1], so that our annotations will not be processed by the underlying DBMS. The '!' character allows our race detector to discern annotations from normal comments. We support two different annotation types:

TAG <*name*> an annotation of this type allows the programmer to unambiguously define a name for a particular SQL query;
SAFE <*name*> this annotation type specifies that a race condition between this query and the query with name <*name*> should not be reported.

---

[1] This is true for MySQL. Should this assumption not be true, it is only a matter of changing the comment character being used.

As an example, consider the queries reported in Figure 4. The programmer has assigned to the **SELECT** statement the name get_all_ids by using the annotation TAG. Then, the report of every race condition that could occur between the first query and the second one has been suppressed with a SAFE annotation. With such annotations, a programmer can easily test his web application with our detector module plugged in, fix the race conditions that are detected and then annotate the concerning queries so that the same races will not be reported again.

3.4   Implementation

We have implemented our detection method in a prototype that handles PHP applications and assumes the MySQL DBMS as their back-end.

The implementation of the query logger module consists of a PHP wrapper procedure around the **mysql_query**() function, so the only preliminary operation required to analyze a web application consists in replacing every call to **mysql_query**() with a call to our **mysql_query_wrapper**() function. Many web applications include a class that provides methods for submitting queries to the underlying database, so abstracting the caller from the particular DBMS being used. Thus, in order to integrate the query logger module, only a very limited number of these methods needs to be modified. Notice that even this operation is made completely automatic by a simple script. Our wrapper function logs into a text file every query that has been submitted to the DBMS together with some meta-information, such as the name of the script that issued that query and a dump of the interpreter's call stack. When a race is detected, such meta-information could help the programmer to easily locate the problem.

After the queries generated by a web application have been logged, the log files are sent to our query analyzer module in order to spot possible race conditions. Our query analyzer module consists in roughly 2000 lines of Python code and it implements the detection model discussed in Section 3.2. Our current prototype only lacks of the constraint solver-based method for determining if the sets of rows identified by two database queries are guaranteed to be disjoint. For parsing MySQL statements, the query analyzer leverages the `DBIx::MyParsePP` PERL module.

3.5   Discussion

The proposed detection algorithm has still some limitations, that can be summarized in the following points:

- our approach is *completely dynamic*, so it can only reason about a *specific* execution path, i.e., the one that has been covered during the observed execution.
- We have no information about the application's semantics other than the query statements submitted to the DBMS. For example, we do not take into account how data retrieved from the database is manipulated by the application.

– Our detection algorithm does not take into account any synchronization method that the application could adopt in order to avoid concurrency problems.

The first limitation could only be overcomed with the application of static or hybrid analysis techniques over the program's source code: by using static or hybrid methods we would be able to reason about the *whole* application rather than a single execution path. Unfortunately, the application of static program analysis methods to an interpreted, object-oriented and dynamic-typed scripting language like PHP is far than easy and it would require to deal with very hard problems, as mentioned in [14]. For example, the analysis of PHP applications requires to perform points-to and alias analyses, that are, in general, undecidable problems [15]. The use of program analysis techniques would also allow us to obtain more information about an application's semantics, thus overcoming our second limitation. We leave such improvements for future work.

The last limitation of our detection algorithm concerns the lack of support for synchronization primitives. Rather than a real limitation, this is an explicit design choice. First, at the application level, to the best of our knowledge, PHP does not provide portable synchronization primitives that are suitable for our needs. For example, PHP supports the **flock**() function that implements a portable file locking mechanism, that can be used for synchronization and mutual exclusion purposes. However, as stated in the PHP manual [16], on some operating systems **flock**() is implemented at the process level, and, on multi-threaded web servers such as Apache, multiple PHP requests can be executed as multiple threads of the *same* process, so making **flock**() completely ineffective. Moreover, **flock**() blocks the caller until the file lock is released unless the LOCK_NB flag is specified. However, this option is not currently supported on Windows systems. PHP does provide wrappers for the System V IPC functions, but this feature is not enabled by default and is not available at all on Windows platforms. Second, at the database level, the available synchronization primitives are highly DBMS-dependent and often too coarse grained. As an example, MySQL, probably the most widely used open source database, supports **LOCK** and **UNLOCK** statements that provide a relation-level locking mechanism. However, such a granularity is often too coarse to be adopted in heavy-loaded web applications. MySQL also supports ACID transactions with row-level locking, but this feature is not available when using MyISAM, the default storage engine. A more suitable mechanism is the GET_LOCK() function[17]: it can be used to simulate record locks by creating named locks. If a name has been locked by one client, GET_LOCK() blocks any request by another client for a lock with the same name. This allows clients that agree on a given lock name to use the name to perform *cooperative* advisory locking. Locks maybe released by calling RELEASE_LOCK().

While there are suitable solutions, these can be used only by programmers that are conscious of the concurrency issue and they require them to code explicitly a synchronization policy. Moreover, the penalty due to the use of synchronization constructs is not always acceptable, because it could drastically reduce the performances of the web application. Thus, we found that synchronization

Table 1. Evaluation of the detection method. FP: False Positives; TP: True Positives (security relevant true positives are reported in brackets). Note that these results have been obtained without using the annotations supported by our system.

Application	Category	Queries	Time	FP	TP
Joomla! 1.5RC4	CMS	4086	90.92 s	0	55 (2)
phpBB 3.0.0	forum	2236	43.09 s	0	35 (4)
WordPress 2.3.2	blog/CMS	3638	47.04 s	0	47 (4)
Zen Cart 1.3.8a	shopping cart	35194	1622.39 s	0	46 (1)

primitives are rarely used in web applications and in our experiments the lack of support for them has not raised the false positive rate. Moreover, the few synchronization attempts we found at the PHP level, have actually been made completely ineffective by the underlying storage engine.

3.6   Evaluation

To prove the effectiveness of our approach in detecting vulnerabilities, we ran our prototype tool on some real word open-source web applications. Of course, the main problem in evaluating our prototype (as with any other dynamic analysis tool) concerns gathering relevant execution traces: the ability of our approach to detect previously unknown race conditions heavily depends on the path coverage rate obtained during the query logging phase. In our experiments, we tried to stimulate the web applications being analyzed as if it was used by a typical user. For example, with forum applications we tried to login by supplying both correct and wrong credentials, we added new users, read some topics, created new topics and polls, sent instant messages to other users, and so on.

We ran our detector on a Linux machine with a dual-core 2.0 GHz Pentium processor and 1GB RAM. In Table 1 we summarize some of the results we obtained during our experiments. The time required to analyze the application's log file of queries is very large, but more than 95% of the whole execution time is spent while parsing SQL statements. Such an overhead is primarily due to the inter-process interactions between our Python detector and the external Perl SQL parser. The runtime overhead for logging SQL queries is negligible and not reported in Table 1. As we already discussed during previous sections, not every race condition we found was actually security relevant. However, we believe the number of security relevant races we found together with the absence of false positives prove the effectiveness of our detection method.

We can briefly summarize some of the vulnerabilities we run into in the following categories:

multiple users. Almost every application we analyzed was found to be vulnerable to a race condition on user uniqueness: a malicious user could register multiple accounts with the same username, thus bypassing application's checks. Of course, the security impact of this vulnerability is highly application-dependent. As an example, it could allow an attacker to take advantage multiple times of a one-time bonus granted by a unique token.

brute forcing. Some applications (e.g., phpBB3), in order to prevent brute forcing attacks, check if the user that is trying to log in has already performed too many login attempts. The procedure used to perform this operation contains a race condition vulnerability that could allow a malicious user to bypass the application's attempts to limit brute forcing password attacks. Depending on the application's logic, such a vulnerability could allow an attacker to perform just a limited number of additional attempts (e.g., when the application ensures that $tries \leq MAX\_TRIES$), or to completely circumvent application's checks (e.g., when a brute force attack is reported only if $tries = MAX\_TRIES$).

multiple poll votes. Web forums and CMSs often implement polls. The applications try to assure that each user does not submit multiple votes to the same poll, but every program was found to be subject to a race that allows a user to vote multiple times by submitting parallel vote requests.

topic flooding. phpBB3 and WordPress include an anti-flooding feature that forces a user that has just submitted a message to wait a couple of seconds before writing another post. Unfortunately, even this control can be easily circumvented by an attacker because of a synchronization issue.

It is worth noting that in the web applications we analyzed we have met very few synchronization attempts. Unfortunately, even in these cases we have been able to find concurrency problems. This confirms that programmers are not aware of the actual impact of race conditions on web-based applications.

4   Countermeasures

Before concluding our paper, in this section we introduce some countermeasures a programmer could employ in order to hamper exploitation attempts.

Probably, the most obvious solution is to completely prevent any concurrency issue by forcing the web server to serve just one client request at a time. Unfortunately, such an approach is typically too drastic and not applicable at all, as it seriously limits the overall efficiency of the whole web-based application.

Another approach consists in employing some application-level or database-level synchronization primitives in order to explicitly serialize the accesses to an application's critical regions. As we already discussed, many of these primitives often hide some subtle platform-specific details that a programmer should accurately consider before deploying his web-based application; otherwise just the migration of the application towards a different server could alter his behavior and introduce new vulnerabilities. During Section 3.5 we pointed out the limitations of PHP/MySQL environments. Obviously, different frameworks could surely offer more efficient and fine-grained locking statements (e.g., row-level database relation locking), but this typically comes at the cost of less efficiency or more resource-consumption.

For example, a table-level locking solution will surely be too coarse grained if applied to the code snippet reported in Figure 1: here the requested transaction could take some time to be executed, thus the application cannot be constrained to serve just a single client for all that time. In this situation, an alternative solution that does not require fine-grained locking primitives consists in moving the **UPDATE** statement just before the execution of the requested transaction, then lock the table before the first **SELECT** query and unlock it both after the **UPDATE** statement and in the *else* branch. This solution is a simple two-phase commit algorithm that requires an additional error handling procedure: the credit is immediately withdrawn from the balance and must be restored if the transaction fails.

Thus, the effectiveness and the efficiency of a synchronization solution is highly application dependent. Automatically fixing race conditions by introducing appropriate locking statements, without affecting the efficiency of the whole application, is surely a rather complex task. In fact, it would be quite simple to blindly insert locking statements around a supposed critical region, but it would be significantly harder to do so also avoiding deadlocks and without reducing the performances of the web-based application. We plan to investigate on similar automatic techniques in future work.

5   Related Work

Race conditions are probably one of the oldest software problems and their implications have extensively been discussed in literature [7]. There has been a substantial amount of research work on the detection of this kind of concurrency problem, both for debugging and for security purposes. To the best of our knowledge, this paper is the first one to focus on the implications of race conditions on web-based application, so in the present section we will discuss alternative solutions directed toward traditional (i.e. non web-based) applications.

Static analysis. Many static race detectors perform compile-time analyses over a program's source code in order to detect if a race condition could occur in *any* possible program execution [18,19]. Other approaches [20,21] modify a programming language's type system so that the resulting language is guaranteed to be race-free. Usually, the major drawback of these tools is an high false positive rate: by reasoning over an application's source code without running it, these approaches are often forced to make some conservative assumptions about possible thread interleavings that could occur at run-time. Moreover, often static methods require a substantial amount of annotation code in order to suppress false positives.

Dynamic analysis. Dynamic methods work by instrumenting and executing a program. These tools are typically easy to use and are more accurate than static methods, as they can observe a concrete execution of the application. On the other side, they are not sound: dynamic approaches can only assert the presence of a synchronization issue on a program path that has been executed, but they cannot prove the absence of race conditions. Several methods [22,23] are based on the dynamic computation of Lamport's *happens-before* relation [24], that outputs a partial ordering on program statements. Other methods [25,26] use *lockset-based* analysis [27], that stem from the assumption that race conditions occur because a programmer forgot to protect a shared variable with an appropriate lock. Basically, each shared variable is associated with a *lockset* that contains locks held during accesses to this variable; if a lockset becomes empty, then a race condition could occur. Some approaches [28,29] have also been proposed that blend together the advantages of both these techniques. Finally, another dynamic method [30] aims to prevent the exploitation of race condition vulnerabilities on filesystem operations, by keeping track of possible interferences between the actions performed by different processes: if a filesystem operation is found to be interfering with another one, then the corresponding process is temporarily suspended.

Model checking. Model checking is a powerful formal verification technique that has also been applied to the detection of concurrency problems [31]. A model checker receives as input a simplified version of an application's source code and exhaustively explores its execution states, searching for possible violations of some asserted conditions. For example, some model checking tools have already been proposed to analyze concurrent Java programs for synchronization issues [32]. Unfortunately, the application of model checking to large software systems is still problematic. Moreover, often a significant effort is required in order to build the simplified model to be supplied to the analysis tool.

Our proposed detection strategy can surely be classified as a completely dynamic detection method. However, the web environment shows some peculiarities that lead to rather different problems than the ones discussed in the aforementioned works. In fact, currently web programmers are not aware of the implications of the lack of proper synchronization on their applications, while traditional concurrent programs are actually written with synchronization in mind. Thus, the approaches discussed above are mainly focused on analyzing the correctness of a programmed synchronization policy. Instead, our work aims to make explicit the implicit interactions among different instances of a sequential code that can be executed concurrently.

6   Conclusions

In this paper we discussed race conditions in web applications. Race conditions are a well-known security problem, but their impact on web-based programs has not been explored sufficiently. We showed that, by exploiting unforeseen interactions between different script instances, a malicious user could be able to alter the behavior of a web application as it was intended by the programmer. We further deep our analysis in order to investigate concurrency issues that could arise because of the interactions between different instances of the same application script when accessing to a SQL-enabled relational database. We proposed a dynamic detection method that allowed us to locate several security-relevant race conditions even in mature and well-tested web applications.

In the future, we plan to refine our detection method by considering how instances of different web application scripts could affect each others. Moreover, we will improve our detection strategy by extracting some additional information from the application through the employment of more sophisticated program analysis techniques, thus overcoming some of the limitations discussed during Section 3.5. Finally, as web programmers will get aware about concurrency problems, they will surely start to try to solve these issues by using some synchronization primitives. So, we plan to improve our analyses to include support for validating their use.

Acknowledgments

The authors would like to thank Lorenzo Cavallaro and the anonymous reviewers for their useful suggestions and comments on this paper.

References

1. NCSA Software Development Group: The Common Gateway Interface (1995)
2. Kunze, M.: Let there be light. LAMP: Freeware web publishing system with database support. c't 12, 230 (1998)
3. Cova, M., Felmetsger, V., Vigna, G.: Vulnerability Analysis of Web Applications. In: Baresi, L., Dinitto, E. (eds.) Testing and Analysis of Web Services. Springer, Heidelberg (2007)
4. Symantec Inc.: Symantec internet security threat report: Volume XII. Technical report, Symantec Inc. (September 2007)
5. Halfond, W.G., Viegas, J., Orso, A.: A Classification of SQL-Injection Attacks and Countermeasures. In: Proceedings of the IEEE International Symposium on Secure Software Engineering, Arlington, VA, USA (2006)
6. CERT: Advisory CA-2000-02: Malicious HTML Tags Embedded in Client Web Requests (2002)
7. Netzer, R.H.B., Miller, B.P.: What are Race Conditions?: Some Issues and Formalizations. ACM Letters on Programming Languages and Systems 1(1), 74–88 (1992)
8. Dean, D., Hu, A.J.: Fixing races for fun and profit: How to use access(2). In: Proceedings of the 13th conference on USENIX Security Symposium (2004)
9. Borisov, N., Johnson, R., Sastry, N., Wagner, D.: Fixing races for fun and profit: How to abuse atime. In: Proceedings of the 14th conference on USENIX Security Syposium (2005)
10. Bishop, M., Dilger, M.: Checking for race conditions in file accesses. Computing Systems 2(2), 131–152 (1996)
11. Abbott, R.P., Chin, J.S., Donnelley, J.E., Konigsford, W.L., Tokubo, S., Webb, D.A.: Security analysis and enhancements of computer operating systems.
12. phpBB Group: phpBB
13. Joomla! Core Team: Joomla!

14. Jovanovic, N.: Web Application Security. PhD thesis, Technical University of Vienna (July 2007)
15. Hind, M.: Pointer analysis: Haven't we solved this problem yet? In: 2001 ACM SIGPLAN-SIGSOFT Workshop on Program Analysis for Software Tools and Engineering (PASTE 2001) (2001)
16. PHP Documentation Group: PHP Manual. [Online; accessed 23-November-2007].
17. MySQL AB: MySQL Reference Manual, http://dev.mysql.com/doc/refman/5.0.
18. Sterling, N.: WARLOCK - A static data race analysis tool. In: Proceedings of the Usenix Winter 1993 Technical Conference, pp. 97–106 (1993)
19. Engler, D., Ashcraft, K.: RacerX: Effective, Static Detection of Race Conditions and Deadlocks. In: Proceedings of the Nineteenth ACM Symposium on Operating Systems Principles, pp. 237–252 (2003)
20. Flanagan, C., Freund, S.N.: Type-based race detection for Java. ACM SIGPLAN Notices 35(5), 219–232 (2000)
21. Boyapati, C., Rinard, M.: A parameterized type system for race-free java programs. In: Proceedings of the 16th ACM SIGPLAN conference on Object oriented programming, systems, languages, and applications, pp. 56–69 (2001)
22. Dinning, A., Schonberg, E.: An empirical comparison of monitoring algorithms for access anomaly detection. In: Proceedings of the Second ACM SIGPLAN Symposium on Principles & Practice of Parallel Programming, pp. 1–10 (1990)
23. Ronsse, M., Bosschere, K.D.: RecPlay: A fully integrated practical record/replay system. ACM Transactions Computer Systems 17(2), 133–152 (1999)
24. Lamport, L.: Time, clocks, and the ordering of events in a distributed system. Communications of the ACM 21(7), 558–565 (1978)
25. Choi, J.D., Lee, K., Loginov, A., O'Callahan, R., Sarkar, V., Sridharan, M.: Efficient and precise datarace detection for multithreaded object-oriented programs. ACM SIGPLAN Notices 37(5), 258–269 (2002)
26. Cheng, G.I., Feng, M., Leiserson, C.E., Randall, K.H., Stark, A.F.: Detecting data races in Cilk programs that use locks. In: Proceedings of the 10th Annual ACM Symposium on Parallel Algorithms and Architectures, pp. 298–309 (1998)
27. Savage, S., Burrows, M., Nelson, G., Sobalvarro, P., Anderson, T.E.: Eraser: A dynamic data race detector for multithreaded programs. ACM Transactions on Computer Systems 15(4), 391–411 (1997)
28. Yu, Y., Rodeheffer, T., Chen, W.: RaceTrack: Efficient detection of data race conditions via adaptive tracking. Technical report, Microsoft Research (April 2005)
29. Pozniansky, E., Schuster, A.: Efficient on-the-fly data race detection in multi-threaded C++ programs. ACM SIGPLAN Notices 38(10), 179–190 (2003)
30. Tsyrklevich, E., Yee, B.: Dynamic detection and prevention of race conditions in file accesses. In: Proceedings of the 12th USENIX Security Symposium (August 2003)
31. Chamillard, A.T., Clarke, L.A., Avrunin, G.S.: An empirical comparison of static concurrency analysis techniques (July 23, 1996)
32. Visser, W., Havelund, K., Brat, G., Park, S.J.: Model checking programs. In: Proceedings of the 15th IEEE International Conference on Automated Software Engineering (September 2000)

On the Limits of Information Flow Techniques for Malware Analysis and Containment[*]

Lorenzo Cavallaro[1], Prateek Saxena[2], and R. Sekar[3]

[1] Dipartimento di Informatica e Comunicazione
Università degli Studi di Milano, Italy
[2] Computer Science Department
University of California at Berkeley, USA
[3] Computer Science Department
Stony Brook University, USA

Abstract. Taint-tracking is emerging as a general technique in software security to complement virtualization and static analysis. It has been applied for accurate detection of a wide range of attacks on benign software, as well as in malware defense. Although it is quite robust for tackling the former problem, application of taint analysis to untrusted (and potentially malicious) software is riddled with several difficulties that lead to gaping holes in defense. These holes arise not only due to the limitations of information flow analysis techniques, but also the nature of today's software architectures and distribution models. This paper highlights these problems using an array of simple but powerful evasion techniques that can easily defeat taint-tracking defenses. Given today's binary-based software distribution and deployment models, our results suggest that information flow techniques will be of limited use against future malware that has been designed with the intent of evading these defenses.

1 Introduction

Information flow analysis has long been recognized as an important technique for defending against attacks on confidentiality as well as integrity [6,8]. Over the past quarter century, information flow research has been concentrated on static analysis techniques, since they can detect *covert channels* (e.g., so-called implicit information flows) missed by runtime monitoring techniques.

Static analyses for information-flow have been developed in the context of high-level, type-safe languages, so they cannot be directly applied to the vast majority of COTS software that is available only in binary form. Worse, software obfuscation and encryption techniques commonly employed in malware (as well as some benign software for intellectual property protection) render any kind of static analysis very difficult, if not outright impossible. Even in the absence of obfuscation, binaries are notoriously hard to analyze: even the basic step of accurate disassembly does not have solutions that are robust enough to work on large x86 binaries. As a result, production-grade tools that operate on binaries rely on dynamic (rather than static) analyis and instrumentation [3,7,17,24,26].

---

[*] This research is supported in part by an ONR grant N000140710928 and an NSF grant CNS-0627687, and was carried out while the first two authors were at Stony Brook University.

Following this observations, several researchers have recently developed dynamic information-flow techniques for COTS binaries [10,15,29,30,36]. These techniques, along with source-to-source based transformation approaches, have enabled accurate detection of a wide range of attacks on trusted software[1] including those based on memory corruption [15,36], format-string bugs, command or SQL injection [2,28,43], cross-site scripting [40], and so on. More recently, researchers have reported significant successes in applying dynamic information flow techniques on existing malware, both from the perspective of understanding their behavior [1], and detecting runtime violation of policies [13,34]. Although dynamic taint analysis technique is quite robust for protecting trusted software, its application to untrusted (and potentially malicious) software is subject to a slew of evasion techniques that significantly limit its utility. We point out that understanding the limitations of defensive techniques is not just an academic exercise, but a problem with important practical consequences: emerging malware does not just employ variants of its payloads by using metamorphic/polymorphic techniques, but instead has begun to embed complex evasion techniques to detect monitoring environments as a means to protect its "intellectual property" from being discovered. For instance, W32/MyDoom [19] and W32/Ratos [38] adopt self-checking and code execution timing techniques to determine whether they are under analysis or not. Likewise, self-modifying techniques — among others — are used as well (W32/HIV [18]) to make malware debugging sessions harder [37,39]. Thus, a necessary first step for developing resilient defenses is that of understanding the weaknesses and limitations of existing defenses. This is the motivation of our work. We have organized our discussion into three major sections as follows, depending on the context in which information flow is being used.

Stand-alone malware. When applied to malware, a natural question is whether the covert channels that were ignored by dynamic techniques could be exploited by adaptive malware to thwart information-flow based defenses. These covert channels were ignored in the context of trusted software since their "capacity" was deemed too small to pose a significant threat. More importantly, attackers do not have any control over the code of trusted software, and hence cannot influence the presence or capacity of these channels. In contrast, malware writers can deliberately embed covert channels since they have complete control over malware code. In this paper, we first show that it is indeed very easy for malware writers to insert such covert channels into their software. These evasion techniques are simple enough that they can be incorporated manually, or using simple, automated program transformation techniques. We show that it is very difficult to defeat these evasion techniques, unless very conservative reasoning is employed, e.g., assuming that any information read by a program could leak to any of its outputs. Unfortunately, such weak assumptions can greatly limit the purposes to which dynamic information flow analysis can be used. For instance, Stinson *et al.* [34] use information flow analysis to detect "remote-control" behavior of bots, which is identified when arguments to security-critical system calls are tainted. If a conservative notion of tainting is used, then all programs that communicate over the network would have to be flagged as "bots," which would defeat the purpose of that analysis.

---

[1] In this paper, the term "trusted software" is used to refer to software that is trusted to be benign.

Malware plug-ins.   Next, we consider recent evolution in software deployment models that has favored the use of plug-in based architechtures. Browser helper objects (BHOs), which constitute one of the most common forms of malware in existence today, belong to this category. Other examples include document viewer plug-ins, media codecs, and so on. We describe several novel attacks that are possible in the context of plug-ins:

- *Attacks on integrity of taint information.* Malware can achieve its goal indirectly by modifying the variables used by its host application, e.g., modifying a file name variable in the host application so that it points to a file that it wants to overwrite. Alternatively, it may be able to bypass instrumentation code inserted for taint-tracking by corrupting program control-flow.

- *Attacks based on violating application binary interface,* whereby malware violates assumptions such as those involving stack layout and register usage between callers and callees.

- *Race-condition attacks on taint metadata.* Finally, we describe attacks where malware races with benign host application to write security-sensitive data. In a successful attack, malware is able to control the value of this data, while the taint status of the data reflects the write operation of benign code.

While conservative notions of tainting could potentially be used to thwart these attacks [33], this would restrict the applicability of information-flow techniques even more.

Analyzing future behavior of malware.   Today's malware is often packaged with software that seems to provide legitimate functionality, with malicious behavior exposed only under certain "trigger conditions", e.g., when a command is received from a remote site controlled by an attacker. Moreover, malware may incorporate anti-analysis features so that malicious paths are avoided when executed within an analysis environment. To uncover such malicious behavior, it is necessary to develop techniques that can reason about program paths that are not exercised during monitoring. While one may attempt to force execution of all program paths, such an approach is likely to be very expensive, and more likely to suffer from semantic inconsistencies that may arise due to forcing execution down branches that are not taken during execution. A more selective approach has been proposed by Moser *et al.* [1] that explores paths guarded by tainted data, rather than all paths. This technique has been quite successful in the context of existing malware. The heart of this approach is a technique that uses a decision procedure to discover memory locations that could become tainted as a result of program execution, and explores branches that are guarded by such data. In Section 4, we show that these trigger discovery mechanisms (and more generally, the technique for discovering which data items can become tainted) can be easily evaded by purposefully embedding memory errors in malicious code.

Paper organization.   Sections 2 through 4 describe our evasion techniques, organized along the lines described above. Where possible, mitigation of these evasions and their implications on information flow analyses are discussed as well. A summary of related work is provided in Section 5, followed by concluding remarks in Section 6.

2 Stand-Alone Untrusted Applications

For the sake of concreteness, we discuss the impact of evasion attacks, as well as mitigation measures, in the context of the "remote control" behavior detection technique presented by Stinson *et al.* [34], although the evasion techniques themselves are applicable against other defenses as well, e.g., dynamic spyware detection [13].

Stinson *et al.* observed that bots receive commands from a central site ("bot-herder") and carry them out. This typically manifests a flow of information from an input operation (e.g., a read system call) to an output operation (e.g., the file named in an open system call). Their implementation relied on *content-based tainting*: i.e., taint was assumed between x and y if their values matched (identical or had large common substrings) or if their storage locations overlapped. As noted by the paper authors, content-based tainting is particularly vulnerable: it can easily be evaded using simple encoding/decoding operations, e.g., by XOR'ing the data with a mask value before its use. However, the authors suggest that a more traditional implementation of runtime information flow tracking [15] would provide "thorough coverage" and hence render attacks much harder. Below, we describe simple evasion measures that allow malware to "drive a truck" through the gaps in most dynamic taint-tracking techniques, and proceed to discuss possible mitigation mechanisms and their implications.

2.1 Evasion Using Control Dependence and Implicit Flows

Dynamic information flow techniques that operate on trusted software tend to focus on *explicit flows* that take place via assignments. It is well known that information can flow from a variable y to another variable x without any explicit assignments. Indeed, a number of covert channels for information flow have been identified by previous research in this area. We demonstrate the ease of constructing evasion attacks using these covert channels. We focus on two forms of non-explicit flow, namely, control dependences and implicit flows.

Control dependence   arises when a variable is assigned within an if-then-else statement whose condition involves a sensitive (tainted[2]) variable, e.g.,

$$\textbf{if } (y = 1) \textbf{ then } x := 1; \textbf{ else } x := 0; \textbf{ endif}$$

Clearly, the value of x is dependent on y, even though there is no assignment of the latter to the former. In particular, the above code snippet enables copying of a single bit from y to x without using direct assignments between them. Using an n-way branch (e.g., a switch statement with n cases) will allow copying of $\log n$ bits. A malware writer can propagate an arbitrarily large amount of information without using explicit flows by simply enclosing the above code snippet within a loop.

Implicit flows   arise by virtue of semantic relationships that exist between the values of variables in a program. As an example, consider the following code snippet that allows copying of one bit of data from a sensitive variable y to w without using explicit flows or control dependences:

---

[2] Typically, the term "taint" is used in the context of integrity, while "sensitive" is used in the context of confidentiality.

1. $x := 0; \ z := 0;$
2. **if** $(y = 1)$ **then** $x := 1;$ **else** $z := 1;$ **endif**
3. **if** $(x = 0)$ **then** $w := 0;$ **endif**
4. **if** $(z = 0)$ **then** $w := 1;$ **endif**

At line 2, if $y = 1$ then x is marked sensitive because of control-dependent assignment in the then-clause. Since there is no assignment to z in the then-clause of line 2, it is not marked sensitive. Moreover, the condition at line 3 will not hold because x was assigned a value of 1 at line 2. But the condition at line 4 holds, so w is assigned the value of 1, but it is not marked sensitive since z is not sensitive at this point. Now, consider the case when $y = 0$. Following a similar line of reasoning, it can be seen that w will be assigned the value 0 at line 3, but it will not be marked sensitive. Thus, in both cases, w gets the same value as y, but it is not marked as sensitive.

As with control dependences, a malware writer can copy an arbitrarily large number of bits using nothing but implicit flow by simply using a slightly more sophisticated example of the above code. It is thus trivial for a malware writer to evade taint-tracking techniques that track only direct data dependencies and control dependencies.

2.2 Difficulty of Mitigating Evasion Attacks

To thwart control-dependence-based evasion, a taint-tracking technique can be enhanced to track control dependences. This is easy to do, even in binaries, by associating a *taint label* with the *program counter (PC)* [13][3]. Unfortunately, this will lead to an increase in false positives, i.e., many benign programs will be flagged as exhibiting remote-control behavior. To illustrate this, consider the following code snippet that might be included in a program that periodically downloads data from the network, and saves it in different files based on the format of the data. Such code may be used in programs such as weather or stock ticker applets:

```
int n = read(network, y, 1);
if (*y == 't')
    fp = fopen("data.txt", "w");
else if (*y = 'i')
    fp = fopen("data.jpg", "w");
```

Note that there is a control dependence between data read over the network and the file name opened, so a technique that flags bots (or other malware) based on such dependence would report a false alarm. More generally, input validation checks can often raise false positives, as in the following example.

```
int n = read(network, y, sizeof(y));
if (sanity_check(y)) {
    fp = fopen("data", "w");
    ...
} else { ... // report error }
```

In the context of benign software, false positives due to control dependence tracking can be managed using developer annotations (so-called endorsement or declassification

---

[3] Specifically, the PC is tainted within the body of a conditional if the condition involves tainted variables. Moreover, targets of assignments become tainted whenever the PC is tainted. Finally, the taint label of the PC is restored at the merge point following a conditional branch.

annotations). We obviously cannot rely on developer annotations in untrusted software; it is also impractical for code consumers, even if they are knowledgeable programmers or system administrators, to understand and annotate untrusted code, especially when it is distributed in the form of binaries.

Mitigating implicit-flow based evasion is even harder. It has been shown that purely dynamic techniques cannot detect implicit flows [42]. This is because, as illustrated by the implicit flow example above, it is necessary to reason about assignments that take place on *unexecuted* program branches. On binaries, this amounts to identify the memory locations that may be updated on program branches that are not taken. Several features of untrusted COTS binaries combine to make this problem intractable:

– Address arithmetic involving values that are difficult to compute statically
– Indirect data references and indirect calls
– Lack of information about types of objects
– Absence of size information for stack-allocated and static objects (i.e., variables)
– Possibility that malicious code may violate low-level conventions and requirements regarding the use of stack, registers, control-flow, etc.

As a result, it is unlikely that implicit flows can be accurately tracked for the vast majority of today's untrusted software that gets distributed as x86 binaries.

2.3 Implications

Evasion measures described above can be mitigated by treating (a) all data written by untrusted code as tainted (i.e., not trustworthy), and (b) all data written by untrusted code as sensitive if any of the data it has read is sensitive. For stand-alone applications, these assumptions mean that all data output by an untrusted process is tainted, and moreover, is sensitive if the process input any sensitive data. In other words, this choice means that fine-grained taint-tracking (or information flow analysis) is not providing any benefit over a coarse-grained, conservative technique that operates at the granularity of processes, and does not track any of the internal actions of a process.

In the context of detecting remote-control behavior, we observe that in the absence of evasion measures, the use of dynamic information flow techniques enables us to distinguish between malicious behavior, which involves the use of security-critical system call arguments that directly depend on untrusted data, and benign behavior. The use of evasion techniques can easily fool taint-tracking techniques that only reason about explicit flows. If the technique is enhanced to reason about control dependences, evasion resistance is improved, but as illustrated by the examples above, many more false positives are bound to be reported, thus significantly diminishing the ability of the technique to distinguish between malicious and benign behaviors. If we further enhance evasion resistance to address all implicit flows, we will have to treat all data used by an untrusted application to be tainted, thereby completely losing the ability to distinguish between benign and malicious behavior.

In summary, the emergence of practical dynamic taint-tracking techniques for binaries enabled high-precision exploit detection on trusted code. This was possible because the presence of explicit information flow from untrusted source to a security-critical sink indicated the ability of an attacker to exert a high degree of control over operations that have a high risk of compromising the target application — a level of control that was unlikely to be intended by the application developer. It seemed that a similar logic could be applied to untrusted code, i.e., a clear distinction could be made between acceptable uses of tainted data that are likely to be found in benign applications from malicious uses found in malware. The discussion so far shows that this selectivity is lost once malware writers adapt to evade information flow techniques.

3   Analyzing Runtime Behavior of Shared-Memory Extensions

A significant fraction of today's malware is packaged as an extension to large softwares such as client-side web applications or the operating system. Applications such as web browsers and email clients are attractive targets for malware authors, because of the ubiquitous use of these applications in online financial transactions and private information exchange.

Nearly all large web browsers have software extension mechanisms that that allow adding various forms of additional functionality, such as better GUI services, automatic form filling, and viewing various forms of multimedia content. We refer to such browser extensions as browser helper objects (BHOs)[4]. Perhaps surprisingly, almost *all* browsers today have extensibility mechanisms that allow extension packages to be shipped with third-party libraries in binary form. Due to the growing user trends towards installing off-the-shelf extensions and due to increasing drive-by-downloads, malware spread in form of BHOs has been rampant.

Recent works [13] have proposed using information flow to track the flow of confidential data such as cookies, passwords and credentials in form-data as it gets processed by web browser. The idea is to monitor the actions of malware masquerading as benign BHOs, which is loaded in the address space of the browser, and to detect if confidential data is leaked by the BHOs. The crux of the problem is to selectively identify malware's actions. Essentially, their technique uses an attribution mechanism to classify actions that access system resources, to trusted and untrusted *contexts*. System calls or operations made directly by the BHO or by a host browser function called on its behalf, are attributed to the untrusted context, while those by the host browser itself belong to the trusted context. In the untrusted context, any sensitive data processed is flagged "suspicious." The presence of this data at output operations that perform writes to networks/files signals the leakage of confidential data effected by the BHO. Although these methods are successful in analysis and detection of current malware, they are not carefully designed to detect adaptive malware that employs evasion techniques against the specific mechanisms proposed in these defenses. Below, we present several such evasion attacks. We remind our readers that the techniques presented in the previous section continue to be available to malware that operates within the address space of a (benign) host application. In this section, our focus is on additional evasion techniques that become possible due to this shared address space.

---

[4] Browser extensions are named in different ways. Internet Explorer uses the terms "BHOs", "extensions" and "toolbars", while Gecko-based browsers (e.g., FireFox) use the terms "plugins" and "extensions". We use the term BHO for all these terms interchangeably in the paper.

3.1   Attacks Using Arbitrary Memory Corruption

Corruption of untainted/insensitive data to effect leakage.   By corrupting the memory used by the host application, a malicious BHO can induce the host application to carry out its tasks outside the untrusted context. For instance, a privacy-breaching malware *does not* necessarily need to read the confidential data itself and pass/copy it to external network interfaces. Instead, it could corrupt the data used by the browser (i.e., the host application) such that the browser unknowingly leaks this information. We present the basic idea for an attack that avoids direct manipulation of any sensitive data or sensitive pointers. Instead, it corrupts higher level untainted pointers that point to the sensitive data. Consider a pointer variable p in the browser code that refers to data items to be transmitted over the network. A malware can corrupt p to point to sensitive data (say s) of its choice, stored within the browser memory. This way a malicious BHO can arrange for s to be transmitted over the network, without being detected by techniques described in [13]. Similarly, a BHO may corrupt a file descriptor as well, so that any write operation using this file pointer will result in the transmission of sensitive data over the network. Vulnerable pointers and data buffers needed for these attacks are rife in large systems. Moreover, they are easily forgeable because of the high degree of address space sharing between the host browser and extensions.

Optimistic assumptions about data originating from untrusted code.   Another basic idea for attack involves using seemingly harmless data, such as constants, which are treated as untainted by most techniques [13,45] for corruption of browser data structures. Treating constants in untrusted code or any data under the control of the malware as untainted is anyway problematic, and specially so in binary code where constants may be addresses. The attack involves overwriting an untainted pointer p, that may initially point to a sensitive data s, with an untainted value such as constant memory address m. When the browser uses m for a critical operation, such as determining the destination for sending s, this threat becomes very significant as shown below.

A real attack.   We now present an example that illustrates how a BHO can corrupt a data pointer to violate a policy that prevents leakage or tampering of sensitive information, like the user's *cookies*, by the BHO. The example has been tested on Lynx, a textual browser which does not have a proper plugin framework support[5]. However, it uses libraries to enhance its functionalities and, as they are loaded into Lynx's address space, they can be considered as untrusted components. In fact, the attack's result could be applied to a different browser application (e.g., Internet Explorer, FireFox) with a full-blown plug-in framework.

The attack consists of modifying the domain name in the cookie, and is illustrated in the figure below. In Lynx, all cached cookies are stored in a linked-list `cookie_list` (note that `cookie_list` is not sensitive as only the sequence of bytes containing cookies value is). Subsequently, when the browser has to send a cookie, the domain is compared using `host_compare` (not shown) which calls `stringcasecmp`. A plug-in can traverse the linked list, and write its intended URL to the `domain` pointer field in cookie record. On enticing the user to visit a malicious web site, such as `evil.com`,

---

[5] Lynx has been chosen to simplify the example.

these cookies would automatically be sent to the attacker web site, thereby subverting the implementation of the Same Origin Policy. The point to note in this example is that the domain pointer will be untainted; the object it points to will be tainted or sensitive. These higher level pointers themselves are not sensitive, therefore they can be corrupted without raising suspicion.

```
typedef struct _cookie {
    char *domain;                            // pointer to the domain this cookie belongs to
    ...
} cookie;

typedef struct _HList {
    void *object;
    HTList *next;
} HTList;
...
extern HTList *cookie_list;                   // declared by the core of the browser
...
void change_domain(void) {                    // untrusted plugin functions
    HTList *p = cookie_list;                  // untainted ptr — — the list itself is not tainted
    char *new_domain = strdup("evil.com");    // untainted string
    for (; p; p = p->next) {                   // iterating over an untainted list gives untainted ptrs
        cookie *tmp = (cookie *)p->object;     // tmp takes the address of a cookie object — — untainted
        tmp->domain = new_domain;              // changing an untainted pointer with an untainted address
    }
}                                             // Function exit
```

Implications

The above example shows how confidential data can leak without being read. The approach proposed in [13] does not deal with this threat. Recall that sensitive data is marked "suspicious"(to use the terminology defined in [13]), only when the untrusted BHO uses the sensitive data itself or propogates it to the external interfaces. Consequently, the malware can overwrite the domain pointer with an address value (which is untainted) of choice, *without* causing the *suspicious flag* to be set.

To detect the aforementioned evasion attacks, an information flow technique needs to incorporate at least the following two features. First, in order to detect the effect of pointer corruption (of pointers such as those used to point to data buffers), the technique must treat data dereferenced by (trusted) browser code using a tainted pointer as if it is directly accessed by untrusted code. Second, it must recognize corruption of pointers with constant values. Otherwise, the above attack will succeed since it overwrites a pointer variable with a constant value that corresponds to the memory location of sensitive data[6]. Considering every write performed by the untrusted BHO to be tainted, as suggested previously (therefore, considering everything written by the untrusted BHO as "suspicious"), may be a too conservative a strategy. It may yield high false positives in the cases where plugins access sensitive data but do not leak it. Though, applying conservative tainting specifically to recognize control data as done in [44] seems reasonable, this may raise significant false positives when applied for identifying all data that is possibly controlled by the plugin.

---

[6] Such pointers reside often enough on global variables whose locations can be predicted in advance and hard-coded as constants in the malware.

3.2 Attacking Mechanisms Used to Determine Execution Context

In a shared memory setting, it is necessary to distinguish the execution of untrusted extension code from that of trusted host application code. To make this distinction, the detection approach needs to keep track of a code execution *context*. The logic used for maintaining this context is an obvious target for evasion attacks: if this logic can be confused, untrusted code could execute with the privileges of trusted code. A more subtle attack involves data exchanged between the two contexts. Since execution in trusted context affords more privileges, untrusted code could achieve its objectives indirectly by corrupting data (e.g., contents of registers and the stack) that is communicated from untrusted execution context to the trusted context.

Although the targets of evasion attack described above are generally independent of implementation details, the specifics of evasion attacks will need to rely on these details. Below, we describe how such evasion attacks can work in the specific context of [13].

Attacking context-switch logic. The approach proposed [13] for context tracking uses the following algorithm. For each instruction, the system checks whether the instruction belongs to the BHO code region. If so, then it saves the value of the current stack pointer as esp_{saved}, and the instruction is executed in untrusted context. Whenever the instruction pointer points outside the code region of the BHO, the system has to determine whether the instruction is executed on behalf of the BHO (i.e., untrusted context) or not. For this, the proposed technique utilizes the fact that on their platform the stack grows downwards and checks if the current stack pointer, $esp_{current}$, is below the esp_{saved}. The context identification logic implicitly assumes a benign call stack model – it assumes that the activation records are pushed on the stack, the stack data belonging to the caller is left unchanged by the callee, and that the callee function cleans up its activation leaving the stack pointer restored after its invocation. We point out that these assumptions are reasonable for calls across benign code modules only. Specifically, if the $esp_{current}$ is not less than esp_{saved}, the context switching logic assumes that the last untrusted BHO code stack frame has been popped off the activation stack and the execution context does not belong to the BHO anymore. This attribution mechanism allows valid (benign) context switches (from untrusted to trusted context) at call/return function boundaries, when the last BHO function f is about to return and there are no other browser functions invoked by f.

Unfortunately, we show that this attribution mechanism is insecure. Malware may employ simple low-level attacks that subvert the control flow integrity of the application at the host-extension interface leading to devastating attacks. The taint analysis approach and the attribution mechanism employed in [13] point out that the mechanism can deal with two threats that may circumvent context attribution – execution of injected code, and attempts to adjust the stack pointer above the threshold limit by changing the ESP register in its code. However, it does not protect against other low-level integrity violations, such as return-into-lib(c) style [31,35] attacks, which aim to eventually execute already present code.

To be concrete, consider the scenario where the malicious BHO corrupts control pointers, such as return addresses pushed by the calling host function, to refer to target locations in the browser or its trusted libraries. It could additionally create a compatible stack layout required for a return-into-lib(c) attack to perform intended action and let its last invoked function simply exit. Changing control pointers such as return address above the recorded threshold stack pointer value, without making any modification to ESP itself, is sufficient and touches no sensitive/tainted data. Such returns from untrusted code trigger control transfers to the attacker controlled target functions, and furthermore, with arbitrarily controlled parameters on the crafted stack layout. As no other BHO instructions are executed after such a return, subsequent code will be executed in the browser context fulfilling the attacker's objectives.

Implications

To counteract such a return-into-lib(c) style attack, a malware analysis has to strengthen the attribution mechanism, to allow information flow to be correctly captured for the different contexts.

Another work in this area, Panorama [45], proposes to label every write operation performed by a BHO for the purpose of being able to track dynamically generated code. But, it seems to rely on a similar attribution mechanism used in [13], and seems vulnerable to the attack presented in the previous section as the attribution mechanism can be circumvented. HookFinder [44], instead, is able to catch every hook implanted into the system by an untrusted binary. To do so, they use an approach which is similar to information flow-based techniques: they label every write operation performed by untrusted binaries, as they want to be able to analyze any hooking attempts (regardless it they are made by benign or potentially malicious modules). This seems to be a promising approach for the attribution problem. In fact, an extension to their strategy, as the one proposed in [33], which marks context as untrusted whenever control transfers involve tainted pointers resolves the issue of correctly attributing context.

3.3 Attacking Meta-data Integrity

Corrupting meta-data maintained by a dynamic information flow technique is another avenue for attack. Typically, meta-data consists of one or more bits of taint per word of memory, with the entire metadata residing in a memory-resident data structure in memory. An obvious approach for corrupting this data involves malware directly accessing the memory locations storing metadata. Most existing dynamic information flow techniques include protection measures against such attacks. Techniques based on emulation, such as [13] can store metadata in the emulator's memory, which cannot be accessed by the emulated program. Other techniques such as [43] ensure that direct accesses to metadata store will cause a memory fault. In this section we focus our attention on *indirect attacks*, that is, those that manifest an inconsistency between metadata and data values by exploiting race conditions.

Attacks based on data/meta-data races. Dynamic information flow techniques need to perform two memory updates corresponding to each update in the original program: one to update the original data, and the other to update the metadata (i.e., the taint information). Apart from emulation based approaches where these two updates can be performed "atomically" (from the perspective of emulated code), other techniques need to rely on two distinct updates. As a result, in a multithreaded program where two threads update the same data, it is possible for an inconsistency to arise between data and metadata values. Assume, for instance, that metadata updates precede data updates, and consider the following interleaved execution of two threads:

$time$	Benign Thread	Malicious Thread
t_1		set tag_x to *tainted*
t_2	set tag_x to *untainted*	
t_3	write *untainted* value to x	
t_k		write *tainted* value to x

Note that at the end, memory location x contains a tainted value, but the corresponding metadata indicates that it is untainted. Such an inconsistency can be avoided by using mandatory locks to ensure that the data and metadata updates are performed together. But this would require acquisition and release of a lock for each memory update, thereby imposing a major performance penalty. As a result, existing information flow tracking techniques generally ignore race conditions, assuming that it is very hard to exploit these race conditions. This can be true for untrusted stand-alone applications, but it is problematic, and cannot be ignored in the context of malware that share their address-space with a trusted application.

To confirm our hypothesis, we experimentally measured the probability of success for a malicious thread causing a sensitive operation without raising an alarm, against common fine-grained taint tracking implementations known today. The motivation of this attack is to show that, by exploiting races between data and metadata updates operations, it is possible to manipulate sensitive data without having them marked as sensitive. To demonstrate the simplicity of the attack, in our experiment we used a simple C program shown below (a) that executes as a benign thread. The sensitive operation open (line 10 (a) column) depends on the pointer fname which is the primary target for the attacker in this attack. We transform the benign code to track control-dependence and verified its correctness, since the example is small.

```
1   char *fname = NULL, old_fname = NULL;
2   void check_preferences () {
3       ...
4       if (get_pref_name () == OK)
5           old_fname = "/.../.mozilla/.../pref.js";
6       ...
7       while (...) {
8           fname = old_fname;
9           if (fname) {
10              fp = open (fname, "w");
11              ...
12      }
13  }
```

```
1   void *malicious_thread(void *q) {
2       int attempts = 0;
3       while (attempts++ < MAX_ATTEMPTS)
4           fname = "/.../.mozilla/.../cookies.txt";
5
6
7
8
9
10
11
12
13  }
```

(a)   (b)

The attacker's thread (b) runs in parallel with the benign thread and has access to the global data memory pointer fname. The attacker code is transformed for taint tracking to mark all memory it writes as "unsafe" (i.e., tainted).

We ran this synthetic example on a real machines using two different implementations of taint tracking. For conciseness, we only present the results for the taint tracking that uses 2 bits of taint with each byte of data, similar to [43], with all taint tracking code inlined, as this minimizes the number of instructions for taint tracking and hence the vulnerability window. Assuming that the get_pref_name call fails to return OK, on a quad-core Intel Xeon machine running Linux 2.6.9 SMP kernel, we found that chances that the open system call executes with the corresponding pointer fname marked "safe" (i.e., untainted) varies from $60\% - 80\%$ across different runs. The reason why this happens is because the transformed benign thread reads the taint for fname on line 8 and sets the control context to tainted scope, before executing the original code for performing conditional comparison on line 9. The malicious thread tries to interleave its execution with the one of the benign thread, trying to achieve the following ordering of operations on the shared variable fname:

Time	Operation	Thread (Line No.)
t_1	read $tag_{fname} \mapsto untainted$	Benign (9)
t_2	write $tag_{fname} := tainted$	Malicious (4)
t_3	write $fname := $ "/home/user/.mozilla/.../cookies.txt"	Malicious (4)
t_4	read $fname$	Benign (9)

If such an ordering occurs, the tag_{fname} read by the benign thread is marked *untainted* as the benign thread has cleared the taint previously, while the data happens to contain an attacker controlled value about user browser cookies. Consequently, contrary to the intention of the instrumentation of tracking control-dependence, the attacker manages to prevent control scope from switching to tainted scope at line 9 in the benign code. In practical settings, the window of time between t_1 and t_4 varies largely based on cache performance, demand paging, and scheduling behaviour of specific platform implementations. Finally, it is worth noting that the attacker could improve the likelihood of success by increasing the scheduling priority of the malicious thread and lower, where possible, those of benign thread.

Implications

Attacks on direct corruption of metadata has been studied before [43] and thwarted by implementations using virtual machines and emulators which explicitly manage the context switches between threads or processors. However, much of the design of such metadata tracking monitors has not been carefully studied in the context of multi-threaded implementations (or multi-processor emulators), and techniques in this section highlight the subtle importance of these.

4   Analyzing Future Behavior of Malware

Several strategies have been proposed to analyze untrusted software. Broadly speaking, these strategies can be divided in two main categories, the ones based on *static* analysis and the others which adopt a *dynamic* analysis approach. While static analysis has the potential to reason about all possible behaviors of software, the underlying computational problems are hard, especially when working with binary code. Moreover, features such as code obfuscation, which are employed by malware as well as some legitimate software, make it intractable in practice. As a result, most practical malware analysis techniques have been focussed on dynamic analysis.

Unfortunately, dynamic analysis can only reason about those execution paths in a program that are actually exercised during the analysis. Several types of malware do not display their malicious behavior unless certain trigger conditions are present. For instance, time bombs do not exhibit malicious behavior until a certain date or time. Bots may not exhibit any malicious behavior until they receive a command from their master, usually in the form of a network input.

In order to expose such trigger-based behavior, Moser *et al.* [1] suggested an interesting dynamic technique that combines the benefits of a static and dynamic information-flow analyses. Specifically, they taint trigger-related inputs, such as calls to obtain time, or network reads. Then, dynamic taint-tracking is used to discover conditionals in the program that are dependent on these inputs. When one of the two branches of such a conditional is about to be taken, their technique creates a checkpoint and a snapshot of the analyzed process, and keeps exploring one of the branch. Subsequently, when the exploration of the taken branch ends or after a timeout threshold is reached, their technique forces the execution of the unexplored branch. Such forcing requires changing the value of a tainted variable v used in the conditional, so that the value of the condition expression is now negated. By leveraging on a *decision procedure* to generate a suitable value for v, the proposed approach also identifies any other variables in the program whose values are dependent on v, and modifies them so that the program is in a consistent state[7]. We observe that this analysis technique has applicability to certain kinds of anti-virtualization or sandbox-detection techniques as well. For instance, suppose that a piece of malware detects a sandbox (or a VM) based on the presence of a certain file, process, or registry entry. The approach proposed can then taint the functions that query for such presence, and proceed to uncover malicious code that is executed only when the sandbox is absent.

Since the underlying problems the analysis proposed by Moser *et al.* has to face are undecidable in general, their technique is incomplete, but seems to work well in practice against contemporary malware. However, this incompleteness can be exploited by a malware writer to evade detection. For instance, as noted by the authors of [1], a conditional can make use of one-way hash function. It is computationally hard to identify values of inputs that will make such a condition true (or false). More generally, malware authors can force the analysis to explore an unbounded number of branches, thereby exhausting computational resources available for analysis. However, the approach proposed in [1] will discover this effort, and report that the software under analysis is suspicious. A human analyst can then take a closer look at such malware. Nonetheless, today's malware writer places high value on stealth, and hence would prefer alternative anti-analysis mechanisms that do not raise suspicions, and we describe such primitives next.

---

[7] This is required, or else the program may crash or experience error conditions that would not occur normally. For instance, consider the code y = x; if (x == 0) z = 0; else z = 1/y; If we force the value of x to be nonzero, then y must also take the same value or else the program will experience a dive-by-zero exception.

4.1 Evasion Using Memory Errors

Binary code is generally hard to analyze, as briefly pointed out in Section 2.2. For instance, this is due to the absence of information about variables boundaries and types, which makes many source-based analyses inapplicable to binaries. We observe that given an arbitrary binary, it is hard to say whether it potentially contains a vulnerability such as a memory error (e.g., buffer overflow), and to determine the precise inputs to exploit it. Exhaustively running the binary on all possible inputs is often infeasible for benign code, leave alone malware which is expected to exploit the exponential nature of exhaustive searches to cause the worst-case hit each run.

Motivated by this observation, we present an attack against dynamic information flow-based analyses used to analyze malware behavior, similar to the one presented in [1]. This attack is able to hide malicious code from being discovered and further strengthen it such that extensions to analysis employed in [1] are unable to detect it. Our attack leverages on the introduction of *memory errors*, as shown in the following example.

```
1   int trigger;
2   ...
3   void procInput(void) {
4       int *p = &buf[0];
5       char buf[4096];
6       ...
7       my_gets(buf);
8       ...
9       *p = 1;
10      ...
11      if (trigger)
12          malcode();
13  }
```

The introduced memory error is a plain stack-based buffer overflow vulnerability[8]. The attacker's goal is to write past the end of buf (line 7) and corrupt the pointer p to make it point to the variable trigger. Eventually, when the vulnerability will be exploited, the malware will set trigger to 1 (line 9) which in turn has the effect to disclose the malicious code represented by malcode() at line 12, guarded by trigger. It can be observed that the lack of proper bound checking in the code snipped shown above is not to be considered as a suspicious pattern by itself. The mere use of an unsafe function as my_gets[9] does not imply that there is a memory error. In fact, bound checking could have been performed elsewhere by the programmer (which justifies the use of an unsafe function), or the programmer knows that at that point the input can never be bigger than buf.

In order to disclose the malicious code during analysis, the variable trigger has to eventually be marked as tainted, so that the code it guards can be further analyzed. The variable trigger is never tainted unless p, which can potentially be corrupted

---

[8] It is important to note that there are no constraints on the type of vulnerability introduced. A generic buffer overflow, an integer overflow, or a (custom) format string vulnerability would have done as well.

[9] This function resembles the well-known libc gets. The malware author can either use its own implementation or the one provided by the C library.

with tainted data by the malware, points to it. The problem of determining whether p could point to `trigger` is undecidable statically, thus augmentations to [1] using some form of static analysis do not help. On the other end, one might argue that the dynamic approach proposed in [1] could potentially accomplish the *detection* of the overflow, at least (while it is unlikely that the correct vulnerability exploitation can be achieved). In fact, given the aforementioned example, it is fairly easy for the analysis technique considered to generate a big-enough input which will eventually corrupt the pointer p. Even if such a technique is employed, we show that we can extend this example to make it even harder – if not unfeasible – to achieve this step.

To this end, it would be desirable to have a function f that is easy to compute, but hard to reason about some properties of it. By doing so, it is possible to modify the previous example in such a way to make it harder for the analyzer to even detect whether a memory error vulnerability is present or not. Such a situation is depicted by the following code snippet (the action performed by this code can be found in benign program as well).

```
...
int trigger;
...
void procInput(void) {
    int pad, n, l;
    char buf[4096+256];
    int *p = &pad;
    char *dst;

    ...
    n = read(s, buf, sizeof (buf));
    l = computespace(buf, n);
    // make sure we have enough room
    dst = alloca(l + 128);
    decode(buf, l, dst);
    ...
    *p = 1;
    ...
    if (trigger)
        malcode();
    ...
}
```

```
int computespace(char *src, int nread) {
    int i, k = 0;
    for (i = 0; i < nread; i++) {
        switch(src[i]) {
            case 0: k++; break;
            ...
            case 255: k++; break;
        }
    }
    return k;
}

void decode(char *src, int nread, char *dst) {
    int i, j;
    for (i = 0, j = 0; i < nread; i++, j++) {
        switch(src[i]) {
            case 0: dst[j] = src[i]; break;
            ...
            case 113: dst[j++] = src[i];
                      dst[j] = src[i];
                      break;
            case 114: dst[j] = src[i]; break;
            ...
            case 255: dst[j] = src[i]; break;
        }
    }
}
```

It is worth noting that the function `computespace` is easy to compute, but is relatively hard to reason about some properties of it. For instance, by looking at the source code, it is easy to understand that at the end of the computation k holds the same value as the length of the data read into the buffer `buf`. On the other end, the same reasoning can be hard to do on binaries and in an automated way. Thus, it is hard to correlate n, the number of read bytes, to l, the minimum number of space to allocate to be sure the function `decode` does not cause overflow. The function `decode` presents a problem by itself, by deliberately introducing the condition for an overflow to occur. In fact, it can cause `dst` to overflow into p if the number of bytes given as input (`buf`) whose

ASCII value is 113 exceed a certain threshold. Only an exhaustive search over all the possible input values and combination would deterministically trigger this memory error. Unfortunately, such an enumeration would be extremely onerous if not impossible to perform. Similar to NP-complete problems which are hard to solve while verification of correct answers is easy, it is rather simple for the attacker to provide the right input which will cause dst to overflow so that p can be corrupted in such a way to eventually disclose the malicious behavior. From the analysis point of view, instead, an exhaustive search will probably start with a sequence of length 1, trying all the possible 256 ASCII values. This does not cause overflow as there is a safe padding of 128 bytes for dst. Following this reasoning, a sequence of length k and 256^k combination have to be tried. For instance, a k equal to 128 can reach the boundaries of dst. This, however, would roughly require to test 256^{127} combinations to try out on average which is a fairly huge number.

Hiding malicious payload using interpreters.   As a final point, we note that the malicious payload need not even to be included in the program. It can be sent by an attacker as needed. We can use the techniques described above to prevent the malware analyzer from identifying this possibility.

One common technique for hiding payload has been based on code encryption. Unfortunately, this technique involves a step that is relatively unusual: data written by a program is subsequently executed. This step raises suspicion, and may prompt a careful manual analysis by a specialist. Malware writers would prefer to avoid this additional scrutiny, and hence would prefer to avoid this step. This can be done relatively easily by embedding an interpreter as the body of the function malcode() in the attack described above. As a result, the body of the interpreter can escape analysis. Moreover, note that interpreters are common in many types of software: documents viewers such as PDF or Postscript viewers, flash players, etc, so their presence, even if discovered, may not be unusual at all. Finally, it is relatively simple to develop a bare-bones assembly language and write an interpreter for it. All of these factors suggest that malware writers can, with modest effort, obfuscate execution of downloaded code using this technique, with the final goal to hide malicious behavior without raising any suspect.

4.2   Implications

The implications on whether dynamic information flow-based techniques can help to disclose, analyze, and understand the behavior of the next-generation of malware is similar to the ones pointed out in the rest of this paper. In fact, to detect the evasion technique proposed in the previous section, an information flow-based approach should ideally be able to trigger *any* memory error which may be present in the analyzed software, and automatically exploit the vulnerability so that interesting (i.e., tainted) previously disabled conditions will be examined. In the previous section we have shown how this could be hard – if not impossible – at all to achieve, if directly faced. Alternatively, information flow analyses could taint *any* memory location, considering all the possible combinations, and see how information is propagated. While this would eventually taint trigger and thus disclose the malicious behavior, it would drop the benefits provided by taint-tracking mechanisms which focus the analysis on *interesting* data, as *every* paths would be forced to be explored. For instance, the resulting analysis would be similar to the one proposed in [9] where, even if the underlying technique is different, the end result is that *every* path can potentially be explored, which of course is a hard task by itself. For instance, one may attempt to force execution of all program paths, but this is likely to be very expensive, and to suffer from semantic inconsistencies that may arise due to forcing execution down branches that are not taken during execution.

5   Related Work

Information flow analysis has been researched for a long time [6,12,14,20,23,32,41]. Early research was focused on multi-level security, where fine-grained analysis was not deemed necessary [6]. More recent work has been focused on language-based approaches, capable of tracking information flow at variable level [27]. Most of these techniques have been based on static analysis, and assume considerable cooperation from developers to provide various annotations, e.g., sensitivity labels for function parameters, endorsement and declassification annotations to eliminate false positives. Moreover, they typically work with simple, high-level languages, while much of security-critical contemporary software is written in low-level languages like C that use pointers, pointer arithmetic, and so on. Finally, it can be noted that despite their benefits static analyses are generally vulnerable to obfuscation scheme, as recently remarked by [22]. Therefore, it is reasonable to rely on dynamic or hybrid approaches, instead. As a result, information flow tracking for such software has been primarily based on run-time tracking of explicit flows that take place via assignments.

Recently, several different information flow-based approaches have been proposed in the literature [11,15,16,30,36,43]. They give good and promising results when employed to protect benign software from memory errors and other types of attacks, by relying on some implicit assumptions (e.g., no tainted code pointers should be dereferenced). The reason is because benign software is not designed to facilitate an attacker task, while malware, as we have seen, can be carefully crafted to embed evasion attacks, such as covert channels, and general memory corruption.

Probably, an ideal solution would require that untrusted binaries would carry proofs that some properties are guaranteed. This is achieved by proof-carrying code [25]. To be successful, this technique relies on some form of collaboration between the code producer and consumer. For instance, Medel *et al.* [21] and Yu *et al.* [46] proposed information flow analyses for typed assembly languages. Likewise, Barthe *et al.* provided non-interference properties for a JVM-like language [4] and dealt with timing attacks by using ACID transactions [5], as well. Unfortunately, it is unlikely that malware writers (i.e., the code producer, in this context) are going to give this form of collaboration which is necessary for the success of these approaches. Therefore, it is unlikely that these strategies would soon be adopted as is in the context of malicious software analysis and containment.

Driven by the recent practical success of information flow-based techniques, several researchers have started to propose solutions based on dynamic taint analysis to deal with malicious or, more generally, untrusted code [1,13,29,34,40,44,45]. During the last years, these techniques have been facing different tasks (e.g., classification, detection, and analysis) related to untrusted code analysis. Unfortunately, even if preliminary results show they are successful when dealing with untrusted code that has not been designed to stand and bypass the employed technique, as we hope the discussion in this paper highlighted, information flow is a fragile technique that has to be supported by new analyses to be more resilient to evasions purposely adopted by ever-evolving malware.

6 Conclusion

Information flow analysis has been applied with significant success to the problem of detecting attacks on trusted programs. Of late, there has been significant interest in extending these techniques to analyze the behavior of untrusted software and/or to enforce specific behaviors. Unfortunately, attackers can modify their software so as to exploit the weaknesses in information flow analysis techniques. As we described using several examples, it is relatively easy to devise these attacks, and to leak significant amounts of information (or damage system integrity) without being detected.

Mitigating the threats posed by untrusted software may require more conservative information flow techniques than those being used today for malware analysis. For instance, one could mark every memory location written by untrusted software as tainted; or, in the context of confidentiality, prevent any confidential information from being read by an untrusted program, or by preventing it from writing anything to public channels (e.g., network). Such approaches will undoubtedly limit the classes of untrusted applications to which information flow analysis can be applied. Alternatively, it may be possible to develop new information flow techniques that can be safely applied to untrusted software. For instance, by reasoning about quantity of information leaked (measured in terms of number of bits), one may be able to support benign untrusted software that leaks very small amounts of information. Finally, researchers need to develop additional analysis techniques that can complement information flow based techniques, e.g., combining strict memory access restrictions with information flows.

References

1. Moser, A., Kruegel, C., Kirda, E.: Exploring Multiple Execution Paths for Malware Analysis. In: IEEE Symposium on Security and Privacy (2007)
2. Nguyen-Tuong, A., Guarnieri, S., Greene, D., Shirley, J., Evans, D.: Automatically Hardening Web Applications Using Precise Tainting. In: 20th IFIP International Information Security Conference (2005)
3. Bala, V., Duesterwald, E., Banerjia, S.: Dynamo: a transparent dynamic optimization system. SIGPLAN Not. 35(5) (2000)
4. Barthe, G., Pichardie, D., Rezk, T.: A certified lightweight non-interference java bytecode verifier. Programming Languages and Systems (2007)
5. Barthe, G., Rezk, T., Warnier, M.: Preventing timing leaks through transactional branching instructions. In: Proceedings of 3rd Workshop on Quantitative Aspects of Programming Languages (QAPL 2005) (2005)
6. Bell, D.E., LaPadula, L.J.: Secure computer systems: Mathematical foundations. Technical Report MTR-2547, vol. 1, MITRE Corp. (1973)

7. Bellard, F.: Qemu, a fast and portable dynamic translator. In: ATEC 2005: Proceedings of the USENIX Annual Technical Conference 2005 on USENIX Annual Technical Conference (2005)
8. Biba, K.J.: Integrity considerations for secure computer systems. Technical Report ESD-TR-76-372, USAF Electronic Systems Division, Hanscom Air Force Base, Bedford, Massachusetts (1977)
9. Cadar, C., Ganesh, V., Pawlowski, P.M., Dill, D.L., Engler, D.R.: Exe: automatically generating inputs of death. In: CCS 2006: Proceedings of the 13th ACM conference on Computer and communications security (2006)
10. Chen, S., Xu, J., Nakka, N., Kalbarczyk, Z., Iyer, R.K.: Defeating memory corruption attacks via pointer taintedness detection. In: IEEE International Conference on Dependable Systems and Networks (DSN) (2005)
11. Chen, S., Xu, J., Nakka, N., Kalbarczyk, Z., Iyer, R.K.: Defeating Memory Corruption Attacks via Pointer Taintedness Detection. In: DSN 2005: Proceedings of the 2005 International Conference on Dependable Systems and Networks (DSN 2005) (2005)
12. Denning, D.E., Denning, P.J.: Certification of programs for secure information flow. Communications of the ACM 20(7) (1977)
13. Egele, M., Kruegel, C., Kirda, E., Yin, H., Song, D.: Dynamic spyware analysis. In: Usenix Tech Conference (2007)
14. Fenton, J.S.: Memoryless subsystems. Computing Journal 17(2) (1974)
15. Newsome, J., Song, D.: Dynamic Taint Analysis for Automatic Detection, Analysis, and Signature Generation of Exploits on Commodity Software. In: Proceedings of the Network and Distributed System Security Symposium (NDSS 2005) (2005)
16. Kong, J., Zou, C.C., Zhou, H.: Improving Software Security via Runtime Instruction-level Taint Checking. In: ASID 2006: Proceedings of the 1st workshop on Architectural and system support for improving software dependability (2006)
17. Luk, C., Cohn, R., Muth, R., Patil, H., Klauser, A., Lowney, G., Wallace, S., Janapa Reddi, V., Hazelwood, K.: Pin: building customized program analysis tools with dynamic instrumentation. SIGPLAN Not. 40(6) (2005)
18. McAfee. W32/hiv. virus information library (2000)
19. McAfee. W32/mydoom@mm. virus information library (2004)
20. McLean, J.: A general theory of composition for trace sets closed under selective interleaving functions. In: IEEE Symposium on Security and Privacy (1994)
21. Medel, R.: Typed Assembly Languages for Software Security. PhD thesis, Department of Computer Science, Stevens Institute of Technology (2006)
22. Moser, A., Kruegel, C., Kirda, E.: Limits of static analysis for malware detection. In: Choi, L., Paek, Y., Cho, S. (eds.) ACSAC 2007. LNCS, vol. 4697. Springer, Heidelberg (2007)
23. Myers, A.C.: JFlow: Practical mostly-static information flow control. In: ACM POPL, pp. 228–241 (1999)
24. Nanda, S., Li, W., Lam, L., Chiueh, T.: BIRD: Binary interpretation using runtime disassembly. In: IEEE/ACM Conference on Code Generation and Optimization (CGO) (2006)
25. Necula, G.C.: Proof-carrying code. In: Proceedings of the 24th ACM SIGPLAN-SIGACT Symposium on Principles of Programming Langauges (POPL 1997) (1997)
26. Nethercote, N., Seward, J.: Valgrind: A framework for heavyweight dynamic binary instrumentation. In: ACM SIGPLAN 2007 Conference on Programming Language Design and Implementation (PLDI 2007) (2007)
27. Perl. Perl taint mode, http://www.perl.org
28. Pietraszek, T., Berghe, C.V.: Defending against injection attacks through context-sensitive string evaluation. In: Valdes, A., Zamboni, D. (eds.) RAID 2005. LNCS, vol. 3858, pp. 124–145. Springer, Heidelberg (2006)

29. Portokalidis, G., Slowinska, A., Bos, H.: Argos: an emulator for fingerprinting zero-day attacks for advertised honeypots with automatic signature generation. SIGOPS Oper. Syst. Rev. 40(4) (2006)
30. Qin, F., Wang, C., Li, Z., Kim, H., Zhou, Y., Wu, Y.: LIFT: A low-overhead practical information flow tracking system for detecting general security attacks. In: IEEE/ACM International Symposium on Microarchitecture (2006)
31. Wojtczuk, R.N.: The Advanced return-into-lib(c) Exploits: PaX Case Study. Phrack Magazine $0x0b(0x3a)$. Phile #$0x04$ of $0x0e$ (2001)
32. Sabelfeld, A., Myers, A.C.: Language-based information-flow security. IEEE J. Selected Areas in Communications 21(1) (2003)
33. Saxena, P., Sekar, R., Puranik, V.: A practical technique for integrity protection from untrusted plug-ins. Technical Report SECLAB08-01, Stony Brook University (2008)
34. Stinson, E., Mitchell, J.C.: Characterizing bots' remote control behavior. In: Hämmerli, B.M., Sommer, R. (eds.) DIMVA 2007. LNCS, vol. 4579, pp. 89–108. Springer, Heidelberg (2007)
35. Clad "RORIV" Strife and Xdream ROJIV Blue. Ret onto Ret into Vsyscalls
36. Suh, G.E., Lee, J.W., Zhang, D., Devadas, S.: Secure Program Execution via Dynamic Information Flow Tracking. In: ASPLOS-XI: Proceedings of the 11th international conference on Architectural support for programming languages and operating systems (2004)
37. Szor, P.: The Art of Computer Virus Research and Defense. Symantec Press (2005)
38. TrendMicro. Bkdr.surila.g (w32/ratos). virus encyclopedia (2004)
39. Vasudevan, A.: WiLDCAT: An Integrated Stealth Environment for Dynamic Malware Analysis. PhD thesis, The University of Texas at Arlington, USA (2007)
40. Vogt, P., Nentwich, F., Jovanovic, N., Kirda, E., Kruegel, C., Vigna, G.: Cross-Site Scripting Prevention with Dynamic Data Tainting and Static Analysis. In: Proceeding of the Network and Distributed System Security Symposium (NDSS) (2007)
41. Volpano, D., Smith, G., Irvine, C.: A sound type system for secure flow analysis. Journal of Computer Security (JCS) 4(3) (1996)
42. Volpano, D.M.: Safety versus secrecy. In: Cortesi, A., Filé, G. (eds.) SAS 1999. LNCS, vol. 1694. Springer, Heidelberg (1999)
43. Xu, W., Bhatkar, S., Sekar, R.: Taint-enhanced policy enforcement: A practical approach to defeat a wide range of attacks. In: USENIX Security Symposium (2006)
44. Yin, H., Liang, Z., Song, D.: Hookfinder: Identifying and understanding malware hooking behaviors. In: NDSS (2008)
45. Yin, H., Song, D., Manuel, E., Kruegel, C., Kirda, E.: Panorama: Capturing system-wide information flow for malware detection and analysis. In: Proceedings of the 14th ACM Conferences on Computer and Communication Security (CCS 2007) (2007)
46. Yu, D., Islam, N.: A typed assembly language for confidentiality. In: Sestoft, P. (ed.) ESOP 2006 and ETAPS 2006. LNCS, vol. 3924, pp. 162–179. Springer, Heidelberg (2006)

Expanding Malware Defense by
Securing Software Installations[*]

Weiqing Sun[1], R. Sekar[1], Zhenkai Liang[2], and V.N. Venkatakrishnan[3]

[1] Department of Computer Science, Stony Brook University
[2] Department of Computer Science, Carnegie Mellon University
[3] Department of Computer Science, University of Illinois, Chicago

Abstract. Software installation provides an attractive entry vector for malware: since installations are performed with administrator privileges, malware can easily get the enhanced level of access needed to install backdoors, spyware, rootkits, or "bot" software, and to hide these installations from users. Previous research has been focused mainly on securing the execution phase of untrusted software, while largely ignoring the safety of installations. Even security-enhanced operating systems such as SELinux and Vista don't usually impose restrictions during software installs, expecting the system administrator to "know what she is doing." This paper addresses this "gap in armor" by securing software installations. Our technique can support a diversity of package managers and software installers. It is based on a framework that simplifies the development and enforcement of policies that govern safety of installations. We present a simple policy that can be used to prevent untrusted software from modifying any of the files used by benign software packages, thus blocking the most common mechanism used by malware to ensure that it is run automatically after each system reboot. While the scope of our technique is limited to the installation phase, it can be easily combined with approaches for secure execution, e.g., by ensuring that all future runs of an untrusted package will take place within an administrator-specified sandbox. Our experimental evaluation has considered over one hundred benign and untrusted software packages. Our technique was able to block malicious packages among these without breaking non-malicious ones.

Keywords: Untrusted code, Malicious code, Software installation, Sandboxing.

1 Introduction

Malware, including adware, spyware, rootkits, backdoors, trojans, and bot software, has become a major security concern on desktop systems over the past few years. Although it was common in the past for software to be executed automatically when users click on attachments or hyperlinks, this practice is no longer that common: execution of

---

[*] This research is supported in part by an ONR grant N000140710928 and NSF grants CNS-0627687, CNS-0716584 and CNS-0551660.

D. Zamboni (Ed.): DIMVA 2008, LNCS 5137, pp. 164–185, 2008.

untrusted software[1] typically requires explicit user consent, or an exploit on web browser or email handler[2].

Software installation provides a more attractive entry vector for malware than competing alternatives such as remote exploits since installations are usually carried out with highest (administrative level) privileges, thereby providing malware the level of access it needs to embed itself deeply and firmly into the system, and to hide its presence from system monitoring utilities. In contrast, programs targeted by exploits (including those embedded in e-mail attachments or browser links) may run with user-level privileges, making it harder for malware to embed itself into the system. Furthermore, security-conscious users can deploy defenses against remote exploits (by using firewalls, buffer overflow defenses such as address-space randomization, etc.) and malicious e-mail attachments and other implicitly downloaded programs (by automatically sandboxing them). In contrast, few defenses are available to secure software installations. Even secure operating systems such as SELinux don't usually impose restrictions during software installs, expecting the system administrator to "know what she is doing." Unfortunately, even the most sophisticated users typically do not understand what goes on when complex software packages are installed. Often, these packages run scripts or other programs with administrative privileges, with the user having no knowledge of these activities. Software installations thus provide an ideal vehicle for malware to surreptitiously inject itself into a host system.

In spite of the threats posed by the installation phase, previous research on untrusted software security [17,4,27,31,22,37,33] has been focused primarily on their execution phase. Relatively little work has been done on securing the installation phase. This paper seeks to address this overlooked problem, and develops a solution that works well with existing techniques for securing the execution phase. Specifically, our technique achieves the following goals that we consider essential for secure software installation:

- *Untrusted software should not interfere with the operation of benign packages.* Sophisticated spyware and rootkits can hide themselves in such a way that trusted components in the system end up executing their malicious payload. Since trusted system components aren't typically sandboxed or carefully monitored, this makes it easier for malware to execute without being noticed.
- *Untrusted software should not be allowed to execute outside a user-specified sandbox or virtualization environment.* Some malware may cause damage during installation, but others may cause damage when they are run. To guard against the latter, our approach can install untrusted code in a manner that it cannot be run outside a sandbox (or a virtualization environment).
- *Untrusted software should be (securely) uninstallable at any time.* Malware may install itself in such a way that uninstallation won't work properly. For instance, they may use scripts to copy files that are unspecified in the package; these files won't be removed during uninstallation.

---

[1] We use the term "untrusted software" to refer to software obtained from untrusted sources on the Internet. Untrusted software may be malicious or non-malicious. On the other hand, benign software, which is obtained from trusted sources, is assumed to be non-malicious.

[2] This observation is supported by a white-paper from Symantec [11], which indicates that most adware and spyware enter desktop systems via an explicit software installation step.

Our technique does not make many assumptions about what constitutes a software installation — it may involve running a software package manager such as RedHat's rpm, Debian's dpkg, running a self-installing executable, installation from a tarball, etc. It may also involve running higher-level GUI-based installers that in turn invoke these lower level installation mechanisms. Our key observation is that once there is an explicit user consent involved, at that point, we can "wrap" the command that is executed for installation so that it runs within our Secure Software Installer (*SSI*).

The rest of this paper is organized as follows. Section 2 describes our threat model. Section 3 presents an overview of our approach and describes the high level design of Secure Software Installer (*SSI*). Section 4 describes the installation policies implemented in *SSI*. Section 5 presents an experimental evaluation of *SSI*. Related work is discussed in Section 6, followed by concluding remarks in Section 7.

2   Threat Model and Defense Overview

Our approach is based on the availability of mechanisms to distinguish between benign and untrusted software. For instance, all software that is digitally signed by a trusted vendor may be classified as benign, while the rest may be deemed untrusted.

We divide the threats posed by untrusted software into three phases: installation phase, execution phase, and uninstallation phase. A variety of solutions are available for securing the execution phase, including runtime policy enforcement (also known as sandboxing) [27,23,17,31,6,4,25,12], isolated execution [22,32,37], and file-label-based integrity protection [33,28]. Therefore, this paper is concerned only with the installation and uninstallation phases. Nevertheless, to demonstrate the end-to-end feasibility of our approach, our implementation includes a defense for the execution phase.

Software installation (and uninstallation) requires a higher level of privilege and access than the execution phase. This makes it difficult to define policies that ensure security objectives without breaking installations. The central contribution of this paper is that of developing policies and enforcement techniques to overcome this challenge.

2.1   Install-Time Threats

We assume that *the goal of malware is to execute some or all of its code while being free of the above-mentioned confinement mechanisms* that are to be employed during the execution phase of untrusted software. Before enumerating possible ways in which this goal can be achieved, it is helpful to have an understanding of the main features of modern software package managers. The specific details given here pertain to RedHat Package Manager (RPM), although the description is applicable (with minor changes) to other package managers such as Debian's dpkg.

An RPM package contains a dozen or more components, most of which are descriptive in nature, e.g., name, version, vendor, copyright, URL, etc. There are five components that are security-relevant:

– *Files contained in the package,* i.e., the files copied by RPM during installation.
– *Scripts.* A package may contain several shell scripts that are run at various stages of installation such as before building a source package, before installation, after installation, etc. RPM runs these scripts at the specified stage.

- *Requires.* This tag specifies dependencies that a package may have. A package may depend on one or more packages. Rather than specifying these dependencies using package names, RPM and Debian permit the use of arbitrary strings. A package that has a dependency *s* will be installed only if there is already another package installed on the system that "provides" *s*. The use of arbitrary strings for dependencies allows for multiple implementations of the same functionality.
- *Provides.* The functionality provided by a package. It will be matched against the "requires" field as described above.
- *Conflicts.* If a package conflicts with one or more packages, those are listed in this section. A new package that conflicts with an existing package will not be installed.

Based on the above description, the following attack avenues are possible that may let untrusted code to escape confinement:

1. *Attacks that perform malicious actions at install time.* RPM does not pose any restrictions on the scripts contained in a package. Thus, in the absence of additional protection, arbitrary attacks on the host are possible. *SSI* performs the installation within a virtual environment, so that these attacks would be isolated from the host.

    The only way in which the host environment is affected in *SSI* is due to copying of files modified during the installation — these files are copied out of the virtual environment onto the host. Hence the rest of the discussion below is concerned with how files may be used to achieve the goals of malicious code.

2. *Attacks that modify files used by benign packages.* By modifying these files, a malicious package may be able to inject its code into the execution flow of a benign application. Since benign applications are not constrained in any way, such an attack would allow malicious packages to escape confinement. There are two cases to consider here:

   - *Existing benign packages.* A malicious package may claim to contain a library or executable that is already used by an existing benign application. As a result, these files may be overwritten when the package is installed, and hence future runs of this benign application may end up executing code that belongs to an untrusted package. It is also conceivable that an attack based on modifying a non-code file (e.g., configuration file used by a benign application) may subvert the operation of a benign application and cause it to execute the code of an untrusted package. *SSI* prevents these attacks by restricting untrusted packages from modifying (or deleting) any existing file other than those previously installed by an untrusted package.
   - *Benign packages installed in the future.* Instead of targeting an existing benign application, a malicious package may target a package that is likely to be installed in the future. Alternatively, it may claim to provide (in the sense of "provides" feature described above) a functionality needed by a future benign package. In these cases, *SSI* would permit the initial installation of these files belonging to the untrusted application. However, at the time of installation of the benign package, *SSI* will detect that a benign package depends on an untrusted package, or contains files belonging to an untrusted package. In either case, *SSI* disallows installation and notifies the user so that he/she can uninstall the untrusted package before attempting to install the benign package (possibly after installing additional benign packages that satisfy the dependencies of the current benign package).

The above discussion assumes that package dependency information is complete. However, it is possible that some optional libraries or configuration files may be omitted in the package specification. Worse, for software installed from tarballs, no dependency information is available. *SSI* employs a second line of defense to prevent untrusted libraries and executables from being directly used by benign applications. It installs libraries in separate directories that are included in the search path used by the dynamic loader for untrusted applications, but not for benign applications[3]. Untrusted executables are installed in such a way that when they are invoked, they are run within a confinement environment.

While our approach copes with missing dependencies on library or executable files, it does not currently implement a complete defense against missing configuration file dependencies. This is partly because we considered it a low-risk, and partly because the threat could be eliminated in the isolation-based execution confinement mechanism used in our implementation. However, as described in Section 5.1, our experiments suggest that a more general solution would be based on restricting the data files written by untrusted applications.

3. *Attacks contained in the files belonging to an untrusted package.* As described above, *SSI* ensures that all executables belonging to the untrusted code are "wrapped" in such a manner that when they are invoked, they would automatically be started up within a sandbox or virtual environment.

4. *Attacks on integrity of package database.* Package managers typically use a few files to maintain a database of packages installed on the system. Since many of the policies described above were based on the content of this database, these policies can be undermined by attacks that compromise the integrity of the database. To preclude these attacks, *SSI* verifies that the database changes resulting from the installation of an untrusted package concern that package only, and do not modify (or insert) information about other packages.

Our discussion in this paper is focused primarily on integrity threats, and does not consider denial-of-service threats[4].

2.2   Uninstall-Time Threats

Software uninstallation is carried out with the same level of privileges as the installation phase. Contemporary package managers run scripts provided by the package. Thus, the threat model parallels that of the installation phase. Specifically, it consists of:

1. *Attacks that perform malicious actions during uninstallation.* These remain the same as during installation, and are addressed in the same way.

---

[3] On Linux, this is done by including these directories in the LD_LIBRARY_PATH environment variable before running an untrusted application, and not including them for benign applications.

[4] This is why "conflicts" did not enter the discussion above — a malicious package may claim to conflict with a large number of packages that are likely to be installed in the future. When a user attempts to install them, she will get an error message. It is expected that in this case, and in other cases involving conflicts or failures relating to untrusted packages, the user will uninstall the untrusted package before proceeding further.

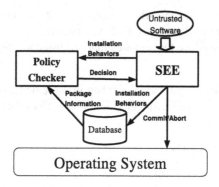

Fig. 1. Design and operation of *SSI*

2. *Attacks that leave behind files after uninstallation.* We do not distinguish in this case between different types of files, or whether these files relate to benign packages in any way. Instead, *SSI* ensures that all files that were installed by an untrusted package are removed on uninstallation.
3. *Attacks that remove files belonging to other packages.* SSI enforces a policy that ensures that only the files copied into the host at installation time can be removed at uninstall-time.
4. *Attacks on the integrity of package database.* The attacks discussed in the installation phase under this category continue to be possible at uninstallation time, and can be prevented using the same high level policies (i.e., ensuring that the database updates are consistent with the package removed.)
5. *Attacks that cause errors during uninstall.* Such attacks are possible if the scripts related to the package perform actions that lead to an error, which in turn cause the package manager to abort uninstallation. While errors would cause a rollback during the installation phase, it is not an option here: we wish to remove the package. Our approach is to use the "force" option provided by package managers to forcibly remove the package from the database. (As mentioned above, *SSI* already ensures that the files installed by the package are removed.)

3   Approach Overview

Our approach consists of the following phases:

– *Initial installation in a virtual environment,* where the installation can proceed without violating host integrity or install-time failures. The actions observed during the installation are logged for further analysis in the policy-checking phase.
– *Policy checking* to detect if the actions observed during initial installation violated the requirements captured by an installation policy.
– *Commit/abort* phase, which propagates the files modified during installation to the host if no policy violations occurred. Otherwise, installation is aborted, leaving the host state as if the installation never took place.

– *Secure execution* phase, during which untrusted software can be invoked within a confinement mechanism that is specified at install time.
– *Secure uninstallation* phase that ensures that untrusted software can be uninstalled safely at any time.

These phases (and their rationale) are described in more detail below. Figure 1 shows the components of *SSI* involved in the installation as well as the uninstallation phase.

3.1   Initial Installation Phase

There are two basic options for protection against attacks during the installation phase. First, the installation could be performed within a sandbox that prohibits the execution of any action that has the potential to compromise host security. Unfortunately, such an *eager enforcement* approach is likely to fail: software installation typically requires writing to system directories, and updating databases that record the software installed on the system. Denying these actions will lead most installations to fail, while permitting them has the potential to damage system integrity. In particular, there is no easy way to determine whether an individual database update is safe or not: it is the end result achieved by a series of updates that can be determined to be "safe" or "unsafe." For this reason, *SSI* determines safety by first performing the installation within a virtual environment, and examining post-installation system state for verifying safety policies. As we describe later, such state-based policies provide a novel capability that is crucial for expressing and enforcing the safety requirements for securing software installations.

We rely on our Safe Execution Environment (SEE) [32] for initial installation. SEEs offer several benefits over the alternative of using virtual machines for this purpose. Chief among them is that of accurate environment reproduction: SEEs are based on one-way isolation, which makes the host state visible inside the SEE. In other words, they provide an initial environment that is exactly the same as the host environment. As such, software installations, which have a number of host dependencies (including those based on previously installed software, their releases and patch versions, and so on) can be successfully installed within the SEE if they can be installed on the host OS. In contrast, virtual machines require significant additional effort for exact duplication of the host environment.

The second important reason for using SEE is that they offer the ability to commit the results of installation onto the host environment. If we relied on virtual machines, there is typically no easy way to migrate the changes made within the VM to the host OS. The obvious approach of rerunning the installation on the host OS after policy verification can turn out to be dangerous: a malicious software package may detect that it is being run within a VM the first time, and may not exhibit malicious behavior. For this reason, our installation policy may hold for the installation within the VM. However, when the installation is rerun on the host, malicious software can detect that it is no longer within a VM, and exhibit malicious behavior that violates our policy. In contrast, with the SEE, the behavior verified against a safety policy is the same one that gets committed to the host, thus ensuring that installation policies cannot be violated.

Our approach can support software installation using means other than package managers, e.g., tarballs and and self-installing executables. This is because our approach has no direct dependency on the tools used for installation — they are simply run inside the SEE, and the resource accesses are observed, and policies enforced on their basis.

SSI uses the Alcatraz tool [22,5] for realizing an SEE. Alcatraz uses copy-on-write to handle file operations, i.e., any host files modified within the SEE are copied into the SEE and modified. The modifications are not visible to host processes unless they are also running within the same SEE. Modifications involving other resources (e.g., mounting files, arbitrary communication with processes outside SEE) are controlled by a policy that forbids most accesses that have the potential to harm host security. More details on SEE implementation (including the containment policies used) can be found in [22,32]. For *SSI*, we made a few modifications to Alcatraz: (a) replacement of manual determination of safety with an automated policy enforcement mechanism, (b) support for the Secure File Container feature described later, and (c) selective relaxation of restrictions on non-file resource accesses within Alcatraz so that software installers can download software from the Internet.

3.2 Policy Checking Phase

Previous work on SEE relied on a manual approach for determining the safety of the actions performed by untrusted software. Unfortunately, such a manual approach is cumbersome and error-prone. We have therefore developed an automated approach for determining the safety of software installations. Safety is defined by a policy, which is derived from the high-level description provided in Section 2. An important innovation in our approach is the development and use of *state-based policies* that can refer to the operations performed during installation, as well as the *actual end result* of installation. Such state-based policies are strictly more powerful than the class of policies that are enforceable using runtime monitoring [29], where decisions regarding permissibility of an operation need to be made without knowing about future operations made by a program. For instance, an installation program may need to add a new userid to the password file, and may do this by creating a copy of the password file, editing it to add a user, removing the original password file and then renaming the copy. A runtime monitoring approach would have to prevent the removal step of the password file, whereas a state-based policy can check that the end result of the program is acceptable: specifically, the difference between the initial and final password file is the addition of a line that corresponds to the new user, respecting other criteria such as the use of previously unused user and groupids, and a permitted shell.

A second innovation in our policies is that of action attribution: instead of requiring policies to be specified entirely in terms of low-level operations (or state changes), our policy framework allows these low-level operations to be mapped to higher-level operations, and the specification of policies in terms of these operations. Taking the userid addition example again, rather than stating a policy that relies on computing file differences between the original and modified password files and verifying certain characteristics of these differences, we can instead correlate the changes to the execution of a program *useradd:* in this case, the policy can be simpler, stating that the execution of `useradd` command with certain arguments is permitted.

Different policies can be associated with different installations — our policy framework provides flexibility in this regard. However, in practice, we expect a small number of policies to be sufficient. One policy would concern benign packages, while a small set of policies may be specified for untrusted packages. (Our implementation uses a single policy for all untrusted applications, although this will need to be changed if we wish to support untrusted applications that require a higher level of access, e.g., servers that get started automatically after reboot.) The specific policies used in our implementation are described in Section 4.

Package Database. The policy checker makes policy decisions by querying a database, which consists of two components:

- Package management database. It is used by an existing package manager such as RPM or Debian to store information about the contents and dependency of all the installed packages.
- *SSI*-database. It is used to maintain package names, trust labels, and information about software installed outside of a package manager, such as tarballs and self-installing executables.

SSI currently supports RPM database, but its dependence on the details of the database is minimal. The implementation needs to be able to query RPM about the packages installed on the system, and their dependencies. For this reason, *SSI* can be easily ported to other package managers such as Debian. Moreover, *SSI* has no dependency on the higher level tools used during installation, e.g., Gnorpm or Synaptic package manager. These tools are simply run inside the SEE, and the safety policies checked against the resulting system state and the actions observed within the SEE.

3.3   Commit/Abort Phase

If the policy checker reports success, then the results of installation are committed. Otherwise, the entire SEE is discarded, which ensures that the host OS state is unchanged by the installation phase. The commit/abort phase is provided by SEE: we made one change, as described below, to ensure that untrusted software would always execute within a user-specified sandbox.

3.4   Secure Execution of Installed Software

An untrusted application may not violate any install-time policy, but may still exhibit malicious behavior when it is run. For instance, a game program may also act as a "bot," polling an attacker-specified network address for malicious actions to carry out. Or, it may communicate with benign processes and may attempt to compromise them. For these reasons, it is important that the untrusted code be monitored at runtime, and its actions confined to ensure that it cannot compromise system security. We consider three options in this regard: sandboxing, isolated execution, and OS-based integrity protection.

Sandboxing. A number of sandboxing and policy confinement techniques have been developed [27,23,17,31,6,4,25,12], and may be used with *SSI*. *SSI* relies on a simple technique to ensure sandboxing of untrusted executables: while copying an executable from the SEE to the host OS, it is renamed, and the execution permission is removed. Libraries used by untrusted applications are stored in non-standard directories to minimize the likelihood that they could be accidentally used by benign applications. A wrapper script is created with the original name of the executable, which is then responsible for properly setting up the search path used by the dynamic loader, and executing the original executable within the sandbox. Note that this simple approach can be defeated by the user, but this is not our concern since we assume that the user is cooperative, i.e., the user will not actively subvert *SSI*.

Development of suitable sandboxing policies is a research problem in itself, and is not the focus of this paper. We simply observe that sandboxing policies are relatively easy to develop for some classes of untrusted code that are most commonly used, namely, document viewers and media players, as they require minimal access to OS resources.

Isolation. Instead of using a sandbox, the execution phase may rely on an isolation-based approach. This is the easiest option in our implementation since we are already using an isolation based technique in *SSI*. To ensure isolated execution of untrusted code, we modified Alcatraz so that it commits the results of untrusted installations to a separate section of the filesystem called a Secure File Container (SFC). The use of SFC ensures that none of the files (libraries, executables, or configuration files) contained in the untrusted software package can be accidentally used by benign applications. We use the same technique as with the sandboxing approach for invoking untrusted executables: a wrapper script is created with the original name of such executables. This wrapper script starts Alcatraz, initializes it with the environment within the SFC, and starts execution of the original executable.

As in the case of sandboxing, there remain some usability issues with isolation-based techniques — this is a topic of ongoing research in safe execution of untrusted software. As advances are made in this area, they can be seamlessly integrated with our approach focused on secure installations.

Information-Flow Based Integrity Protection. *SSI* will work seamlessly with information-flow based integrity techniques for Linux [33,28,21]. Indeed, *SSI* has been developed so that, together with the PPI integrity technique described in [33], it can provide a comprehensive defense against malware. In particular, *SSI* can simply label the files belonging to untrusted application with low integrity, while files belonging to benign packages are labelled with high integrity. Since PPI ensures that information cannot flow from low-integrity sources to high-integrity sinks, it makes sure that benign processes and the files used by them won't be corrupted by untrusted applications.

3.5   Secure Uninstallation Phase

Secure uninstallation is supported for untrusted packages. If a package A is to be uninstalled, we go ahead and uninstall all other packages that depend on A. Since our policies do not permit benign packages to depend on untrusted packages, uninstallation of untrusted packages can always be performed without breaking benign packages.

The threats relating to uninstallation phase and the approach for mitigating them were already discussed in Section 2, while the specifics of our policy are described in Section 4.2.

Within *SSI*, uninstallation first runs the normal package uninstallation process (e.g., rpm -e). It then determines if the actions performed during the uninstallation are permitted by the uninstallation policy specified in Section 4.2. Otherwise, *SSI* forces the package manager to remove the package from its database (without actual uninstallation), and then deletes all the files installed by the untrusted package.

4   Installation Policies

4.1   Policy Framework

One of the main difficulties with policy-based approaches is the difficulty of policy development. Sandboxing policies can routinely get quite large and complex since (a) they are stated in terms of low-level primitives (which files can be accessed and which ones can't be), and (b) there are a large number of files on the system, and it is time-consuming (and error-prone) to identify all files that an application should be permitted to access. Moreover, a different policy is needed for each application, as the set of allowable and/or required resource accesses differ for different applications.

We observed that the principal reason for policy complexity is the large gap between high-level policy objectives such as those stated in the Introduction, and the low-level policies that can actually be enforced, which deal with specific resources that can be accessed, and the operations that are permissible. To combat this problem, we developed an approach that enables automated generation of lower-level policies from higher level policies. The specific techniques and mechanisms used to support higher level policies are described below.

Deriving low-level, enforceable policies from software package dependencies. We leverage the contents of software packages to ensure that untrusted packages cannot modify or corrupt files used by benign packages. Specifically, the following pieces of information can be obtained from a software package: (a) the files contained in the package, and (b) the names of other packages that this package depends on. The second type of information is readily available for RPM or Debian packages, but not for tarballs or self-installing executables. This has not been a serious problem in practice since we need (b) only for benign packages, which are typically from an OS distribution vendor that uses a package manager such as RPM or Debian. However, if it becomes necessary to install a benign package that arrives in the form of a tarball, the following work-around could be used to obtain an approximation for dependency information. In particular, the application can be executed within a virtual environment (e.g., our SEE) and its file accesses observed. The application then has a dependency on all the packages that contain one or more of the files accessed by the application. We note that the list obtained in this way may not be complete, but is clearly an improvement over the alternative of assuming no dependencies. Moreover, as described in Section 2, our approach incorporates a second line of defense to guard against attacks that may be possible due to incomplete dependence information.

To use the above procedure, benign packages need to be identified. We expect this information to remain the same across a given OS version, although it is conceivable that individual users[5] may have some differences in terms of the sources they are willing to trust. Such differences may be captured by appropriately modifying a configuration file that specifies this information.

In our implementation, where RPM is the default package manager, we query the installed packages on the system, and based on the signature of the RPM package, a trust label is assigned and recorded in the *SSI*-database. We verify that installed benign packages only depend on other benign packages. (If this is not true, there is an inconsistency, and user input is needed to resolve it.) For packages that are installed outside of the package manager, their contents (and optionally, dependencies) are maintained in the *SSI*-database.

State-based policies. Another important reason for the complexity of typical sandboxing policies is due to the need to ensure that each permitted action leaves the system in a safe state. This requires explicit consideration of all possible operations that can be performed by an application, and their possible operands, and identification of those operation/operand combinations that are safe. Since there can be many ways for an attack to achieve the same objective, the size (and complexity) of policies can correspondingly increase. Moreover, as illustrated using the user addition example earlier, some sequence of operations may first take the system to an unsafe state before bringing it back to a safe state.

For the reasons mentioned above, *SSI* uses state-based policies that can reference (a) the final state of the system, (b) the initial state of the system, and (c) the sequence of operations that took the system from the initial to the final state. This enables powerful policies to be specified, e.g., we can capture any sequence of operations that allow "a file f to be updated to an f' such that f and f' differ in at most k lines, and all these lines match a regular expression R."

The power offered by our post-execution analysis framework has steered us towards an extensible approach for verifying state-based policies, where new policy primitives could be defined by essentially writing scripts that operate on the state within the SEE, and return *true* or *false* indicating whether the policy was satisfied. We have chosen this alternative for expediency, as opposed to defining a special-purpose policy language.

Providing safe exceptions using action attribution. Sometimes, the installation of a package may require modifications to some files whose integrity is critical. For instance, /etc/ld.so.cache file needs to be updated after installing new shared libraries. Similarly, some packages may need to create new users. Arbitrary changes to files such as /etc/ld.so.cache and /etc/passwd will harm the system, so *SSI* needs to provide mechanisms to perform controlled updates to these files that ensure safety.

One approach for permitting safe changes was described in the previous paragraph: by comparing modifications to the file, and defining safety criteria for these modifications. However, an alternative approach may be preferable in some cases. This approach

---

[5] Our intent is that the "user" is a system administrator — e.g., an OS distribution vendor may provide the list of benign and untrusted packages, or they may be maintained by user communities.

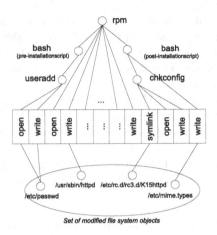

Fig. 2. Behavior of Apache Installation

exploits the fact that often, the system already provides utilities for safely updating certain critical pieces of information. Examples include the `ldconfig` program to update the `ld.so.cache` file, `useradd` and `groupadd` programs to create new users or groups, and `chkconfig` program to enable or disable automatic startup of a specified service.

Based on the above observation, our approach allows specification of policies that permit execution of such utility programs, with constraints on argument values. Such an approach avoids the need for writing policies that need to "understand" the format of configuration files. For instance, instead of describing the format of a "safe" entry in `/etc/passwd`, we can state that it is safe to call the `useradd` program with certain parameters, e.g., with a userid other than 0, and not belonging to any existing group.

Policies in terms of higher-level actions such as `useradd` are supported by the policy checker as follows. First, a raw log of operations performed within SEE is obtained. The policy checker analyzes this log to derive parent-child relationships between processes, the programs executed by each process, and the resource accesses made by them. This information can be represented using a tree structure shown in Figure 2. In this tree, the internal nodes represent processes, while the leaves represent modification operations. The program corresponding to the root process of this tree is `rpm`, as we used `rpm` from the command-line in this example.

If the policy states that `useradd` can be used with certain restrictions on parameters, the policy checker first verifies if the invocation of this program in the SEE log conforms to these restrictions. It also makes sure that the program did not interact with any untrusted components, other than being invoked from an untrusted script with the arguments as permitted by the policy. If these checks succeed, all operations in the log that can be attributed to `useradd` or one of its children are deleted. Policies regarding resource accesses are checked after this step.

The power of the attribution mechanism is easier to illustrate in the context of more complex software packages. For this reason, Figure 2 shows the attribution tree for Apache. The scripts of this packages are executed in child processes of the `rpm` process.

The pre-installation script is executed first, adding a user account though the `useradd` command. Then `rpm` copies the contents of the package into their destination. Finally, a post-installation script uses `chkconfig` to start up Apache automatically at boot time, and then updates `/etc/mime.types` file.

4.2 Policy for Installing Untrusted Packages

Our installation policy consists of the following components. These components correspond directly to the threat model described in Section 2. We also describe the enforcement of these policies based on the mechanisms and techniques described above.

We remark that the policy described below is exactly the same as the one used in our evaluation.

1. *Attacks that perform malicious actions at install time.* These are prevented by policies that are already enforced by SEE, which confine non-file accesses made within SEE. We made two modifications to the default policy: the installer application is permitted to access the network, so that it can download packages from the Internet if needed. We also make an exception for communication with the X-server. (Alternatively, untrusted applications may be directed to a nested X-server using the Xnest [3]. This option ensures that the primary X-server is not compromised by untrusted code.)

2. *Attacks that modify files used by benign packages.*
   - *Files that an existing benign package depends on.* SSI ensures that an untrusted package does not modify or delete any existing file, except possibly those installed by an untrusted package.
   - *Files that a future benign package depends on.* As mentioned earlier, this is prevented by enforcing a policy that restricts benign packages from (a) having dependencies on untrusted packages, and (b) containing files that belong to untrusted packages. The contents of the package manager database and SSI database are used to compute the complete list of files that are within a package, as well as the complete list of files that it depends on.
   - *Files used by a benign package without specifying dependency.* Since we do not know that such a file would be used by an existing or future package, no install-time policy can be specified to preclude this. Instead, this possibility is avoided at the time of execution of benign software. The exact mechanisms differ, depending upon the technique used during execution phase, and were described in Section 3.4.

3. *Attacks contained in files belonging to untrusted package.* These attacks are contained using a confinement mechanism during the execution of untrusted software. The choices for doing this were described in Section 3.4.

4. *Attacks on integrity of package database.* We enforce a policy that ensures that the changes to the package database are consistent with the files actually copied into the system. In particular, (a) the package contents should include all and only the files that were reported as having been created or modified within the SEE, and (b) any files that were reported as having been deleted within the SEE must be part of the package. Moreover, information regarding all other packages in the database should remain unchanged.

5. *Granting exceptions based on attribution.* Updates to the file /etc/ld.so.cache using ldconfig are always permitted. Addition of a new MIME type in the file /etc/mime.types is permitted as long as it conforms to the state-based policy described before. These exceptions are recorded in *SSI* database so that their inverse operations can be permitted during uninstallation.

4.3   Policy for Uninstallation of Untrusted Packages

The uninstallation policy follows the outline specified in Section 2.

1. *Attacks that perform malicious actions during uninstallation.* These remain the same as during installation.
2. *Attacks that leave behind files after uninstallation.* The contents of the package database are queried to obtain the list of files installed by an untrusted package. If all these files are not removed during uninstallation, they are forcibly removed.
3. *Attacks that remove files belonging to other packages.* Once again, the contents of the package database are queried for the list of files installed by the untrusted application. Only these files are permitted to be deleted at commit time.
4. *Attacks on the integrity of package database.* These are thwarted by checking that the only change to the database is the removal of the untrusted package, and that none of the information relating to other packages have been changed.
5. *Attacks that cause errors during uninstall.* These attacks are handled as described in Section 3.5.
6. If *SSI* database indicates that exceptions were granted, operations that have the inverse effect are permitted.

Currently, there is no general way to identify how to "invert" an operation. Instead, we manually specify how to invert an operation on a case-by-case basis. For instance, for an operation that adds a MIME type, we specify that inverse operation has the effect of deleting the added MIME type.

4.4   Installation Policy for Benign Packages

The only policy enforced is that *benign packages should not depend on untrusted packages.* No policies are enforced during uninstallation of benign packages.

5   Evaluation

We have implemented *SSI* on RedHat Linux (CentOS 4.1). Our implementation uses a publicly available tool Alcatraz [5] as the SEE. The implementation of the policy checker and the user interface consists of 7K lines of Java code. In this section, we present an evaluation of the functionality and performance of this implementation.

5.1   Evaluation of Functionality

The goal of this section is to evaluate the utility of *SSI* in securing real-world software packages. In this regard, we considered four cases: (a) installation of malicious packages, (b) installation of nonmalicious untrusted packages, (c) installation of benign packages, and (d) secure uninstallation. Of these, (a) and (b) use the policies described in Sections 4.2, (c) uses policies from Section 4.4, while (d) uses policies from Section 4.3.

Real-world packages don't embody all aspects of malicious behavior considered in Section 2. As a result, they do not stress our policies. In other words, confidence in the security provided by our approach is more a function of the completeness of the threat model and the soundness of the policies described earlier rather than the experimental evaluation. However, our experiments on nonmalicious and benign software involved a much larger number of packages, so they do demonstrate that our policies do not lead to false positives for typical untrusted packages.

Installation of Malicious Packages

Ideally, *SSI* would be evaluated by experimenting with a large collection of malware samples. Unfortunately, such an evaluation is not feasible on our chosen platform (Linux) since malware is relatively uncommon on Linux. What we have been able to do is to evaluate *SSI* using rootkits that are available from [1] — these were the only malware collection that we were able to obtain. In addition, since these rootkits are easily detected by our technique, we developed two additional test cases that embody a more sophisticated attack strategy.

More generally, we observe that most malware is designed so that it runs in the background, and is started up automatically at boot time. This requires modification of startup files, e.g., files within /etc/init.d/ on Linux. Since these files belong to benign packages, *SSI* will likely detect such attempts and abort the installation of such packages.

- *Disguised rootkit.* In this experiment, we downloaded all the rootkits that were available from [1]. There were a total of 10, of which 8 were applicable to Linux. Of these 8, four (mood-nt, adore-ng, suckitdid and cd00r) expect users to knowingly run them each time, and hence are not persistent. Our tool is not designed to prevent a knowledgeable user from knowingly running malware, but is rather aimed at malware that is installed surreptitiously. We were then left with four rootkits: bobkit, tuxkit, lrk5 and portacelo. During installation, all these rootkits modified files belonging to benign packages, such as ls, find, du, ps and init. The installation analysis determined that these actions are in conflict with the security policy that only untrusted files can be overwritten by untrusted packages. Hence the installation was aborted cleanly.
- *Fake patch from Redhat.* We tried to install the patch for fileutils that was suggested in the phish email from Redhat [24]. This fake patch was stopped by *SSI*, as the installation policy identified that the patch tried to create a privileged user with no password. On seeing this violation, the installation was aborted.
- *"Malicious" rpm package.* The Fedora package build system [16] suggests three possible attack scenarios from the malicious package writer. Of these, a malicious rpm-scriptlet is a serious threat. To test the effectiveness of *SSI* under this threat, we crafted a "malicious" rpm package. This package is named glibsys in RPM format. During the installation phase, the package tried to overwrite system files

/lib/libc.so and /bin/gcc. By running the installation inside *SSI*, the policy checker captured these unsafe behaviors and aborted the installation.

Installation of Nonmalicious Packages from Untrusted Sources

For this test, we installed untrusted (but nonmalicious) packages from sources that might be considered untrustworthy, such as freshrpms and ATrpms. We report our experiences in installing and using these packages with *SSI*. In particular, we downloaded 335 packages from Atrpms and 152 packages from freshrpms. Only 144 of these 487 packages could be installed on our system *even in the absence of SSI* — this was because of dependencies that were not satisifed. Of these 144, 11 were server applications that required a higher level of trust, so we were left with 133 packages in all. Below are some examples of these applications.

- *Multimedia and Document Viewers:* gthumb, graphviz, ggv, xmms and xpdf.
- *Games, Web Agents, IM:* gnapster, ltris, xifrac, ymessenger and gaim.
- *Archive Creation and Related Utilities:* jpeg2ps, f2c, flac, unrar and pdfmerge.
- *File Organization and Album Creation:* hardlink++ and mkpp.
- *Editors:* bluefish, glabels, screem and gedit.

All of these 133 packages could be installed successfully without any problems within *SSI*. Thus, there were no false positives due to *SSI* in this experiment. Although we currently do not restrict the data files (e.g., configuration or documentation files) belonging to untrusted applications, we observed that we could do so fairly easily. In particular, we noticed that all these files had the name of the untrusted package, and were created within certain directories such as /usr/share/doc and /usr/share/info/-nasm.info.gz. There were about half-a-dozen such locations. Based on this observation, we plan to constrain data files written.

Installation of Benign Packages

For this evaluation, we chose a set of 38 rpm packages from the official repository, and tried to install them within *SSI*. It turned out that 37 of them were installed successfully, and one of them (ethereal) complained that it was dependent on package libnet which was untrusted. On seeing this, we replaced the untrusted version of libnet with a benign version obtained from the official repository and repeated the installation process. During this second attempt, ethereal was installed without problems.

Secure Uninstallation

We did not find any package that comes with malicious uninstallation scripts, so we hand-crafted some test cases to evelute the ability to perform secure uninstallation. In particular, we crafted a package which tried to delete /etc/passwd in its uninstallation script. This action was captured by *SSI* and it was a violation of the policy specified in Section 4.2. Therefore, this action was aborted, and *SSI* verified that the set of files installed were actually removed from the file system.

We then tried to uninstall the nonmalicious packages installed before. We randomly chose 10 of them and ran uninstallation operation within *SSI*, it turned out all of them were successfully uninstalled without any violations to the uninstallation policy.

Table 1. Performance overhead of *SSI*. All numbers are in seconds.

	Original Installation	SSI Installation	
	Time	Time	Overhead
Mozilla installer (binary)	3.285	4.127	26%
Gnuchess (tar ball)	15.868	18.98	20%
Yahoo! Messenger (rpm)	2.433	4.813	98%

5.2 Performance Evaluation

The result of performance evaluation is summarized in Table 1. We evaluated *SSI* using three types of installation packages: binary installer, tar ball distribution, and rpm distribution. Mozilla installer is a self-contained binary, and it performed 8716 file modifications using 6 child processes. It incurred an overhead of 26%. The installation of gnuchess package (tgz format) had a 20% overhead, and its operation included three steps: `configure`, `make`, and `make install`. The entire procedure involved creation of 1935 new processes and 5325 modification operations on the file system. Finally, the installation of Yahoo messenger (rpm package) forked 6 child process and involved overall 42650 modification operations on the file system, and it incurred a 98% overhead. The average overhead across these three packages is about 50%, which is moderate but we believe to be acceptable in the context of *SSI*. Moreover, the primary performance bottleneck is the Alcatraz tool that provides our SEE. It uses `ptrace`-based system call interception, which frequently introduces 100% overheads on programs.

To estimate the performance benefits achievable using a more efficient system call interposition mechanism, we made an enhancement to Alcatraz that uses in-kernel system call interception mechanism for operations that don't require processing by Alcatraz, e.g., read and write operations. With this modification, overheads due to context switches are decreased to about a third of the figures reported above. For instance, the overhead for installing Yahoo messenger rpm becomes 38% as compared to 98% which we observed using original Alcatraz.

6 Related Work

Software Installation. A number of recent research efforts have focused on the problem of software installation, but they are mainly concerned with handling dependencies and conflicts among packages.

Checkinstall [15] is a tool to build installation packages such as RPM from an installation script. Nix [14] presents a comprehensive solution for deploying software, but its focus is on functionality rather than security.

RPMShield [34] is a tool aimed at securing the process of software installation. It uses policies based on the notion of ownership of files by packages. A file is said to be owned by a package if it is part of that package. However, it does not address the problem of dependencies between benign and untrusted packages, nor does it satisfy any of the goals for secure software installation that we outlined in the Introduction.

SoftwarePot [20] incorporates a secure software circulation model for software deployment. The software to be run is encapsulated with a file system that is transferred from the code producer to consumer. The operations from the software are confined within the "pot." It can be thought of as a combination of sandbox and software distribution model. But it constrains users into using one single way of software installation and execution confinement method. As a result, it is not possible to utilize existing package formats or sandboxing tools and policies with this approach. In contrast, *SSI* is compatible with existing software installation methods, and it is flexible in allowing users to choose different execution confinement tools. More importantly, SoftwarePot requires policy development efforts to support new software, while *SSI* uses a single installation policy for all untrusted applications. For securing untrusted applications during execution, *SSI* can leverage confinement policies that may already be available in widely used sandboxing tools such as systrace.

Virtualization and Isolation Approaches. Virtual Machines (VMs) [35,13,9] provide a coarse-granularity approach for dealing with untrusted software: such software could be run inside a virtual machine, while benign software runs on the host OS. FreeBSD jails [19], Linux VServer [2] and Solaris Zones [26] provide light-weight virtualization, where the same OS kernel is shared across the VMs, while still providing strong isolation between applications running on different VMs.

The main problem with virtualization approaches is that typically, users want to use untrusted software to operate on their files, and other resources that are part of the host OS. To derive the same utility within the VM, the host environment has to be duplicated inside the virtual machine. This is quite time-consuming — for instance, most standard (and typically benign) packages would have to be installed on both the host OS and the VM. Moreover, files needed by untrusted applications would need to be explicitly copied into the VM. As a result of this inconvenience, users frequently end up installing untrusted software directly on the host OS. Techniques such as Alcatraz [22] and FVM [37] (and the closely related product called Software Virtualization Solution (SVS) [7]) mitigate the overhead of environment duplication by using one-way isolation, wherein the host OS files are visible within the isolated environment, but the files written within the isolated environments aren't visible on the host OS. However, usability issues still remain: if users want to make use of the outputs produced by untrusted software, they have to explicitly copy them back into the host systems.

DTE and Sandboxing. Boebert and Kain proposed Domain and Type Enforcement (DTE) [10,36]. Subjects (processes) are associated with domains, while objects (e.g., files) are associated with types. DTE policies specify which domains can access which types. They also specify domain transitions (if any) that should take place when a certain program is executed. Use of DTE to defeat rootkit attacks is described in [8]. SELinux [23] security is primarily based on DTE policies that have been developed with the goal of enforcing the principle of least privilege.

A number of so-called "sandboxing" approaches that have been developed to address untrusted code security [17,12,4,25,30,27] are conceptually similar to DTE. Motivated by simplicity, many of these systems typically use policies that are based on program names and file names, eliminating the intermediary notions of types and domains. While this loses some generality, it seems acceptable in the context of untrusted software.

All of the above approaches can potentially be used during the resident phase of untrusted software. However, they do not provide the power or flexibility of *SSI* during the installation phase. First, all these techniques are only capable of enforcing safety properties [29], which require that every operation leaves the system in a "safe" state. As described in Section 3, software installations typically involve intermediate states that are not safe. This motivated the development of state-based policies in *SSI*. Second, one of the biggest challenges in using DTE and sandboxing techniques is the difficulty of policy development. In contrast, *SSI* uses a single high-level policy that is enforced on all untrusted package installations.

Information-flow based Approaches. There has been a resurgence of interest in information-flow based approaches for preserving host integrity. PPI [33] and SLIM [28] enforce information flow policies that ensure that high integrity objects and subjects are not compromised by interacting with low-integrity objects and subjects. While policy development has been a challenge that has impeded deployment of mandatory access control (MAC), recent efforts such as UMIP [21] and PPI [33] have begun to address this problem by developing techniques to synthesize MAC policies.

SSI complements the above techniques: while the above techniques can protect host integrity from the execution of untrusted software, they do not provide a good solution for the installation phase. However, they do provide a strong foundation for *SSI* since they can answer questions regarding the trustworthiness of every file on the system. As a result, some of the potential gaps in *SSI* policies that arise due to missing information in software packages can be avoided.

Back to the Future system [18] uses information flow techniques to detect the presence of malware. Their approach does not constrain malware during its installation; instead, it is detected when its files are used by a benign application. Its main advantage is that it can recognize any attempt by malware to inject itself into inputs consumed by benign applications. Its drawback is that it allows host integrity to be compromised (as a result of malware installation), and this change has to be undone when malware is detected. This rollback may cause delays, and moreover, can introduce subtle file system consistency issues.

7   Conclusion

Software installations provide an attractive avenue for spyware and rootkits to embed themselves deeply into the operating system. In this paper, we proposed an approach for securing this entry point by developing a framework that confines accesses made by untrusted packages during their installation. Our technique can support a diversity of software installation mechanisms. It can also work with different approaches for confining untrusted software after the installation phase. A key novelty in our approach is the development of a high-level policy framework that largely eliminates the need for developing application specific installation policies. Instead, a single, intuitively simple high level policy can be used for a wide range of untrusted applications. Our experimental results demonstrate that our approach is effective, and achieves the goals set out in the Introduction.

Acknowledgments

We thank Joy Dutta, Milan Manavat, and Kumar Thangavelu for their work on early versions of SSI, and Anupama Chandwani and Abhishek Dhamija for discussions on Redhat/Debian package managers. We also thank our shepherd John McHugh and the anonymous reviewers for their insightful comments and suggestions.

References

1. Linux rootkits,
   http://www.eviltime.com/download.php?page=hacking&subpage=rootkits
2. Linux v-server, http://linux-vserver.org
3. Xnest, http://www.xfree86.org/4.2.0/Xnest.1.html
4. Acharya, A., Raje, M.: Mapbox: Using parameterized behavior classes to confine applications. In: USENIX Security Symposium (2000)
5. Alcatraz, http://www.seclab.cs.sunysb.edu
6. Alexandrov, A., Kmiec, P., Schauser, K.: Consh: A confined execution environment for internet computations (1998)
7. Altiris. Software virtualization solution (2005), http://www.altiris.com
8. Badger, L., Sterne, D.F., Sherman, D.L., Walker, K.M., Haghighat, S.A.: A domain and type enforcement unix prototype. In: USENIX Computing Systems, pp. 127–140 (1995)
9. Barham, P., Dragovic, B., Fraser, K., Hand, S., Harris, T., Ho, A., Neugebauer, R., Pratt, I., Warfield, A.: Xen and the art of virtualization. In: ACM Symposium on Operating systems principles, pp. 164–177 (2003)
10. Boebert, W.E., Kain, R.Y.: A practical alternative to hierarchical integrity policies. In: Proceedings of the 8th National Computer Security Conference, pp. 18–27 (1985)
11. Chien, E.: Techniques of adware and spyware. Symantec (April 2005)
12. Dan, A., Mohindra, A., Ramaswami, R., Sitaram, D.: Chakravyuha: A sandbox operating system for the controlled execution of alien code. Technical report, IBM T.J. Watson research center (1997)
13. Dike, J.: A User-Mode port of the linux kernel. In: Proceedings of the 4th Annual Showcase and Conference (LINUX 2000), Berkeley, CA, October 10–14, 2000, pp. 63–72 (2000)
14. Dolstra, E., de Jonge, M., Visser, E.: Nix: A safe and policy-free system for software deployment. In: LISA, pp. 79–92 (2004)
15. Eduardo, F.: Checkinstall (2004),
    http://asic-linux.com.mx/~izto/checkinstall/
16. The fedora.us buildsystem,
    http://enrico-scholz.de/fedora.us-build/html/
17. Goldberg, I., Wagner, D., Thomas, R., Brewer, E.A.: A secure environment for untrusted helper applications: confining the wily hacker. In: USENIX Security Symposium (1996)
18. Hsu, F., Ristenpart, T., Chen, H.: Back to the future: A framework for automatic malware removal and system repair. In: Jesshope, C., Egan, C. (eds.) ACSAC 2006. LNCS, vol. 4186. Springer, Heidelberg (2006)
19. Kamp, P.H., Watson, R.N.M.: Jails: Confining the omnipotent root. In: Proceedings of the 2nd International SANE Conference (2000)
20. Kato, K., Oyama, Y.: Softwarepot: An encapsulated transferable file system for secure software circulation. In: Okada, M., Pierce, B.C., Scedrov, A., Tokuda, H., Yonezawa, A. (eds.) ISSS 2002. LNCS, vol. 2609, pp. 112–132. Springer, Heidelberg (2003)

21. Li, N., Mao, Z., Chen, H.: Usable mandatory integrity protection for operating systems. In: IEEE Symposium on Security and Privacy (2007)
22. Liang, Z., Venkatakrishnan, V.N., Sekar, R.: Isolated program execution: An application transparent approach for executing untrusted programs. In: Omondi, A.R., Sedukhin, S. (eds.) ACSAC 2003. LNCS, vol. 2823, pp. 182–191. Springer, Heidelberg (2003)
23. Loscocco, P., Smalley, S.: Integrating flexible support for security policies into the Linux o perating system. In: Proc. FREENIX track of the 2001 Usenix Annual Technical Conference (2001)
24. PHCN. Fedora-redhat fake security alert / trojan source code analysis (2004), http://www.phcn.ws/main/include.php?path=content/articles.php&contentid=120&PHCN=
25. Prevelakis, V., Spinellis, D.: Sandboxing applications. In: Proceedings of Usenix Annual Technical Conference: FREENIX Track (2001)
26. Price, D., Tucker, A.: Solaris zones: Operating system support for consolidating commercial workloads. In: LISA, pp. 241–254. USENIX (2004)
27. Provos, N.: Improving host security with system call policies. In: Proceedings of the 11th USENIX Security Symposium, pp. 257–272 (2003)
28. Safford, D., Zohar, M.: A trusted linux client (tlc) (2005)
29. Schneider, F.B.: Enforceable security policies. ACM Transactions on Information and System Security 3(1), 30–50 (2000)
30. Scott, K., Davidson, J.: Safe virtual execution using software dynamic translation. In: Proceedings of Annual Computer Security Applications Conference (2002)
31. Sekar, R., Venkatakrishnan, V.N., Basu, S., Bhatkar, S., DuVarney, D.C.: Model carrying code: a practical approach for safe execution of untrusted applications. In: Proceedings of 19th ACM symposium of Operating Systems Principles (SOSP), Bolton Landing, New York (October 2003)
32. Sun, W., Liang, Z., Venkatakrishnan, V.N., Sekar, R.: One-way isolation: An effective approach for realizing safe execution environments. In: NDSS (2005)
33. Sun, W., Sekar, R., Poothia, G., Karandikar, T.: Practical proactive integrity preservation: A basis for malware defense. In: IEEE Symposium on Security and Privacy (May 2008)
34. Venkatakrishnan, V.N., Sekar, R., Kamat, T., Tsipa, S., Liang, Z.: An approach for secure software installation. In: Proceedings of the 16th Systems Administration Conference (LISA 2002), Philadelphia, PA, November 3-8, 2002, pp. 219–226 (2002)
35. Walters, B.: VMware virtual platform. j-LINUX-J 63 (July 1999)
36. Young, W.D., Telega, P.A., Boebert, W.E., Kain, R.Y.: A verified labeler for the Secure Ada Target. In: Proc. National Computer Security Conference, pp. 55–61 (1986)
37. Yu, Y., Guo, F., Nanda, S., Lam, L.c., Chiueh, T.c.: A feather-weight virtual machine for windows applications. In: Proceedings of the 2nd ACM/USENIX Conference on Virtual Execution Environments (VEE 2006) (June 2006)

FluXOR: Detecting and Monitoring Fast-Flux Service Networks

Emanuele Passerini, Roberto Paleari, Lorenzo Martignoni, and Danilo Bruschi

Università degli Studi di Milano
{ema,roberto,lorenzo,bruschi}@security.dico.unimi.it

Abstract. *Botnets* are large groups of compromised machines (*bots*) used by miscreants for the most illegal activities (e.g., sending spam emails, denial-of-service attacks, phishing and other web scams). To protect the identity and to maximise the availability of the core components of their business, miscreants have recently started to use *fast-flux service networks*, large groups of bots acting as front-end proxies to these components. Motivated by the conviction that prompt detection and monitoring of these networks is an essential step to contrast the problem posed by botnets, we have developed FluXOR, a system to detect and monitor fast-flux service networks. FluXOR monitoring and detection strategies entirely rely on the analysis of a set of features observable from the point of view of a victim of the scams perpetrated thorough botnets. We have been using FluXOR for about a month and so far we have detected 387 fast-flux service networks, totally composed by 31998 distinct compromised machines, which we believe to be associated with 16 botnets.

1 Introduction

A malware is a program written with malicious intents. Today, the main motivation behind malware writing and their use is the easy financial gain. Smart miscreants write malware and sell them in the wealthy underground market to other miscreants [1]. These malicious programs are "installed" on machines all around the world, without any permission of the users, and transform these machines into *bots*, i.e., hosts completely under to control of the attackers. Bots are then used to steal computational resources and confidential information, to relay spam email messages, to mount distributed denial of service (DDoS) and other attacks, to host phishing websites, and for other kinds of scams. To maximise the profit from these activities, multiple "infected" machines are grouped together in a *botnet* (a network of bots) and used simultaneously to achieve the same purpose [2]. With a single command, miscreants can control hundreds or even thousands of bots [3]. The botnet problem is so extensive nowadays that it has made headlines several times [4,5].

The most well known botnets are those related with the Warezov and the Storm worms [6,7]. These botnets are infamous for the huge amount of spam emails they have been generating, often containing links to malicious web servers hosting various frauds as well as malicious web pages able to infect the machines

D. Zamboni (Ed.): DIMVA 2008, LNCS 5137, pp. 186–206, 2008.
© Springer-Verlag Berlin Heidelberg 2008

of the visitors with malware. Of particular interest is the technique used by those botnets to masquerade the identity of the malicious web servers in order to maximise the availability of the service. If these web servers are difficult to identify, they are difficult to shutdown, and they can hit more and more victims. This technique, known as *fast-flux service network*, is very simple and consists in associating the canonical hostname of a malicious web server (e.g., www.factvillage.com) with multiple IP addresses corresponding to the addresses of a subset of the bots of the botnet. Each victims' request to visit the web server will thus reach one of the bots and the bot will proxy the request to the real server, making impossible to discover the identity of the malicious web server without having full control of one of these bots. The association between the hostname of the web server and the IP addresses of the bots acting as front-end proxies is updated very frequently such that newly compromised machines can immediately take part in the game and dead bots are excluded without affecting the availability of the service [8].

The impact that botnets using fast-flux service networks have on the Internet community is tremendous [9]. Although the average lifetime of domains used for malicious purposes, including the domains associated with fast-flux service networks, is very short, the lifetime of botnets using those domains is much longer. As the identity of the hosts associated with those domains is well protected and the bots that are part of the networks are difficult to track, botnets are difficult to eradicate. Authorities put a lot of efforts to take down the domains registered for malicious purposes, but these efforts are worthless because the bots are not isolated. Before the domain is suspended, a new one is registered and associated with the same set of bots, to replace the old one. Consequently, miscreants can continue their malicious activity through their botnets without interruption.

The natural approach to monitor and detect botnets activity and the bots involved is to passively analyse the network traffic. Unfortunately, that requires the access to a significant network segment [10,11,12,13,14,15,16]. Fast-flux service networks are interesting from the research point of view because they allow to "observe" the botnet phenomenon from a completely different prospective, the prospective of a victim of the botnet. In fact, the visibility a victim has on the botnet is quite significant. More precisely, imagine a recidivous victim that visits very frequently a malicious web site associated with a botnet and served through a fast-flux service network. At each visit the victim is likely to access the web site through a different bot (recall that the canonical hostname of the web server is resolved into the IP address of one of the bots). After a large number of visits, the recidivous victim will have discovered the IP addresses of the majority of the active bots of the botnet.

This paper presents FluXOR, the system we have developed to detect and monitor fast-flux service networks. Given a suspicious hostname, FluXOR, by behaving like a recidivous victim, tries to detect if the hostname conceals a fast-flux service network. Hostnames associated with fast-flux service networks are then continuously monitored to find out all the IP addresses of the compromised machines that are part of the botnet associated with the service network itself.

FluXOR detection strategy is based on the combined analysis of nine distinguishing features describing some properties of (I) the domain the suspicious hostname belongs to, (II) the degree of availability of the potential fast-flux service network, and (III) the heterogeneity of the potential hosts of the network.

We have been using FluXOR since the beginning of January 2008 to monitor potential fast-flux service network whose hostnames were collected from spam emails. So far the system correctly classified all the analysed hostnames (4961) and 7.8% of them (387) turned out to be associated with fast-flux service networks, involving 31998 distinct compromised machines located all around the world. Real-time results of the analysis are available on-line at http://fluxor. laser.dico.unimi.it.

To summarise, this paper makes the following contributions:

- Identification of the features that, combined together, allow to precisely detect whether or not a suspicious hostname conceals a fast-flux service network (Section 3 and 4).
- Implementation of a strategy to monitor a fast-flux service network and to detect the majority of the bots that are in the network (Section 5).
- Empirical analysis of the fast-flux service network phenomenon (Section 6).

2   Problem Description and Solution Overview

A *fast-flux service network* is a network of compromised hosts that is used to carry out malicious activities, for example to deliver malware to users, to distribute illegal materials or to steal users' credentials [8]. The service network is identified by one or more fully qualified domain names (FQDNs) that are resolved to multiple (hundreds or even thousands) different IP addresses, belonging to unaware compromised hosts, the *fast-flux agents* (or *bots*). The fundamental characteristic of a fast-flux service network is *high availability*, which is provided by continuously updating the pool of agents serving the network. Newly compromised hosts are inserted into the network, inactive or unreliable hosts are removed, and victims are always redirected to the active and most reliable agents. The key is a combination of a very short time-to-live (TTL) of the DNS resource records that associate the canonical name of the service network with the set of IP addresses of the agents and a round-robin selection of these records [17,18]. In the common setup, the agents do not carry out the malicious activities, but they simply redirect received requests to the *fast-flux mother-ship*, the controlling element of the network, whose identity must be kept secret. With this setup, it is not possible to identify the mother-ship without having complete control of one of the agents.

Imagine that the fully qualified domain name www.factvillage.com conceals a fast-flux service network composed of hundreds of agents and that it is used to attract users, with the promise of very cheap drugs, and to infect their machines with malware. Figure 1 shows how our sample malicious contents provider leverages the fast-flux service network to serve the victims. A victim, wishing to visit the on-line drugstore, queries a name server (usually a non-authoritative name

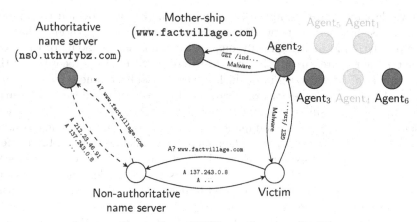

Average time-to-live of DNS resource records: 300 s.
Number of distinct IP addresses in the network: 253.

Fig. 1. An example of the fast-flux service network used by our sample malicious web server `www.factvillage.com`, the entities involved and the communication between these entities (nodes in gray denote hosts under the control of the miscreants and shaded agents denote those that are not currently serving the network)

server which recursively queries the authoritative one) to resolve the hostname of the website. The name server returns the addresses of a subset of the agents currently active in the network, and the victim connects to one of them. The agent then proxies the victim's requests to the mother-ship, which in turn delivers the malicious contents. In background, the mother-ship, or another entity controlled by the miscreants, continuously monitors the status of the agents and updates the resource records of the authoritative name server of the domain (in the example the authoritative name server is `ns0.uthvfybz.com`), to distribute the network across the reliable agents. The short time-to-live associated to the DNS resource records prevents non-authoritative name servers to cache for too long the records that define the subset of agents currently serving the network. When the cache expires the name server contacts again the authoritative name server for the domain and gets the new list of agents serving the network. These agents are selected from the set of all active agents in a round-robin fashion, to balance their load.

Our goals are, given a fully qualified domain name, to verify whether it conceals a fast-flux service network and, in such a case, to identify all the agents that are part of the network. The prompt identification and isolation of all the agents is important because if the service network is shutdown but the agents remain under the control of miscreants, a new service network of the same extent can be created by simply registering a new domain and reusing the same agents. Moreover, these agents can be used for other malicious purposes (e.g., they can be used as DDoS zombies, to steal personal information from the hosts they are running on, and to act as spam bots). FluXOR is the name of the system we have developed to accomplish these goals. The key idea behind the system is that a fast-flux service network has *multiple distinguishing features* that are not typically found in benign fully qualified domain names. Some of the most characteristic features are (I) the time-to-live of DNS resources records, (II) the large number of IP addresses into which the canonical hostname is resolved, and (III) the heterogeneous set of organisations that own these addresses. Clearly, these features taken singularly are not enough to distinguish between benign and malicious hostnames. As an example let us compare our sample malicious hostname `www.factvillage.com` with the benign hostname `database.clamav.net`. The latter is a typical example of how DNS resources records with very small time-to-live and round-robin can be used to distribute the load across multiple mirrors (in this case the mirrors are used to distribute updates for the database of signatures of the ClamAV anti-virus [19]). Moreover, as mirrors are hosted by universities and companies, the hosts running a mirror belong to different networks, owned by different organisations, and are distributed around the world. Despite hosts like `database.clamav.net` have most of the characteristics of a fast-flux service network, FluXOR, by monitoring the suspicious hostname for a small period of time and by combining the extracted features using a naïve Bayesian classifier [20], can precisely distinguish between hostnames that are associated with fast-flux service networks from those that are not. It is worth noting that the chosen approach works well also when some of the selected features are not available.

When a fast-flux service network is detected, FluXOR continuously monitors the service network, behaving like a victim and periodically querying various DNS servers to resolve the canonical name of the network for the purpose of enumerating the IP addresses of the compromised hosts that, even for a small period of time, are used as agents.

A fast-flux service network, like the one described in this section, is known in the literature as a *single-flux* network. More complex setups are possible, an example is a *double-flux* network [8]. FluXOR handles indifferently any kind of fast-flux service network, but unfortunately the current implementation does not distinguish between the various types.

For the remaining of the paper, for conciseness, we will refer to the FQDNs associated with a fast-flux service network as malicious and to all the others as benign, although what in the paper is considered benign could be an hostname created for other malicious purposes but not associated with a fast-flux service network. Moreover, we will refer to any hostname whose maliciousness has not been established yet as suspicious.

3   Characterising Fast-Flux Service Networks

The features used by FluXOR to distinguish between benign and malicious hostnames are summarised in Table 1 and discussed in detail in the remaining of the section. The features are grouped in three categories: (I) features characterising the domain name to which the suspicious hostname belongs to, (II) features

Table 1. Summary of the features used to distinguish between benign and malicious hostnames, grouped by category

Category	#	Description
Domain name	F_1	Domain age
	F_2	Domain registrar
Availability of the network	F_3	Number of distinct DNS records of type "A"
	F_4	Time-to-live of DNS resource records
Heterogeneity of the agents	F_5	Number of distinct networks
	F_6	Number of distinct autonomous systems
	F_7	Number of distinct resolved qualified domain names
	F_8	Number of distinct assigned network names
	F_9	Number of distinct organisations

characterising the degree of the availability of the network that is potentially associated with the suspicious hostname, and (III) features characterising the heterogeneity of the potential agents of the network. Some of the features might appear similar initially, but, as shown later, each of them tells us something important about the suspicious hostname, especially because some features might not be always available and because there is no well known convention about how some of them are attributed.

3.1 Features Characterising the Domain Name

Domain age (F_1). Benign domains are usually characterised by a relatively long age. Domains used for malicious purposes instead are typically active only for short periods of time. As soon as they are identified, they are deactivated by the authority in charge of the corresponding top-level domain. Thus, miscreants have to register new domains and start to use them right away, to successfully achieve their malicious purposes. The average age of a benign domain is much older than the average age of malicious domain. Indeed, during our experiments, we have estimated that the average age of malicious hostnames is less than five weeks.

Domain registrar (F_2). We empirically observed that most of the domains used to implement fast-flux service networks are registered through a limited number of registrars, typically located in countries with a lax legislation against cybercrime. Our hypothesis is that these registrars perform almost no check when domains are registered. Miscreants can easily complete the registration process using false identities and paying with stolen credit card numbers, making impossible, for the authorities, to identify the person who has effectively registered a domain. On the other hand, the set of registrars used to register benign domains is more heterogeneous and is not likely to overlap with the set of registrars used by miscreants.

3.2   Features Characterising the Degree of Availability of the Network

Number of distinct DNS "A" records (F_3). Fast-flux service networks are generally composed by a large number of agents. The authoritative name server for the malicious domain, when queried, returns the set of active agents (i.e., the subset of agents currently serving the network) by returning multiple DNS "A" records, each one containing the IP address of a specific agent. These resource records are periodically updated by the fast-flux mother-ship to put in the network newly compromised agents and to remove the faulty ones. Thus, after a reasonable long span of time, the number of distinct DNS records of type "A" (i.e., agents IP addresses) that had or have been associated with a malicious FQDN is rather large. The higher the number of distinct DNS records of type "A" associated to the same FQDN, the larger the number of potential agents, and the higher the probability that the FQDN conceals a fast-flux service network.

Time-to-live of DNS resource records (F_4). The fundamental characteristic of fast-flux service networks is the high frequency at which the set of active agents is updated. Most of the agents are end-user machines and consequently it is reasonable to expect that they will appear on-line and disappear very frequently. Thus, to guarantee the high availability of the service offered through the fast-flux network, the set of active agents has to be updated as soon as one of them changes its state. Moreover, the update must be promptly propagated across the Internet, down to the victims. To achieve this goal, the authoritative name server for the malicious domain associates a very short time-to-live to the DNS resource records of the domain. That forces non-authoritative name servers, used by the victims, to flush their cache and to query the authoritative name server very frequently, that in turn returns a different set of active agents every time. The higher the time-to-live associated to the various DNS resource records of a domain, the lower the probability that the domain is malicious. Unfortunately the converse is not always true. Several authoritative name servers for benign domain names associate very short time-to-live to their records for various purposes.

3.3   Features Characterising the Heterogeneity of the Agents

Number of distinct networks (F_5). Fast-flux agents are usually randomly compromised hosts scattered all around the globe. Thus, a malicious FQDN is resolved to many different IP addresses belonging to hosts that very likely belong to different networks. On the other hand, when a benign FQDN encompasses multiple hosts, for load-balancing purposes, these hosts often belong to the same network because they are owned by the same company and physically very close to each other. The higher the number of distinct networks associated to the same FQDN, the more scattered the hosts are, and the more likely these hosts have been compromised and have been used as fast-flux agents. As an example compare the networks associated with the benign FQDN `hp.com` with those associated with the malicious FQDN `www.factvillage.com`, reported respectively

Table 2. Comparison of the host specific features (F_5 to F_9) characterising two benign and one malicious FQDNs (the entries in bold are those common to multiple IP addresses)

IP address	F_5	F_6	F_7	F_8	F_9
15.216.110.140	**15.0.0.0/8**	**AS9218**	**polyserve.com**	**HP-INTERNET**	**Hewlett-Packard**
15.192.45.22	**15.0.0.0/8**	**AS9218**	**polyserve.com**	**HP-INTERNET**	**Hewlett-Packard**
15.200.30.24	**15.0.0.0/8**	**AS9218**	**polyserve.com**	**HP-INTERNET**	**Hewlett-Packard**

(a) `hp.com` (benign)

IP address	F_5	F_6	F_7	F_8	F_9
67.228.112.196	67.228.0.0/16	**AS36351**	avast.com	SOFTLAYER-4-5	**SoftLayer Tech.**
216.12.205.130	216.12.192.0/19	AS36420	**avast.com**	EVRY-BLK-4	Everyone Internet
74.86.245.119	74.86.0.0/16	**AS36351**	avast.com	SOFTLAYER-4-4	**SoftLayer Tech.**

(b) `www.avast.com` (benign)

IP address	F_5	F_6	F_7	F_8	F_9
61.18.66.?	61.18.0.0/16	AS9908	hkcable.com.hk	HKCABLE-HK	HK Cable TV
218.47.195.?	218.47.0.0/16	AS4713	ap.plala.or.jp	PLALA	Plala Net. Inc.
81.173.151.?	81.173.151.0/24	AS8422	netcologne.de	NC-DIAL-IN-POOL	NetCologne

(c) `www.factvillage.com` (malicious)

in Table 2(a) and Table 2(c). The IP addresses associated with the former all belong to the same network (15.0.0.0/8), while the addresses associated with the latter belongs to completely different networks. As shown in the example of Table 2(b) where each IP address associated with `www.avast.com` belongs to a separate network, this is not always the case.

Number of distinct autonomous systems (F_6). An autonomous system (AS) is a connected group of one or more IP prefixes run by one or more network operators with a single and clearly defined routing policy [21]. Thus, distinct networks, but physically very close, might be connected to the Internet through the same AS. As with the previous feature, the majority of benign FQDNs are mapped to hosts located in a circumscribed geographical area and are all part of the same autonomous system. On the other hand, as the agents of a fast-flux network are scattered across all the countries, they typically belong to distinct autonomous systems. As an example let us compare the autonomous systems associated with the benign FQDN `www.avast.com`, with those associated to `www.factvillage.com` (Tables 2(b) and 2(c) respectively). In the first case we have three distinct networks but only two autonomous systems. In the second case, each host, as located in a different country, is part of a different AS.

Number of distinct resolved qualified domain names (F_7). Even if a FQDN is associated with multiple hosts scattered around the globe and part of distinct networks and autonomous systems, the hosts might still be owned by the same company or organisation and thus they can share the same qualified domain name. As an example let us compare the benign FQDNs of Tables 2(a) and 2(b) with the malicious `www.factvillage.com` of Table 2(c). In the first two cases both hostnames are resolved into multiple IP addresses, but these addresses are in turn resolved into canonical hostnames belonging to the same domain (i.e., `polyserve.com` and `avast.com` respectively). The example of `www.avast.com` clearly indicates that all the IP addresses found are legitimate. Unfortunately, that is not completely evident in the case of `hp.com` because the domain name (`polyserve.com`) does not match the domain name of the suspicious FQDN under analysis. Nevertheless, all the IP addresses found are part of the same domain, which is not common for malicious FQDNs. Indeed, fast-flux agents are compromised hosts belonging to distinct organisations, and the canonical hostnames associated with their IP addresses are solely under the control of the respective owners of the networks and the attacker cannot control in any way these information. In the case of `www.factvillage.com`, each of the three IP addresses found, probably used by dial-up hosts, is resolved into a hostname with a distinct qualified domain, corresponding to that used by the ISP providing the service.

Number of distinct assigned network names (F_8). The network name is the name assigned to a network by the registration authority. Multiple network addresses can be logically grouped under the same network name. This is often the case when the different network addresses are owned by the same company or organisation. Like the other three previous features, the number of distinct network names is an indication of the degree of scattering of the hosts associated with the suspicious FQDN.

Number of distinct organisations (F_9). Each network is assigned to an organisation, but as with network names, same organisation can own multiple networks with one or multiple names. As an example let us consider the benign domain `avast.com` analysed in Table 2(b). Each network is assigned a distinct network name, but two of these networks belong to the same organisation (i.e., Soft-Layer Technologies Inc.). Clearly, fast-flux agents randomly distributed around the world share a limited number of organisations.

4   Combining the Features for Detection

FluXOR initially monitors suspicious hostnames for a short period of time, after which the selected features are analysed to determine whether the domain is malicious or not. The number of domains is incredibly growing. Indeed, it has been estimated that several hundreds of thousands of generic second-level domains (e.g., .com, .org, .net) are registered daily [22]. Consequently, the number of suspicious hostnames to monitor can be very large and it is essential that a precise classification can be accomplished in the shortest period of time, to reduce the workload of the system, but also to promptly intervene to mitigate the damage fast-flux service networks and their bots can cause to the Internet community.

Table 3 shows a comparison of the features of three FQDNs, associated with as many distinct fast-flux service networks, with those of three benign hostnames.

Table 3. Comparison of three sample benign and malicious FQDNs using the selected features (F_1 is measured in weeks) and comparison of the features of the average benign and malicious FQDNs (computed from a set of about 75 benign and 215 malicious hostnames monitored for about three hours)

	FQDN	F_1	F_2	F_3	F_4	F_5	F_6	F_7	F_8	F_9
Benign	www.avast.com	539	NetworkSolutions	12	3600	5	3	1	5	2
	adriaticobishkek.com	65	Melbourne IT	21	1200	1	1	1	1	1
	google.com	542	MarkMonitor	3	300	2	1	1	1	1
	Mean	**493.27**	N/A	**2.86**	**4592.53**	**1.27**	**1.11**	**1.08**	**1.21**	**1.07**
	Standard dev.	**289.27**	N/A	**3.89**	**7668.74**	**0.65**	**0.36**	**0.74**	**0.58**	**0.25**
Malicious	www.eveningher.com	18	PayCenter	127	300	83	49	33	71	54
	www.factvillage.com	2	PayCenter	117	300	81	46	34	67	54
	www.doacasino.com	2	NameCheap	33	180	19	14	11	19	14
	Mean	**4.85**	N/A	**98.13**	**261.49**	**63.75**	**38.36**	**27.98**	**53.58**	**41.47**
	Standard dev.	**4.9**	N/A	**37.27**	**59.64**	**23.91**	**12.34**	**8.5**	**18.73**	**15.41**

Note that the features reported in the table were extracted after only three hours of monitoring. From a quick glance at the numbers in the table it should be clear that each of the selected features effectively tells us something important about the maliciousness of a hostname. Although it is easy to spot by hand benign and malicious hostnames, the numbers in the table show a high variability in the most intuitive features (e.g., F_3 and F_4). For all the analysed hostnames reported in the table it was possible to extract all the selected features. In the general case some of these features might be missing, but nevertheless the system must be able to correctly discern between malicious and benign hostnames. Furthermore, hosts associated with malicious hostnames tend to be rather scattered, but the degree of the scattering and the number of fast-flux agents might depend on the amount of time the fast-flux service network has been active. If hosts are compromised and turned into agents using a self-propagating malware (e.g., that identifies targets using weak random scanning), it is reasonable to believe that, in the early stage, the agents are rather localised and limited in number. Our goal is to be able to detect if a hostname is malicious as soon as possible, even when the number of agents involved is very small.

For these reasons the detector tries to achieve the best accuracy by combining the selected features using a naïve Bayesian classifier [20]. Given the features of a suspicious hostname, the classifier returns the class (i.e., benign or malicious) to which the hostname is most likely to belong to. The classifier was trained with a set of malicious and benign FQDNs that we manually classified, with the help of data obtained after a week of monitoring. The set of malicious hostnames was composed of hostnames found in spam emails. The set of benign hostnames was composed of hostnames found in spam and non-spam emails. Furthermore, the latter set was extended, to make it more heterogeneous, by adding the address of some randomly selected websites we recently visited. The assumption that the features are completely independent, made by this type of classifier, might appear to simplistic (e.g., features like F_5, F_6, F_8, and F_9 could be correlated). Nevertheless, this approach turned out to have very good performance in many real-world situations and the work of Zhang has shown that the efficacy of naïve

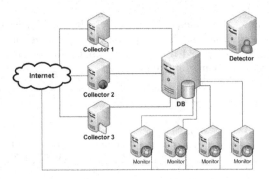

Fig. 2. Typical deployment of the system. Multiple collectors and monitors can be used to distribute the workload and to uniformly blend the system in the victims.

Bayesian classifiers has some theoretical foundations [23]. In our context, as discussed later in Section 6, this approach gives very accurate results (for this reason we decided not to evaluate other classifiers). Our hypothesis is that, in practise, no real correlation between the alleged correlated features (F_5, F_6, F_8, and F_9) exists because no convention regulates how ISPs should partition their address space. For example the network associated with a single autonomous system (F_6) could be divided into sub-networks and multiple sub-networks (F_5) can be assigned to the same organisation (F_9).

5   Architecture and Implementation of the System

The architecture of FluXOR is very simple. The system is divided in three components and each one accomplishes a very specific task: (I) one or more *collectors* of suspicious hostnames, (II) one of more *monitors* of suspicious and malicious hostnames, and (III) a *detector* of fast-flux service networks. Figure 2 shows the typical deployment of the system.

FluXOR is entirely developed in Python and consists of about 2150 LOC, without including the code of the web interface used to display the results of the analysis.

5.1   Collector

The *collector* harvests from various sources hostnames that could be associated with fast-flux service networks. Examples of sources are unsolicited emails, instant messages and post in public web forums and blogs. The current implementation of FluXOR only supports harvesting of suspicious hostnames from emails. In the future this component will be extended to support other sources, for example using web crawlers and honeypots. Newly collected hostnames are flagged as suspicious and are considered as such and monitored until the detector classifies them.

5.2   Monitor

The *monitor* is responsible for monitoring suspicious and malicious hostnames. Benign FQDNs, instead, do not need to be monitored (recall that benign hostnames are those already monitored in the past and classified as such). The distinguishing features used by FluXOR to detect fast-flux service networks are extracted from data obtained by querying two different sources: (I) non-authoritative name servers and (II) WHOIS servers. Once a malicious hostname is detected, instead, it is sufficient to perform a subset of the queries used to monitor suspicious hostnames, that is, those used to extract features describing the heterogeneity of the agents. For statistical and analysis purposes other information about the agents are also collected (e.g., the country in which the hosts are located and their geographical location). A description of the queries performed follows.

Features characterising the domain name (F_1 and F_2). Given a FQDN like `www.factvillage.com`, the age of the domain and the registrar in charge for the domain are determined through WHOIS queries on the name of the second-level domain (e.g. `factvillage.com`). Although the query is conceptually trivial, it presents a serious challenge from the practical point of view. The WHOIS protocol does not define the format in which replies to queries have to be formatted and registries are free to choose the format they like more [24]. Moreover, some registration authorities omit to publish part of the information needed by our analysis. Today the entire IPV4 address space is assigned to 10 different registries. Things are more and more complicated for top-level domains because each domain is assigned to a different registry[1]. Currently we are using a custom WHOIS client that is able to parse the format used by the most common registration authorities. To deal with the registries not currently supported by our client, we rely on a commercial service, that extracts WHOIS information and convert them in XML and offers a free limited number of queries per day. In the future we will extend our client to make the system completely independent from third parties.

Features characterising the degree of availability of the network (F_3 and F_4). The natural approach to enumerate all the resource records of type "A" associated with a particular FQDN (i.e., the IP addresses of the potential fast-flux agents) and the time-to-live of the various records would be to query directly the authoritative name server for the suspicious domain. Although at each query we would always obtain "fresh" records and we would have the highest chance to see previously unseen records (i.e., in the ideal case records are rotated at each query and always have the highest time-to-live), the malicious authoritative name server could easily correlate the high number of queries with a system like FluXOR and consequently fool the analysis by returning fake resource records.

---

[1] Obviously, a malicious registrar returning (directly or indirectly) fake answers to our WHOIS queries could fool our system. However, in our opinion, that is very improbable: top-level domain registrars are accredited directly by ICANN and they risk to compromise their entire business if they are found to be malicious.

The solution currently adopted by FluXOR is to collect the information by issuing recursive queries through multiple public non-authoritative name servers, such that FluXOR queries are blended in the victims' queries. To estimate the maximum time-to-live of the resource records, to maximise the number of agents seen, and to minimise the network traffic, non-authoritative name servers are queried immediately after the cached records have expired.

Features characterising the heterogeneity of the agents (F_5 to F_9). The remaining features are specific to the IP addresses into which a suspicious FQDN is resolved to. The number of distinct networks (F_5) associated with the same FQDN is computed by enumerating the distinct networks associated with the IP addresses of the potential fast-flux agents. This information can be obtained through a WHOIS query, one for each IP address, directed the respective registry. Similarly, the number of distinct autonomous systems associated with the same FQDN (F_6), is obtained by querying the databases of the regional registries for the AS to which each IP address belongs to. The number of distinct domain names associated with the IP addresses of the potential fast-flux agents (F_7) are obtained by querying name servers for pointer (PTR) resource records associated with each IP address (this kind of query is commonly known as "reverse lookup"). The hostnames obtained are subsequently split to extract the domain name. The network name and the organisation owning the network (F_8 and F_9) are obtained through WHOIS queries. Unfortunately some of the information from which we extract the features of interest are not always available. An example are PTR records associated with the IP addresses of the potential agents.

5.3   Detector

The *detector* of malicious hostnames feeds the set of collected features of the suspicious hostname to the naïve Bayesian classifier for the classification. The classifier is built on top of Weka [25], using the classification algorithm called "NaiveBayesSimple", which models numeric attributes by a normal distribution.

6   Experimental Results

We have been running FluXOR since the beginning of January, but unfortunately the system has been working without interruption only since mid January. Currently the monitor and the detector are located on the same machine, an AMD Athlon XP 1.8GHz with 384Mb of RAM, running GNU/Linux and using MySQL for the persistent storage. The detector has been trained with three different data-sets, containing features extracted after one, two, and three hours of monitoring respectively. The three training sets were composed by 50 benign and 75 malicious FQDNs manually analysed and classified. The collector was located on the mail server of our laboratory and processed all the spam emails forwarded by the mail server of our department. Malicious FQDNs were all extracted from

Table 4. Summary of the results obtained using FluXOR to monitor the suspicious hostnames found in spam emails. Note that the number of agents is the number of distinct IP addresses. Dial-up hosts using dynamically assigned addresses might use multiple addresses and multiple hosts might share some addresses.

Description	#
Processed spam email messages	44804
Extracted URLs	15281
Active FQDNs (whose hostname could be resolved)	4961
Fast-flux service networks	**387**
Fast-flux agents	**31998**
Botnets	**16**

spam emails, while benign hostnames were extracted from emails (both spam and non-spam) and from the history of our browsers.

Table 4 summarises the most important numbers of our experiments: the volume of spam email messages processed, the number of URLs extracted, the number of FQDNs active at the time the emails were received, the number of fast-flux service networks detected, the number of distinct fast-flux agents, and the number of hypothetical botnets the detected fast-flux agents were part of. About 7.8% of the active FQDNs turned out to conceal fast-flux service networks served by 31998 distinct fast-flux agents, which we believe to belong to 16 distinct botnets (we considered two fast-flux service networks associated with the same botnet if they were pointing to the same website).

We evaluated the detection accuracy automatically, before training the classifier, and manually by comparing the output of the detector with our belief. Although during the manual analysis we found some corner case benign and malicious hostnames, the detector always classified the suspicious hostnames correctly. That is, we had *zero* false-positives. We also tried to correlate the data collected in the last month to understand the botnet phenomenon by observing botnets activity from the prospective of a victim, starting from hostnames associated with fast-flux service networks found in spam emails.

6.1   Detection Accuracy

We evaluated the accuracy of our detection strategy following two different strategies: (I) an automatic cross-validation with the three training data-sets and (II) a manual analysis of a random subset of the active FQDNs extracted from the emails.

Part of our training data-set was used to estimate the accuracy of the model using cross-validation, with 5 and 10 folds [26]. No hostname was misclassified. The manual analysis was performed by comparing the response of the detector with our belief about the maliciousness of the hostnames. Hostnames whose maliciousness was difficult to attest were monitored for a day. The detector was invoked three times on each sample, the first time with the features extracted after one hour of monitoring and the corresponding model, the second and the third time with the features extracted after two and after three hours of monitoring, and the corresponding model, respectively. Note that the amount of active hostnames processed were rather large and impossible to analyse manually in its entirety. Thus, we pruned the set using a filter to identify all the hostnames that were undoubtedly benign (i.e., those, after three hours of monitoring, associated with only two or less IP addresses and classified as benign). The manual analysis confirmed the correctness of our classifier, no hostname was misclassified.

During the manual analysis of the accuracy of the detector we came across some peculiar benign hostnames that had some of the characteristic of malicious hostnames. Two examples of these hostnames are `imageshack.us` and `database.clamav.net`. These hostnames are associated with very small time-to-live and are resolved in multiple IP addresses, 129 and 21, respectively[2]. All the 129 distinct IP addresses associated with the first hostname belong to the same network. That makes us believe that the hosts are hosted in a server farm somewhere and that load-balancing is implemented using DNS round-robin. On the other hand, the IP addresses associated with `database.clamav.net` (see the discussion in Section 2) are located in 12 distinct networks, because mirrors are voluntarily hosted by companies and universities. Both hostnames belong to domains registered several years ago through registrars that are not commonly used by miscreants. In both cases FluXOR correctly classified the hostnames, even when the detection was performed using the features collected during one hour of monitoring only. Other examples of correctly classified benign hostnames that share some of the features of hostnames used for fast-flux service networks are `pool.ntp.org` and `en.wikipedia.org.nyud.net` (Wikipedia mirrored through Coral Content Distribution Network).

We also identified several very young (or not very active) fast-flux service networks for which, after an hour of monitoring, we only saw from three to five distinct agents. After three hours of monitoring the size of the network was still very small and reached only seven or eight agents. Despite the small number of agents, the hostnames were always classified as malicious, even when detection was performed using the data collected in an hour of monitoring. Not completely convinced of the response of the detector, we continued to monitor the hostnames. After several days the service networks encompassed hundred of hosts.

Three observations are worth mentioning. First, the detector is surprisingly precise. Second, in less than three hours we can precisely tell if a FQDN is malicious or not. Third, the current status of the fast-flux service network might not reflect the status of the network in the future (e.g., a hostname can be used for any kind of purpose at the beginning and then associated with a fast-flux service network in the future). The detector can only classify the current status

---

[2] The hostname `database.clamav.net` is resolved into different IP addresses according to the country from which the request comes from. During our experiments we used a public DNS located in the U.S., which is the country with the highest number of IP addresses associated with the hostname.

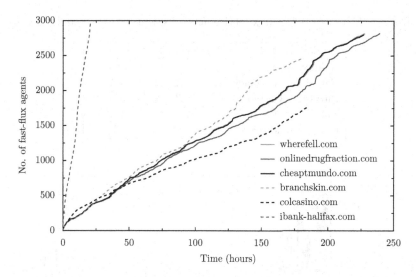

Fig. 3. Number of fast-flux agents, serving some representative fast-flux service networks, detected during the time

of the hostname and, in order to detect a change of the status, the hostname must be monitored and classified again.

6.2 Empirical Analysis of the Fast-Flux Service Networks Phenomenon

Although we collected suspicious hostnames from a single source only and the number of hostnames collected was rather small, the number of detected fast-flux service networks and the number of their agents is unexpectedly very large. About 7.8% of the hostnames analysed were malicious. In the following paragraphs we briefly summarise some results we believe are interesting. Real-time and complete results of the analysis can be found on-line at `http://fluxor.laser.dico.unimi.it`

Figure 3 shows the number of fast-flux agents, belonging to six distinct networks, detected during the time. The number of agents detected depends on many factors. For example the time-to-live of the DNS resource records, the number of records returned at each query, and the frequency at which the set of active agents is updated. The case of `ibank-halifax.com` is very impressive. In less than a day we detected about 3000 agents. The turnaround of agents in the average fast-flux service network is much smaller. The average number of new agents detected daily was about 122.

We visited some of the websites served thorough the detected fast-flux service networks and found out that several FQDNs were associated with the same website. The networks were probably pointing to the same mother-ship. Our hypothesis is that, to improve the availability of the system, miscreants registered multiple domains. If a domain was shutdown, victims could still be served

Table 5. Some of the fast-flux service networks detected, grouped by botnet

Botnet (Website)	# networks	# agents
Halifax scam	1	13958
Canadian Pharmacy	312	4773
EuroPrimeCasino	7	3242
Cheap EOM Software	1	2371
PosteItaliane scam	1	50

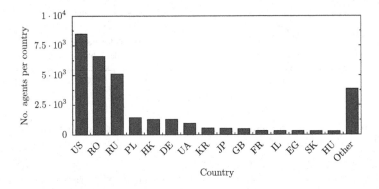

Fig. 4. Geographical distributions of the detected fast-flux agents

through the other domains. Thus, it is more difficult for the authorities to eradicate the scam. Besides the common website, this hypothesis is further corroborated by the fact that multiple fast-flux service networks are served by the same set of agents. Figure 3 shows that the number of agents detected during the time for the FQDNs `wherefell.com` and `cheaptmundo.com` is growing symmetrically. We also observed that the two domains share the same authoritative name servers and also about 81% of the agents. We believe it is reasonable to assume that all the fast-flux networks pointing to the same website, and thus used for the same fraud, are served by agents belonging to the same botnet. Table 5 shows some of the hypothetical botnets associated with the detected fast flux service networks, and their extent in number of agents (the name assigned to the botnet is derived from the title of the main page of the website).

Figure 4 shows the geographical distribution of the detected agents. Their heterogeneous geographical distribution testifies that the scale of the problem is world-wide.

7   Related Work

The botnet problem has been studied by the research community mainly from two different prospectives: from the prospective of the bot, to study its code and its behaviours, and from the prospective of the network, to study the traffic generated by these bots. The approach proposed in this paper studies the phenomenon from the prospective of a victim of the scams perpetrated by these botnets.

The first analysis and characterisation of fast-flux service networks was presented by the HoneyNet project [8]. The report analysed the two types of networks seen so far (i.e., single-flux and double-flux service networks) and analysed the behaviour of a malware with the capabilities of a fast-flux agent. The problem of detecting and mitigating fast-flux service networks was concurrently addressed by Holz et al. [27]. Our work and theirs are very similar. They also propose a detection method based on the observation of some features common in fast-flux service networks. However, while we employ 9 different features, Holz et al. focus on just three features (i.e., the number of DNS "A" records, the number of DNS "NS" records, and the number of distinct autonomous systems fast-flux agents belongs to), one of which (the second) does not seem to be used at all for the classification. We believe such a limited set of distinguishing features could lead to several false-positives, mostly because such features are also typical of domains that employ some DNS load-balancing techniques (e.g., such as pool.ntp.org). Our extensive evaluation has shown that FluXOR is undoubtedly robust and very efficient. The work of Rajab et al. differs from ours in term of techniques and goals. However, the point of view from which botnets are observed is similar to ours [28]. We detect and monitor fast-flux service networks by performing simple DNS and WHOIS queries. Similarly, in their work, Rajab et al. tracked botnets by infiltrating in IRC channels and by measuring the cache-hit rate of the DNS servers queried by the bots to contact their control centre.

The analysis of the network traffic generated by compromised machines transformed into bots and the traffic generated by bot "management" open several opportunities for understanding the phenomenon and for detection. Rishi, by monitoring the network traffic for unusual IRC communications like connection to uncommon servers and ports and use of suspicious nicknames, detects machines infected with bots [11]. Karasaridis et al. developed a transport and application layer traffic analyser to detect IRC based bots on wide-scale [13]. Cooke et al. studied the effectiveness of detecting botnets by directly monitoring IRC communications and other command and control activities. Unfortunately their work demonstrated that a more comprehensive approach, based on the correlation of data coming from multiple sources, is required to precisely detect botnets. BotHunter correlates alerts coming from different types of sensors to identify the communication sequences that occur during the infection process (i.e., target scanning, infection exploit, binary egg download, and outbound scanning) [12]. Dagon et al. used DNS redirection to detect machines part of specific botnets and to understand how time and geographical location affect the spread dynamics of these botnets [14]. The problem of understanding how challenging is to estimate the size of botnets were addressed by Rajab et al. [3]. A similar problem was subsequently addressed by Dagon et al. [10]. They proposed several metrics to measure the utility of botnets for various activities and presented a taxonomy of botnets based on these metrics and on the topological structure of the networks.

Many researchers have studied botnets by studying how bots behave and how they are implemented. These bots can be analysed using dynamic, static, or a hybrid dynamic and static analysis. BotSwat characterises and detect the typical behaviours of bots using dynamic taint analysis [29]. Barford *et al.* statically analysed the codebase of four of the most common IRC bots to understand their propagation methods, the mechanism used for their remote control, the delivery and the obfuscation mechanisms used [30]. Other specific bots have been thoroughly analysed to understand the new techniques used and the best method to block them [31,32,7].

8   Conclusion

Botnets represent one of the major threats for the Internet community. In this paper we have presented FluXOR, the system we have developed to detect and monitor fast-flux service networks. Fast-flux service networks are used by the miscreants, controlling the biggest and most powerful botnets, to hide and to maximise the availability of the core components of their business. Fast-flux service networks offer researchers the possibility to observe a botnet from the outside, by simply observing what a victim of these botnets could observe. Through FluXOR we have demonstrated that, by tracking fast-flux service networks with very simple queries any end-user can perform, we were able to detect, in a very short period of time, more than thirty thousands compromised machines remotely controlled by miscreants and used for various on-line frauds.

Acknowledgements

We would like to thank our shepherd, John McHugh, and the anonymous reviewers for their useful comments and suggestions.

References

1. Franklin, J., Perrig, A., Paxson, V., Savage, S.: An inquiry into the nature and causes of the wealth of internet miscreants. In: Proceedings of the 14th ACM conference on Computer and communications security (CCS 2007), pp. 375–388. ACM, New York (2007)
2. Ször, P.: The Art of Computer Virus Research and Defense. Addison Wesley Professional, Reading (2005)
3. Rajab, M.A., Zarfoss, J., Monrose, F., Terzis, A.: My Botnet is Bigger than Yours (Maybe, Better than Yours): Why Size Estimates Remain Challenging. In: Proceedings of the first conference on First Workshop on Hot Topics in Understanding Botnets (HotBots 2007), Berkeley, CA, USA. USENIX Association (2007)
4. Furst, M.: Expert: Botnets No. 1 Emerging Internet Threat. CNN Technology (2006)

5. Markoff, J.: Attack of the Zombie Computers Is a Growing Threat, Experts Say. The New York Times (January 2007)

6. Corporation, F.S.: Malware Information Pages: Warezov (2006), http://www.f-secure.com/v-descs/warezov.shtml

7. Porras, P., Saidi, H., Yegneswaran, V.: A Multi-perspective Analysis of the Storm (Peacomm) Worm. Technical report, SRI International (October 2007)

8. The Honeynet Project & Research Alliance: Know Your Enemy: Fast-Flux Service Networks (2007)

9. Gaudin, S.: Storm Worm Erupts Into Worst Virus Attack In 2 Years (2007)

10. Dagon, D., Gu, G., Lee, C., Lee, W.: A taxonomy of botnet structures. In: Proceedings of the 23 Annual Computer Security Applications Conference (ACSAC 2007) (December 2007)

11. Goebel, J., Holz, T.: Rishi: identify bot contaminated hosts by irc nickname evaluation. In: Proceedings of the first conference on First Workshop on Hot Topics in Understanding Botnets (HotBots 2007), Berkeley, CA, USA. USENIX Association (2007)

12. Gu, G., Porras, P., Yegneswaran, V., Fong, M., Lee, W.: BotHunter: Detecting malware infection through ids-driven dialog correlation. In: Proceedings of the 16th USENIX Security Symposium (Security 2007) (August 2007)

13. Karasaridis, A., Rexroad, B., Hoeflin, D.: Wide-scale botnet detection and characterization. In: Proceedings of the first conference on First Workshop on Hot Topics in Understanding Botnets (HotBots 2007), Berkeley, CA, USA. USENIX Association (2007)

14. Dagon, D., Zou, C., Lee, W.: Modeling botnet propagation using time zones. In: Proceedings of the 13th Annual Network and Distributed System Security Symposium (NDSS 2006) (2006)

15. Ramachandran, A., Feamster, N., Dagon, D.: Revealing botnet membership using dnsbl counter-intelligence. In: Proceedings of the 2nd conference on Steps to Reducing Unwanted Traffic on the Internet (SRUTI 2006), Berkeley, CA, USA. USENIX Association (2006)

16. Cooke, E., Jahanian, F., Mcpherson, D.: The Zombie Roundup: Understanding, Detecting, and Disrupting Botnets. In: Workshop on Steps to Reducing Unwanted Traffic on the Internet (SRUTI), pp. 39–44 (June 2005)

17. Mockapetris, P.: Domain names – concepts and facilites. RFC 1034, Internet Engineering Task Force (November 1987)

18. Mockapetris, P.: Domain names – implementation and specification. RFC 1035, Internet Engineering Task Force (November 1987)

19. Kojm, T.: Clam AntiVirus, http://www.clamav.net

20. John, G.H., Langley, P.: Estimating continuous distributions in Bayesian classifiers. In: Proceedings of the 11th Conference on Uncertainty in Artificial Intelligence, pp. 338–345. Morgan Kaufmann, San Francisco (1995)

21. Hawkinson, J., Bates, T.: Guidelines for creation, selection, and registration of an autonomous system (as). RFC 1930, Internet Engineering Task Force (March 1996)

22. DomainTools.com: Domain Counts & Internet Statistics, http://www.domaintools.com/internet-statistics/

23. Zhang, H.: The Optimality of Naïve Bayes. In: Proceedings of the Seventeenth International Florida Artificial Intelligence Research Society Conference. AAAI Press, Miami Beach (2004)

24. Daigle, L.: WHOIS protocol specification. RFC 3912, Internet Engineering Task Force (March 2004)

25. Witten, I.H., Frank, E.: Data Mining: Practical machine learning tools and techniques, 2nd edn. Morgan Kaufmann, San Francisco (2005)
26. Kohavi, R.: A Study of Cross-Validation and Bootstrap for Accuracy Estimation and Model Selection. In: Proceedings of the Fourteenth International Joint Conference on Artificial Intelligence, pp. 1137–1145. Morgan Kaufmann, San Francisco (1995)
27. Holz, T., Gorecki, C., Freiling, F., Rieck, K.: Detection and Mitigation of Fast-Flux Service Networks. In: Proceeding of the 15th Annual Network & Distributed System Security Symposium (NDSS 2008) (February 2008)
28. Rajab, M.A., Zarfoss, J., Monrose, F., Terzis, A.: A multifaceted approach to understanding the botnet phenomenon. In: Proceedings of the 6th ACM SIGCOMM conference on Internet measurement (IMC 2006), pp. 41–52. ACM, New York (2006)
29. Stinson, E., Mitchell, J.C.: Characterizing Bots' Remote Control Behavior. In: Proceedings of the Conference on Detection of Intrusions and Malware, and Vulnerability Assessment, pp. 89–108. Springer, Heidelberg (2007)
30. Paul, B., Vinod, Y.: An Inside Look at Botnets. In: Malware Detection. Advances in Information Security, vol. 27. Springer, Heidelberg (2007)
31. Chiang, K., Lloyd, L.: A case study of the rustock rootkit and spam bot. In: Proceedings of the first conference on First Workshop on Hot Topics in Understanding Botnets (HotBots 2007), Berkeley, CA, USA. USENIX Association (2007)
32. Daswani, N., Stoppelman, M.: The anatomy of clickbot.a. In: Proceedings of the first conference on First Workshop on Hot Topics in Understanding Botnets (HotBots 2007), Berkeley, CA, USA. USENIX Association (2007)

Traffic Aggregation for Malware Detection

Ting-Fang Yen[1] and Michael K. Reiter[2]

[1] Carnegie Mellon University
tingfang@cmu.edu
[2] University of North Carolina, Chapel Hill
reiter@cs.unc.edu

Abstract. Stealthy malware, such as botnets and spyware, are hard to detect because their activities are subtle and do not disrupt the network, in contrast to DoS
attacks and aggressive worms. Stealthy malware, however, does communicate to
exfiltrate data to the attacker, to receive the attacker's commands, or to carry out
those commands. Moreover, since malware rarely infiltrates only a single host in a
large enterprise, these communications should emerge from multiple hosts within
coarse temporal proximity to one another. In this paper, we describe a system
called TĀMD (pronounced "tamed") with which an enterprise can identify candidate groups of infected computers within its network. TĀMD accomplishes this by
finding new communication "aggregates" involving multiple internal hosts, i.e.,
communication flows that share common characteristics. We describe characteristics for defining aggregates—including flows that communicate with the same
external network, that share similar payload, and/or that involve internal hosts
with similar software platforms—and justify their use in finding infected hosts.
We also detail efficient algorithms employed by TĀMD for identifying such aggregates, and demonstrate a particular configuration of TĀMD that identifies new
infections for multiple bot and spyware examples, within traces of traffic recorded
at the edge of a university network. This is achieved even when the number of infected hosts comprise only about 0.0097% of all internal hosts in the network.

1 Introduction

It is clearly in the interest of network administrators to detect computers within their
networks that are infiltrated by spyware or bots. Such stealthy malware can exfiltrate
sensitive data to adversaries, or lie in wait for commands from a bot-master to forward
spam or launch denial-of-service attacks, for example. Unfortunately it is difficult to detect such malware, since by default it does little to arouse suspicion: e.g., generally its
communications neither consume significant bandwidth nor involve a large number of
targets. While this changes if the bots are enlisted in aggressive scanning for other vulnerable hosts or in denial-of-service attacks—in which case they can easily be detected
using known techniques (e.g., [38, 27])—it would be better to detect the bots prior to
such a disruptive event, in the hopes of averting it. Moreover, such easily detectable
behaviors are uncharacteristic of significant classes of malware, notably spyware.

We hypothesize that even stealthy, previously unseen malware is likely to exhibit
communication that is detectable, if viewed in the right light. First, since emerging malware rarely infects only a single victim, we expect its characteristic communications,
however subtle, to appear roughly coincidentally at multiple hosts in a large network.

D. Zamboni (Ed.): DIMVA 2008, LNCS 5137, pp. 207–227, 2008.

Second, we expect these communications to share certain features that differentiate them from other communications typical of that network. Of course, these two observations may pertain equally well to a variety of communications that are not induced by malware, and consequently the challenge is to refine these observations so as to be useful for detecting malware in an operational system.

In this paper we describe such a system, called TĀMD, an abbreviation for "Traffic Aggregation for Malware Detection". As its name suggests, TĀMD distills *traffic aggregates* from the traffic passing the edge of a network, where each aggregate is defined by certain characteristics that the traffic grouped within it shares in common. By refining these aggregates to include only traffic that shares multiple relevant characteristics, and by using past traffic as precedent to justify discarding certain aggregates as normal, TĀMD constructs a small set of new aggregates (i.e., without previous precedent) that it recommends for examination, for example, by more targeted (e.g., signature-based) intrusion detection tools. The key to maximizing the data-reducing precision of TĀMD is the characteristics on which it aggregates traffic, which include:

- **Common destinations:** TĀMD analyzes the networks with which internal hosts communicate, in order to identify aggregates of communication to busier-than-normal external destinations. Spyware reporting to the attacker's site or bot communication to a bot-master (e.g., with IRC, HTTP, or another protocol) might thus form an aggregate under this classification.
- **Similar payload:** TĀMD identifies traffic with similar payloads or, more specifically, payloads for which a type of edit distance (*string edit distance matching with moves* [8]) is small. Intuitively, command-and-control traffic between a bot-master and his bots should share significant structure and hence, we expect, would have a low edit distance between them.
- **Common internal-host platforms:** TĀMD passively fingerprints platforms of internal hosts, and forms aggregates of traffic involving internal hosts that share a common platform. Traffic caused by malware infections that are platform-dependent should form an aggregate by use of this characteristic.

Alone, each of these methods of forming traffic aggregates would be far too coarse to be an effective data-reduction technique for identifying malware, as legitimate traffic can form aggregates under these characterizations, as well. In combination, however, they can be quite powerful at extracting aggregates of malware communications (and relatively few others). To demonstrate this, we detail a particular configuration of TĀMD that employs these aggregation techniques to identify internal hosts infected by malware that reports to a controller site external to the network. Indeed, botnets have been observed to switch controllers or download updates frequently, as often as every two or three days [19, 11]; each such event gives TĀMD an opportunity to identify these communications. We show that with traffic generated from real spyware and bot instances, TĀMD was able to reliably extract this traffic from all traffic passing the edge of a university network, while the number of other aggregates reported is very low.

In addition to identifying aggregates and ways of combining them to find malware-infected hosts, the contributions of TĀMD include algorithms for computing these aggregates efficiently. Our algorithms draw from diverse areas including signal processing, data mining and metric embeddings. We will detail each of these algorithms here.

2   Related Work

Botnet detection. Previous approaches to botnet detection rely on heuristics that assume certain models of botnet architecture or behavior, such as IRC-based command-and-control [7, 4, 26, 11], the presence of scanning activities, long idle time and short response time for bots compared to humans [32], etc. Karasaridis et al. [19] proposed an approach for identifying botnet controllers by combining heuristics that assume the use of IRC communication, scanning behavior, and known models of botnet communication. BotHunter [14] models all bots as sharing common infection steps—namely target scanning, infection exploit, binary download and execution, command-and-control channel establishment, and outbound scanning—and then employs Snort with various malware extensions to raise an alarm when a sufficient subset of these are detected. Thus, malware not conforming to this profile (e.g., spyware or bots engineered differently) would seemingly go undetected by their approach. Ramachandran et al. [36] observed that botmasters lookup DNS blacklists to tell whether their bots are blacklisted. They thus monitor lookups to a DNS-based blacklist to identify bots.

We believe our approach to be fundamentally different from the above approaches in the following respect. While these approaches work from models of malware behavior (not unlike signature-based intrusion detection), our approach simply seeks to identify new aggregates of communication that are not explained by past behavior on the network being monitored. Like all anomaly-detection approaches, our challenge is to demonstrate that the number of identified anomalous aggregates is manageable, but it has the potential to identify a wider range of as-yet-unseen malware. In particular, the assumptions underlying previous systems present opportunities for attackers to evade these systems by changing the behavior of botnets, and these systems will fail to detect other types of malware (e.g., spyware) that do not meet these assumptions.

Independently of or subsequently to our work [37], other works have begun to incorporate aspects of using aggregation for detecting bots. For example, BotSniffer [15] looks for infected hosts displaying spatial-temporal similarity. It identifies hosts with similar suspicious network activities, namely scanning and sending spam emails, and who also share common communication contents, defined by the number of shared bi-grams. BotMiner [13] groups together hosts based on destination or connection statistics (i.e., the byte count, the packet count, the number of flows, etc.), and on their suspected malicious activities (i.e., scanning, spamming, downloading binaries, or sending exploits). BotMiner is more similar to TĀMD in the sense that they both identify hosts sharing multiple common characteristics, but the characteristics on which TĀMD and BotMiner cluster hosts are different. BotSniffer seeks to identify known bot activities, such as scanning or spamming, and limits its attention only to bots using IRC or HTTP to communicate with a centralized botmaster.

Various prior works on botnet detection use honeypots (e.g., [2, 33]). As honeypots can only approximately mimic (at best) real user behavior, they may not attract spyware or bots that rely on human action to infect users' machines. Our approach, in not requiring a honeypot, places no assumptions about the infection vector by which attacks occur and whether these vectors present themselves in a honeypot. In doing so, we hope to make our approach as general as possible.

Techniques. The techniques we employ for aggregation, specifically on the basis of external subnets to which communication occurs, include some drawn from the signal processing domain. While others have drawn from this domain in the detection of network traffic anomalies, our approach has different goals and hence applies these techniques differently. Coarsely speaking, past approaches extract packet header information, such as the number of bytes or packets transferred for each flow, counts of TCP flags, etc., in search of volume anomalies like denial-of-service attacks, flash crowds, or network outages [39, 3, 22]. Lakhina et al. [25] studied the structure of network flows by decomposing OD flows (flows originating and exiting from the same ingress and egress points in the network) using Principal Component Analysis (PCA). They expressed each OD flow as a linear combination of smaller "eigenflows", which may belong to deterministic periodic trends, short-lived bursts, or noise, in the traffic. Terrell et al. [40] focused on multi-variate data analysis by grouping network traces into time-series data and selecting features of the traffic from each time bin, including the number of bytes, packets, flows, and the entropy of the packet size and port numbers. They applied Singular Value Decomposition (SVD) to the time-series data. From examining the low-order components, they were able to detect denial-of-service attacks. In general, transient and light-weight events would go unnoticed by these approaches, such as spammers that send only a few emails over the course of a few minutes [35]. Our work, on the other hand, is targeted at such lighter-weight events and so employs these techniques differently, not to mention techniques from other domains (e.g., metric embeddings, passive fingerprinting). Ramachandran et al. [34], in assuming that spammers exhibit similar email-sending behaviors across domains, constructed patterns corresponding to the amount of emails sent to each domain by known spammers. The patterns are calculated from the mean of the clusters generated through spectral clustering [6]. This is similar to our method of finding flows destined to the same external subnets; however, they do not look at other aspects of spamming besides the destination.

Another technique we employ is payload inspection, specifically to aggregate flows based on similar content. Payload inspection has been applied within methods for detecting worm outbreaks and generating signatures. Many previous approaches assume that malicious traffic is significantly more frequent or wide-spread than other traffic, and so the same content will be repeated in a large number of different packets or flows (e.g., [38, 21, 29, 18, 30]); we do not make this assumption here. Previous approaches to comparing payloads includes matching substrings [28, 18] or n-grams [42, 29, 15], hashing blocks of the payload [38, 22], or searching for the longest common substring [24]. Compared to these methods, our edit distance metric is more sensitive and accurate in cases where parts of the message are simply shifted or replaced. Goebel et al. [11] inspected packet payload to find IRC bots with formatted nicknames. They observed that often IRC bots have nicknames with common patterns, such as long random numbers or country codes. However, this approach can only detect bots for which the nickname format is known. ARAKIS from CERT Polska (http://www.arakis.pl) is an early-warning system that generates signatures for new threats. Assuming new attacks will have payloads not seen previously, they examine traffic from honeypots and darknets to cluster flows with similar content (determined by comparing Rabin hashes) not seen before, and that are performing similar activities, i.e., port scanning. A signature is generated from the longest common substrings of the similar flows. However, ARAKIS currently only focuses on threats that propagate through port scanning.

Another tool for intrusion analysis is the commercial product StealthWatch from Lancope (http://www.lancope.com). StealthWatch monitors all traffic at the network border, checking for policy violations or signs of anomalous behavior by looking for higher-than-usual traffic volumes. Although this is similar to our approach of using past traffic as a baseline for identifying busier-than-normal external destinations, they does not refine this information using, e.g., payload or platform aggregation as we do here. Thus, it is primarily useful for detecting only large-volume anomalies like port scanning and denial-of-service attacks.

3 Defining Aggregates

Given a collection of bi-directional flow records observed at the edge of an enterprise network, our system aims to identify infected internal hosts by finding communication "aggregates", which consist of flows that share common network characteristics. Specifically, TĀMD deploys three aggregation functions to identify flows with the following characteristics: those that contribute to busier-than-usual destinations, that have payloads for which a type of edit distance is small, or that involve internal hosts of a common platform.

The aggregation functions take as input collections of flow records, Λ, and output either groups (aggregates) of internal hosts that share particular properties or a value indicating the amount of similarity between the input flow record collections. We presume that each flow record $\lambda \in \Lambda$ includes the IP address of the internal host λ.internal involved in the communication and the external subnet λ.external with which it communicates. λ also includes some portion of the payload λ.payload of that communication, packet header fields, and the start and end time of the communication.

3.1 Destination Aggregates

Previous studies show that the destination addresses with which a group of hosts communicates exhibit stability over time, both in the amount of traffic sent and in the set-membership of the destinations [1, 23]. Malware activities are thus likely to exhibit communication patterns outside the norm, i.e., contacting destinations that the internal hosts would not have contacted otherwise.

The destination aggregation function $\mathsf{ByDest}^\tau(\Lambda, \Lambda_{\mathsf{past}})$ takes as input two sets $\Lambda, \Lambda_{\mathsf{past}}$ of communication records. The variable τ is a parameter to the function, as described later in this section. By analyzing the external addresses with which internal hosts communicate in Λ and Λ_{past}, the function outputs a set SuspiciousSubnets of destination subnets for which there is a larger number of interactions with the internal network, using Λ_{past} as a baseline. The function also outputs an integer numAggs and a set Agg_i ($1 \le i \le \mathsf{numAggs}$), where Agg_i are internal hosts (IP addresses) that originated traffic in Λ, and who contributed to larger-than-usual number of interactions with an external destination subnet in SuspiciousSubnets.

At a high level, the set SuspiciousSubnets of selected "suspicious" external destinations is determined after filtering out periodic and regular activities in the communications of the network as represented in the past traffic Λ_{past}. External destinations observed in Λ that do not follow the norm, i.e., that according to Λ_{past} are busier than usual or have not been contacted before, are thus output in SuspiciousSubnets.

Below we describe the three processing steps in $\text{ByDest}^{\tau}(\Lambda, \Lambda_{past})$: (i) Trend filtering, which selects the set of suspicious external destinations; (ii) Dimension reduction, which first characterizes each host by a vector indicating which suspicious destinations it interacted with, and then reduces the dimensionality of these vectors while preserving most of the information; and (iii) Clustering, which forms clusters of the vectors (i.e., internal hosts) by the destinations they contacted.

Trend Filtering. Trend filtering aims to remove regular and periodic communications from Λ, so that external destinations showing behavior outside the norm are identified. In particular, the "norm" is defined, for each external destination subnet, by the average number of internal hosts that communicate with that subnet in various periodic intervals, as recorded in Λ_{past}. For example, periodic patterns, such as Windows machines connecting to the Windows update server on a weekly basis or banking websites experiencing traffic spikes on pay day each month, can be inferred from Λ_{past}. The change in activity of a destination in Λ can then be measured by how much more traffic it received in Λ compared to its average values for previous time intervals in Λ_{past}. In the current implementation, a destination is selected to be in SuspiciousSubnets if no internal host has been seen to communicate with it for all previous periodic time intervals in Λ_{past}.

Dimension Reduction. Given SuspiciousSubnets, each internal host can be represented as a binary vector $v = (v[1], v[2], \cdots, v[k])$ for which the dimensionality k is equal to the number of destinations in SuspiciousSubnets. A dimension $v[i]$ is set to 1 if the internal host communicated with destination i in SuspiciousSubnets (according to Λ), and 0 otherwise. However, the dimensions may be redundant or dependent on one another; e.g., retrieving a web page can cause other web servers to be contacted. To identify such relationships between the destinations and to further dimension reduction, we apply Principal Component Analysis (PCA).

PCA [17] is a method for analyzing multivariate data. It enables data reduction by transforming the original vectors onto a new set of orthogonal axes, i.e., principal components, while preserving most of the original information. This is done by having each principal component capture as much of the variability in the data as possible.

While a vector originally has length equal to the number of suspicious destinations, the transformed vector after PCA has a dimensionality that is the number of selected principal components, with each dimension now representing a linear combination of the external destinations. The number of selected principal components depends on the amount of variance we want to capture in the data, denoted as the parameter τ. The more variance to be captured, the more accurate the transformation represents the original data, but, at the same time, more principal components are needed, increasing the dimensionality.

Clustering. PCA reduces the vector dimensionality significantly, after which hosts connecting to the same combinations of destinations can be identified efficiently through clustering. $\mathsf{ByDest}^\tau(\Lambda, \Lambda_{\mathsf{past}})$ forms clusters of the vectors (i.e., internal hosts) whose traffic is present in Λ using a K-means clustering algorithm [20], which does not require the number of clusters to be known in advance.

1. Randomly select a vector as the first cluster hub. Assign all vectors to this cluster.
2. Select the vector furthest away from its hub as a new cluster hub. Re-assign all vectors to the cluster whose hub it is closest to.
3. Repeat step 2 until no vector is further from its hub than half of the average hub-hub distance.

Cosine distance is used for comparing vector distances, i.e., $\mathsf{CosineDist}(v_1, v_2) = \cos^{-1}((v_1 \bullet v_2)/(|v_1||v_2|))$, for two vectors v_1 and v_2, where the symbol $\bullet$ is the dot product between the two vectors, and $|v_1|$ is the length of vector v_1. Cosine distance is essentially a normalized dot product of the vectors, where a particular dimension would contribute to the final sum if and only if both vectors have a nonzero value in that dimension. In our case, each vector represents a particular internal source host, and each dimension represents a linear combination of destination subnets. Cosine distance thus captures well the relationship between source hosts based on the common destinations they contacted.

Let $\mathsf{numAggs}$ denote the number of clusters from the above algorithm, and let Agg_i ($i = 1 \ldots \mathsf{numAggs}$) denote the hosts whose vectors comprise the i-th cluster. As such, Agg_i is an aggregate of internal hosts interacting with the same busier-than-usual external subnets. Again, all of $\mathsf{SuspiciousSubnets}$, $\mathsf{numAggs}$ and $\{\mathsf{Agg}_i\}_{1 \leq i \leq \mathsf{numAggs}}$ are output from $\mathsf{ByDest}^\tau(\Lambda, \Lambda_{\mathsf{past}})$.

3.2 Payload Aggregates

Payload inspection algorithms for malware detection have previously focused on either modeling byte-frequency distributions (e.g., [38, 21, 29, 18]), which assumes that malicious traffic should exhibit an observably different byte-frequency distribution from that of normal traffic, or substring matching (e.g., [42, 28]). In contrast to these approaches, our measure of payload similarity is *edit distance with substring moves*, which we choose because it is capable of capturing syntactic similarities between strings, even if parts of one string are simply shifted or replaced. To our knowledge, ours is the first work that detects malicious traffic by computing (a type of) string edit distance between payloads, and that develops techniques to scale these computations to high data rate environments.

For two character strings s_1 and s_2, $\mathsf{EditDist}(s_1, s_2)$ is defined as the number of character insertions, deletions, substitutions, or substring moves, required to turn s_1 into s_2. Given a string $s = s[1] \cdots s[\mathsf{len}(s)]$, a substring move with parameters i, j, and k transforms s into $s[1] \cdots s[i-1], s[j] \cdots s[k-1], s[i] \cdots s[j-1], s[k] \cdots s[\mathsf{len}(s)]$ for some $1 \leq i \leq j \leq k \leq \mathsf{len}(s)$. For example, swapping labeled parameters in a parameter list would be a substring move in a command string.

The payload comparison function $\mathsf{ByPayload}^{\delta_{\mathsf{Ed}}}(\Lambda)$ that we introduce for use in Section 4 takes as input a set Λ of communication records, and outputs a value in the range $[0, 1]$. It is parameterized by an edit distance threshold δ_{Ed} that determines if communication records λ, λ' are "close enough", i.e., if $\mathsf{EditDist}(\lambda.\mathsf{payload}, \lambda'.\mathsf{payload}) \leq \delta_{\mathsf{Ed}}$. Its output indicates from among all pairs $(\lambda, \lambda') \in \Lambda \times \Lambda$ such that $\lambda.\mathsf{external} = \lambda'.\mathsf{external}$ (i.e., that involve the same external subnet) and $\lambda.\mathsf{internal} \neq \lambda'.\mathsf{internal}$ (i.e., that are not from the same internal host), the (approximate, see below) fraction for which $\mathsf{EditDist}(\lambda.\mathsf{payload}, \lambda'.\mathsf{payload}) \leq \delta_{\mathsf{Ed}}$.

Since Λ can be large, computing $\mathsf{ByPayload}^{\delta_{\mathsf{Ed}}}(\Lambda)$ by computing $\mathsf{EditDist}(\lambda.\mathsf{payload}, \lambda'.\mathsf{payload})$ for each relevant (λ, λ') pair individually can be prohibitively expensive, i.e., requiring time proportional to $|\Lambda| \cdot |\Lambda|$, where $|\Lambda|$ denotes the cardinality of Λ. A contribution of our work is an algorithm for approximating the fraction of relevant record pairs (λ, λ') that satisfy $\mathsf{EditDist}(\lambda.\mathsf{payload}, \lambda'.\mathsf{payload}) \leq \delta_{\mathsf{Ed}}$ in time roughly proportional to $|\Lambda|$ if δ_{Ed} is small.

To perform this approximation, we first *embed* the EditDist metric within L1 distance L1Dist, where for two vectors $v_1 = v_1[1 \ldots m]$, $v_2 = v_2[1 \ldots m]$, $\mathsf{L1Dist}(v_1, v_2) = \sum_{i=1}^{m} |v_1[i] - v_2[i]|$. That is, we transform each $\lambda.\mathsf{payload}$ into a vector v_λ so that if $\mathsf{EditDist}(\lambda.\mathsf{payload}, \lambda'.\mathsf{payload}) \leq \delta_{\mathsf{Ed}}$ then $\mathsf{L1Dist}(v_\lambda, v_{\lambda'}) \leq \delta_{\mathsf{L1}}$ for a known value δ_{L1}. We do so using an algorithm due to Cormode et al. [8] called *Edit Sensitive Parsing* (ESP). For this algorithm, the ratio of δ_{L1} over δ_{Ed} is bounded by $O(\log n \log^* n)$, where n is the length of $\lambda.\mathsf{payload}$.[1] In our evaluation in Section 5, $n = 64$ and we set $\delta_{\mathsf{L1}} = \delta_{\mathsf{Ed}} \cdot \log_{10} 64$.

The embedding of EditDist into L1Dist is essential to our efficiency gains, since it enables us to utilize an approximate nearest-neighbor algorithm called *Locality Sensitive Hashing* (LSH) [10] to find vectors (and hence payload strings) near one another in terms of L1Dist (and hence in terms of EditDist), in time roughly proportional to $|\Lambda|$. Briefly, LSH hashes each vector using several randomly selected hash functions; each hash function maps the vector to a *bucket*. LSH ensures that if $\mathsf{L1Dist}(v_1, v_2) \leq \delta_{\mathsf{L1}}$, then the buckets to which v_1 and v_2 are hashed will overlap with high probability (and will overlap with much lower probability if not), where probabilities are taken with respect to the random selection of the hash functions. Consequently, we hash v_λ for each $\lambda \in \Lambda$, and explicitly confirm that $\mathsf{EditDist}(\lambda.\mathsf{payload}, \lambda'.\mathsf{payload}) \leq \delta_{\mathsf{Ed}}$ only for pairs (λ, λ') for which v_λ and $v_{\lambda'}$ hash to at least one overlapping bucket.

While edit distance may not be meaningful for encrypted messages, we can generalize the payload comparison function to define encrypted payload (e.g., detected by its entropy) as "similar". Exploring payload aggregation using other metrics is part of ongoing work; see Section 6.

3.3 Platform Aggregates

Forming traffic aggregates based on platform can be useful in identifying malware infections that are platform dependent. That is, suspicious traffic common to a collection of hosts becomes even more suspicious if the hosts share a common software platform.

Much host platform information can be inferred from traffic observed passively. Passive tools, unlike active fingerprinting tools like Nmap (http://insecure.org),

---

[1] $\log^* n$ denotes the *iterated logarithm* of n, i.e., the number of times the logarithm must be iteratively applied before the result is less than or equal to one.

do not probe hosts, but rather listen silently. The most comprehensive passive operating system fingerprinting tool of which we are aware is p0f (`http://lcamtuf.coredump.cx/p0f.shtml`), which extracts various IP and TCP header fields from SYN packets and uses a rule-based comparison algorithm. However, p0f cannot be applied to traffic traces in the flow-record format available to us (see Section 5), since most individual packet information (including for SYN packets) is not retained.

At the time of this writing, TĀMD employs two heuristics for fingerprinting internal host operating systems passively. The first employs time-to-live (TTL) fields witnessed at the network border in packets from internal hosts. It is well-known that in many cases, different operating system types select different initial TTL values (e.g., see `http://secfr.nerim.net/docs/fingerprint/en/ttl_default.html`). With a detailed map of the internal network, the observed TTL values can be used to infer the exact initial TTL value and so narrow the possibilities for operating system the host is running. However, a detailed map is typically unnecessary, as routes in most enterprise networks are sufficiently short that witnessing TTLs of packets as they leave the network enables the initial TTL values to be inferred well enough.

The second heuristic employed in TĀMD watches for host communications characteristic of a particular operating system platform. For example, Windows machines connect to the Microsoft time server by default during system boot for time sychronization, and the FreeBSD packages FTP server is more likely to be accessed by FreeBSD machines to install software updates. Once characteristic communications for platforms are identified, TĀMD can monitor for these to learn the platform of an internal host.

There are at least three limitations of such passive fingerprinting approaches for our purposes. First, DHCP-assigned IP addresses can be assigned to hosts with different operating systems over time, leading to inconsistent indications of the host operating system associated with an IP address. This suggests that TĀMD should weigh recent indications more heavily than older (and hence potentially stale) indications. Second, a machine with a compromised kernel could, in theory, alter its behavior to masquerade as a different operating system. In the absence of a possible IP address reassignment (e.g., for address ranges not assigned via DHCP), such a shift in behavior should itself be detectable evidence that a compromise may have occurred. In general, however, this limitation is intrinsic to *any* fingerprinting technique, passive or active, except those based on attestations from trusted hardware (e.g., TCG's Trusted Platform Module, `https://www.trustedcomputinggroup.org/groups/tpm/`). While we are unaware of malware that employs such a masquerading strategy, should platform-based aggregation for malware detection become commonplace, such systems would presumably need to migrate to attestation-based platform identification as it matures, in order to detect kernel-level compromises. User-level compromise should not affect platform-based aggregation using conventional fingerprinting techniques, however. The third limitation to forming aggregates based on platform is that it is likely for an enterprise to have the majority of its hosts running the same operating system. Thus ByPlatform would be more effective for networks with a diverse host population; for example, in a university setting.

Presently TĀMD uses the aforementioned heuristics based on TTL values and communication with characteristic sites to identify platforms. For use in Section 4, we embody this in a function ByPlatform(Λ) that returns the largest fraction of internal hosts in Λ (i.e., among the hosts $\{\lambda.\text{internal} : \lambda \in \Lambda\}$) that can be identified as having the same operating system, based on these heuristics applied to the traffic records Λ.

4   Example Configuration

In this section, we detail a configuration of TĀMD that identifies internal hosts infected by malware by employing the functions described in Section 3. This configuration identifies platform-dependent malware infections that report to common sites, e.g., IRC channels for receiving commands, public servers for downloading binaries, denial-of-service victims to attack, or database servers for uploading stolen information. This configuration is based on several observations about such malware:

O1. For even moderately aggressive malware, it is rarely the case that only a single victim exists in a large enterprise network, and so we hypothesize that stealthy malware is likely to generate traffic that appears within the same, coarse window of time (e.g., within the same hour) from multiple infected hosts. Moreover, we would expect that the controller site is located in a subnet that would not be a common one with which benign hosts interact, as major services with substantial client populations are typically better managed. As such, malware interacting with the controller site should generate a noticeable increase in the number of interactions with the controller's subnet in that window of time.

O2. We expect that the multiple instances of the malware communication to the controller site would be syntactically similar to each other, since the malware instances are communicating using the same protocol, and likely to be receiving or responding to similar commands.

O3. In the case of platform-dependent malware, the malware communications to the controller site will involve internal hosts all having the same host platform.

Using these observations, we have assembled the aggregation functions described in Section 3 into an algorithm FindSuspiciousAggregates to identify such malware infections, shown in Figure 1. The input to this function is a set Λ of traffic records observed in a fixed time interval (e.g., one hour) at the border of the network, and a set Λ_{past} of records previously observed at the border of the network. FindSuspiciousAggregates assembles and returns (in line 108) a set SuspiciousAggregates comprised of suspicious aggregates, where each aggregate is a set of internal hosts (IP addresses) that is suspected of being infected by malware.

FindSuspiciousAggregates first exploits observation O1, using ByDest$^{\tau}$ from Section 3.1 to find suspicious external subnets SuspiciousSubnets responsible for noticeably greater communication with the monitored network than in the past, and to find aggregates $\{\text{Agg}_i\}_{1 \leq i \leq \text{numAggs}}$, each of which includes internal hosts that interacted with one or more of these subnets. In line with observation O2, each aggregate is tested in line 105 to determine if distinct hosts in the aggregate communicate with suspicious subnets using similar payload. Finally, as motivated by observation O3, for each aggregate that has survived these tests, the platforms of the hosts in the aggregate are

FindSuspiciousAggregates(Λ, Λ_{past})

100: SuspiciousAggregates $\leftarrow \emptyset$
101: (SuspiciousSubnets, numAggs, $\{\text{Agg}_i\}_{1 \leq i \leq \text{numAggs}}$) $\leftarrow$ ByDest$^\tau$(Λ, Λ_{past})
                /∗ Form aggregates by external subnet ∗/
102: **for** $i = 1 \ldots$ numAggs **do**
103: $\Lambda_i \leftarrow \{\lambda \in \Lambda : \lambda.\text{internal} \in \text{Agg}_i\}$ /∗ Traffic from hosts in Agg$_i$ ∗/
104: $\Lambda_i^{\text{susp}} \leftarrow \{\lambda \in \Lambda_i : \lambda.\text{external} \in \text{SuspiciousSubnets}\}$
          /∗ Traffic from hosts in Agg$_i$ to suspicious subnets ∗/
105:   **if** ByPayload$^{\delta_{\text{Ed}}}$(Λ_i^{susp}) > 0.3 **then**
         /∗ Keep if traffic to same external subnet is self-similar ∗/
106:   **if** ByPlatform(Λ_i^{susp}) > 0.9 **then**
         /∗ Keep if most of aggregate consists of one platform ∗/
107:    SuspiciousAggregates $\leftarrow$ SuspiciousAggregates $\cup \{\text{Agg}_i\}$
108: **return** SuspiciousAggregates

Fig. 1. The function used to find suspicious aggregates in the example construction given in Section 4. ByDest$^\tau$ (line 101), ByPayload$^{\delta_{\text{Ed}}}$ (line 105), and ByPlatform (line 106) are defined in Sections 3.1, 3.2 and 3.3, respectively.

inferred using ByPlatform and, if the aggregate is adequately homogenous (line 106), then it is added to SuspiciousAggregates (line 107).

There are numerous constants in Figure 1 that we have chosen on the basis of our evaluation that we will present in Section 5. These constants include $\tau = 90\%$ or 95% for ByDest$^\tau$, 0.3 in line 105 and 0.9 in line 106. In addition, as we will describe in Section 5, the data on which we perform our evaluation includes 64 bytes of payload per record λ, for which we found $\delta_{\text{Ed}} = 15$ to be an effective value. However, we emphasize that all of these constants can be adjusted in order to make this configuration of TĀMD more conservative or liberal in its selection of suspicious aggregates, and we plan to continue evaluation of the alternatives in ongoing work. That said, in Section 5, we show that with traffic generated from real spyware and bot instances, and traces from real bots captured in a honeynet, this configuration of TĀMD was able to reliably extract malware traffic from all traffic passing the edge of a university network, while the number of other aggregates reported is very low. This reliability is achieved even in tests where the number of simulated infected hosts comprise only about 0.0097% of the total number of internal hosts in the network, calculated as the maximum number of internal IP addresses observed communicating in any one hour period during our data collection (see Section 5), which was over 33,000.

5   Evaluation

We present an evaluation of the particular configuration of TĀMD described in Section 4, using traffic from real spyware and bot instances, which are overlaid onto flow records recorded at the edge of a campus network. The performance of TĀMD as observed in this evaluation is described in Appendix C.

5.1 Data Collection

Our network traffic traces were obtained from the edge routers on the Carnegie Mellon University campus network, which consists of two /16 subnets. The packets are organized into bi-directional flow records by Argus (Audit Record Generation and Utilization System, http://www.qosient.com/argus), which is a real time flow monitor based on the RTFM flow model [5, 16]. Argus inspects each packet and groups together those with the same attribute values into one bi-directional record. In particular, TCP and UDP flows are identified by the 5-tuple (source IP address, destination IP address, source port, destination port, protocol)[2], and packets in both directions are recorded as a summary of the communication, namely, an Argus flow record.

The fields extracted from Argus records are listed in Table 1. The rate of the traffic from the edge of our campus network is about 5000 flow records per second. The traces were collected for

Table 1. Extracted Flow Fields

IP Header	Transport Header	Flow Attribute
Source IP	Source Port	Byte Count
Destination IP	Destination Port	Packet Count
Protocol	TCP Sequence Number	Payload (64 bytes)
TTL	TCP Window Size	

three weeks in November and December 2007. In our evaluation, we focused on TCP and UDP traffic.

We also obtained network traffic traces for several malware. The malware traces used for testing are grouped into two sets, Class-I and Class-II, as described below.

Class-I Traces. We obtained four instances of malware from the internet: Bagle, IRCbot, Mybot and SDbot, and collected their traffic by infecting virtual machines hosts with each malware. The virtual hosts were all running the Windows XP Professional operating system with the same VMWare image file. Each run of traffic collection is one hour long, and includes the communications from eight instances of Bagle, three instances of IRCbot, five instances of Mybot, or five instances of SDbot. These numbers of instances were chosen to represent a very small fraction of the total campus hosts, specifically at most 0.0097% based upon the number of campus hosts observed sending traffic in the busiest hour, which has over 33,000 distinct IP addresses. The characteristics of these malware are described in Appendix A.

For testing, we overlaid flows from these malware instances onto one hour of our recorded campus network traffic, and assigned the malware traffic to originate from randomly selected internal hosts observed to be active during that hour. This makes our testing scenario much more realistic, since the internal hosts to be identified still exhibit their normal connection patterns, in addition to subtle malware activities.

Class-II Traces. We also obtained network traces of botnets gathered from honeynets, including an IRC-based Spybot, a HTTP-based botnet (similar to the Bobax worm[3]),

---

[2] Since Argus records are bi-directional, the source and destination IP addresses are swappable in the logic that matches packets to flows. However, the source IP address in the record is set to the IP address of the host that initiated the connection.

[3] http://www.secureworks.com/research/threats/bobax/

and a large IRC botnet captured in the wild. The Spybot trace contains communications from four bots for the duration of 32 minutes; the HTTP-bot trace contains communications from four bots over the course of three hours; and the large botnet trace contains traffic from more than three hundred bots over seven minutes.

These botnet traces were then overlaid onto each hour of our recorded campus traffic, in the same way as the Class-I traces. For the trace that spans multiple contiguous hours, i.e., the HTTP botnet trace, we overlaid it onto the same number of contiguous hours in the campus network traffic, performed analysis on each of the hours "covered" by the malware trace, and reported the hour that TĀMD detected the malware aggregate. This time window was then shifted by one hour, and the experiment repeated until we reached the end date of our campus traffic collection.

In our initial tests, we found that these malware-infected hosts were obscured by certain unknown hosts with highly unusual behavior, which turned out to be PlanetLab (http://www.planet-lab.org) and Tor (http://tor.eff.org) nodes. The experience of identifying these hosts and their exclusion from our dataset for the experiments reported in Section 5.2 is described in Appendix B. In practice, a system administrator can remove such hosts known for unusual behavior prior to performing analysis using TĀMD.

5.2   Detecting Malware

As described in Section 5.1, TĀMD was given all TCP and UDP traffic collected at the edge of our university network in hourly batches, overlaid with malware traffic assigned to randomly selected internal hosts. The same analysis steps were repeated for each hour over three weeks in November and December 2007.

The granularity of external destinations was set to be /24 subnets. While the communication records from the current hour were given to FindSuspiciousAggregates as Λ, the set Λ_{past} was selected from communication records in the past (specifically, from the beginning of our traffic collection dating to the first week of September 2007) that represented the general trend and the periodicity in the traffic. Specifically, Λ_{past} consisted of traffic from, in reference to the time frame for Λ, (i) the same hour from the same days of the week, (ii) the same hour from the same days of the month, (iii) the same hour from the previous two days, and (iv) the previous two hours. For example, if Λ consists of traffic from 2 to 3 PM on Wednesday, November 28th, then Λ_{past} will include traffic from 2 to 3 PM every Wednesday before that, from 2 to 3 PM in the previous two days (November 27th and 26th), and from 12 to 2 PM on November 28th.

In all experiments, TĀMD was able to identify all the infected hosts (with the exception of the Class-II large IRC trace, as described later) while the number of additional aggregates reported was only about 1.23 per hour on average. For the Class-II HTTP-botnet trace that spans multiple hours, TĀMD always detected the infected hosts in the very first hour. For the case of the Class-II large IRC botnet trace, which contains 340 infected bots, TĀMD was able to identify 87.5% of the bots on average, and these bots were all grouped in a single aggregate. We suspect that the reason not every bot in the botnet was detected is due to the randomness in our choice of selected internal hosts to which the malware traffic was assigned, such that a selected internal host that was

Malware traces	ByDest$^{\tau}$ (line 101)	ByPayload$^{\delta Ed}$ (line 105)	ByPlatform (line 106)
Class-I			
Bagle	47.46 ($\pm$ 23.13)	4.19 ($\pm$ 2.34)	2.55 ($\pm$ 1.33)
IRCbot	35.10 ($\pm$ 20.51)	2.74 ($\pm$ 1.41)	1.98 ($\pm$ 0.98)
Mybot	45.60 ($\pm$ 25.10)	3.19 ($\pm$ 1.76)	2.13 ($\pm$ 1.09)
SDbot	52.15 ($\pm$ 43.87)	3.55 ($\pm$ 1.88)	2.34 ($\pm$ 1.16)
Class-II			
Spybot	39.18 ($\pm$ 22.31)	2.95 ($\pm$ 1.44)	2.04 ($\pm$ 0.92)
HTTP bot	53.97 ($\pm$ 26.54)	3.31 ($\pm$ 1.91)	2.22 ($\pm$ 1.21)
Large IRC bot	44.54 ($\pm$ 16.16)	4.39 ($\pm$ 2.75)	2.39 ($\pm$ 1.32)

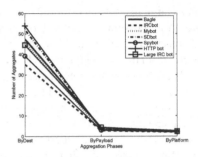

Fig. 2. Mean number of aggregates ($\pm$ std. dev.) remaining after each function in Figure 1

also contacting other suspicious subnets (not relevant to the botnet) is likely to bias the dimension reduction and clustering algorithms.

Figure 2 shows for each malware experiment (the rows), the number of aggregates remaining after applying each aggregation function (the columns), averaged over all test hours. The number of aggregates is reduced after each aggregation function, as they become more refined to satisfy multiple characteristics. The single aggregate consisting solely of infected hosts was always identified, in every malware experiment. As shown in the figure, even for homogeneous networks where the majority of internal hosts are of the same platform, applying ByDest$^{\tau}$ and ByPayload$^{\delta Ed}$ would still yield good results.

5.3 Unknown Aggregates

As indicated in Figure 2, our methodology detected a small number of unknown aggregates (about 1.23 per hour, on average) in addition to the one aggregate of infected hosts that we overlaid on the trace. We found that some of these same unknown aggregates regularly appeared for that hour of input data, across different malware experiments. Further investigation based on the 64 bytes of flow payload available to us, port numbers, and protocol field (for privacy reasons, the IP addresses were anonymized), showed that these aggregates included NetBIOS messages on port 137, DNS name server queries, SMTP connection timeout messages, and advertising-related HTTP requests; several of these suggest that additional investigation may be warranted. Others included connections to online game servers and large flows over high-order ports, which we suspect to be peer-to-peer (P2P) transfers. All of these aggregates consisted of internal hosts contacting rare sites, and often consisted of less than five hosts sharing one or two common destination subnets.

In theory, a group of internal hosts visiting a new popular website (i.e., the "slashdot" effect) could also form an aggregate. However, it is unlikely that all of the hosts would come from the same platform, and in our experiments, we believe we saw very few such aggregates. We thus believe that TĀMD is a useful data reduction tool for malware identification.

6   Discussion and Ongoing Work

Approaches by which malware writers might attempt to avoid detection by our techniques include encrypting their malware traffic, so that our payload comparisons will be ineffective. To accommodate encryption, our techniques can be generalized to define encrypted content (which itself is generally easy to detect) as "similar"; we are exploring the impact of this adaptation in ongoing work. Malware writers could go further and have their malware communicate steganographically, though at the cost of greater sophistication and lower bandwidth. Detecting steganographic communication is itself an active area of research (e.g., [31]) from which TĀMD could benefit.

A second way that malware writers could try to avoid detection by TĀMD is with alternative botnet architectures. Although the vast majority of spyware and botnets found today use a centralized IRC command-and-control server, other botnet architectures have been reported, such as P2P botnets (Phatbot[4], Trojan.Peacomm bot [12], Sinit P2P trojan[5]) or HTTP-based botnets (Clickbot.A [9]). Still others have been proposed, such as hybrid P2P and centralized botnets [41, 43].

Even among these alternative architectures, a large number exhibit characteristics that we believe should be detectable via FindSuspiciousAggregates in Section 4. For example, Trojan.Peacomm bots, while using a P2P network to transfer addresses of compromised web servers among them, still connect to these web servers to download malicious executables for sending spam or performing DoS attacks. This activity of collectively contacting web servers matches the behavior that our techniques successfully detected in our evaluations. The same detection method can also be applied to HTTP-based bots, such as Clickbot.A [9], which commit click frauds by having bots connect to a compromised web server for a list of websites and search keywords, or for a URL to download updated bot versions. Vogt et al. [41] suggested a "super-botnet", where the botnet is composed of individual smaller centralized botnets, and the controllers from each smaller botnet peer together in a P2P network. Since the individual smaller botnets still use a centralized architecture, this should be still be detectable via our techniques. Wang et al. [43] proposed a hybrid P2P botnet where each bot maintains its own peer list and polls other bots periodically for new commands. However, in order to monitor the IP address and resources of each individual bot, the botnet supports a command by which the botmaster can solicit all bots to report to a specific compromised server. Again, this behavior should be detectable by FindSuspiciousAggregates.

That said, some P2P bots avoid contacting a common server for the transfer of executables or other tasks, such as Phatbot and the Sinit trojan. While Phatbots find peers by registering themselves as Gnutella clients, the Sinit trojan sends out random probes for peer discovery. In both cases, forming aggregates based on payload similarity should remain effective, provided that similarity is generalized as described above to accommodate encrypted traffic (which Phatbot utilizes). Similarly, platform-based aggregation should also be effective, as both are platform-dependent. We are evaluating these directions in ongoing work, as well as alternative aggregation methods to help identify these types of malware.

---

[4] See http://www.secureworks.com/research/threats/phatbot
[5] See http://www.secureworks.com/research/threats/sinit

7 Conclusion

In this paper, we presented TĀMD, a system that identifies hosts within a network that are possibly infected by stealthy malware by finding those that share common and unusual network communications. TĀMD employs three aggregation functions to group hosts based on the following characteristics. First, the destination aggregation function, ByDest$^\tau$, forms aggregates of internal hosts that contact the same combination of busier-than-usual external destinations. A binary vector is formed for each internal host, with each dimension representing one of the selected external destinations. The vectors are processed by PCA for dimension reduction, and clustered by K-means clustering. New clusters are selected as those that do not conform to preceding communication patterns. Second, the payload aggregation function, ByPayload$^{\delta_{Ed}}$, identifies communications with similar payloads in terms of a type of edit distance. This is done by first embedding the payload strings into vectors in L1 space, and then finding close vectors by an approximate nearest-neighbor algorithm. Third, the platform aggregation function, ByPlatform, forms aggregates that involve hosts running on common platforms, as inferred using TTL values or platform-specific sites to which they connect.

We detailed a configuration of TĀMD that employs these functions in combination to identify platform-dependent malware infections that report to common sites. A common site might be an IRC channel for receiving commands, a public webserver for downloading binaries, a denial-of-service victim they are instructed to attack, or a database server for uploading stolen information, as is typical of most bots and spyware. Our experiments showed that, with traffic generated from real spyware and bot instances, this configuration of TĀMD reliably extracted malware traffic from all traffic passing the edge of a university network, while the number of other aggregates reported is very low. This is achieved even in tests where the number of simulated infected hosts comprised only about 0.0097% of over 33,000 internal hosts in the network.

Acknowledgements

We are grateful to Moheeb Rajab and other members of the Johns Hopkins Honeynet Project (http://hinrg.cs.jhu.edu/jhuhoneynet/) for providing malware binaries that we used in our evaluations, and to Wenke Lee, Guofei Gu, David Dagon, and Yan Chen for providing botnet traces. We are also grateful to Chas DiFatta, Mark Poepping and other members of the EDDY Initiative (http://www.cmu.edu/eddy/) for facilitating access to the network traffic records from Carnegie Mellon University used in this research. This research was supported in part by NSF awards 0326472 and 0433540.

References

[1] Aiello, W., Kalmanek, C., McDaniel, P., Sen, S., Spatscheck, O., Van der Merwe, J.: Analysis of communities of interest in data networks. In: Proceedings of Passive and Active Measurement Workshop (2005)

[2] Bächer, P., Holz, T., Kötter, M., Wicherski, G.: Know your enemy: Tracking botnets. Technical report, The Honeynet Project and Research Alliance (2005)

[3] Barford, P., Kline, J., Plonka, D., Ron, A.: A signal analysis of network traffic anomalies. In: Proceedings of ACM SIGCOMM Internet Measurement Workshop (2002)

[4] Binkley, J.R., Singh, S.: An algorithm for anomaly-based botnet detection. In: Proceedings of the Workshop on Steps to Reducing Unwanted Traffic on the Internet (2006)

[5] Brownlee, N., Mills, C., Ruth, G.: Traffic flow measurement: Architecture. RFC 2722 (1999)

[6] Cheng, D., Kannan, R., Vempala, S., Wang, G.: A divide-and-merge methodology for clustering. ACM Transactions on Database Systems 31(4) (2006)

[7] Cooke, E., Jahanian, F., McPherson, D.: The zombie roundup: Understanding, detecting, and disrupting botnets. In: Proceedings of the Workshop on Steps to Reducing Unwanted Traffic on the Internet (2005)

[8] Cormode, G., Muthukrishnan, S.M.: The string edit distance matching problem with moves. In: Proceedings of the ACM-SIAM Symposium on Discrete Algorithms (2002)

[9] Daswani, N., Stoppelman, M.: The Google Click Quality, and Security Teams. The anatomy of clickbot.A. In: Proceedings of the 1st Workshop on Hot Topics in Understanding Botnets (2007)

[10] Datar, M., Immorlica, N., Indyk, P., Mirrokni, V.S.: Locality-sensitive hashing scheme based on p-stable distributions. In: Proceedings of the Symposium on Computational Geometry (2004)

[11] Goebel, J., Holz, T.: Rishi: Identify bot contaminated hosts by IRC nickname evaluation. In: Proceedings of the 1st Workshop on Hot Topics in Understanding Botnets (2007)

[12] Grizzard, J.B., Sharma, V., Nunnery, C., Kang, B.B., Dagon, D.: Peer-to-peer botnets: Overview and case study. In: Proceedings of the 1st Workshop on Hot Topics in Understanding Botnets (2007)

[13] Gu, G., Perdisci, R., Zhang, J., Lee, W.: Botminer: Clustering analysis of network traffic for protocol- and structure-independent botnet detection. In: Proceedings of the USENIX Security Symposium (August 2008)

[14] Gu, G., Porras, P., Yegneswaran, V., Fong, M., Lee, W.: BotHunter: Detecting Malware Infection Through IDS-Driven Dialog Correlation. In: Proceedings of the USENIX Security Symposium (2007)

[15] Gu, G., Zhang, J., Lee, W.: Botsniffer: Detecting botnet command and control channels in network traffic. In: Proceedings of the 2008 ISOC Network and Distributed System Security Symposium (February 2008)

[16] Handelman, S., Stibler, S., Brownlee, N., Ruth, G.: New attributes for traffic flow measurement. RFC 2724 (1999)

[17] Jolliffe, I.T.: Principal Component Analysis. Springer, Heidelberg (1986)

[18] Karamcheti, V., Geiger, D., Kedem, Z., Muthukrishnan, S.M.: Detecting malicious network traffic using inverse distributions of packet contents. In: Proceedings of the ACM SIGCOMM Workshop on Mining Network Data (2005)

[19] Karasaridis, A., Rexroad, B., Hoeflin, D.: Wide-scale botnet detection and characterization. In: Proceedings of the 1st Workshop on Hot Topics in Understanding Botnets (2007)

[20] Kaufman, L., Rousseeuw, P.J.: Finding Groups in Data. An Introduction to Cluster Analysis. Wiley, Chichester (1990)

[21] Kim, H., Karp, B.: Autograph: Toward automated, distributed worm signature detection. In: Proceedings of the USENIX Security Symposium (2004)

[22] Kim, S.S., Reddy, A.L.N., Vannucci, M.: Detecting traffic anomalies using discrete wavelet transform. In: Proceedings of the International Conference on Information Networking (2004)

[23] Kohler, E., Li, J., Paxson, V., Shenker, S.: Observed structure of addresses in IP traffic. IEEE/ACM Transactions on Networking 14(6) (2006)

[24] Kreibich, C., Crowcroft, J.: Honeycomb - creating intrusion detection signatures using honeypots. In: Proceedings of the ACM SIGCOMM Workshop on Hop Topics in Networks (2003)

[25] Lakhina, A., Papagiannaki, K., Crovella, M.: Structural analysis of network traffic flows. In: Proceedings of ACM SIGMETRICS/Performance (2004)

[26] Livadas, C., Walsh, B., Lapsley, D., Strayer, T.: Using machine learning techniques to identify botnet traffic. In: Proceedings of the IEEE LCN Workshop on Network Security (2006)

[27] Moore, D., Voelker, G.M., Savage, S.: Inferring internet denial-of-service activity. In: Proceedings of the USENIX Security Symposium (2001)

[28] Newsome, J., Karp, B., Song, D.: Polygraph: Automatic signature generation for polymorphic worms. In: IEEE Security and Privacy Symposium (2005)

[29] Parekh, J.J., Wang, K., Stolfo, S.J.: Privacy-preserving payload-based correlation for accurate malicious traffic detection. In: Proceedings of the ACM SIGCOMM Workshop on Large Scale Attack Defense (2006)

[30] Perdisci, R., Gu, G., Lee, W.: Using an ensemble of one-class SVM classifiers to harden payload-based anomaly detection systems. In: Proceedings of the International Conference on Data Mining (2006)

[31] Provos, N., Honeyman, P.: Detecting steganographic content on the Internet. In: Proceedings of the 2002 ISOC Network and Distributed System Security Symposium (NDSS) (February 2002)

[32] Racine, S.: Analysis of Internet Relay Chat Usage by DDoS Zombies. Master's thesis, Swiss Federal Institute of Technology Zurich (2004)

[33] Rajab, M.A., Zarfoss, J., Monrose, F., Terzis, A.: A multifaceted approach to understanding the botnet phenomenon. In: ACM SIGCOMM/USENIX Internet Measurement Conference (2006)

[34] Ramachandra, A., Feamster, N., Vempala, S.: Filtering spam with behavioral blacklisting. In: Proceedings of the ACM conference on Computer and Communications Security (2007)

[35] Ramachandran, A., Feamster, N.: Understanding the network-level behavior of spammers. In: Proceedings of ACM SIGCOMM (2006)

[36] Ramachandran, A., Feamster, N., Dagon, D.: Revealing botnet membership using DNSBL counter-intelligence. In: Proceedings of the Workshop on Steps to Reducing Unwanted Traffic on the Internet (2006)

[37] Reiter, M., Yen, T.: Traffic aggregation for malware detection. Technical Report CMU-CyLab-07-017, Carnegie Mellon University (2007)

[38] Singh, S., Estan, C., Varghese, G., Savage, S.: Automated worm fingerprinting. In: Proceedings of the Symposium on Operating Systems Design and Implementation (2004)

[39] Taylor, C., Alves-Foss, J.: NATE - network analysis of anomalous traffic events, a low-cost approach. In: Proceedings of the New Security Paradigms Workshop (2001)

[40] Terrell, J., Zhang, L., Zhu, Z., Jeffay, K., Shen, H., Nobel, A., Donelson Smith, F.: Multivariate SVD analyses for network anomaly detection. In: Poster Proceedings of ACM SIGCOMM (2005)

[41] Vogt, R., Aycock, J., Jacobson Jr., M.J.: Army of botnets. In: Proceedings of the Network and Distributed System Security Symposium (2007)

[42] Wang, K., Parekh, J.J., Stolfo, S.J.: Anagram: A content anomaly detector resistant to mimicry attack. In: Proceedings of the 9th International Symposium on Recent Advances in Intrusion Detection (2006)

[43] Wang, P., Sparks, S., Zou, C.C.: An advanced hybrid peer-to-peer botnet. In: Proceedings of the 1st Workshop on Hot Topics in Understanding Botnets (2007)

A   Class-I Malware Instances

For our testing described in Section 5, traffic from four malware instances was collected using virtual machine hosts infected with each malware. The virtual hosts were all running the Windows XP Professional operating system with the same VMWare image file. Each run of traffic collection is one hour long.

Bagle[6] is spyware that, on execution, runs as a background process and attempts to download other malicious executables from various sites, while generating pop-up windows and hijacking the web browser to advertising websites. As with other types of spyware and adware, Bagle initiates connections to numerous destinations that are set up to exclusively host advertisements or other malicious content. We collected Bagle traffic by simultaneously running eight instances of Windows XP virtual machine hosts infected with Bagle.

IRCbot[7] is a backdoor trojan that connects to an IRC server and waits for commands from the attacker. In addition, after successfully connecting to the command-and-control center, the bot downloads an update executable from a designated webserver, and goes on to scan the local /16 subnet attacking other machines with the LSASS vulnerability on port 445[8] and the NetBIOS vulnerability on port 139[9]. We collected traffic from two instances of IRCbot running on two Windows XP virtual machine hosts.

Mybot[10] is spyware, a worm, and a bot that connects to an IRC server to wait for commands, and also records keystrokes and steals other personal information on the victim host. This malware is especially subtle in its communications. When it is only waiting for commands on the IRC server, the bot initiates one connection every 90 seconds, in the form of IRC PING/PONG messages. In the hour of our traffic collection, Mybot simply waited for commands on the IRC channel, and its only outbound connections were these PING/PONG messages. We collected traffic for five Mybot instances.

SDbot[11] is a trojan and a bot that opens a back door to connect to an IRC server. Similar to Mybot, when it is waiting for commands from the attacker, SDbot only makes outbound connections once every 90 seconds, in the form of IRC PING/PONG messages. We collected SDbot traffic from simultaneously running five instances of Windows XP virtual machine hosts infected with this malware.

B   Outlier Hosts

In the early stages of our analysis described in Section 5, we found that often TĀMD failed to detect the malware-laden hosts, but rather identified other internal hosts as

---

[6] http://www.trendmicro.com/vinfo/virusencyclo

[7] http://www.symantec.com/enterprise/security_response/
threatexplorer/threats.jsp

[8] http://www.microsoft.com/technet/security/Bulletin/MS04-044.
mspx

[9] http://msdn2.microsoft.com/en-us/library/ms913275.aspx

[10] http://www.sophos.com/security/analyses/w32rbotxf.html

[11] http://www.symantec.com/enterprise/security_response/
threatexplorer/threats.jsp

more symptomatic of malware. Upon further inspection, we identified the internal hosts that resulted in these false alarms: PlanetLab nodes (`http://www.planet-lab.org`) and a Tor node (`http://tor.eff.org`).

In the case of PlanetLab nodes, we noticed that during the destination aggregation function, the vectors after PCA analysis often had very low dimensionality, e.g., two, where two principal components were able to cover over 90% of the data variance. Clustering these vectors resulted in a few outliers forming their own individual clusters, unlike any of the other vectors in Λ (i.e., the "new vectors"), or even those from Λ_{past} (the "old vectors"). This is shown in Figure 3. The two axes correspond to the top two principal components on which the original data is projected. The

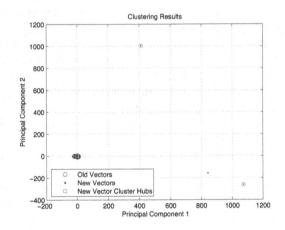

Fig. 3. Clustering results after dimension reduction by PCA. The three outliers were found to be PlanetLab nodes.

outliers were found to be PlanetLab nodes, which, being a development and testing platform, exhibit behavior deviating from other hosts. Their existence was also the reason why PCA analysis was able to reduce the vector dimensionality down to only two, since PlanetLab nodes' behavior is so different from other hosts that only two principal components were needed to capture most of the data variance.

In another example from experiments involving the Bagle trojan spyware, we noticed that even though TĀMD was able to form a final aggregate containing all spyware traffic and spyware traffic only, at times it also combined another unknown host into the spyware-hosts aggregate, both in the ByDest and the ByPayload functions. Similar investigations revealed that this additional node is a Tor router inside the campus network. Tor offers online anonymity by routing packets over random routes between Tor servers so that the source and destination of the packet is obfuscated. Because the traffic comes from different anonymous hosts, it is possible that, even though the Tor router itself is not infected, another host routing traffic through the Tor node may be a spyware victim.

For this work, we removed PlanetLab and Tor nodes from our analysis.

C   Performance

The top half of Table 2 shows the run times in seconds for each aggregation function and for each malware instance, averaged over the week's worth of traffic (in one-hour intervals) we used to performed our experiments. In our present implementation of TĀMD, ByDest$^{\tau}$ is implemented in Matlab, and ByPayload$^{\delta_{Ed}}$ and ByPlatform are

Table 2. Mean run times of each phase in seconds of algorithm in Figure 1 and means of measures impacting performance ($\pm$ std. dev.)

Malware traces	ByDest$^\tau$ (line 101)	ByPayload$^{\delta Ed}$ and ByPlatform (lines 105, 106)	Total time	Size of SuspiciousSubnets	Internal hosts contacting SuspiciousSubnets
Class-I					
Bagle	79.48 ($\pm$ 264.54)	14.08 ($\pm$ 18.07)	93.48 ($\pm$ 271.51)	701.87 ($\pm$ 596.78)	754.73 ($\pm$ 812.75)
IRCBot	94.67 ($\pm$ 350.13)	20.19 ($\pm$ 16.78)	114.86 ($\pm$ 356.72)	927.23 ($\pm$ 561.33)	742.13 ($\pm$ 836.55)
Mybot	63.82 ($\pm$ 177.34)	10.96 ($\pm$ 15.28)	70.93 ($\pm$ 183.43)	686.03 ($\pm$ 565.11)	728.45 ($\pm$ 708.65)
SDbot	102.34 ($\pm$ 355.25)	10.21 ($\pm$ 19.51)	112.55 ($\pm$ 359.23)	749.01 ($\pm$ 577.49)	952.96 ($\pm$ 1191.66)
Class-II					
Spybot	86.30 ($\pm$ 276.81)	63.42 ($\pm$ 38.56)	151.15 ($\pm$ 286.99)	850.14 ($\pm$ 609.19)	777.71 ($\pm$ 848.43)
HTTP bot	83.12 ($\pm$ 278.76)	15.75 ($\pm$ 20.62)	99.31 ($\pm$ 287.11)	697.36 ($\pm$ 609.15)	776.76 ($\pm$ 848.43)
Large IRC Bot	110.64 ($\pm$ 253.78)	46.00 ($\pm$ 34.78)	156.64 ($\pm$ 260.42)	760.83 ($\pm$ 548.48)	1104.42 ($\pm$ 799.58)

implemented in C. For the numbers reported in Table 2, ByDest$^\tau$ was run on a PC with a Pentium IV 3.2 GHz processor and 3 GB of RAM, and ByPayload$^{\delta Ed}$ and ByPlatform were run on a Dell PowerEdge server with dual core 3 GHz processors and 4 GB of RAM.

The running times of the aggregation functions depend on several factors, including the number of external destinations identified as suspicious (i.e., SuspiciousSubnets as computed by ByDest$^\tau$) and the number of flows to those suspicious destinations; averages for these numbers are also listed in Table 2. The amount of traffic in Λ_{past} is especially critical to the performance of ByDest$^\tau(\Lambda, \Lambda_{\text{past}})$, since it accesses significant amounts of historical data (i.e., Λ_{past}) to define the "normal" behavior for this network. While the implementation of TĀMD is not yet optimized, retrieving historical data from the database contributed to the majority of the slowdown. This problem can be alleviated in the future by performing these calculations in advance and storing them statically, only updating incrementally as more data is collected.

The Contact Surface:
A Technique for Exploring Internet Scale
Emergent Behaviors

Carrie Gates[1] and John McHugh[2]

[1] CA Labs
Islandia, NY, USA
carrie.gates@ca.com
[2] Dalhousie University
Halifax, NS, Canada
mchugh@cs.dal.ca

Abstract. Large scale internet data analysis often concentrates on statistical measures for volume properties or is focused on the epidemiology of specific malcodes. We have developed a high level abstraction that we call the contact surface that allows us to visualize internet scale connection behaviours across the border of a monitored network. The contact surface is a time series of contact lines, each line plotting the number of outside sources that contact a specific number of inside hosts in a given time interval (typically an hour). In general, the lines follow a power law in the mid range with distinct outliers at the one destination per source and the hundreds to thousands of destinations per source ends. During some periods, however, the lines are perturbed with what appears to be a persistent bump or waterfall. We have studied two such episodes, one that persisted from at least January 2003 until August 2003 and another that appeared on February 11, 2004 and lasted until May 31, 2004. The exact cause of the former is unknown, however the later appears to have been caused by the Welchia.B worm. Similar activities are currently being reported by other observers. We hypothesize that the cause of the perturbation is low frequency periodic scanning by a small population of hosts scanning at the same rate. We have created simulations to explore the range of activities that might be observable and find reasonable agreement with the observed phenomena.

1 Introduction

In 2003 and 2004, we had access to NetFlow data from the border of a composite network (multiple, disjoint network blocks) that covered address space that was equivalent to multiple /8s in aggregate. The network is sparsely populated but contains several million active hosts. As part of the preliminary efforts to investigate schemes for detecting coordinated distributed scans, we became interested in "typical" host to host connection behavior. Many of the papers that examine the characteristics of network traffic focus on packet properties such

D. Zamboni (Ed.): DIMVA 2008, LNCS 5137, pp. 228–246, 2008.

as counts of hosts, protocols, port usage, payload size and characterization, etc. Other papers, inspired by work in social networks attempt to map communications patterns on the physical structure of the internet, overlooking the fact that from the standpoint of an IP layer user, the internet is flat and fully connected.

Our fundamental question was essentially "Is there any regularity in cross border connection behaviour?" We were interested in determining how many of the outside hosts generating traffic into the network connect to (or attempt connections to) one service, two services, three services, etc. In the beginning, we were concerned only with the quantitative nature of the connecting populations and not with the identity of the participants. In this case, the initial investigation was restricted to TCP and a service was defined as the combination of a host IP address and a service port.

One of the tools that we used for studying this traffic was a visual representation that we call a *contact surface*. This is a three dimensional time series of lines in which each line shows the number of outside sources, Y vertical, that contact a specific number of internal addresses (or address-service combinations[1]) on the inside of the network, X horizontal. Time is into the page, Z. Because of the large dynamic range ov values represented, we present the contact surface as a log-log plot. The lines represent hourly flows and the shading separates days of the week.

The first period for which we developed a contact surface was a week of data from January, 2003. This data manifested a "bump" or standing wave (perturbation) in the surface as seen in Figure 1. This phenomenon was observed from January 2003, the earliest data available to us, until mid August 2003 when it abruptly disappeared. A similar phenomena appeared in mid February 2004 and persisted through the end of May, 2004. We have been told that similar phenomena are present in recent data, but we lack current access to the data source.

To a first approximation in the absence of a disturbance, the data for each hour can be represented as a straight line of the form $\log(y) = A + B\log(x)$ and we plot the x and y values on logarithmic scales. Figure 2a shows an example of the undisturbed contact surface while Figure 2b shows the regression line superimposed on several aggregated lines. These are discussed in more detail is Section 2.

This paper discusses our present views of this phenomenon. Section 2 discusses the initial observations and analysis with separate discussions of the 2003 and 2004 perturbations. We hypothesize that this phenomenon was related to the appearance of scanning worms that exhibited particular timing characteristics and consider the minimum amount of address space that must be monitored in order to observe this phenomenon in Section 3. Recent observations of similar perturbations resurrected our interest in the wave feature and in the visualizations.

---

[1] An address-service combination is a unique combination of an IP address and a service. For TCP and UDP a service is the combination of the protocol and the destination port. For other protocols, the notion may vary with the protocol, but these are sufficiently rare so we can assume a single service per protocol.

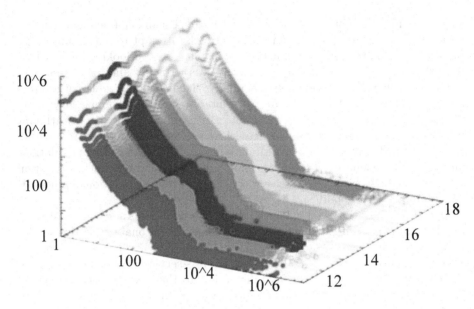

Fig. 1. Contact surface for January 11-18, 2003. Vertical axis is count of outside sources. Horizontal axis is count of inside services targeted by each outside source. Time is into the page.

Although we do not have access currently to either the historical or current data from this source, we have developed a simulation that provides a plausible explanation for the observed phenomena. Described in Section 4, this allows us to vary the background and perturbing parameters to examine the effects of altering the perturbing population, its probe rate, the size of the monitored network and the percentage of the probes that are observed. Related work is presented in Section 5 and our conclusions and future plans in Section 6.

2   Observed Phenomenon

NetFlow traffic from the border routers of a large ISP was collected using the SiLK [1] collection system. The network was heterogeneous and globally distributed, with routers at multiple locations within the United States and in several other countries. The majority of traffic is generated within the United States. The network consists of a number of discontinuous address blocks assigned to subcomponents of the ISP. Asymmetric routing policies were commonly used, so that traffic from host A to host B does not cross the border via the same router used for traffic from host B to host A. In any event, NetFlow is unidirectional and the two sides of a bidirectional connection are collected and stored separately. Both incoming and outgoing flow traffic was collected, but matching of forward and reverse flows is not usually done. Traffic that was sent to the null interface on the router as specified by an access control list (ACL) was also collected, however it was not analyzed for this paper. Null routed traffic consists primarily of traffic destined for TCP or UDP ports known to contain vulnerabilities.

The SiLK tools[2] [1] were used for the collection system. SiLK stores a subset of the information contained in the NetFlow records: source IP address, destination IP address, source port, destination port, protocol, number of packets, number of bytes, start time and duration of each flow. The records are compacted to use the minimum number of bits necessary to represent the recorded information and are organized into hourly files with each hour being partitioned in ways that make many searches more efficient. The archive data is unsorted and serial search is required to extract all records matching a given search criteria within a given hour.

Network traffic from January 2003 through early June 2004 was analyzed. We developed a variety of visualizations to help us understand this data. One of these is the *contact line*, which shows the number of external hosts that contacted a specific number of internal hosts during a specified time interval. Figure 1 demonstrates the *contact surface* that was generated by processing only incoming, routed[3], TCP flows over one week in September 2003. Each hour of the data results in an hourly contact line and the 168 hourly lines are plotted as a surface. The X and Y axes are plotted on log scales, while the Z axis, time, is linear.

The initial analysis was computationally intensive, involving creating a text file for each hour that contains only the source and destination IP addresses for the incoming routed TCP data collected at the border router (so that source IP addresses are always external to the monitored network while destination IP addresses are always internal to the monitored network, regardless of who initiated the session). The result was sorted by source IP and then destination IP, passing the sorted data through uniq to remove duplicates, using cut to remove the destination IPs leaving only the source, and using uniq -c to count the number of destinations associated with each source. Using cut again to remove the sources, sorting the counts and, again, using uniq -c, counting the number of occurrences of each value. Applied to data from one hour, this gives a single line, which we call a *contact line*. Plotting a time series of contact lines as a pseudo three dimensional plot gives a *contact surface*. These lines and surfaces form the underlying basis for our analyses.

This contact surface (see Figure 2a) has several interesting properties. The first is a persistent linear relationship between the $\log(x)$ and $\log(y)$ values. This is examined in more depth later. The second is a distinct diurnal pattern, particularly observable at $x = 2$. This demonstrates that traffic fluctuates in a predictable pattern with the time of day. (We note that this pattern is much more distinctive for $x = 2$ than for $x = 1$ because the graph was plotted on a log

---

[2] SiLK stands for System for Internet Level Knowledge, and is named in honour of its creator, the late Suresh L. Konda.

[3] Our data was divided into two partitions: packets that were routed and packets that were dropped due to access control restrictions (e.g., packets destined for particular ports were dropped).

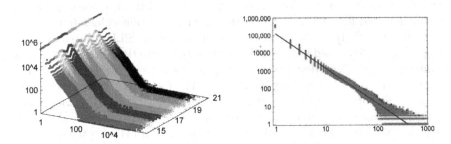

Fig. 2. The contact surface for a week in September of 2003 and its regression line. The y-axis is the number of outside hosts that contacted x inside hosts. The z-axis is time.

scale and so the fluctuations at $x = 1$ were not great enough to be observable at that resolution.) The third is a substantial jump in the number of external hosts that contact only one host per hour when compared to the numbers that contact two or more hosts per hour. While the number of hosts making 2 contacts per hour is about twice the number making 3 contacts per hour, the number making 1 contact per hour is ten times the number making 2 contacts per hour. The large amount of singleton traffic is also seen in traffic from other sources (e.g.Figure 11). The nature and sources of this traffic are the subject of a current investigation. The fourth is the spreading or flat area that occurs for a small number of sources that contact hundreds to hundreds of thousands of destinations per hour. Sources for this area are mostly high volume scanners.

The straight line in the log / log scale exhibits a power-law relationship. We fit a regression line to the week's data shown in Figure 2a. The line has the form $y = e^{11.763367} \times x^{-1.957496}$. in the x, y reference framework or approximately $\log(y) = 5.11 - 1.96 \log(x)$ in the log / log framework. Figure 2b, shows the regression line superimposed on the aggregated contact lines from the five weekdays from Figure 2a. The outliers at count 1 and the spreading at high counts are easily seen. We were somewhat surprised to find a power law relationship here, but note that they describe many other internet traffic characteristics[4]. Faloutsos *et al.* [2] have observed this relationship with regards to out-degree and hop-count.

2.1   The 2003 Disturbance

Our first experience with this traffic was from an earlier time period, the week of January 12 – 18, 2003. The contact surface for this week is shown in Figure 1. This traffic exhibits all of the general characteristics discussed above, except that the one contact outlier is less extreme. In addition, it has an additional property, a perturbation that appears as a "bump" or "waterfall." This perturbation was present across the entire week of data. We examined additional data to determine

---

[4] It has been observed that everything follows a power law if you graph it with a fat enough marker.

the duration of the perturbation. It was present in the earliest data we had for January 2003. The perturbation was continuously present is all the samples that we examined through early August 2003, however the shape of the wave changed slightly and the 1 contact outlier grew to upwards of a million hosts per hour in July. The perturbation disappeared on August 11, 2003. This is shown in Figure 3a, where one week of data is provided, providing context surrounding August 11.

Figure 3b focuses on the area of the perturbation, with only the Y axis shown on a log scale. The graph shows that the perturbation (two different bumps) is present for the four days previous to August 11, and that it has disappeared for the four days subsequent to August 11, 2003. The largest deviation (or bump) is the second one, which occurs at roughly 20 to 35 external source IP addresses each contacting approximately 150 to 350 internal destination IP addresses per hour.

This traffic was examined further by extracting the source IP addresses that contacted between 150 and 350 destination IP addresses per hour. We discovered that the bulk of the traffic in this region came form three /8 networks, two in the Asian registry, one in the Latin American registry. This distribution was present in each of the weekly samples that we analyzed with roughly constant proportions. The traffic was largely untargeted TCP SYN packets (SYN packets directed at hosts or services that did not exist) destined for port 80. We examined the target distribution for a week in July and found that the targets were not randomly distributed throughout the monitored network. 49% of the flows for this week went to one of the 60 /16s that were being monitored within a single /8 (the remaining 196 /16s are not part of the monitored network), with 14% going to a single /16.

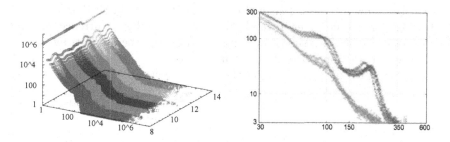

Fig. 3. Wave disappearance details, contact surface and selected lines The y-axis is the number of outside hosts that contacted x internal hosts. The z-axis represents August 9–14.

Given the consistency of this behavior over time, we speculated that the hump was caused by coordinated activity that would exhibit regular temporal behaviour. We attempted to analyze the distribution of the interarrival times for the flows, expecting to see a clustering around the interval (24 seconds for 150 hosts) that would account for the observations if only the monitored network was being targeted.

Our analysis did not support our original hypothesis. The largest cluster (with approximately 5,000,000 observations) shows less than 1 second between successive flows. The detailed analysis did reveal another interesting structure, a scalloping that occurred at regular intervals from about 15 to 70 seconds, after which the decrease becomes more linear (on a log-linear scale). This scalloping indicates a periodic behaviour from some of the sources that we were unable to explain at the time.

2.2   The 2004 Disturbance

In February of 2004, a perturbation in the contact surface was again observed. It started to reappear on February 11, 2004. Figure 4a shows the average traffic patterns for each day from Sunday, February 8, to Saturday, February 14, 2004. The bump first increases in amplitude and then slides to the right during its developmental phase. The number of sources detected peaks at around 50 at the beginning of the period and at about 75 by the end, but the effects of the process can be seen in terms of displacement of Monday / Tuesday baseline. The total number of disturbing hosts involved would be the integral between the baseline and the disturbed line and contains up to 1500 source IP addresses contacting up to 100 or so destinations each. The disturbed behavior continues until June 1, 2004, when it abruptly disappears (see 4b). An examination of source addresses during the disappearance, indicates that the activity ceased as the May 31 / June 1 dividing line progressed around the world.

It is also interesting to note that Figures 4a and 4b display another disturbance in the contact line, a small spike at 150 destinations per hour. We did not examine its sources during our investigation, but, as a result of our simulations, believe that we now know its cause. This will be discussed further in Section 4.1.

There are some differences in the behavior between this occurrence and the previous perturbation. As shown in Figure 5, this time the hump is more pronounced, and there is only one. Both perturbations were caused by traffic to port 80, primarily SYN-only flows. Two of the three /8 networks that had the most

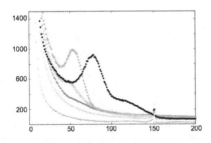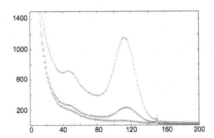

Fig. 4. 2004 perturbation appearance (February) and disappearance (June) details. The y-axis is the number of outside hosts that contacted x internal hosts.

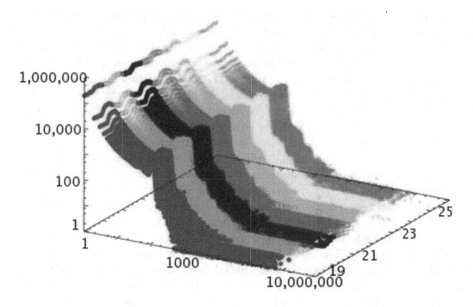

Fig. 5. Contact Surface for April 19 – 25, 2004. The y-axis is the number of external hosts that contacted x internals hosts. The z axis represents time.

sources in the first perturbation appear as the primary contributors to the second perturbation. The third /8 network also contains a large number of sources, however is not in the top three contributing /8 networks. The destination sets, however, were different, with 23% of the traffic targeting a different /8 network from the first perturbation.

3 Hypotheses

At the time this type of perturbation was first observed, the authors were interested in scanning activity. The initial contact surface graph displayed the connection behaviour of the entire monitored network. We hoped to determine whether scanning activity could be easily separated from legitimate network connections. We expected to find a large number of external hosts each of whom contacted a small number of internal hosts, and that this would represent legitimate traffic. We also expected that there would be a small number of external hosts who contacted a large number of internal hosts, and that this would represent scanning activity.

As we note in Section 2, what was actually observed was a power law relationship in the count of external hosts that contact a given number of internal addresses per hour in the central portion of the contact surface with outliers at the one destination per hour end of the line and a high degree of spreading at small source count end of the line. In retrospect, this linear relationship is not surprising. However, the perturbation was not expected and is particularly interesting because of its variable nature — consistently present or absence for months at a time, with sudden onset and disappearance.

The perturbation was present in the earliest data that we analyzed (January 2003). The perturbation persisted until August 11, 2003, when it abruptly disappeared. Blaster was released on August 11, 2003, and this might be related to the change in behavior that we observed. At first, we thought Blaster might have caused data loss at our sensors, suppressing the data that gave rise to the perturbation. The nature of NetFlow collection using routers is such that substantial data can be lost under heavy load as NetFlow is sacrificed to routing under router overload. In addition, NetFlow is transmitted to the collection point using UDP which also suffers under network load. Had the losses been significant, the entire surface would have been displaced downward and, we suspect, the perturbation reduced, but not eliminated. It is also possible that the sources of the perturbation were taken off line by Blaster. If that were the case, we would expect the systems to resume their previous activity when brought back on-line. This did not happen. The most likely explanation is that the remote systems were also infected with Blaster, which caused them to be taken off the network, patched, and cleaned to remove all sources of malicious activity. We suspect that this cleaning removed the cause of the unusual behavior observed at our monitoring points and that the patching prevented the source from reestablishing the behaviour. We suspect a scanning worm of some kind, possibly exploiting a vulnerability in port 80 that was patched at the same time as the DCOM vulnerability[5] used by Blaster, but have not identified a specific candidate.

The 2004 perturbation appeared on 11 February and disappeared as June 1 arrived. In December of 2004, Alfred Huger of Symantec noted that the dates of the appearance and disappearance of 2004 perturbation exactly matched the onset and demise of the worm Welchia.B[6]. Welchia.B contained a "suicide" timer that accounted for its demise along the dateline between May 31 and June 1. We were able to persuade a colleague to examine a corpse of Welchia.B and discovered that the main scanning loop of the worm contained a "sleep" system call with a delay constant that appeared to account for the disturbance when the scanning rate and the percentage of the total IPv4 address space being monitored were taken into account.

At this point, we had a plausible explanation for our observations, but lacked a confirmation. Not too long afterwards, we took other positions and subsequently lost access to the data source, so that further analysis was not possible. In 2007, we learned from former colleagues that the perturbation phenomena had reappeared. Development of code to visualize the contact surface is part of an unrelated analysis project, and we decided to revisit the original problem to refine our hypotheses and determine whether we could develop a simulation that provided a plausible explanation for the earlier observations. Based on the

---

[5] http://www.cve.mitre.org/cgi-bin/cvename.cgi?name=CAN-2003-0352

[6] W32.Welchia.B.worm was a relatively minor threat, in the general scheme of things. See http://www.symantec.com/security_response/writeup.jsp?docid=2004-021115-2540-99 for additional details.

earlier work, we developed several hypotheses that serve to focus the analyses and simulations.

Hypothesis 1. *The perturbation of the contact surface is caused by the presence of persistent scanning behavior (such as would be exhibited by a worm-infected host) with a fixed time delay between each scan probe. This delay is constant across the infected population.*

Note that this hypothesis implies a coordinated activity, however, the coordination may well be preprogrammed. All that is required is that each participant scan at the same rate.

Hypothesis 2. *The targets of the scanning are essentially random so that they are not easily observed without a network telescope with an aperture that encompasses substantial address space (several /8s or more).*

There is a tradeoff between the strength of the observed signal and the telescope aperture. For example, a single source emitting 1 randomly addressed probe per second would be seen about once every 4 minutes if the aperture is the equivalent of a /8 while it would be seen about once every 10 days if the aperture is a /24. If the scans are targeted so that the percentage of the total probes that are intercepted is disproportionate to the address space monitored, the signal strength increases.

We noted in Subsection 2.2 that we observed a small spike at 150 addresses that was consistent over time. While we did not investigate that spike further to determine the characteristics of the IP addresses generating the spike, we believe that it was due to scanning activity from several sources whose targets were largely within the monitored address space. This gives rise to an additional hypothesis.

Hypothesis 3. *Sharp spikes in the contact surface are due to a group of hosts that all scan addresses within the monitored address space at a fixed rate.*

Note that there are several limiting cases here. A small number of dropped packets are equivalent to a scan that largely, but not completely, targets the monitored address space. In addition, scans that target one or more complete subnets and are carried out so rapidly that all addresses are probed within the interval of the analysis (one hour in our case), will also generate spikes. If all probes from all sources scanning full subnets are observed, the spike becomes a point whose amplitude is the number of scanners and whose position on the target count axis reflects the size of the scanned subnets.

In the next section, we explore these hypotheses using a combination of simulation and analysis of data from a /22 network that we have monitored for several years.

4   Analysis and Simulation

The correlation between the onset and demise of Welchia.B and the 2004 perturbation provided evidence that the observations could be due to regular behaviours of a small population of infected machines. The discovery of a timed scanning loop in Welchia.B provided a mechanism for regular behaviour. We decided to see if we could reproduce the observed perturbations in a controlled manner. In order to do this, we needed to generate appropriate background behaviour and perturb it according to our hypotheses. Because we were not analyzing flow data *per se* in constructing the contact surface, we can avoid the task of simulating millions of individual hosts and concentrate on the essential characteristics of the background traffic as seen in the contact surface. This admits some simplifications.

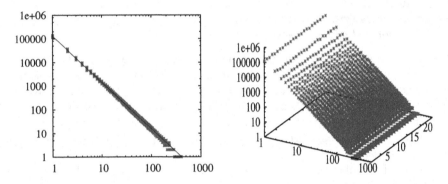

Fig. 6. Base traffic simulation, 2D (6a) and 3D (6b) views, 4% of IPv4 monitored (12 /8s), 40% noise spread, 24 hours with no perturbations. Vertical axis is number of outside addresses seen per hour. Horizontal axis is number of inside addresses targeted per outside address. Time is into the page in the 3D case.

In Section 2, we noted that there is always an outlier at the 1 host per hour portion of the fit. Far more outside hosts make single contacts than would be predicted by the model. A similar phenomenon occurs at the other end of the scale where a few (typically less than 5) hosts contact each of a very large number (thousands to hundreds of thousands) of destinations per hour. We believe that, in the undistributed (no perturbation) case, that the contact lines represent three independent phenomena. The excess of single destination hosts represents a very low frequency noise component. For about a year, we have been analyzing NetFlow data from a local /22 network that is about 10% occupied. In a typical hour, on the order of five thousand external sources each contact single inside addresses. Extending the filtering period to a day gives an average of about 62 thousand, with a little over a million external addresses contacting a single internal address in the course of a month. For the year, there are slightly over 10 million external addresses that each contact a single inside address and more than half (5.4 million) are active in only a single hour of the observation period. For reasons that we are still investigating, the diurnal variations in this low frequency component are much smaller than those in the main portion of the traffic, and the diurnal variations in the regular data are suppressed by the log scale presentation of their sum. Inspection of other end of the scale indicates that the spreading is due to a substantial number of bulk scanners who systematically probe the monitored network. We do not include either the low frequency or bulk scanning components in our base model.

The simulation is written in Snobol-4[7], enhanced with a Mersenne Twister random number generator[8]. The simulator produces scripts for the **gnuplot** graphics program. The simulation is constructed in two parts. The first uses the regression line, $e^{11.763367} \times x^{-1.957496}$, noted above and generates the expected number of sources contacting each destination count. Noise is added using a triangular distribution that spreads each point by a fixed percentage of its value (constant width on a log / log scale). It is important to note that the sole purpose of this portion of the simulation is to provide a **realistic appearing** base and **not** to emulate the processes that actually produce the base. The noise spread is included in the base so that the injected perturbations will not be completely obvious at low levels of disturbance. We have not included the diurnal and weekly variations found in the real data. Figures 6a and 6b show two and three dimensional views of the base traffic. These were created by setting the perturbation parameters to zero and assuming the fit parameter, 4% of the IPv4 address space associated with the regression line. It is interesting to compare Figure 2b with Figure 6a. In the central region, the figures are sufficiently similar so that we can claim that the base traffic generation is adequate. This base traffic is used for all of the subsequent simulations, normalized for different monitored percentages as necessary.

To simplify the simulation of the perturbation process, we assume that the perturbers scan at a constant rate, dictated by some delay loop. We also assume that they generate random IP addresses, over some portion of the Internet, up to and including all of the IPv4 address space, $0 \cdots (2^{32} - 1)$. If this is the case, our monitoring network will collect a fraction of the probes, based on the amount of address space being monitored and the percentage of probes that target that space. The simulator allows us to specify these parameters as well as the number of probers and the rate at which they probe. We have run a series of sensitivity analyses in which we vary the coverage, i.e. the percentage of the Internet being monitored, from 4 /24s to 20 /8s, assuming 1000 probers each sending 2 probes per second. Similar runs vary the number of probers or the probe rate while holding other parameters constant. The simulation is "brute force" in that we simulate each prober separately. For each scanner, we generate a random number in $\{0.0 \cdots 1.0\}$ for each scan it would have emitted during the hour. The number of observed probes is the count of random numbers with values below the monitored network percentage adjusted for the assumed probe range[9]. This number is the number of destinations reached by the prober and we add 1 to the appropriate base cell in the array holding the contact line.

---

[7] Phil Budne's C implementation, version 1.1 from http://www.snobol4.org

[8] http://www.math.sci.hiroshima-u.ac.jp/~m-mat/MT/emt.html

[9] If we assume that the probes target just the monitored network, or some portion of it, this count will approach the probe rate.

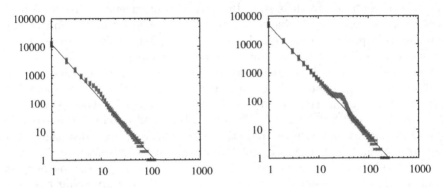

Fig. 7. Simulation of 1000 perturbers at 1800 probes per hour. 1 /16 (7a) and 1 /8 (7b) monitored.

Figures 7a and 7b indicate that a perturbing population of of 1000 sources at one probe per 2 seconds each *might* be visible if a single, relatively quiet /16 was being monitored but should be quite visible if a /8 is being monitored. This appears to confirm hypothesis 2 and provides guidance for future investigations of observed perturbations.

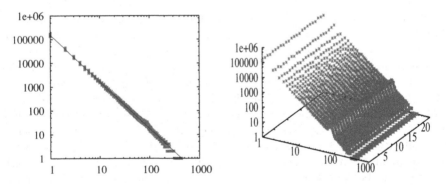

Fig. 8. Simulation of 100 (8a - 2D) and 1000 (8b - 3D) perturbers at 1800 probes per hour, 12 /8s monitored

Similarly, Figures 8a and 8b indicate that 100 sources at 1 probe per 2 seconds *might* be visible if 12 /8s are being monitored and that 1000 will be clearly visible. Note that the disturbance moves downslope and grows in amplitude as the coverage increases while the amplitude of the disturbance grows in place as the number of probers increases. In both cases, the width of the disturbance reflects the randomness of the interception process.

Figures 9a and 9b indicate that a disturbance caused by a population of 1000 probers each issuing one probe per 10 seconds (360 per hour) is barely visible in

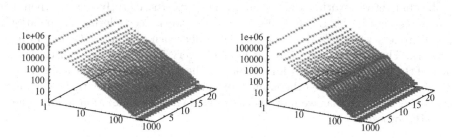

Fig. 9. Simulation of 1000 perturbers at 360 (9a) and 900 (9b) probes per hour, 12 /8s monitored

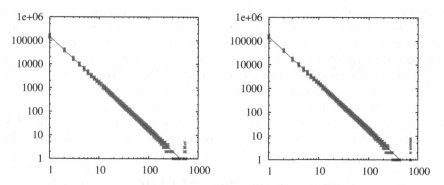

Fig. 10. Simulation of 20 perturbers at 720 probes per hour, 75% (10a) and 99% (10b) hit rate, 12 /8s covered

the artificial background, while a similar population is easily seen with a probe rate of one per 4 seconds. Again, the disturbance moves down slope and increases in amplitude with increasing probe rate. The above examples serve to describe the approximate limits of visibility for regular probes as a function of probe population and rate and observational coverage. In this part of the analysis, we assume that the percentage of probes seen is equal to the percentage of the address space that is being monitored. While this is true for a number of random scanning strategies, targeted scans will manifest differently. The simulated perturbations embody the strategies implicit in Hypothesis 1. The resemblance to the observed data is gratifying, but we cannot say conclusively that these are the only assumptions capable of producing the observed phenomena.

4.1   The Minor Spike

Figures 4a and 4b show minor spikes at the 150 contacts per hour point in addition to the broad disturbances seen earlier. We did not have an opportunity to analyze these at the time, but realized that the simulation also provides a plausible explanation for these as well. If the probing strategy is such that the probes fall entirely within the monitored network, the disturbances sharpen as can be seen in Figures 10a and 10b. In this case, we are considering a population of 20 probers with 75% and 99% of the probes being seen in the monitored network. The probe rate is 720 per hour (1 every 5 seconds) per source. Note that, if the hit rate were 100% for all sources, the spike would become a single dot whose amplitude indicated the number of sources. We see exactly this behaviour in the /22 network that we have been monitoring. This simulation is consistent with Hypothesis 3.

4.2 Full Subnet Scanning on a /22

Figure 11 shows contact data for a month from the /22 that we have been monitoring. The data was first filtered to retain only traffic from an external source address to a destination addresses within the monitored network then sorted by flow start time. The data was then filtered using a Bloom filter so that only the first record for each unique source IP / destination IP pair was kept for subsequent analysis. The retained data was passed through to the SiLK `rwbag` program and a bag or multiset made for the source IP addresses. This bag counts the number of internal addresses contacted by each external address. Inverting this bag provides the data pairs used to produce the contact line. The line is similar to those composing the contact surface seen in the Figure 2a.

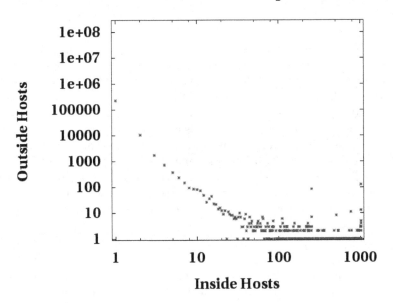

Fig. 11. Observed Contact line for a /22 in April 2006

The general shape of the curve is similar to those for the larger network. Several hundred thousand external addresses appear associated with only a single internal address. In other months, this number is as much as a million. At the bottom of the figure, one to three addresses contact most of the host counts between 50 or so and 1016[10].

Notable at the right hand end of the figure are high points, approaching 100 sources at 254 and 1016 destinations with smaller peaks at 508 and 762. A closer inspection shows that significant numbers of sources attempt to connect to one to four of the monitored subnets. Most probe all of the monitored addresses, but smaller numbers contact nearly all, missing only one or two, resulting in secondary points, as well. Inspection of the corresponding daily and hourly traffic shows that the full scans are distributed throughout the month and are not easily seen on a shorter time scale. These observations appear to be consistent with the limiting cases of Hypothesis 3. The singleton traffic is the subject of a current investigation. We note that during the 14 that months we have analyzed, nearly 13 million outside sources contacted the network. About 42% of these generated only a single flow record and over 90% generated 10 or fewer flows.

5   Related Work

The contact surface described in this paper was first shown in a paper by McHugh and Gates [3] on locality. However, at that time, the disturbance in the contact surface was only noted, but not analyzed nor was it presented as a subject for speculation. At that point it was not known that the perturbation would disappear in August 2003. It appeared again in a later paper by McHugh et al. [4], however at that point the cause of the perturbation was still unknown and, again, the disturbance was not analyzed. Since that time the suspected cause of the 2004 perturbation was discovered, and the contact surface was the subject of several invited presentations but not of any publications.

While we know of no other work that has demonstrated a contact surface, nor demonstrated observed effects of security-related phenomena on large-scale traffic analysis, some work related to the contact surface can be found in the network traffic analysis literature. Network traffic analysis traditionally has focused on an examination of traffic volumes or round-trip-times. For example, Paxson and Floyd found that WAN traffic was largely self-similar in nature [5], exhibiting fractal-like scaling behavior and a heavy-tailed distribution over various time scales. Feldmann et al. [6] studied this further, relating the impact of the local networks on the traffic characteristics to the physical construction of the network. Later, Chen modeled traffic volumes using an ARIMA (Auto-Regressive Integrated Moving Average) model [7]. He analyzed traffic based on subnetworks, such as analyzing all http traffic in isolation (rather than by LAN,

---

[10] While the /22 contains 1024 addresses, the maximum count that we see is 1016. Addresses 0 and 255 in each /24 do not appear, having been "absorbed" within the instrumented router.

as done by Feldmann *et al.*), and suggests aggregating each of these subnetworks together to better model overall network traffic. Traffic volumes have also been analyzed for security events (*e.g.*, denial-of-service attacks) and failures, using approaches such as signal processing [8]. Lee and Fapojuwo review several statistical techniques for analyzing network traffic [9]. However, these studies and others have not examined the interhost communication characteristics we observe in the contact surface.

Some work has been done on analyzing host-to-host communications. For example, Epsilon *et al.* [10] examined host-level network traffic characteristics for ATM traffic at an ISP, finding that host traffic is highly non-uniform (with a few servers accounting for the most traffic). They also analyzed connection information in terms of typical traffic volumes, however no analysis was performed on typical connection patterns (such as how many servers a typical client accessed). Sarvothan *et al.* [11] do a similar connection-level analysis, noting that there are two types of traffic — alpha and beta — where alpha traffic is dominated by a few flows transferring large amounts of data over high-bandwidth connections whereas beta traffic consist of the remaining flows with smaller data transfers and lower bandwidths. Lakhina *et al.* [12] examined OD (origin-destination) flows on backbone networks using PCA, however they defined the origin as a network ingress point and the destination as a network egress point, rather than as the source and destination hosts respectively. Lakhina *et al.* [13] also examined network traffic using clustering and entropy approaches on source and destination IP addresses, but did not combine the two as done in the contact surface. Dübendorfer *et al.* [14] analysed the effect of worm traffic on an internet backbone, where they aggregated the number of unique sources seen over time. However, they did not split this into the third dimension, aggregating again by number of destinations contacted. Karagiannis *et al.* [15] do examine network traffic at what they term the "social level", analyzing the communication of a single host with regards to the number of destination IPs contacted for particular types of traffic (*e.g.*, web, p2p, malware and mail), however they do not aggregate this information across multiple sources.

Visualization software has been developed to help administrators better understand their network traffic and better detect anomalies. Such visualizations have typically focused on host to host behavior, such as providing three dimensional graphs indicating the traffic relationships between external host, internal host and destination port (see, for example, [16] and [17]). Goodall *et al.* [18] developed a Time-based Network traffic Visualizer (TNV) demonstrating context and time for network traffic. TNV provides a visual representation of the network traffic between hosts, but does not aggregate in the form shown in the contact surface, instead focusing on traffic between individual hosts. Oberheide *et al.* [19] present a similar tool, showing traffic volumes per host, or non-aggregated interhost relationships. Interestingly, they show how the Dabber worm appears using their interface, along with traffic both before and after a slashdot event. However, as they do not look at the aggregated traffic, they do not observe the same phenomena presented in this paper.

6   Conclusions and Acknowledgments

We have developed a graphic representation for large scale Internet connection behavior and have used it to investigate two outbreaks of what appears to be synchronized activity by significant populations of scanning hosts. It appears that the synchronization arises from a "design time" choice of a delay constant in the scanning loop and that this allows a small population of scanners to create a pronounced disturbance in the midst of the activities of millions of others. We have explored the phenomena through simulation and believe that we have plausible explanations for a number of features that appear in observed contact lines. We realize that there is some risk in publishing this kind of result. It would be trivial to modify the scanning mechanism so as to avoid the observed phenomena. As part of our future work in this area, we will investigate the effect of such changes, noting that both increases and decreases work against the scanner, raising detectability or reducing effectiveness. Given access to suitable data, we expect to discover additional periodic phenomena, as well. In addition, the development of the techniques used to display and analyze this phenomena has aided us in performing more immediate tasks as well as serving to identify other research areas of interest. The reviewers of the paper made a number of helpful suggestions, including the performance of more detailed analyses of the 2003 and 2004 outbreaks. We agree that these analyses should be performed, but we no longer have access to this data and know of no comparable sources to which we might obtain access. Thus far, we have been unable to persuade individuals who have current access to collaborate. We want to thank Tom Longstaff for his encouragement when we were all at CERT, Michael Collins and Mark Thomas for the initial and continuing support of the SiLK tools. We owe a debt of gratitude to the late Suresh L. Konda for the vision that made our discoveries possible.

References

1. Gates, C., Collins, M., Duggan, M., Kompanek, A., Thomas, M.: More NetFlow tools: For performance and security. In: Proceedings of the 18th Large Installation Systems Administration Conference (LISA 2004), Atlanta, Georgia, USA, pp. 121–132 (November 2004)
2. Faloutsos, M., Faloutsos, P., Faloutsos, C.: On power-law relationships of the internet topology. In: Proceedings of the 1999 ACM SIGCOMM Conference, Cambridge, MA, USA, August 31 - September 3, pp. 251–262 (1999)
3. McHugh, J., Gates, C.: Locality: A new paradigm for thinking about normal behavior and outsider threat. In: Proceedings of the 2003 New Security Paradigms Workshop, Ascona, Switzerland, pp. 3–10 (August 2003)
4. McHugh, J., Gates, C., Becknel, D.: Situational awareness and network traffic analysis. In: Proceedings of the Gdansk NATO Workshop on Cyberspace Security and Defence: Research Issues, Gdansk, Poland, pp. 209–228 (September 2004)
5. Paxson, V., Floyd, S.: Wide area traffic: The failure of Poisson modeling. IEEE/ACM Transactions on Networking 3(3), 226–244 (1995)

6. Feldmann, A., Gilbert, A., Willinger, W.: Data networks as cascades: investigating the multifractal nature of internet wan traffic. In: Proceedings of the ACM SIG-COMM 1998 Conference on Applications, Technologies, Architectures, and Protocols for Computer Communications, Vancouver, British Columbia, Canada, pp. 42–55 (1998)

7. Chen, Y.W.: Traffic behavior analysis and modeling of sub-networks. International Journal of Network Management 12(5), 323–330 (2002)

8. Barford, P., Kline, J., Plonka, D., Ron, A.: A signal analysis of network traffic anomalies. In: Proceedings of the 2nd ACM SIGCOMM Workshop on Internet Measurement, Marseille, France, pp. 71–82 (2002)

9. Lee, I., Fapojuwo, A.: Statistical methods for computer network traffic analysis. IEE Proceedings Communications 153(6), 939–948 (2006)

10. Epsilon, R., Ke, J., Williamson, C.: Analysis of ISP IP/ATM network traffic measurements. ACM SIGMETRICS Performance Evaluation Review 27(2), 15–24 (1999)

11. Sarvotham, S., Riedi, R., Baraniuk, R.: Connection-level analysis and modeling of network traffic. In: Proceedings of the 1st ACM SIGCOMM Workshop on Internet Measurement, San Francisco, CA, USA, pp. 99–103 (2001)

12. Lakhina, A., Papagiannake, K., Crovella, M., Diot, C., Kolaczyk, E., Taft, N.: Structural analysis of network traffic flows. In: Proceedings of the 2004 Joint International Conference on Measurement and Modeling of Computer Systems (SIG-METRICS/Performance), New York, NY, USA, June 12-16, pp. 61–72 (2004)

13. Lakhina, A., Crovella, M., Diot, C.: Mining anomalies using traffic feature distributions. In: Proceedings of the ACM SIGCOMM 2005 Conference on Applications, Technologies, Architectures, and Protocols for Computer Communications, Philadelphia, PA, USA, pp. 217–228 (2005)

14. Düberdorfer, T., Wagner, A., Hossmann, T., Plattner, B.: Flow-level traffic analysis of the blaster and sobig worm outbreaks in an internet backbone. In: Proceedings of the 2005 Conference on Detection of Intrusions and Malware and Vulnerability Assessment, Vienna, Austria, pp. 103–122 (2005)

15. Karagiannis, T., Papagiannaki, K., Faloutsos, M.: BLINC: Multilevel traffic classification in the dark. In: Proceedings of the ACM SIGCOMM 2005 Conference on Applications, Technologies, Architectures, and Protocols for Computer Communications, Philadelphia, PA, USA, pp. 229–240 (2005)

16. van Riel, J.P., Irwin, B.: Inetvis, a visual tool for network telescope traffic analysis. In: Proceedings of the 4th International Conference on Computer Graphics, Virtual Reality, Visualization and Interaction In Africa, Cape Town, South Africa, pp. 85–89 (2006)

17. Lakkaraju, K., Yurcik, W., Lee, A.J.: NVisionIP: NetFlow visualizations of system state for security situational awareness. In: Proceedings of 2004 CCS Workshop on Visualization and Data Mining for Computer Security, Washington, DC, USA, pp. 65–72 (October 2004)

18. Goodall, J., Lutters, W., Rheingans, P., Komlodi, A.: Preserving the big picture: visual network traffic analysis with tnv. In: Proceedings of the 2005 IEEE Workshop on Visualization for Computer Security, Minneapolis, MN, USA, pp. 47–54 (October 2005)

19. Oberheide, J., Goff, M., Karir, M.: Flamingo: Visualizing internet traffic. In: Proceedings of the 10th IEEE/IFIP Network Operations and Management Symposium, Vancouver, BC, Canada, pp. 150–161 (2006)

The Quest for Multi-headed Worms

Van-Hau Pham, Marc Dacier, Guillaume Urvoy-Keller, and Taoufik En-Najjary

Institut Eurecom, Sophia–Antipolis, France
{pham,dacier,urvoy,ennajjar}@eurecom.fr

Abstract. In [6], Pouget et al. have conjectured the existence of so-called multi-headed worms and found a couple of them on attack traces collected on a single honeypot. These worms take advantage of several distinct attack techniques to propagate but they use only one of them against a given target. From a victim's viewpoint, they are therefore indistinguishable from the other classical worms that always propagate using the same attack vector or same sequence of attack vectors. This paper aims at confirming the existence of these worms by studying a very large dataset. The validation process led to three important contributions. First, we establish the existence and assess the importance of three distinct classes of attacks seen in the wild. Second, we propose a new method to correlate attack traces time series and apply it to search for multi-headed worms. Third, we offer and discuss results of the analysis of 15 months of data gathered over 28 different platforms located all over the world.

1   Introduction

The concept of worm, as a programming paradigm, has been introduced more than 25 years ago [8] and has been used to propagate malicious code on a large scale as early as September 1988 with the first ADM worm targeting the DNS infrastructure [3] and with the so called Morris worm, also known as the Internet worm, hitting the Internet in November 1988 [9,2]. However, one had to wait more than ten years to see worms routinely used by hackers and various techniques used to speed up their propagation on the Internet [10]. We refer the interested reader to the taxonomy of worms published in [12]. The authors provide several examples of worms, classifying them according to various viewpoints, namely worm target discovery and selection strategies, worm carrier mechanisms, worm activation, possible payloads, and plausible attackers who would employ a worm. As indicated in [12], worm authors are not so much interested anymore in gaining faith for having created the fastest worm or the worm having compromised the largest amount of machines. Instead, worm spreading is now seen as a preliminary phase to conduct other fraudulent activities to gain money using various techniques (spam relays, extortion with DDoS threats, pay-per-click fraud, etc.). Therefore, worms are now designed to make their propagations as stealthy as possible.

Multi-headed worms, identified by Pouget et al. in [6], belong to a new class of worms designed with stealthiness in mind. These sophisticated programs can break into target machines using several different techniques. This, by itself, is not new. The Morris worm [9], in 1988, already had this feature. It was propagating using attacks against three different services: rshd, fingerd and sendmail. The Morris worm, after

D. Zamboni (Ed.): DIMVA 2008, LNCS 5137, pp. 247–266, 2008.

having selected a target, was trying all three attacks, one after another, interrupting the process only in the case of a successful intrusion. Several other worms have, since then, used the same strategy. They all are fairly easy to identify thanks to the known sets (or sequences) of attacks they try against their targets. Multi-headed worms, as defined in [6], use a very different strategy: they probe each target with only one of the attacks they are capable of. This strategy decreases their chance of success but increases their stealthiness. Indeed, there will be no trace left anywhere highlighting the fact that a new worm has been created combining attacks X, Y and Z as they will never be tried together by a given attacker against a given attackee.

In [6], the authors had used traces left on a simple low interaction honeypot to highlight the existence of a couple of such multi-headed worms propagating in the Internet. At that time, only one of them, Nachia, had been acknowledged by intrusion detection and antivirus vendors. This seminal work had been carried out on a single platform and, therefore, was not able to assess the seriousness of the threats posed by this new class of worms.

In this paper, we carry out a systematic identification of multi-headed worms in attack traces collected thanks to 28 distinct low interaction honeypot platforms, located in 15 different countries, over a 15 month period. In order to perform this experiment, we had to design a different method than the one originally proposed in [6] because of algorithmic complexity issues. The application of this validation process led to three important contributions: i) we establish the existence and assess the importance of three distinct classes of attacks seen in the wild; ii) we offer a new generic method to correlate attack traces time series that could be applied to other kinds of datasets; iii) we offer and discuss results of the analysis of 15 months of data gathered over 28 different platforms located all over the world.

The paper is structured as follows. Section 2 reviews the state of the art and describes the two main reasons why the solution provided in [6] does not scale. Section 3 presents the three distinct steps of the new method we propose: (i) Identification and selection of attack classes (ii) Identification of correlated platforms (iii) Root causes identification. Section 4 provides a summarized description and discussion of the most interesting results obtained. Section 5 concludes the paper.

2   Problem Statement

In this section, we describe the original solution provided in [6] for the identification of multi-headed worms and explain the two main reasons why this solution does not scale. For the sake of completeness, we first start by briefly describing the data collection environment considered in that work as well as some definitions of terms used throughout this paper.

2.1   The Leurré.com Environment

The Leurré.com environment is a distributed setup of low interaction honeypots. As of now, there are approximately 50 different partners that host a so-called *platform*. All platforms are configured exactly the same way. Each platform emulates, thanks to honeyd [7], three virtual machines: a Windows 98 machine, a Windows NT Server, and a Linux RedHat 7.3. These platforms are located in 30 different countries covering the five continents. They are hosted by different types of institutions (academic, industrial, government, defense, SME, etc.). Most platforms have been active for more than 24 months; the oldest one has been running since January 2003.

Each platform captures tcpdump traces of all packets sent to and from it. These files are uploaded, on a daily basis, in a centralized Oracle database accessible to all partners to carry out various kinds of analysis. The entity relationship diagram of the database is fairly complex and its description lies outside the scope of this paper. However, a few key concepts must be precisely defined in order to avoid any misunderstandings.

- **Platform:** A physical machine, hosting three virtual machines, connected directly to the Internet and collecting tcpdump traces in the context of the Leurré.com environment.
- **Source:** A source corresponds to an IP address that has sent at least one packet to, at least, one platform. It is important to understand that a given IP address can correspond to several distinct sources. Indeed, a given IP remains associated to a given source as long as there is no more than 25 hours between 2 packets received from that IP. After such a delay, a new identifier will be assigned to the IP. By grouping packets by sources instead of by IPs, we minimize the risk of gathering packets sent by distinct physical machines that have been assigned the same IP dynamically after 25 hours.
- **Ports Sequence:** A ports sequence is a time ordered sequence of ports (without duplicates) a source has contacted on a given virtual machine. For example, if an attacker sends the following packets: icmp, 135 TCP, 135 TCP, 139 TCP to a given virtual machine, the associated ports sequence will be represented by the string $ICMP|135T|139T$. Each source can have, at most, three distinct ports sequences associated to it, per platform. As of now, we have observed around 40,000 distinct unique ports sequences on all Leurré.com platforms.
- **Cluster:** A cluster is made of a group of sources that have left highly similar traces on all platforms they have been seen on. Clusters have been precisely defined in [5]. They aim at grouping together attackers that are likely launching attacks with the very same attack tool. Traces present in a given cluster have 7 features in common, one of them being to have targeted the same ports sequence as defined here above. As of now, we have observed more than 154,900 different clusters.
- **Cluster time series:** A Cluster time series represents the amount of sources, on a daily basis, associated to a given cluster on a given platform. In other words, there are, for a given cluster, as many cluster time series as platforms.
- **Global Cluster time series:** A global cluster time series represents the sum of all cluster time series associated to a given cluster. In other words, there is a single global cluster time series associated to a given cluster.
- **Platform time series:** A platform time series represents the sum of all cluster time series associated to a given platform. In other words, there is a single platform time series associated to a given platform.

2.2 Seminal Work on the Identification of Multi-headed Worms

Pouget et al. have proposed in [6] a method to discover multi-headed attack tools. In that paper, the authors explain that sources compromised by a multi-headed worm leave, by definition, distinct traces on the honeypots depending on which attack they choose to launch against them. As a result, the sources will be classified into as many different clusters as there are different possible attacks for the worm. However, the various cluster time series associated to a given multi-headed worm should evolve over time in a similar way as they all are a function of the total amount of machines compromised by that multi-headed worm at any point in time. Therefore, by identifying cluster time series that are very similar to each other appears to be a simple yet efficient way to identify multi-headed worms. In [6], the authors have used the SAX technique [4] to calculate the distance between all pairs of cluster time series data.

The authors have shown, by means of data extracted from a single platform, the existence of a couple of interesting multi-headed worms. Having a much larger dataset at our disposal, we were interested in verifying their results on a worldwide scale. Unfortunately, we found out that the detection method in [6] does not scale to that level for two main reasons. First, the most straightforward way to generalize the approach to data collected on several platforms, instead of one, is to measure the distance between different global cluster time series. Experience shows, as discussed below, that this approach does not work when a large number of platforms located in many different places in the world are considered. The reason lies in the fact that worms do not spread in an uniform way across the IP space. Therefore, we must measure distances between cluster time series observed on distinct platforms instead of global cluster time series. Second, the authors in [6] considered a fixed time window of 1 year to assess the distance between time series. This approach works for some extreme cases but, as we demonstrate hereafter, is also likely to miss many interesting phenomena, the existence of which is only visible during a couple of weeks. Therefore, their fixed time window must be replaced by a sliding window.

Measuring distance between cluster time series on many platforms by means of a sliding window leads to an algorithmic complexity problem. In the next three sections, we provide examples of the two problems described above and offer a formal complexity analysis of these issues. Section 3 proposes a new solution to address these identified drawbacks of the original method.

Fixed time window vs sliding time window. The top plot in Figure 1 presents the global cluster time series for two distinct clusters, over a period of more than 450 days. The first (resp. second) one represents sources belonging to cluster number 15715 (resp. 60231) only. The corresponding ports sequence of cluster 15715 (resp. 60231) is 1433TCP (resp. 5900TCP). The SAX distance, computed as described in [6], i.e., over the whole observation period, would lead us to consider that these two cluster time series are not correlated. However, when looking at the bottom plot in Figure 1, it is clear that these curves are highly correlated between day 60 and 90. The reason why SAX gives a low similitude is mostly due to the activities happening before day 60 as well as after day 200. It can well be that the existence of the multi-headed worm can only be detected during a limited period of time. This is especially true for multi-headed

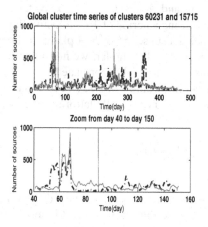

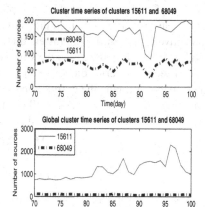

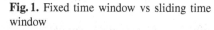

Fig. 1. Fixed time window vs sliding time window

Fig. 2. Global cluster time series vs. cluster time series

worms that are using attacks that were already frequently observed when the multi-headed worm got launched. As a consequence, one cannot simply rely on the usage of a large fixed time window, as proposed in [6] to detect those worms. Using a sliding time window is obviously the way to go in order to address this issue.

Global cluster time series vs. cluster time series. The top plot in Figure 2, shows two distinct cluster time series on platform 18 over a period of 30 days. The first (resp. second) one represents the evolution of cluster number 15611(resp. 68049). The bottom plot in Figure 2 represents the corresponding global cluster time series (over all platforms) over the same period for these two clusters. These figures highlight the fact that, on platform 18, the two cluster time series are highly correlated between day 70 until day 100 whereas the corresponding global cluster time series are not. This can be explained by the fact that a multi-headed worm is not necessarily observed everywhere in the world. If the multi-headed worm is reusing attack vectors that are frequently observed elsewhere, its existence will remain hidden if we use global cluster time series instead of carrying out the analysis on each platform independently.

Working with global cluster time series is thus not an option. One of the contribution of this paper will be to demonstrate that, unlike global clusters, platform time series carry enough information so as to uncover correlations among cluster time series. This is an important finding as it enables us to reduce the computational cost of the correlation search phase as shown in the next section.

2.3 Complexity Analysis

From the previous two examples, it comes out that, in order to deal with these two issues, we should apply the method proposed in [6] between all cluster time series, for every platform, over a sliding time window. Intuitively, this leads to a very large amount of computations that we detail hereafter.

Let $S = \{S_i\}, i = 1..N$, be the set of platforms and $A = \{cl_i\}, i = 1..K$ be the set of distinct clusters observed on all the platforms during a period of T consecutive days. Our objective is to identify all clusters that targeted a subset $S' \subset S$ of platforms over a period of $T' \leq T$ consecutive days in a similar way. By similar, we mean that the selected cluster time series on any two platforms of S' are highly correlated.

To do so, we compute the correlation over a sliding window of size L. For a total of M time series ($M \leq K \times N$ as not all clusters are observed on all platforms), the total number of correlations to be computed is given by:

$$C_1 = \frac{M \times (M-1)}{2}(T - L)$$
$$C_1 = O(M^2 T)$$

We postpone until Section 4 the details of the numerical results obtained from the experiments but, for now, the reader should be aware that M amounts to more than 59,000 in the 15 months period considered. Clearly the simplistic generalization of the method described in [6] is too expensive.

Our solution to reduce the complexity is twofold. First, we find an automated way to select a subset M' from M such that $M' \ll M$. The reduction technique is presented in Section 3.1. Experimentally, we found out that M' can be an order of magnitude smaller than M. After such selection, the complexity comes down to $C_2 = O(M'^2 T)$ and $C_2 \ll C_1$. However, the cost C_2 remains prohibitive and this leads to the second step of our method where we compute filtered platform time series corresponding to the sum of activities corresponding to these M' time series per platform. We then look for similitude between these filtered platform time series instead of between cluster time series. The cost to pay for finding similar platform time series comes down to

$$C_3 = \frac{N \times (N-1)}{2}(T - L)$$
$$C_3 = O(N^2 T)$$

This leads us to the identification of a certain amount P (with $P \ll T - L$) of periods in which we have a group of G_i (with $i = 1..P$ and for $\forall i | G_i | \ll N$) correlated platform time series. For each period, we have to find the cluster responsible for the identified similarity. In other words, for each period, we must compare the M' cluster time series with, at maximum, N filtered platform time series. This leads to the identification of the root causes of the similarity on each platform. If we define $G = max G_i | i = 1..P$, an upper bound of the cost of this operation can be given by $C_4 = P \times G \times M'$. Thus, the total cost of this method is equal to $C_5 = C_3 + C_4$ and we have $C_5 = O(N^2 T + PGM')$. In the general case, nothing ensures, a priori, that $C_5 \ll C_2 \ll C_1$ but, as we expect the values of N, P and G to be very small compared to M and M', this justifies the choice of this solution. Experimental results presented in Section 4 validate this choice.

3   Methodology

We detail in this section the three steps of our methodology we have eluded to in the previous Section:

1. All attack traces can be grouped into three distinct families. Only one of them is likely to contain traces due to multi-headed worms. Therefore, the method starts by selecting in our dataset those traces that belong to the sole interesting family.

2. Our platforms observe a limited number of hits per day. If at some points in time two platforms become the target of a multi-headed worm, we make the assumption that this will significantly impact the overall platform time series on that period. Therefore, the method identifies groups of platform time series strongly correlated over different periods of time and identifies the root causes for those similitudes. Similarly to the approach followed in [6], if a similitude is caused by many attack tools, we believe this reveals the existence of a multi-headed worm. Obviously, if the intensity of the attack is not high enough that it impacts the platform time series of at least two platforms, our method will miss it. The validity of the method is further discussed while presenting the experimental results in Section 4.

3. We search for the root causes, i.e. the clusters that are responsible, if any, for the similar shape of the filtered platform time series in each group. Once we have found them, we verify that they did not also existed on other platforms than the ones we had in the group under study. This can happen if the influence of these clusters on the other filtered platform time series was not strong enough to include them in the group of similar platforms.

3.1   Construction of Filtered Platform Time Series

As explained before, the first step of our technique aims at reducing the number of cluster time series we need to focus on. Our method to reduce the size of the problem is based on our experience with attack traces collected in the Leurré.com project. We have observed that cluster time series can be categorized into 3 distinct families[1]:

1. **Peaked family:** Time series in this family exhibit a significant peak of values during a very small period of one or two days and almost no activity otherwise. In most cases, the corresponding cluster is observed on a single platform only. We leave for future work a more in depth study of this specific type of phenomena and we thus exclude those time series when building platform time series.

2. **Stable family:** Time series in this family have a roughly constant behavior during the whole observation period. As we make assumption that correlated clusters due to multi-headed worms exhibits time series having similar noticeable variations over time, stable clusters are meaningless in the context of this analysis. We can simply remove them from our dataset. Note that removing the stable ones has little impact on the shape of the platform time series. However, as a very large number of time series falls into the stable family, removing them from our initial set dramatically reduces the computational cost.

3. **Strongly varying family:** Time series in this family are characterized by wide amplitude variations over long periods of time. Our objective is to uncover phenomena

---

[1] There is no reason to believe that the findings described hereafter are not also applicable to datasets collected by other projects. If that were the case, it would certainly be worth investigating the reasons why.

that involve several cluster time series over periods of time larger than a few days, we restrict our attention to those time series in the remaining of this paper.

We proceed as follows to classify each cluster time series into one of the three families introduced above. We first compute the standard deviation of the time series over the whole observation period. If it is smaller than a threshold δ, then we flag the time series as belonging to the stable family. Otherwise, we filter out the outlier values from the time series. Outliers are defined as the two greatest and smallest values of the time series. Then we compute the standard deviation of newly obtained time series. If the standard deviation is now smaller than δ, we declare the time series as being a peaked time series. Otherwise, we declare the time series as belonging to the strongly varying family and we thus keep it in our set of cluster time series. In the above procedure, we used $\delta = 2$, which is intended to be a conservative value, based on the visual inspection of a lot of cluster time series.

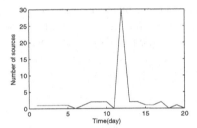

Fig. 3. Example of the peaked family time series

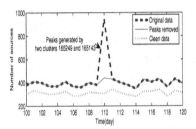

Fig. 4. Data Pre-processing

Figure 3 illustrates the algorithm for a cluster time series that spans over 20 days. The standard deviation of the time series is 6.51. Since it is greater than 2, our algorithm can not declare this time series as a stable one upfront. We next filter the extreme values from this time series , which for the case of Figure 3 boils down to cutting the peak on day 12. The resulting time series is obviously smoother than the initial one and its standard deviation is 0.46, which is smaller than the threshold 2. Hence, our algorithm eventually flags the time series of Figure 3 as belonging to the peaked family.

The cost of the above filtering process comes on top of the complexity evaluated in the previous Section but it is very small compared to C_1 since its complexity is linear with respect to the number of clusters and the algorithm involved for each cluster is much cheaper to run than the evaluation of the correlation between two clusters (over sliding windows), as discussed before.

Figure 4 illustrates our pre-processing technique. We plot three platform time series for platform 18. *Original data* is the platform time series obtained using all clusters. It is made of 6162 clusters in this specific case. *Peaks removed* is obtained once the peaked time series have been filtered out. It is made of 6108 clusters as 54 clusters were peaks in this example. *Clean data* is the platform time series data once the peaked and stable time series have been removed. It is made of only 39 clusters! This highlights the usefulness of the preprocessing phase.

Figure 4 clearly shows that *original data* is quite different from *clean data* due to the two peaks at the same position (110). These peaks (clusters number 165249 and 165143) were created by 510 sources. This attack was neither observed before or after day 80, nor was it observed on any other platform. As we can see, the *peaks removed* and *clean data* time series have a very similar shape. They differ only with respect to their amplitude. However, we remind the reader that the *peaks removed* time series contain 6108 clusters and that only 39 (strongly varying) time series remain in *clean data*.

3.2   Groups of Correlated Filtered Platform Time Series

In this section, we explain how we identify correlated groups, i.e. groups of platforms for which any two filtered platform time series are mutually correlated for a given period of T' days. Obviously, one wants to maximize the number of platforms involved and the duration T' over which each group exists. The proposed algorithm is made of three successive steps described in the following subsections: i) pairwise comparison of filtered platform time series, ii) construction of groups of correlated platforms within a given time period and iii) reorganization of the time periods to maximize them on a group by group basis.

Pairwise correlation of filtered platform time series. The first step of our algorithm consists in computing the correlation of any two platform time series using a sliding window of L days. Consider two time series Φ and Ψ. Let $cor(A, B)$ be the coefficient of correlation of two vectors A and B. The correlation vector C of Φ and Ψ is computed as follows:

$$C[k] = cor(\Phi[k, k + L], \Psi[k, k + L]), \quad k = 1, \ldots T - L$$

Φ and Ψ are considered to be correlated in the interval $[t_1, t_2]$ if $C[k]$ is greater than a given threshold for every k value in the interval $[t_1, t_2 - L]$. We use as a measure of correlation the Pearson coefficient of correlation [11].

An important parameter of our procedure is the choice of the threshold to declare that two time series are correlated. Again, we rely on experience, i.e. visual inspection of a lot of cases, to choose our threshold. We end up having a threshold of 0.75. We note that this is a high, and thus safe, value as 0.4 is already considered as a significant correlation value in the statistical literature.

Figure 5 illustrates the first step of our procedure. The platform time series for platforms 2 and 15 are deemed correlated in the interval $[t_1, t_3]$ as their correlation vector is greater than the threshold of 0.75 in the period $[t_1, t_2] = [t_1, t_3 - L]$.

Application of the above procedure to all the pairs of platform time series leads to the identification of a set of correlated pairs of platforms over different periods of time. Figure 6 illustrates the situation at the end of the first phase. It shows that platform time series 4 and 7 (curve 4&7) are correlated from day 1 to day 4, platform time series 1 and 8 (curve 8&1) are correlated from day 1 to day 6, etc.

Correlated groups extraction per time interval. Based on this first result, our next objective is to divide the time line from 0 to T into a set of time intervals such that the

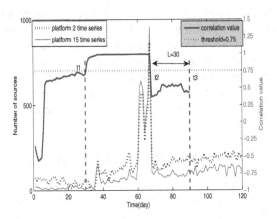

Fig. 5. Example of correlated platform time series

pairs of platforms associated to one interval are correlated over the whole duration of this interval. Within each interval, we want to identify groups of platforms such that all platforms in the group are correlated to all others. The algorithm we use to achieve this task can be summarized as follow:

1. $i = 1, T_{start,i} = 1, T_{end,i} = 1$, L is the sliding window parameter.
2. We define S_i as being the set of pairs of correlated platforms at time $T_{start,i}$.
3. We exclude from S all pairs of correlated platforms that are not correlated until, at least, $T_{start,i} + L$.
4. We define $T_{end,i}$ as being the first end point of the pairwise correlations in S. Interval i is then defined as $[T_{start,i}, T_{end,i}]$; We proceed to the next interval $i \rightarrow i + 1$
5. We define $T_{start,i}$ as being the first start point of a pairwise correlations not yet present in S.
6. If $T_{start,i} \leq T - L$, we reinitialize S to $\emptyset$ and go back to step 2; if not the algorithm terminates.

Applying this algorithm to the case described in Figure 6, leads to the identification of the three periods defined in Table 1 when we chose L=3.

Table 1. Periods

$T_1 = [T_{start,1}, T_{end,1}] = [1, 4]$	$S_1 = \{(4, 7), (8, 1), (1, 2), (2, 8)\}$
$T_2 = [T_{start,2}, T_{end,2}] = [3, 6]$	$S_1 = \{(8, 1), (1, 2), (2, 8), (9, 10)\}$
$T_3 = [T_{start,3}, T_{end,3}] = [4, 8]$	$S_1 = \{(5, 1), (1, 2), (2, 5)\}$

Having identified time intervals, we now need to group together all platforms that are correlated with each other. If we use a graph representation of the correlated pairs identified in the previous stage of our algorithm, the problem corresponds to the identification of cliques[2] within the graph. We generate one graph per period. Nodes in a

---

[2] A clique in an undirected graph G is a set of vertices V such that for every two vertices in V, there exists an edge connecting the two.

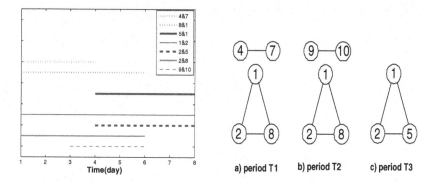

Fig. 6. Correlated pairs of platform time series over time

Fig. 7. Correlated groups extraction

graph represent platform time series and if two platform time series are correlated in that period, their edges are connected. Figure 7 depicts the graphs we obtain for the periods T_1, T_2 and T_3 extracted from Figure 6. The clique extraction problem [1] is an NP-complete one. In our case, this is not an issue as the number of nodes (platforms) per period is very small, typically less than 20.

Reorganization of the time periods. From the example given above, it is clear that our algorithm generates overlapping time intervals and that the very same group of correlated platforms can be found in these overlapping periods. For instance, the correlated group consisting of platforms 1,2 and 8 appears in period T_1 and also in period T_2 in Figure 7.

In the last step, we revisit the various groups obtained and, on a group by group basis, merge time intervals whenever the same group is found in two consecutive or overlapping periods. This eventually leads to the following time periods (Table 2) and groups for the preceding example.

Table 2. Groups

$T_1 = [1, 4]$	$G_1 = (4, 7)$
$T_2 = [1, 6]$	$G_2 = (1, 2, 8)$
$T_3 = [3, 6]$	$G_3 = (9, 10)$
$T_4 = [4, 8]$	$G_4 = (1, 2, 5)$

3.3   Root Cause Analysis and Hidden Correlations

The most intuitive explanation behind the existence of correlated groups of platforms is that those platforms are targeted by the same tool, launched from a diverse set of sources in a loosely coordinated way. In that case, the same clusters(s) should be found on each platform of the group as being the root cause of the correlation of the platform time series. We could, therefore, simply search for the root causes on one platform per group.

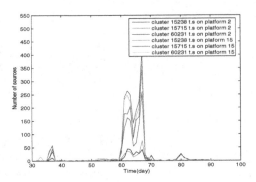

Fig. 8. cluster time series for the clusters uncovered during the root cause analysis for platforms 2 and 15

However, as explained in [6], multi-headed worms could hit platform X with cluster 1 and platform Y with cluster 2. Therefore, we take the stance of not assuming a priori that the traces left by a given attack tool are the same on the platforms of a correlated group. We thus look for the root causes behind a correlation independently for each platform in a correlated group. This means that for a period of T' days associated to a correlated group, we look, for each platform, for the set of cluster time series that are correlated with the platform time series. Here too, we use a sliding window as one can imagine that the platform time series are correlated due to two distinct and consecutive, or overlapping phenomena. Section 4.2 shows an example of such a situation found in our dataset.

The correlated group in Figure 5 (between day 31 and day 91) provides an illustration of when the attack tool leaves the same fingerprint on each platform of a correlated group. Indeed, our root cause analysis technique identifies three clusters numbered 15238, 15715 and 60231 on both platform 2 and platform 15 as the root causes behind the observed correlation. Figure 8 depicts the cluster time series over the corresponding interval. Table 3 summarizes the correlation values obtained between the different cluster time series for each pair of platforms in the extended group of platforms formed by platforms {2,15}. As we can see, the correlation coefficients between those clusters are extremely high (greater than 0.85) in this period.

We can observe the highly synchronized behavior of the activities targeting the two platforms.

Hidden Correlations. The root cause analysis technique described above enables us to find a set of candidate clusters associated to each correlated group for each platform in that group. However, since we initially identify correlation based on the platform time series, it is possible that a tool targeted x platforms but the effect of the tool is only strongly influencing a subset of $y < x$ platform time series (e.g due to the activity of other local malwares) To uncover all possible hidden correlations, we check if all clusters identified as root causes for a period of T' days for a correlated group are correlated with their siblings on the platforms that are not in the correlated group.

Table 3. Correlation coefficient between clusters

cluster t.s	2 15238	2 15715	2 60231	15 15238	15 15715	15 60231
15238-2	1.0000	0.8521	0.8422	0.8916	0.8631	0.8550
15715-2	0.8521	1.0000	0.9863	0.9248	0.9938	0.9908
60231-2	0.8422	0.9863	1.0000	0.9260	0.9873	0.9873
15238-15	0.8916	0.9248	0.9260	1.0000	0.9154	0.9121
15715-15	0.8631	0.9938	0.9873	0.9154	1.0000	0.9969
60231-15	0.8550	0.9908	0.9873	0.9121	0.9969	1.0000

4   Results

We experimented our algorithms for a period of $T = 467$ days (15 months) and for 28 platforms, whose up time rate was above 90% for the considered period. Those 28 platforms are located in 15 different countries. We applied the methodology described in Section3.2 to a large dataset. It enables us to confirm the existence of multi-headed attack tools, but it also leads to a better understanding of the specific behavior of other interesting classes of attack tools. A summary of these findings is presented hereafter.

4.1   Overview

For our specific dataset, we identified 28 groups involving 111 cluster time series before the hidden correlation identification phase and 130 cluster time series after that. The groups were found in 23 distinct periods, lasting between 30 and 117 days. Figure 9 provides the distribution of number of clusters per correlated group. We observe from Figure 9 that 18 out of 28 correlated groups (ie. 64%) have been associated to more than one root cause. Table 4 lists all the clusters related to at least one correlated group. The first column contains the cluster id. The second column lists the corresponding ports sequences. If a cluster contacts two (resp. three) machines it will have two (resp. three) ports sequences separated by a comma. The last column indicates the number of groups that the cluster is involved in. Figure 10 shows the distribution of the size of correlated groups. We observe from Figure 10 that most of the groups have a small size: 90% of the groups have less than 7 platforms. This observation relates to the fact that malware attack processes are in general not uniform over the IP address space. The observed phenomena appear to be localized. This is confirmed by Figure 11 which shows that most phenomena target a single /8 network. However, we observe that 21 out of the 28 platforms are involved in at least one correlated group showing that these phenomena are visible all over the world. These 21 platforms are located in 13 (resp 12) out of 15 countries (16 /8 networks).

4.2   Root Causes Analysis

Based on the nature of correlated groups, we classify them into four different families as follows: single root cause, variant signature attack tools, fingerprint worm, and multi-headed worm.

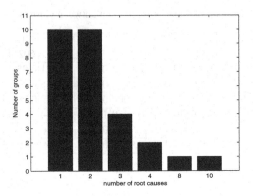

Fig. 9. Distribution of number of clusters

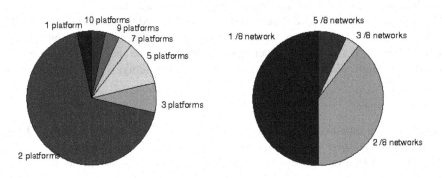

Fig. 10. Platform size distribution   **Fig. 11.** /8 network distribution

Single root cause. Table 5 presents all single root cause groups. They correspond to phenomena where a single, and always the same, cluster is the root cause of the correlation of platform time series. They could have been easily detected by computing the correlation (still using a sliding window approach) between all the cluster time series corresponding to the same cluster on each platform. This is in contrast with the multi-headed tools that require comparisons between cluster time series that do not correspond to the same clusters.

As an example, the top plot of Figure 12 represents the attacks corresponding to cluster number 170309 on two platforms 7 and 27 from day 194 to day 290 (group 7 in Table 5), targeting Symantec System Center Agent (SSC Agent) service on port 2967 TCP. As we can see, its cluster time series on these two platforms are almost the same. The bottom plot represents the highly correlated attacks on the same two platforms and also during the same period, but related to cluster 60231, targeting Virtual Networking Computing service on port 5900 TCP (group 6 in Table 5). The interesting thing is that the attacks of these two clusters are totally dissimilar. This shows the usefulness of the sliding window technique during the root cause identification phase. We can see other groups related to these 2 platforms around the same period. A more in-depth analysis

Table 4. Cluster description

Cluster Id	Ports sequences	Number of groups
15611	**ICMP**	7
15715	1433T	6
17466	135T	5
14647	445T	4
60231	5900T	4
60943	$ICMP, ICMP$	4
0	unclassified	3
17718	$ICMP\vert445T$	3
175309	2967T	3
15238	139T	2
15610	**ICMP**	2
54623	1025T	2
65710	$1026U, 1026U, 1026U$	2
75851	$ICMP\vert445T\vert139T\vert445T\vert139T\vert445T$	2
75853	$ICMP\vert445T\vert139T\vert445T\vert139\vert T445T$	2
136244	$ICMP\vert445T\vert139T\vert445T\vert139T\vert445T$	2
136323	$ICMP\vert445T\vert139T\vert445T\vert139\vert T445T$	2
17470	1026U	1
65862	$1026U, 1026U$	1
72377	1028U	1
76768	$445T\vert5000T\vert445T\vert5000T$	1
81280	$5900T, 5900T$	1
145554	$445T\vert5000T\vert445T\vert5000T\vert135T\vert5000T$ $135T\vert5000T\vert135T\vert5000T\vert135T$	1
147436	$ICMP\vert445T\vert80T$	1
147476	$ICMP\vert445T\vert80T$	1
150691	$2967T, 2967T, 2967T$	1
164629	$2967T, 2967T$	1
168772	$1027U\vert1028U\vert1026U$	1
171073	$1027U\vert1026U\vert1028U$	1
174163	$1026U\vert1028U\vert1027U$	1

of these identified groups and clusters would reveal interesting findings, from a forensic point of view, highlighting relationships between phenomena which, otherwise, would have been studied isolated from each other. Instead, our grouping can help those in charge of attributing attacks to malicious actors, on the basis of their modus operandi.

Variant signature attack tools. Our clustering algorithm classifies sources into clusters on a basis of a set of attributes such as the number of packets sent by the sources to our platforms, the ports sequences, the number of virtual hosts contacted,etc. Not all attack tools have a deterministic behavior. Some may probe ports in a random order, a variable number of times, etc. As a result, traces left by such tools will appear in distinct clusters that will appear in correlated groups. Table 6 lists them with the value "Y" in

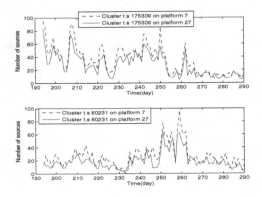

Fig. 12. Single root cause example

Table 5. Single root cause

group	platforms	root causes	start,end dates
1	6 8 22 24 26	17466	13,116
2	24 26	0	2,119
3	2 15	17466	31,91
4	7 27	15715	194,290
5	7 27	54623	198,263
6	7 27	60231	194,290
7	7 27	175309	194,290
8	6 8 17 22 26	17515	241,286
9	2 3 8 9 10 12 15 24 26	0	241,286
10	2 3 8 9 10 12 15 24 26	14647	412,452

the column labeled "Variant". In this specific dataset, we found two reasons for which clusters can be "splitted".

The first one is that they have contacted a different number of targets (marked Y(1) in Table 6). One cluster contacts only 1 honeypot and the other cluster contacts two honeypots. By our observation, two-honeypot-contacted clusters have a smaller number of sources than the one-honeypot-contacted clusters. It may be explained as follows: if one source randomly chooses its target in a network, the probability for it to hit only one of our machines is much higher than to hit two (or even three) of them. As an example, the left plot of Figure 13 represents the attacks of all cluster time series related to group 26 in Table 6. The middle plot of Figure 13 represents only the attacks of two clusters 15611 and 60943 on platform 5. Cluster 15611 contacts 1 honeypot and cluster 60943 contacts two honeypots.

The other case is that the attack tool sends different amount of packets each time it attacks our platform. These groups are marked 'Y(2)' in the "Variant" column. The right plot of Figure 13 represents the attacks of three clusters numbered 75851, 75853 and 136323 also on platform 5. The three clusters have the same ports sequence:

$ICMP|445T|139T|445T|139T|445T$. The difference resides in the number of packets sent by each source in these clusters.

Fingerprint worm. OS fingerprint is a well-known attack tactic. The idea is that before launching the attack, the attacker checks the type of target system it faces and then launches, or not, the appropriate attack. We have found worms that automatized this idea. We call them "Fingerprint worm". If a fingerprint worm learns that it is attacking a non vulnerable host (w.r.t its attack model), it gives up. Since on our platforms, we deploy two kinds of virtual machines: Windows and Linux, the fingerprint worms will leave different traces on these two platforms. In terms of ports sequences, fingerprint worms may leave two different ports sequences on two kinds of virtual machines. One ports sequence may be the prefix of the other. We have found 5 cases of fingerprint worm in our dataset. They are presented in Table 6 with the value "Y" in the column "fingerprint". For instance, we plot 4 clusters numbered 75851, 75853, 136323, and 17718 of platform 5 from, again, group 26 (in Table 6) on Figure 14. The three clusters numbered 75851,75853 and 136323 (resp. 17718) have the corresponding ports sequence $ICMP|445T|139T|445T|139T|445T$ (resp. $ICMP|445T$). Cluster 17718 is mostly observed on the Linux machine (296 sources). There are only 64 sources that

Table 6. Multiple root cause groups

group	platforms	root causes	start,end dates	Multi-headed	Finger-print	Var-iant
11	5 13	15610 15611 17718 60943 75851 75853 136244 136323	52,119		Y	Y(1,2)
12	5 13	15611 17718	157,194		Y	
13	27	0 14647 145554	316,364		Y	
14	10 21	14647 15611 76768	332,364		Y	
15	9 27	72377 168772 171073 174163	371,408			Y(2)
16	24 26	15611 60943	419,452			Y(1)
17	7 27	175309 164629	73,119			Y(1)
18	8 11	17470 65862	156,202			Y(1)
19	7 27	60231 81280	316,364			Y(1)
20	1 2 3 6 10 12 15 22 24 26	15611 60943	2,119			Y(1)
21	6 8 10 17 22 24 26	150691 175309	56,91			Y(1)
22	9 23	15611 65710	405,448	Y		
23	2 15	15238,15715,60231	31,91	Y		
24	2 15	14647 15238 15715 17466	246,286	Y		
25	6 8 17 22 26	15715 17466	253,286	Y		
26	5 13 28	15610 15611 17718 60943 75851 75853 136244 136323 147436 147476	120,156	Y	Y	Y(1,2)
27	2 15	15715 17466 60231	163,194	Y		
28	7 8 27	54623 65710	214,245	Y		

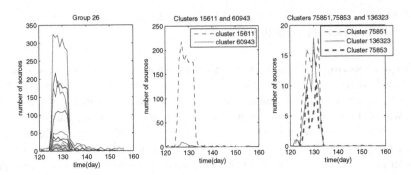

Fig. 13. Example variant worm

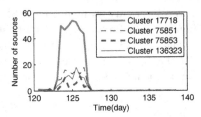

Fig. 14. Example Fingerprint worm

sent packets to the other two windows machines. The three other clusters however, are only observed on the two windows machines (251 sources in total). The explanation is that since port 445TCP is closed on the Linux machine, the attack tool is "intelligent enough" not to try port 139 TCP since it knows that the target is not vulnerable w.r.t its attacks. The fact that 64 sources have contacted the two Windows machines but have given up can probably be explained by packet losses, either in the network (e.g packet losses, firewall filters,etc..) or at the host (e.g congestion while launching too many scans in parallel). Here too, the identification of this class of attacks helps in understanding the threats on the Internet.

Multi-headed attack tools. As being mentioned before, attack tools belonging to the multi-headed family have different attack techniques, but each time they use only one of them against the victim. The services targeted are usually different. Table 6 indicates all the multi-headed groups we found. They have the "Y" value in the column labeled "Multi-headed". As an example, group 23 in Figure 8 consists of three clusters targeting Microsoft NetBios Service (port 139 TCP), Virtual Network Computing service (port 5900 TCP) and Microsoft SQL Server (port 1433 TCP). The coordinated attacks of these three clusters spanned from day 31 to day 91. The top plot of Figure 15 represents group 24. It consists of four clusters numbered 14647(port 445 TCP), 15238 (port 139 TCP), 15715 (port 1433 TCP) and 17466(135 TCP). Their time series on platforms 2 and 15 are highly correlated from day 246 to day 286. As a sanity check, we found very low correlation coefficient between these cluster time series when computing their

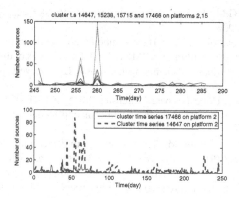

Fig. 15. Example of multi-header worm

correlation coefficients over the whole period. For instance, the bottom plot of Figure 15 shows the dissimilitude of two cluster time series 17466 and 14647 on platform 2 from day 1 to day 245 (the interval just before the correlation). We could not have discovered this group if we had applied the algorithm for the whole period.

5 Conclusion

In this paper, we revisit the problem of discovering multi-headed worms mentioned in [6], but in the context of a larger dataset collected from a distributed honeypot network. Compared to the approach in [6] where correlation was investigated over the whole period of observation, our technique is able to look for correlation over smaller periods of time. To avoid comparing all possible cluster time series over different time windows, which is very costly, we worked around this issue by using filtered platform time series. Our expectation was that the phenomena we were looking for would be enough spatially and timely localized so as to be visible in the filtered platform time series over some periods of time. Applying our technique to a 15 month dataset, we are not only able to confirm the existence of multi-headed worms (on many places), but also bring to the community insight knowledge about worm behaviours. Besides that, the results obtained can also be used to improve our clustering algorithm. However, work remains to take full advantage of the obtained result in order to carry out a systematic analysis of the identified phenomena and to help in studying the so called attack attribution problem.

References

1. Bron, C., Kerbosch, J.: Algorithm 457: finding all cliques of an undirected graph. Commun. ACM 16(9), 575–577 (1973)
2. Eichin, M.W., Rochlis, J.A.A.: With microscope and tweezers: An analysis of the internet virus of november 1988. In: Proceedings of the 1989 IEEE Computer Society Symposium on Security and Privacy, Oakland, Ohio (1989)

3. Hoglund, G., Graw, G.M.: Exploiting Software: How to Break Code. Addison-Wesley Professional, Reading (2004)
4. Lin, J., Keogh, E., Lonardi, S., Chiu, B.: A symbolic representation of time series, with implications for streaming algorithms. In: DMKD 2003: Proceedings of the 8th ACM SIGMOD workshop on Research issues in data mining and knowledge discovery, pp. 2–11. ACM Press, New York (2003)
5. Pouget, F., Dacier, M.: Honeypot-based forensics. In: AusCERT2004, Brisbane, Australia, May 23 - 27, 2004. AusCERT Asia Pacific Information technology Security Conference (May 2004)
6. Pouget, F., Keller, G.U., Dacier, M.: Time signatures to detect multi-headed stealthy attack tools. In: 18th Annual FIRST Conference, June 25-30, Baltimore, USA (June 2006)
7. Niels Provos. Home page of honeyd, http://www.honeyd.org/
8. Shoch, J., Hupp, J.: The worm programs: Early experience with a distributed computation. Commun. ACM 25(3), 172–180 (1982)
9. Spafford, E.H.: The internet worm program: an analysis. SIGCOMM Comput. Commun. Rev. 19(1), 17–57 (1989)
10. Staniford, S., Paxson, V., Weaver, N.: How to own the internet in your spare time. In: Proceedings of the 11th USENIX Security Symposium, Berkeley, CA, USA, pp. 149–167. USENIX Association (2002)
11. Trochim, W., Donnelly, J.P.: The Research Methods Knowledge Base. Atomic Dog (December 2006)
12. Weaver, N., Paxson, V., Staniford, S., Cunningham, R.: A taxonomy of computer worms. In: WORM 2003: Proceedings of the 2003 ACM workshop on Rapid malcode, pp. 11–18. ACM Press, New York (2003)

A Tool for Offline and Live Testing of Evasion Resilience in Network Intrusion Detection Systems

(Extended Abstract)

Leo Juan[1], Christian Kreibich[2], Chih-Hung Lin[1], and Vern Paxson[2]

[1] Institute For Information Industry, Taipei City, Taiwan
{lichou,chlin}@nmi.iii.org.tw
[2] International Computer Science Institute, Berkeley, USA
{christian,vern}@icir.org

Abstract. In this work we undertake the creation of a framework for testing the degree to which network intrusion detection systems (NIDS) detect and handle evasion attacks. Our prototype system, idsprobe, takes as input a packet trace and from it constructs a configurable set of variant traces that introduce different forms of ambiguities that can lead to evasions. Our test harness then uses these variant traces in either an *offline configuration*, in which the NIDS under test reads traffic from the traces directly, or a *live* setup, in which we employ replay technology to feed traffic over a physical network past a NIDS reading directly from a network interface, and to potentially live victim machines. Summary reports of the differences in NIDS output tell the analyst to what degree the NIDS's results vary, reflecting sensitivities to (and possible detections of) different evasions. We demonstrate idsprobe using two popular open-source NIDSs and report on their respective abilities in dealing with evasive traffic.

1 Introduction

Network intrusion detection systems (NIDS) monitor network traffic for potential threats and successful exploits. However, such monitoring faces a fundamental problem: the traffic as observed by an intermediary such as a NIDS does *not* necessarily appear to the recipient in the same semantic terms. Instead, the recipient may either observe a *different* pattern of traffic or may impose an alternative *interpretation* on ambiguous traffic (such as two packets spanning the same sequence range in a TCP flow, but offering different payload bytes for that sequence). While attackers can actively exploit such ambiguities to confuse NIDS, ambiguities unfortunately also arise in traffic streams for benign reasons, requiring valuable analyst time for ascertaining whether the condition constitutes a threat.

Given the fundamental significance of evasion attacks for network intrusion detection, it is striking how little has been documented regarding the efficacy with which modern NIDS address the threat. Vendors publish extensive performance testing results regarding linespeed and breadth of attacks detected by a given system, but little information regarding its resilience to evasion. Because evasion constitutes a fundamental

D. Zamboni (Ed.): DIMVA 2008, LNCS 5137, pp. 267–278, 2008.

problem, however, for vendors to ignore it risks building a "house of cards": their products increasingly provide more of an appearance of security than a reliable foundation. Recently, third-party testing of NIDS products has begun to include an assessment of evasion vulnerabilities [1]. This testing environment, however, is proprietary: it is not available for inspection, modification and extension by others. In this work, we argue that there is significant utility for the network security community at large to have an easy-to-use, transparent, open-source environment for testing NIDS for resilience in the presence of evasion.

To this end, we have designed and implemented a framework, termed `idsprobe`, to facilitate the creation of evasion test-cases in a pluggable fashion, coupled with fully automated testing of different NIDS on the resulting test-cases. In the next section, we describe the requirements that guided our system development. In § 3 we present the architecture of the overall framework, and in § 4 some initial experimental results obtained with using it. We discuss related work in § 5, and offer final thoughts as well as a look at important future work in § 6.

2   Requirements

For our evasion-testing environment we consider two sets of requirements: creating test cases, and then applying those test cases to evaluate a given NIDS.

For the former, we have the following considerations. First, the framework should support both trace-based test cases and live network operation. Trace-based test cases offer very large advantages in terms of repeatability, portability, and ease of inspection and verification of correctness. However, some forms of evasion testing *require* live testing. These include: *(i)* NIDS that gain information from end systems [2,3,4]; *(ii)* NIDS that employ some form of traffic *modification* to remove ambiguities to prevent evasions from exploiting them [5,6]; and *(iii)* evasion attacks that rely on *resource exhaustion* thus causing it to drop packets and consequently miss an attack. Second, the framework needs to accommodate elementary and modular traffic transformations across the relevant layers of the protocol stack. For example, a single test case might include network-layer (e.g., fragmentation), transport-layer (e.g., ambiguous TCP retransmissions) and application-layer (e.g., ambiguous HTTP character encoding) evasions all together.

To use the resulting test cases for evaluating a NIDS, we desire the following. First, reusability of the generated test traces for live testing. On-the-fly introduction of evasive actions to live traffic is complicated by the fact that it requires selectiveness as well as careful sequencing. The ability to leverage input traces containing ready-made evasions in live environments both reduces effort and improves reliability. Second, automation of the process of executing the NIDS and capturing its full set of outputs, including summaries of differences among individual runs. Finally, suitable postprocessors to inspect these differences to highlight patterns corresponding to susceptibility to or thwarting of evasion attempts, particularly to shed light on *architectural* issues reflected in the results (such as whether a given NIDS lacks sufficient state).

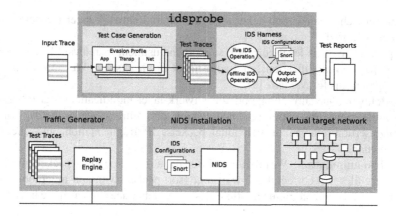

Fig. 1. The `idsprobe` framework. Top: offline testing, bottom: live environment.

3 Framework Architecture

Figure 1 illustrates the current architecture of the `idsprobe` framework, which accommodates both offline and live testing.

3.1 Overview

For simplicity, we limit the presentation of the framework to reflect a single set of related test cases. The process begins with a single, non-evasive trace which contains some attribute, such as a particular payload string in a particular context, for which we can configure a NIDS to detect its presence. We then repeatedly apply a series of *transformation profiles* to copies of this trace to yield a set of variants, each of which reflects a particular potential evasion. After generating these traces, we then employ a "test harness" to run a set of NIDS-under-test against the traces (including the original, unmodified trace), capturing their outputs, from which we then construct a set of reports summarizing the NIDS's behavior in the presence of different evasions.

3.2 Test Case Generation

To support modularity, we encapsulate a set of elementary transformations in scripts that can be individually invoked and then subsequently composed. Each script takes as input (from a file or *stdin*) a `libpcap` trace and produces as output a new trace (to a given output file or *stdout*). In addition, the `idsprobe` framework transparently manages any temporary storage a script requires to perform the transformation, which facilitates chained application of transformations.

We currently provide tools for the following transformations:

Application layer. We support rewriting of application-layer contents using the framework developed in our previous work [7] built upon the Bro intrusion detection system [8]. This framework allows application-level specification of trace transformations that are then reflected down to the transport layer (adjustment of sequence numbers, checksums, and acknowledgments) and network layer (repacketization where required).

Transport layer. This level currently supports adjustment of relevant header control bits, payload modifications, and adjustment of checksums. We implement these using plug-ins for *Netdude* [9].

Network layer. Our current support for network-layer modifications—also based on Netdude plug-ins—comprises modification of arbitrary header fields, duplication/insertion/removal of individual packets, IP fragmentation, and checksum correction.

Trace file manipulation. We provide additional plug-ins to *(i)* adjust packet timestamps in trace files, *(ii)* correct the flow of time (sort packets with non-monotonic timestamps), and *(iii)* recombine multiple sets of packets/traces into a single trace file.

We emphasize that the scripting interface to the transformation tools can readily accommodate other tools that can provide trace manipulation at different semantic levels.

Finally, we also note a somewhat subtle point regarding composition of different evasions: multiple types of evasions need to be applied "top down" in terms of network protocol layering. That is, we must first apply application-layer transformations, then transport-layer ones, and finally those operating at the network-layer. The reason for this is that tools that manipulate one layer generally assume that the lower layer is unambiguous (and thus the tool is free to rewrite it accordingly).

3.3   Offline Evasion Testing

Once a set of test traces have been generated, the `idsprobe` framework then enables automated assessment of a number of NIDS against the suite. Adding a NIDS is a simple process: all that is required is to provide a shell script that will invoke the NIDS given a number of environment variables including, among others, the trace file to be analyzed. The test harness then invokes the script repeatedly to execute the NIDS across each of the traces in the variant set, storing the generated files separately. After execution, `idsprobe` invokes *diff*-based file-differencing to determine the degree to which the NIDS's behavior changed for given variants. Once differenced, the results currently require manual inspection to assess their significance.

3.4   Live Evasion Testing

As mentioned in Section 2, some forms of evasion testing require live tests. To facilitate these, we extended the `idsprobe` framework to function in live environments, while allowing us to re-use the evasive test traces generated for offline testing whenever possible. Three components, connected via a physical link, facilitate live testing: *(i)* a traffic generator, which establishes connections to the victim machine(s) and drives the data exchange; *(ii)* a NIDS installation which monitors the link; and *(iii)* a virtual target network which hosts the victim machines, responding to the traffic sent by the traffic generator.

The key challenge for the traffic generator is enabling re-use of the existing test traces. Our approach is to replay traces *adaptively*, relying on the causality of exchanged application data units (ADUs) at the application level and to ignore the actual content of the responder's ADUs, while patching up the sequence and acknowledgement numbers in the input trace's packets to keep the TCP exchange working. We used the scapy packet processing tool [10] to build this replay functionality.

We used honeyd [11] to realize the virtual target network. honeyd provides the major benefits of allowing easy adjustment of the network topology (for example in order to introduce additional routers for reachability evasions relying on the IP TTL field), while providing flexible victim responder configurations. ranging from simple shell scripts to forwarding to live external systems via honeyd's subsystem mechanism.

4   Initial Experimental Results

As a preliminary evaluation of the idsprobe framework, we developed an initial set of 10 different types of test cases. We evaluated each against the *Snort* [12] (version 2.6.1.4) and *Bro* [8] (version 1.2.1) NIDSs.

4.1   Test Cases

In all test cases, we use a set of traces of entire, full-packet TCP connections. Each contains a single HTTP request with lengths ranging from 8 to 256 bytes, and a corresponding HTTP response. The main objective is to determine whether the NIDS under test can match a signature (not necessarily of an attack) that we *know* is present in the generated, evasive traffic, while also checking for any signs of evasion or other unusual activity that the NIDS might signal. idsprobe automatically generated 196 test traces based on 5 input traces. Table 1 shows the sets of transformations.

4.2   NIDS Configurations

For the Bro NIDS, we used its default configuration settings. We instructed it to monitor all TCP traffic (-f tcp) and loaded the mt, frag, and signatures analyzers. We configured signatures for the HTTP requests in the input traces, with each signature matching exactly one of the HTTP requests. For Snort, we removed the large list of signature file include directives, since none of the listed rule sets were actually included in the Snort distribution, verified that the frag3 and stream4 preprocessors were enabled, and that evasion-related alerts would be generated.

4.3   Findings

Output of idsprobe-generated traces. Table 2 summarizes our findings based on the idsprobe-generated evasive packet traces. Overall, Bro and Snort performed similarly as far as signature detection is concerned. They differ, however, in the amount of detail delivered in addition to the relevant alerts. After excluding from file-differencing Bro's .state directories (which remain empty) and Snort's *tcpdump* log files, the total amount of difference in Bro's output amounts to 1,665 lines, as opposed to 17,018 for

Table 1. Test cases used for evaluating `idsprobe`

- **TC1** A single, consistent, and immediate retransmission 1 μsec after the original of a TCP segment carrying the signature-bearing application-layer payload. This test case checks whether the NIDS performs a simple form of TCP stream reassembly correctly.
- **TC2** Like TC1, but the retransmission consists of only part of the original TCP segment. We retransmit a right-aligned part of the original segment with correct checksum and sequence number. This constellation likewise presents neither threat nor ambiguity.
- **TC3** Like TC1, but we change the TCP payload on the first (subtest TC3a) or the second (subtest TC3b) variant of the duplicated packet, respectively, without any checksum corrections. This test does not pose any actual ambiguity.
- **TC4** Like TC3, except now the checksums are corrected. Our payload modification is *careless*, thus leading to a different checksum value. This test case represents the first truly ambiguous traffic. The NIDS needs to decide which version of the byte stream to analyze, and ideally should note the inconsistency.
- **TC5** Like TC4, but we change the TCP payload *carefully*, leaving the checksum unchanged. We achieve this by swapping 16-bit fields, though one could derive more complex modifications due to the incremental nature of the checksumming algorithm. As with TC3, this presents a real ambiguity, requiring the NIDS to compare the actual payloads.
- **TC6** We duplicate one of the IP datagrams in the TCP flow, setting its IP fragment offset to a non-zero offset value (adjusting the IP header checksum to reflect the change) on the first (subtest TC6a) or second (subtest TC6b) variant, respectively. This test case creates an ambiguous, malformed fragment.
- **TC7** We duplicate one of the IP datagrams in the TCP flow and set its IP TTL value to a number of different values (again with header checksum updated) on the first (subtest TC7a) or second (subtest TC7b) variant, respectively. This test case does not introduce a serious ambiguity but can confuse NIDS evasion detection that examines TTL values for anomalies.
- **TC8** We consistently fragment one of the IP datagrams in the TCP flow carrying the signature-bearing payload, using various different fragment sizes. This test case tests whether the NIDS correctly processes well-formed fragments.
- **TC9** Like TC8, but we duplicate one of the fragments, and alter its payload in the first (subtest TC8a) or second (subtest TC8b) variant, respectively. The alteration is again careless, i.e., reassembly of the datagram using the modified payload leads to an incorrect TCP checksum for the full datagram.
- **TC10** Like TC9, but with a careful payload alteration, i.e., reassembly of the datagram using the modified payload leaves the TCP checksum unchanged. Figures 2 and 3 present the workings of TC10 in detail.

Snort. Ignoring Snort's verbose summary output reported on *stdout* and *stderr* reduced the differential data volume to 1,329 lines.

In TC2, Snort erroneously reported a TCP checksum change on a retransmission, where in fact no divergent payload was transferred. In the event of careful payload alterations that do not affect the TCP checksum (TC5/TC10), however, Snort fails to notice the (rather likely) evasion attempt. Bro handled both cases correctly, remaining silent on the former but alerting on the latter case. Snort also generated a total of 60 potential evasive TCP FIN detections in 4 of the test cases. A number of the values reported in these alerts are nonsensical, such as IP TTL values of 240, IP ToS fields with values

```
00:01:37.427628 10.48.0.1.2013 > 10.48.0.81.80: . 1:158(157) ack 1 win 32768
0x0000   4500 00c5 7566 0000 4006 f01b 0a30 0001     E...uf..@....O..
0x0010   0a30 0051 07dd 0050 0000 092a 3838 4e57     .0.Q...P...*88NW
0x0020   5010 8000 0fc2 0000 4745 5420 2f31 6162     P.......GET./1ab
0x0030   6364 6566 6768 696a 6b6c 6d6e 6f70 7172     cdefghijklmnopqr
0x0040   7374 7576 7778 797a 3261 6263 6465 6667     stuvwxyz2abcdefg
0x0050   6869 6a6b 6c6d 6e6f 7071 7273 7475 7677     hijklmnopqrstuvw
0x0060   7879 7a33 6162 6364 6566 6768 696a 6b6c     xyz3abcdefghijkl
0x0070   6d6e 6f70 7172 7374 7576 7778 797a 3461     mnopqrstuvwxyz4a
0x0080   6263 6465 6667 6869 6a6b 6c6d 6e6f 7071     bcdefghijklmnopq
0x0090   7273 7475 7677 7879 7a35 6162 6364 6566     rstuvwxyz5abcdef
0x00a0   6768 696a 6b6c 6d6e 6f70 7172 7320 4854     ghijklmnopqrs.HT
0x00b0   5450 2f31 2e31 0d0a 484f 5354 3a6e 6f6e     TP/1.1..HOST:non
0x00c0   650d 0a0d 0a                                e....
```

Fig. 2. *tcpdump* output for relevant packet from the TC10 input trace. A single TCP segment contains the relevant application-layer content, "`GET /1abcdef`".

```
00:01:37.427628 10.48.0.1.2013 > 10.48.0.81.80: [|tcp] (frag 30054:8@0+)
00:01:37.427629 10.48.0.1 > 10.48.0.81: tcp (frag 30054:8@8+)
00:01:37.427630 10.48.0.1 > 10.48.0.81: tcp (frag 30054:8@16+)
0x0000   4500 001c 2006 4006 d0c2 0a30 0001     E...uf..@....O..
0x0010   0a30 0051 0fc2 0000 4745 5420           .0.Q...GET.
00:01:37.427631 10.48.0.1 > 10.48.0.81: tcp (frag 30054:8@24+)
0x0000   4500 001c 7566 2003 4006 d0c1 0a30 0001     E...uf..@....O..
0x0010   0a30 0051 2f31 6162 6364 6566               .0.Q/1abcdef
00:01:37.427632 10.48.0.1 > 10.48.0.81: tcp (frag 30054:8@24+)
0x0000   4500 001c 7566 2003 4006 d0c1 0a30 0001     E...uf..@....O..
0x0010   0a30 0051 2f31 6364 6162 6566               .0.Q/1cdabef
00:01:37.427633 10.48.0.1 > 10.48.0.81: tcp (frag 30054:8@32+)
0x0000   4500 001c 7566 2004 4006 d0c0 0a30 0001     E...uf..@....O..
0x0010   0a30 0051 6768 696a 6b6c 6d6e               .0.Qghijklmn
00:01:37.427634 10.48.0.1 > 10.48.0.81: tcp (frag 30054:8@40+)
00:01:37.427635 10.48.0.1 > 10.48.0.81: tcp (frag 30054:8@48+)
...
00:01:37.427650 10.48.0.1 > 10.48.0.81: tcp (frag 30054:8@168+)
00:01:37.427651 10.48.0.1 > 10.48.0.81: tcp (frag 30054:1@176)
```

Fig. 3. *tcpdump* output of resulting TC10 evasive traffic. The TCP segment shown in Figure 2 has its application-layer content rewritten, fragmented into 24 8-byte fragments, with a duplicate fragment with the original TCP stream content inserted after the third fragment. The sensitive payload is now spread across three IP datagrams. The payload variation preserves the TCP checksum's validity. Finally, `idsprobe` patches the packet timestamps to preserve chronological ordering.

Table 2. Bro's vs. Snort's results on 10 test cases generated by `idsprobe`. The first line per NIDS summarizes signature detection, the second reports evasion-related alerts or messages. The numbers reflect the following: ① "RetransmissionInconsistency". ② "WeirdActivity" of type "fragment_inconsistency". ③ Bad checksums in weird.log. ④ "WeirdActivity" of type "excessively_small_fragment" for fragments of 32 bytes or less. ⑤ "Possible evasive FIN detection" with nonsensical parameters. ⑥ "TCP checksum changed on retransmission". ⑦ "Fragmentation overlap".

	Output	TC1	TC2	TC3a/b	TC4a/b	TC5a/b	TC6a/b	TC7a/b	TC8	TC9a/b	TC10a/b
Bro	Sig. match	✓	✓	✓	✗/✓	✗/✓	✓	✓	✓	✗/✓	✗/✓
	Evasion			③	①	①				④	②④	②④
Snort	Sig. match	✓	✓	✓	✗/✓	✗/✓	✓	✓	✓	✗/✓	✗/✓
	Evasion	⑤	⑥		⑤			⑤		⑦	

0x10, and IP IDs of 0. None of these values exist in the FIN packets in question; in addition, none of the traces actually reflects an ambiguous TCP FIN packet.

Bro correctly reports TCP retransmission inconsistencies, IP fragment inconsistencies, the presence of bad checksums, and the presence of excessively small IP

```
08:00:09.176192 IP 10.48.0.1.2010 > 10.48.0.81.80: . 1:13(12) ack 1 win 32768
        0x0000:  4500 0034 f178 0000 4006 749a 0a30 0001   E..4.x..@.t..O..
        0x0010:  0a30 0051 07da 0050 0000 092a 3392 88d8   .0.Q...P...*3...
        0x0020:  5010 8000 4582 0000 4745 5420 2f31 6162   P...E...GET./1ab
        0x0030:  6364 7878                                 cdxx
08:00:09.176194 IP 10.48.0.1.2010 > 10.48.0.81.80: . 11:14(3) ack 1 win 32768
        0x0000:  4500 002b f178 0000 4006 74a3 0a30 0001   E..+.x..@.t..O..
        0x0010:  0a30 0051 07da 0050 0000 0934 3392 88d8   .0.Q...P...43...
        0x0020:  5010 8000 80f0 0000 6566 67               P.......efg
```

Fig. 4. *tcpdump* of inconsistent retransmission not reported by Snort 2.8.0.1

fragments. For Snort, the only correct evasion-related output concerns IP fragmentation overlap.[1]

During the course of our work, new releases of Snort appeared. We experimented with the latest release available, Snort version 2.8.0.1, to see how its behavior might have changed. The erroneous evasive FIN alerts have been repaired. However, the new stream reassembly module stream5 introduced new issues: a partially overlapping retransmission (shown in Figure 4) is not reported, while Snort 2.6.1.4 did report a changed TCP checksum on the retransmission.

Output after long-term operation. To better understand the usability of evasion/anomaly-related events reported by different IDSs, we ran Bro 1.2.1 along with Snort 2.6.1.4 and 2.8.0.1 on a 24-hour, 21 GB trace recorded at ICSI on 16 March 2007. The NIDSs were not configured to detect attacks, but only to report anomalous or potentially evasive activity.

Table 3 summarizes our findings. The absence of consensus in the reported events is striking, particularly between Bro and the Snort versions, but to a lesser degree even between two different Snort releases. TCP SYNs with payload data seem a rare case where there is near-consensus, with the three NIDSs reporting 460, 458, and 461 instances, respectively. Bro reports a single retransmission inconsistency (which we have verified to be correct, but it does not reflect a malicious evasion). Snort 2.6 reports this as one of 36,873 "possible EVASIVE RST detection" events, and Snort 2.8 as 3 of the 5 "Data sent on stream after TCP Reset" events recorded. For the 22,137 flow reassembly issues reported by Bro ("ContentGap" and "AckAboveHole"), which have direct significance for content-based analysis, there is no apparent corresponding alert in either of the Snort logs. These events account for the main reason why Snort 2.8 reports fewer events than Bro, whose output volume is almost an order of magnitude below Snort 2.6's.

5   Related Work

The fundamental problem of NIDS evasion was first framed in the seminal paper by Ptacek and Newsham [13]. Aspects of the problem also appear in the discussion of the Bro system [8], particularly in the context of inconsistent TCP retransmissions. In response to the threat of evasion, researchers have developed several types of countermeasures,

---

[1] Even that is not the best description of the problem, since IP fragments can overlap for rare-but-benign reasons. Better would be to highlight that the overlap is inconsistent.

Table 3. Aggregate summaries of anomalies and evasion-related events reported by the NIDSs under test, on the 24h ICSI trace.

BRO 1.2	SNORT 2.6	SNORT 2.8
14,591 ContentGap	161,862 possible EVASIVE FIN detection	4,844 TCP Timestamp is outside of PAWS window
7,546 AckAboveHole	36,873 possible EVASIVE RST detection	2,058 Data sent on stream not accepting data
2,249 window_recision	27,384 TCP CHECKSUM CHANGED ON RETRANSMISSION	807 Bad segment, adjusted size $<= 0$
735 bad_TCP_checksum	1,933 Possible RETRANSMISSION detection	461 Data on SYN packet
460 SYN_with_data	458 DATA ON SYN detection	67 WARNING: ICMP Original IP Header Truncated!
311 possible_split_routing	67 WARNING: ICMP Original IP Header Truncated!	30 WARNING: TCP Data Offset is less than 5!
290 data_before_established	30 WARNING: TCP Data Offset is less than 5!	18 Truncated Tcp Options
98 bad_ICMP_checksum	18 Truncated Tcp Options	12 Experimental Tcp Options found
85 above_hole_data_without_any_acks	12 Experimental Tcp Options found	5 Data sent on stream after TCP Reset
35 connection_originator_SYN_ack	2 Tcp Options found with bad lengths	2 Tcp Options found with bad lengths
30 bad_TCP_header_len	1 WARNING: ICMP Original IP Fragmented and Offset Not 0!	1 WARNING: ICMP Original IP Fragmented and Offset Not 0!
18 inappropriate_FIN		
15 SYN_seq_jump		
15 premature_connection_reuse		
9 active_connection_reuse		
8 data_after_reset		
3 SYN_inside_connection		
3 SYN_after_reset		
3 bad_SYN_ack		
2 TCP_christmas		
1 RetransmissionInconsistency		
1 FIN_advanced_last_seq		
1 bad_UDP_checksum		
26,509	228,640	8,305

such as traffic normalization [5,6], active mapping [2], passive fingerprinting [4], and the use of host-based context [3].

Several tools have been developed for testing NIDS for vulnerabilities to evasion. Fragrouter[2] implements some network-layer evasions based on IP fragmentation. Unlike our framework, it modifies live traffic only. The libwhisker[3] library provides basic functionality for testing HTTP implementations. Nikto[4] leverages the library, adding HTTP content obfuscation techniques. Both tools primarily target live-traffic operation.

Regarding systematic evaluation of NIDS in the presence of possible evasions, Vigna and colleagues present a framework for NIDS testing based on traffic transformation [14]. Rather than testing the NIDSs' awareness of evasion, they emphasize evaluating the robustness of individual signatures used by such NIDSs. Their system takes as input an attack trace, to which it applies semantically invariant transformations and then and monitors for changes in the alerts generated by the NIDSs. Similarly, Rubin et al. developed a framework to facilitate traffic transformations on different network layers [15], again aiming to produce variants of a specific attack. Marty [16] similarly proposed a platform for subjecting NIDS to automatically generated variations of attack traffic. His system exclusively operates on live traffic.

In contrast to these efforts, our framework does not assume the existence of an attack, but instead determines the general effects of traffic transformations. This allows us to separate the NIDS's specific attack detection logic from its architectural analysis limitations. In addition, the work of Rubin et al. develops a formal model of possible transformations, which allows them to exhaustively test a NIDS against attack variants. Our work, on the other hand, aims to facilitate a public, open-source effort for developing NIDS evasion test suites, with a related emphasis for our framework on modularity and a plug-in architecture.

6 Discussion and Future Work

The `idsprobe` framework does *not* attempt to provide "turnkey" evaluation of NIDS evasion vulnerabilities. Rather, our aim is to provide the means for an experienced assessor to more readily construct good test cases, and more efficiently apply those test cases in a repeatable fashion across a set of NIDS under consideration. We also do not strive to ourselves provide a *comprehensive* set of evasion tests; rather, we aim to facilitate that others can *collectively* work towards such a goal. These considerations motivate our open-source, modular/plug-in approach.

The focus of our future work is to devise methodologies for assessing live-traffic evasions based on overloading NIDS resources and to assess the efficacy of on-line anti-evasion technology.

---

[2] Per http://www.securityfocus.com/tools/176, nominally available at http://www.anzen.com/research/nidsbench/, but in fact that location no longer resolves.

[3] http://www.wiretrip.net/rfp/libwhisker/

[4] http://www.cirt.net/code/nikto.shtml

7   Summary

We have designed and implemented the `idsprobe` framework to facilitate the creation of offline as well as live evasion test-cases in a pluggable fashion, coupled with fully automated testing of different NIDS on the resulting test-cases. We aim for the system to encourage extension and broad use by the community, and to this end will provide the software to others upon request, and ultimately aim to maintain it in as a public open-source resource.

Acknowledgments

This work was partially supported by the iCAST project sponsored by the National Science Council (NSC), Taiwan, under Grants 95-3114-P-001-002-Y02, 95-3114-P-307-003-Y, 96-3114-P-001-002-Y, 95-2221-E-017-007, 95-3113-P-017-001, as well as by the Ministry of Economic Affairs, Taiwan, under Grant 96-EC-17-A-31-F1-0824, and by the US National Science Foundation, under grant NSF-0433702. Christian Kreibich was supported by a postdoctoral grant provided by DAAD. The opinions expressed in this work are solely those of the authors and should not necessarily be considered to be the opinions of any government, funding agency, or other organization.

References

1. Group, N.: Network IPS Testing Procedure (V4.0) (2006),
   http://www.nss.co.uk/certification/ips/nss-nips-v40-testproc.pdf
2. Shankar, U., Paxson, V.: Active mapping: resisting NIDS evasion without altering traffic. In: Proc. Symposium on Security and Privacy, pp. 44–61 (2003)
3. Dreger, H., Kreibich, C., Paxson, V., Sommer, R.: Enhancing the accuracy of network-based intrusion detection with host-based context. In: Julisch, K., Krügel, C. (eds.) DIMVA 2005. LNCS, vol. 3548. Springer, Heidelberg (2005)
4. Taleck, G.: Ambiguity Resolution via Passive OS Fingerprinting. In: Vigna, G., Krügel, C., Jonsson, E. (eds.) RAID 2003. LNCS, vol. 2820, pp. 192–206. Springer, Heidelberg (2003)
5. Handley, M., Paxson, V., Kreibich, C.: Network Intrusion Detection: Evasion, Traffic Normalization, and End-to-End Protocol Semantics. In: Proc. USENIX Security Symposium (2001)
6. Watson, D., Smart, M., Malan, G.R., Jahanian, F.: Protocol Scrubbing: Network Security through Transparent Flow Modification. IEEE/ACM Transactions on Networking 12(2), 261–273 (2004)
7. Pang, R., Paxson, V.: A High-Level Programming Environment for Packet Trace Anonymization and Transformation. In: Proceedings of the ACM SIGCOMM Conference (August 2003)
8. Paxson, V.: Bro: A system for detecting network intruders in real-time. Computer Networks 31(23-24), 2435–2463 (1999)
9. Kreibich, C.: Design and Implementation of Netdude, a Framework for Packet Trace Manipulation. In: Proc. USENIX Technical Conference, FREENIX track (2004)
10. Biondi, P.: Scapy, a powerful interactive packet manipulation program,
    http://www.secdev.org/projects/scapy/

11. Provos, N.: A Virtual Honeypot Framework. In: Proceedings of the 13th USENIX Security Symposium, pp. 1–14 (2004)
12. SourceFire: Snort, the Open Source Network Intrusion Detection System, http://www.snort.org/
13. Ptacek, T., Newsham, T.: Insertion, evasion, and denial of service: Eluding network intrusion detection. Secure Networks, Inc. (January 1998)
14. Vigna, G., Robertson, W., Balzarotti, D.: Testing network-based intrusion detection signatures using mutant exploits. In: Proceedings of the 11th ACM Conference on Computer and Communications Security, pp. 21–30 (2004)
15. Rubin, S., Jha, S., Miller, B.: Automatic Generation and Analysis of NIDS Attacks. In: Proceedings of the 20th Annual Computer Security Applications Conference (ACSAC 2004), vol. 00, pp. 28–38 (2004)
16. Marty, R.: Thor – A Tool to Test Intrusion Detection Systems by Variations of Attacks. Master's thesis, Swiss Federal Institute of Technology, Zurich, Switzerland (2002)

Author Index